Revolution from above

The demise of the Soviet system

David M. Kotz with Fred Weir

ROUTLEDGE

London and New York

First published 1997
by Routledge
11 New Fetter Lane, London EC4P 4EE

Simultaneously published in the USA and Canada
by Routledge
29 West 35th Street, New York, NY 10001

Typeset in Palatino by Pure Tech India Ltd, Pondicherry

Printed and bound in Great Britain by
Redwood Books, Trowbridge, Wiltshire

British Library Cataloguing in Publication Data
A catalogue record for this book is available from the British Library

Library of Congress Cataloging in Publication Data
Kotz, David M. (David Michael),
    Revolution from above: the demise of the Soviet system / David M. Kotz
    with Fred Weir.
        p.   cm.
    Includes bibliographical references (p.) and index.
    1. Soviet Union—Economic conditions—1985–1991. 2. Soviet Union
    —Politics and government—1985–1991. 3. Former Soviet republics
    —Economic conditions. I. Weir, Fred.   II. Title.
HC336.26.K668   1997
338.947—dc20

                                                                96–7570
                                                                CIP

ISBN 0–415–14316–0 (hbk)
ISBN 0–415–14317–9 (pbk)

Contents

Figures

Tables

Preface

One of the authors of this work, David Kotz, is an economics professor at the University of Massachusetts at Amherst, and the other, Fred Weir, is a journalist based in Moscow. In the late 1980s, from our separate vantage points, we both observed with interest the economic and political reforms taking place in the Soviet Union. At that time it appeared that Mikhail Gorbachev's policy of perestroika might be giving birth to the world's first democratic socialist system. Perhaps, buried beneath the Soviet Union's repressive state and rigidly centralized economy, some genuine socialist remnants might have survived from the ideas that had originally inspired the Russian Revolution. It seemed possible that Gorbachev's reforms would succeed in liberating what was good in the Soviet past while expunging the unsavory aspects of the Soviet system.

Events in the former Soviet Union did not follow such a course. Gorbachev's attempt to reform the Soviet system instead led to its disintegration. By the end of 1991, some six years after Gorbachev's rise to power, the Soviet state was dissolved, replaced by fifteen newly sovereign nation-states, and an effort to build capitalism superseded Gorbachev's project of reforming and democratizing Soviet socialism. This was a remarkable turn of events, which almost no one had predicted.

The authors of this book first met in Moscow in the summer of 1991. We discussed the Soviet demise unfolding around us. The Western media were filled with stories of a popular assault from below toppling the Soviet system, as its inevitable economic collapse suddenly left the Soviet elite unable any longer to protect and save the system. However, this did not accord with what we saw. We looked at the process of the Soviet demise from the perspective of our particular intellectual training and experience, and we found the received explanations to be implausible and inconsistent with the evidence.

David Kotz is an economist who specializes in the process of institutional change in economic history, in the former Soviet Union and elsewhere. This specialty requires knowledge of the factors that promote

economic growth and those that retard it, of the interplay of technological development and class interest, of the roles of economics and
politics in social change. He had spent years studying the factors that
make for continuity in socioeconomic systems and those that produce
either incremental or radical change. As Kotz observed the Soviet
demise in 1991, the difficulties of the economy of the USSR, serious
though they were, did not seem to provide a satisfactory explanation
for the rapid unravelling of the Soviet system. Other forces were at work
besides economic decline.

Fred Weir is the Moscow correspondent for the *Hindustan Times* of
India and a regular contributor to Canadian Press, Canada's national
news service. He had studied Russian and Soviet history up to the
graduate level at the University of Toronto, taking a special interest in
ideas for modernizing and democratizing the state socialist system. He
travelled widely in the USSR and Eastern Europe in the 1970s and early
1980s, before coming to live in the Soviet Union to work as a journalist in
1986. He married Mariam Shaumian, a Russian–Armenian woman, in
1987. Weir travelled throughout the country and reported weekly on the
progress, disappointments, and disasters of perestroika. He came to
know personally, as well as in the line of work, many members of the
Soviet Union's intellectual and political elite. He found a widespread
cynicism among them. Contrary to the claim that the Soviet elite sought
to defend the system to the end, it appeared to Weir that by 1991 many
of them not only failed to support the effort to reform socialism but were
ready to embrace capitalism.

The two of us discussed these puzzling events and how they could be
understood. We came to the view that the Soviet system had been
dispatched, not by economic collapse combined with a popular uprising,
but by its own ruling elite in pursuit of its own perceived interests. In
1992 we decided to write a book exploring, and explaining, this uncon-
ventional interpretation of the Soviet demise.

It took several years to complete the research, which came to cover not
just the Soviet demise but its sequel, in the twists and turns of Russian
economic and political development that followed the disintegration of
the Soviet Union. We interviewed dozens of contemporary figures,
including former Soviet government and Communist Party leaders, policy advisors, political leaders from across the spectrum of independent
Russia, economists and other academics, new private businessmen,
trade union leaders, and foreign (non-Soviet/Russian) specialists (a list
of people interviewed is found in the Appendix). We studied Soviet and
Russian history and read contemporary accounts and analyses by
Soviet/Russian and foreign sources.

As always happens, the research process modified and revised our
initial views in various ways. However, we found that our central

hypothesis was supported by the evidence and that it explained features of the Soviet demise and its aftermath that were otherwise very difficult to understand. We hope that the interpretation offered here will clear away some of the myths that have arisen about these events and make it possible to discover the real lessons of the now defunct Soviet experiment.

Some explanation of our division of labor is in order. The two of us together developed the main ideas and the organizational plan of the book. We planned the research and interviewing together. Apart from the few chapters that deal strictly with economic developments, we jointly planned how each chapter would be organized and presented. Journalists face constantly recurring deadlines, while academics are afforded time for research and writing. Thus, contrary to what one might have expected from a team consisting of an economist and a journalist, Kotz, the economist, wrote the chapter drafts, while Weir provided comments and revisions. Kotz also conducted the interviews specifically for this book, during seven visits to the Soviet Union/Russia, although we also drew upon information from Weir's many previous interviews of important figures in Soviet life. The phrasing 'David M. Kotz with Fred Weir' is intended to convey this particular version of primary and secondary authorship.

David M. Kotz and Fred Weir, May 1996

Acknowledgements

Many individuals provided assistance of one kind or another on the project that produced this book. Generous sharing of contacts and/or help in arranging interviews were provided by Ludmila Bulavka, Alexander Buzgalin, Stephen F. Cohen, John Helmer, Tatyana Koryagina, Nicholas Kozlov, Bernard Lown, Robert J. McIntyre, Stanislav Menshikov, Anatoly I. Miliukov, Vladimir Panchekhin, John Simmons, Vladimir Sucharev, Albert Toussein, Lynn Turgeon, and Ludmila Vartazarova. Unpublished data, papers, or other important information were given to us by Gennady Ashin, Vladimir Gimpelson, Sergei Grigoriev, Grigory Kotovsky, Olga Kryshtanovskaya, Chris Lane, David Lane, Vadim Radaev, Maxim Shuvalov, and Stephen White. We received helpful comments on part or all of the manuscript from Karen Pfeifer, Ronald Suny, William Taubman, Thomas Weisskopf, and two anonymous readers for Routledge. Other forms of assistance in conducting the research and preparing the manuscript came from Karen Graubart, David Hotchkiss, Merrilee Mardon, Robert Rothstein, and Elizaveta Voznessenskaya. Of course, any shortcomings in the results are our own responsibility. Financial support was provided by the University of Massachusetts Faculty Research Grant program and the Deans of the Graduate School and the Faculty of Social and Behavioral Sciences.

A note on transliteration of Russian names

The English language spelling of Russian names found in the text of this book was based on the system of transliteration most commonly used in books that are not aimed solely at specialists in Russian studies (known as "System I"). This transliteration system gives the English spelling of well-known Soviet/Russian individuals' names that is likely to be familiar to most readers. However, this system does not accommodate a reader wishing to locate a copy of a book or article cited here. Thus, Russian names in the bibliography and in endnote citations were transliterated following a Library of Congress system ("System II", the Library of Congress system with diacritical marks omitted). As a result, there are some slight differences in the spelling of Russian names between the text and bibliographic citations in this book.

demise (dĭ-mīz′) *n.* 1. Death. 2. The transfer of an estate by will or lease.

From *The American Heritage Dictionary* (1985) Second College Edition, Boston: Houghton Mifflin Company, p. 379.

Chapter 1

Introduction

In 1917 the Soviet Union was born in a poor, largely agricultural country.[1] Its predecessor, the Russian Empire, had played a role on the world stage, owing to its large population, huge land mass, and strategic location straddling Europe and Asia. But an underdeveloped economy and crumbling autocratic government had condemned pre-Revolutionary Russia to the position of weak relation to the dominant world powers – Britain, France, Germany, and the United States. Large factories had grown up in its western cities, a development largely propelled by infusions of West European capital. But in 1917 the Russian economy lagged far behind the dynamic capitalism of the great powers.

In 1980, some sixty years after the Russian Revolution, the Soviet Union was one pole of a bipolar world. It had been transformed into an urban, industrialized country of 265 million people. By such measures as life expectancy, caloric intake, and literacy, the Soviet Union had reached the ranks of the developed countries.[2] It gave economic and military aid to many countries around the world. It was a leader in many areas of science and technology. It launched the first space satellite. In some more prosaic fields, ranging from specialized metals, to machines for seamless welding of railroad tracks, to eye surgery equipment, it was a world leader. Its performing artists and athletes were among the world's best. With its Warsaw Pact allies, it was the military equal of the United States-led Nato alliance.

The undeniable economic achievements of the Soviet Union existed side by side with persistent failures. Resources were used inefficiently. Many Soviet products, particularly consumer goods, were of low quality. Shoppers often faced long lines for ordinary goods in the notoriously inefficient system of retail distribution. Consumer services, from haircuts to appliance repair, were abysmal, if they were available at all. Construction projects seemed never to reach a conclusion. And the environmental cost of Soviet economic development mounted steadily.

Western commentators generally stressed the failures, yet it must be admitted that the achievements were impressive. Third World audiences particularly noticed the speed of Soviet industrialization. The Soviet leap from rural, agricultural society to urban, industrial one was among the most rapid in history.[3]

These transformations and achievements of the Soviet Union took place under a socioeconomic system that was radically different from capitalism. While capitalist systems, such as those of the United States, Germany, and Japan, differ from one another in many details, they share a common set of fundamental institutions. In all three most production is carried out by private business firms that are owned largely by wealthy shareholders. Market forces serve as the main coordinator of economic activity, and the profit motive acts as the propellant force. The Soviet system relied on none of those institutions. In the Soviet Union nearly all production took place in enterprises owned by the government. State plans devised in Moscow, rather than decentralized market forces, coordinated the economy. Directives aimed at fulfilling the central plan, not the pursuit of profit, set economic activity in motion. What would be a normal business in New York or Tokyo would, if conducted by a Soviet citizen, be criminal activity in Moscow.

Western analysts called this system "Communism." Soviet officials, reserving that term for a future stateless and classless society, called it "socialism." Generations of Western socialists, repelled by the authoritarian, repressive nature of the Soviet state, questioned its identification as socialist. Perhaps the most neutral and accurate label is "state socialism," which suggests the economic institutions of public ownership and economic planning that are usually associated with socialism, combined with the extreme centralization of economic and political power in an authoritarian state that characterized the Soviet system.[4]

During 1990–91, in the space of two short years, the mighty system built by Lenin and his successors collapsed. The huge Soviet Communist Party, which had exercised unchallenged rule for seventy years, was disbanded. The state socialist system which it ran was dismantled, replaced by an effort to install capitalism in its place. Even the nation-state of the Soviet Union disintegrated, replaced by 15 new nations, some of which soon were locked in cross-border warfare or internal rebellion. The former Soviet Union lay prostrate, its economy collapsing, its people suddenly impoverished, its cultural achievements withering, its athletes and scientists emigrating, and its superpower status vanished.

To call this development surprising would be a vast understatement. Great powers have declined often before in history – but never so rapidly and unexpectedly. The sudden demise of such an economically and militarily powerful entity as the Soviet Union, in the absence of external invasion or violent internal upheaval, is unprecedented in modern history.

This raises a host of questions. Why did the attempt to reform the Soviet system, known as "perestroika," lead instead to its demise? Why was perestroika attempted in the first place? Why was the demise of the Soviet system followed by such a rapid economic and social decline? Why is the attempt to make a transition to democracy and capitalism in the former Soviet Union proving to be so difficult? What do these events tell us about the feasibility of alternative modes of development to modern capitalism? Do they demonstrate that in the modern world capitalism is the only viable socioeconomic system, and that any attempt to build a more cooperative and egalitarian system is doomed to failure?

Soviet specialists in the West have proposed various interpretations of the Soviet demise, but two explanations have dominated the popular understanding. One is the view that the Soviet demise resulted from the non-viability of a socialist economic system. According to this interpretation, the Soviet planned economy stopped functioning and was impossible to reform, leaving capitalism as the only alternative.[5] The view of socialism as economically unworkable dates back to the 1920s, when a literature arose claiming that a planned economy could not function.[6]

A serious problem with this explanation of the Soviet demise lies in the evidence that Soviet state socialism produced rapid economic development for some sixty years before succumbing. While it did encounter increasing economic difficulties in the 1970s and 1980s, it continued to yield economic growth, although at reduced rate, through to the end of the 1980s.[7] As we shall argue in Chapter 5, the evidence does not support the claim that a collapse of the Soviet planned economy due to its own internal contradictions explains the demise of the system.[8]

The second dominant interpretation of the Soviet demise stresses the role of popular opposition to the system from below. According to this view, a society based on repression could only last as long as its leaders had the will to use the coercive instruments at their command. The first serious attempt at liberal reform gave the people an opportunity to break their bonds. As it became clear that Soviet President Mikhail Gorbachev would not use force to preserve the system, a popular movement from below peacefully dismantled it, through elections, mass demonstrations, strikes, and secessionist movements.[9] Oppressed people voted in capitalism, and oppressed nationalities gained freedom from Moscow's yoke.

While it is true that many ordinary Soviet citizens actively expressed their dissatisfaction with the system, this second explanation also has serious shortcomings. While much of the Soviet population, along with Gorbachev and his associates, favored an expanded role for market forces in the Soviet economy, polling evidence shows that only a small minority in the former Soviet Union wanted the sort of capitalism found in the United States.[10] The rapid rush to capitalism does not appear to have flowed from a popular desire for this direction of development.

It also appears that a large majority of the people in the former Soviet Union, with the exception of some of the smaller republics, wanted to preserve the Union. A referendum on preserving the Union won with 76.4 per cent of the vote only nine months before the Union was dismantled.[11] While the people wanted economic and political change, they apparently did not want either the capitalist transformation or the political disintegration that were visited upon them.[12] This calls into question the view that popular pressure or popular revolution can explain the demise and transformation of the Soviet system.

The explanations offered by supporters of Soviet state socialism are no more persuasive than the foregoing claims of inevitable economic collapse or popular revolution. Some Soviet officials complained that foreign pressure destabilized the Soviet Union.[13] But the major Western powers had done their best to apply whatever pressure they could to defeat the Soviet system since its inception. If they were unable to do so during the decades when the Soviet Union was still weak and underdeveloped, is it plausible that they could succeed after the Soviet Union had reached the peak of its power and achievement?

Other supporters of the old regime cited betrayal at the very top within the former Soviet Union. According to this view, President Gorbachev, hiding under a cloak of reform and renewal of the Soviet system, actually set about to destroy it.[14] But a careful reading of the record supports the sincerity of Gorbachev's claim that he wanted to reform socialism, not replace it with capitalism. Even after the failed coup of August 1991, when Gorbachev had nothing to gain from clinging to socialism, he insisted on doing just that. And he struggled to the end to keep the Union intact.

There is a grain of truth in each of the above four views. The particular form of economic administration adopted in the Soviet Union under Stalin, and never fundamentally changed prior to perestroika, did have severe flaws, which grew more serious over time. The Soviet people's yearning for freedom and democracy did play an important role in the demise of the system. So also did Western pressure. And, if not Gorbachev himself, some of his top aides did abandon any belief in socialism while still occupying influential positions. However, none of these factors, individually or together, can adequately explain the course of events.

This book offers a different explanation. In the mid-1970s the performance of the Soviet economy deteriorated significantly. After ten years of minor adjustments had failed to improve economic performance, a new leadership under Mikhail Gorbachev set off on the path of major structural reform, the aim being to democratize and renew

Soviet socialism. However, unforeseen by Gorbachev and his fellow reformers, the economic, political, and cultural reforms they carried out unleashed processes that created a new coalition of groups and classes that favored replacing socialism with capitalism.

Boris Yeltsin, who became the chief executive of the Russian Republic[15] within the Soviet Union in 1990, emerged as the leader of this coalition. To win power, this coalition had to elbow aside two rival groups – those who wanted to reform socialism, led by Mikhail Gorbachev, and the Old Guard who wanted to preserve the state socialist system with only minor changes, typified by the leaders of the attempted coup of August 1991. The political victory of the group favoring capitalism was made possible by the support it gained from an apparently unlikely source – the party–state elite of the Soviet system.

The vast territory and many nationalities which made up the Soviet Union had been held together by the centralized economic and political institutions of state socialism. As Gorbachev's perestroika transformed those institutions, the multinational Soviet state began to weaken. A new union might have been stitched together – and, indeed, nearly was in 1991 – but this aim clashed with the political ambitions of the emerging dominant political coalition in Russia, which found that it could consolidate its power only by separating Russia from the other Soviet republics. This spelled the end of the Union.

Although no one predicted this chain of events in advance, one can see how the basic structure of Soviet state socialism made this outcome a likely one. While many accidental events played a role in this process, the victory of the political coalition favoring capitalism was not the result of pure chance. The success of Gorbachev's bold venture of reforming and democratizing socialism depended not just on the technical feasibility of the reform plans, but on whether Gorbachev and his associates could gather the necessary political support to carry them out. As the reforms reduced the power of the very top leadership of the hierarchical Soviet system, the broader party–state elite became the decisive power broker.[16]

The Old Guard leaders who sought to preserve the old system with only cosmetic changes found little support within the elite. As a result, the coup plotters of the summer of 1991 soon found themselves very isolated. But Gorbachev and the others promoting the reform of socialism also had difficulty rallying the elite to their program, as the elite grew increasingly skeptical of their reform plans. The bulk of the elite concluded that a democratized form of socialism had little to offer them. That direction of change threatened to reduce their power and material privileges. Once the future course of the Soviet system was opened to serious internal debate by the policy of glasnost (openness), support for capitalism grew with astonishing speed within this elite, because that path appeared to offer the only way to maintain, and even increase, its power and privileges.

The political significance of Boris Yeltsin has been widely misunderstood in the West, where he has been seen primarily as a supporter of democracy. A rising star of the early perestroika period who had been cast out of his job as Moscow Party boss, Yeltsin took advantage of the new openness to campaign against the leadership, calling initially for ill-defined radical political and economic change. This stance brought him support from democratic intellectuals and from ordinary voters. But, once chosen as leader of the Russian Republic in May 1990, his subsequent victory over Gorbachev and over the Old Guard depended most importantly on his ability to win the support of a decisive part of the party–state elite. He accomplished this by clearly signalling to the elite his intention to rapidly sweep away socialism and head full-speed toward a capitalist future for Russia. Thus, the ultimate explanation for the surprisingly sudden and peaceful demise of the Soviet system was that it was abandoned by most of its own elite, whose material and ideological ties to any form of socialism had grown weaker and weaker as the Soviet system evolved. It was a revolution from above.[17]

Members of the party–state elite played various roles in the process of abandonment of socialism in favor of building capitalism. Some, as early as 1987, used their connections and access to money and other resources to start private businesses. Others became political leaders of the drive to bring capitalism to the USSR. The switch from defense of socialism to praise for capitalism appeared to require a drastic change of worldview for the old elite. Many Western observers have been puzzled, and a bit suspicious, at the sudden mass conversion of thousands of former Soviet Communist officials. But since Stalin's day the Soviet leadership had gone through frequent sharp reversals on key policy issues. By the 1980s ideology had long since ceased to have any real significance for most of the Soviet elite. Exchanging Communist ideology for advocacy of private property and free markets did not prove to be difficult for the highly pragmatic members of this group. No deeply held political beliefs had to be abandoned, because they had had none in the first place. There were exceptions – true believers in some form of socialism were present within the elite of the Soviet system – but they turned out to be a small minority.

The idea that the Soviet Communist elite played the key role in bringing capitalism to the former Soviet Union runs contrary to deeply held beliefs in the West.[18] Western analysts spent decades documenting the evils of the Soviet system, and the Soviet Communist elite was seen as the ultimate perpetrator of those evils. When the Soviet system suddenly met its end, Western analysts naturally tended to interpret it as a victory over the former Soviet elite. According to the dominant Western view, as the Soviet planned economy finally began to collapse, the Soviet elite made every effort to save it, but was unable to do so. When the Soviet people began to demonstrate and vote for democracy and capitalism, the Soviet elite is presumed to have resisted to the end but to have been ultimately defeated. That this very same elite might have played the leading role in bringing about the Soviet demise in order to install Western-style capitalism would appear implausible to most Western analysts of the Soviet system.[19]

It has not escaped the notice of Western analysts that some former Communist officials turned up as capitalists in the new Russia. However, this has been explained as making the best of a situation they had sought to prevent. It has even been suggested that the former Communist elite has been trying to hijack the popular revolution for capitalism. In our view, the elite did not have to hijack someone else's revolution, since they were the ones who made it in the first place.

The interpretation of the Soviet demise as a capitalist revolution carried out with the support of the Soviet party–state elite is not a conspiracy theory of secret maneuvers by a few top officials. What took place was a complex political battle that involved many groups in Soviet society. As we shall see, supporters of capitalism arose from various sectors of Soviet society in addition to the party–state elite. Some of those who came to support capitalism did so consciously and stated their new goal quite openly.[20] Many others who called for private ownership of business and free markets believed that the terms "socialism" and "capitalism" had become outmoded and did not use the term "capitalism" to describe the new system they favored. However, since the combination of private business and relatively free markets defines the system that has traditionally been called "capitalism," it is reasonable for the social analyst to refer to such a position as pro-capitalist, whether or not all of those holding such views think of it in those terms.[21] It is also worth noting that, while perceptions of material self-interest played a major role in the growing support for capitalism, the new supporters of that direction of change generally believed that it would be good for the country as well as for their own individual interests.

Although it may be uncongenial to the currently dominant beliefs in the West, in our view the evidence supports an interpretation of the Soviet demise as a revolution from above. Unlike other explanations, this one accounts for the extremely rapid, and relatively peaceful, character of the process. Furthermore, this interpretation of the Soviet demise helps to explain the enormous difficulties that have arisen with the plan to install capitalism in independent Russia, as well as helping to clarify the complex political battles that have dominated Russia since its independence in 1992.

This book recounts the major developments in the Soviet Union, showing how, and why, the world-shaking events of the demise of state socialism and of the Soviet Union took place. Part I provides the necessary background for analyzing the Soviet demise. It takes a look at the state socialist system, to show where it came from, what it was, and how it worked. It examines the turn from rapid growth to economic stagnation in the mid-1970s, and it shows how this prepared the way for Gorbachev's rise to power and the adoption of his reform program of perestroika.

Part II investigates the process by which perestroika, which was conceived as a socialist reform program, ended up instead producing the demise of the Soviet system. Perestroika had three main dimensions – glasnost, or openness; economic reform; and democratization of political institutions. Each of these is examined in turn. The manner in which these policies were carried out contributed, in ways never expected by the leadership, to the eventual defeat of the reform effort. Part II examines how and why a decisive part of the party–state elite came to support the pro-capitalist position by 1991. It traces the complex political battle in the Soviet Union during 1989–91, to learn why it ended with victory for the pro-capitalist coalition and the disintegration of the Soviet state. The relation between the battle for power by the groups favoring capitalism and the rise of nationalist movements is also considered.

Part III concerns the aftermath of the Soviet demise. It analyzes developments from 1992 through 1995 in Russia, the largest and most influential successor state to the former Soviet Union.[22] It examines Russia's adoption of the "shock therapy," or neoliberal, program for rapidly building a capitalist economy. It looks into the severe economic problems that followed and considers the reasons for those problems. It examines the political evolution of Russia since 1991, including the growing authoritarianism of the Yeltsin government and the remarkable rise from the grave of the Communist Party. It is by no means obvious that the current attempt to build Western-style democratic capitalism will succeed in Russia. The future of Russia's economic and political system remains highly uncertain.

Part III concludes with a consideration of the implications of these events for the feasibility of a democratic, cooperative, egalitarian alternative to capitalism. The dominant interpretation of the demise of Soviet state socialism holds that it represents the final victory of capitalism over socialism. It is said that the failure of socialism has now been acknowledged by those who tried it the longest; the future belongs to capitalism, there being no alternative.

We will argue that this conclusion is premature. What met its end in the former Soviet Union was a particular variant of socialism – one that was undemocratic, repressive, and in its economic organization, greatly overcentralized. It had some achievements to its credit, particularly its rapid industrialization without enormous extremes of wealth and poverty. But it was far removed from the system of popular ownership and control of society's productive institutions envisioned by Marx and generations of Western socialists. That the Soviet attempt to transform undemocratic state socialism into democratic socialism failed does not demonstrate that the latter system is either unworkable or unattainable. The Soviet experience, and the process by which the Soviet system met its end, hold important lessons for the shape of any viable socialist system that may arise in the future.

The analysis offered in the following chapters is not a fully comprehensive one. Probably the most important omission concerns the demise of state socialism elsewhere in Eastern and Central Europe. The latter process was related, in complex ways, to the Soviet demise. Beyond a few limited observations, we do not take account of this interdependence, due to constraints of time and expertise. We also cannot comment here on the ways in which the process of collapse in Eastern Europe may have been similar, and the ways in which it may have differed, from the process that unfolded in the Soviet Union. The full story of the demise of state socialism remains to be written. But this system originated in the Soviet Union, there it struck its deepest roots, and there it lasted the longest. Understanding the internal forces that propelled the Soviet demise seems a worthwhile goal in its own right.

Part I

The Soviet system

INTRODUCTION TO PART I

The demise of the Soviet system was a product of that system's particular features and history. Part I concerns the origins of the Soviet system and its evolution, through Mikhail Gorbachev's rise to power. Chapter 2 examines the socialist critique of capitalism and vision of an alternative socioeconomic system, which formed the background for the Bolshevik Revolution of 1917. After the revolution a decade passed before a clear shape emerged for the new society. The decision to build a particular model of socialism in the Soviet Union at the end of the 1920s, and the main features of the Soviet system that emerged, are considered in this chapter. The nature of the new elite which arose in the Soviet Union is analyzed.

For many decades the Soviet system appeared to be bringing rapid economic progress, despite serious and persistent economic problems. Chapter 3 looks at the evidence on Soviet economic growth, including the recent challenge to the conventional wisdom on this issue. Chapter 3 presents a case that, after 1975, Soviet economic performance significantly worsened and considers explanations for this development. Gorbachev's reform program, perestroika, is found to be a response to both the long-standing problems of the Soviet economy and the post-1975 deterioration in economic performance.

Chapter 2

Socialism and the Soviet system

As Soviet President Mikhail S. Gorbachev battled unsuccessfully to preserve the Soviet Union in the months following the failed coup of August 1991, he repeatedly mentioned the "socialist choice" of 1917. This was a reference to the Soviet Union's birth in one of the major revolutions of the twentieth century. After the Bolsheviks seized power in Petrograd in 1917, the Bolshevik leader Vladimir Ilich Lenin declared, "we must now set about building a proletarian socialist state in Russia."[1]

This "socialist choice" in Russia was the first victory of a political movement that had sprung to life some 70 years earlier. In 1848 Karl Marx and Friedrich Engels's pamphlet, the *Communist Manifesto*, announced to the world that "A spectre is haunting Europe – the spectre of Communism."[2] Marx and Engels denounced capitalism and foresaw a workers' uprising that would replace it with a new, more just social system. Attracted to this vision, workers and dissident intellectuals formed socialist parties in every major European country, as well as in North America, in the second half of the nineteenth century. What was the vision which led them to condemn the existing order and call for something radically different, a vision which was to inspire the Russian Revolution some 70 years later?

THE IDEA OF SOCIALISM

It often comes as a great surprise to those who have never read the *Communist Manifesto* to learn that it contains some of the highest praise for capitalism ever found in print, such as the following:

> The bourgeoisie ... has been the first to show what man's activity can bring about. It has accomplished wonders far surpassing Egyptian pyramids, Roman Aqueducts, Gothic cathedrals ... The bourgeoisie cannot exist without constantly revolutionizing the instruments of production ... The bourgeoisie, during its rule of scarce one hundred

years, has created more massive and more colossal productive forces than have all preceding generations together.[3]

But Marx and Engels believed the impressive accomplishments of capitalism had a dark side – they rested on the exploitation of the class that labored to produce these great works. A life of poverty and insecurity was the reward the working class received for its role in these accomplishments. The capitalists who owned the means of production, Marx and Engels insisted, captured all the benefits. The Medieval era's aristocracy of birth had been replaced by one of money.

The socialist critique went beyond the inequality that characterized early capitalism. It condemned the periodic economic depressions, when production stopped despite the continuing need for more goods. It pointed out the wastefulness and pain of unemployment for the new working class, many of whom still remembered the previously more stable life of the small farmer or town artisan. It abhorred the treatment of workers as simple commodities for the production of wealth.[4]

Unlike their predecessors the utopian socialists, Marx and Engels believed the next, higher stage in human social evolution would come not by intellectuals convincing the rich and powerful of the merits of social change but from the political and economic struggles of the central victims of capitalism, the working class. Lenin's reference to "a proletarian socialist state" is based on this vision of social change. The proletariat, or working class, was destined to follow a path from self-organization for material improvement to a struggle for power. Eventually the working class would overthrow the capitalist system and build a new society in its place.

Marx and Engels did not give any detailed blueprint for the socialist society they foresaw and advocated. They concentrated instead on analyzing capitalism and its tendencies of development, which, they were convinced, held the secret of building the new society. Only a few comments on what a future socialism might be like are found scattered through their writings. The new society would have stages, beginning with a lengthy period during which the vestiges of capitalism, and its imprint on social institutions and individual psychology, would remain relatively strong. But eventually a new classless society would evolve. Marxian socialists traditionally used the term "socialism" for the first stage, reserving "communism" for the final stage.[5]

Prior to the Russian Revolution, socialists debated about the details of what the new society would look like. But there was wide agreement that three key economic institutions would characterize a socialist system. First, society's instruments of production – factories, machines, power and mass transportation systems, and so forth – would become public property, rather than belonging to private owners. This would end exploitation of workers by the owners of capital. Henceforth no one would be able to gain an income simply by owning property.

Second, production would be guided by an economic plan rather than market forces. Marx and Engels contrasted the planning and order that exist *within* each capitalist enterprise with what they viewed as the "chaos" of market exchange relations.[6] Just as the individual capitalist plans the activities that are to take place within an enterprise, the working class as a whole, once in power, would use a system of planning to direct the economic process in society as a whole. They believed that economic planning would abolish the unemployment and periodic business depressions that had characterized capitalism.

Third, socialism would do away with production for profit. Capitalists decide what to produce, and how to produce it, based on what they expect will bring the greatest profit. Competition among capitalists seeking to make profits is the source of technological progress and economic growth in capitalism, but Marx and Engels viewed it as less than an ideal way to bring progress. Socialism would replace production for profit with "production for use." Socialist enterprises would produce to meet people's needs, using the most up-to-date technologies, not to gain profits but to benefit society. With no need for trade secrets, knowledge could be widely shared among enterprises, and technological progress and product quality would surpass the admittedly impressive performance that capitalism had registered.

The early socialists had less to say about the political structure of a future socialism than about its economic structure. In Marx and Engels's view, governments had always been instruments by which one class rules over and dominates another. Even in a democratic republic in a capitalist society, socialists argued that genuine majority rule did not obtain. The great wealth and economic power of the capitalist class prevented the working-class majority from exercising real political sovereignty.[7]

It was assumed that after taking power the working class would become the new ruling class, using state power to ensure that the defeated capitalist class could not stage a comeback or interfere with the construction of socialism. Marx and Engels used the phrase "dictatorship of the proletariat" to express the idea of the workers as the new ruling group, parallel to their view of the capitalist state as a "dictatorship of the bourgeoisie." But most socialists expected that, in the relation between the workers and the socialist state, democracy would prevail. After all, how could the majority class of workers serve as the ruling class, except through democratic institutions that would enable the members of that class to freely express their views and arrive at collective decisions? It was expected that such a "workers' democracy," having no class of wealthy property owners to subvert democratic principles, would be a more genuine democracy than the world had previously seen.

The institutions of public ownership, economic planning, production for use, and a democratic workers' state were supposed to embody and promote certain social values appropriate to a socialist society – equality, economic security, cooperation, and democracy. It was believed that socialism would quickly eliminate poverty, as a more egalitarian distribution of income accompanied a more rapid development, and more full use, of society's productive capacity. The wastefulness and insecurity resulting from unemployment and periodic business depressions would be banished through economic planning. Cooperation would replace the dog-eat-dog competition of capitalism.

After a period of further economic development and the disappearance of the remnants of the old system, society would finally reach communism. At this stage, classes would be fully eliminated for the first time in human history since the days of primitive hunter–gatherer bands. In place of class conflict, Marx and Engels foresaw "an association, in which the free development of each is the condition for the free development of all."[8] Distinctions between town and country, and between manual and mental labor, would fade away. The state as an instrument of coercion would disappear. Once the new society was achieved in all the major countries of the world, ending the world-wide capitalist rivalry for control of resources and markets, war would become a thing of the past.

Socialists argued that capitalism was not oppressive only to the working class. Even the capitalists were seen as not truly free. They are subject to the laws of motion of the system over which they preside, as much as are the workers. Capitalists must seek profits over all else; they must accumulate capital. Those who fail to do so effectively are always in danger of falling behind in the battle of competition and ending up as ex-capitalists. Socialism was supposed to be fundamentally different. It would be a new stage of human development, in which for the first time people would achieve conscious control over the principles of operation of their society, rather than be controlled by it.[9]

THE RUSSIAN REVOLUTION

Human motivations are always complex, but more than any other factor it was a belief in the socialist critique of existing society and vision of an alternative – not a desire for fame, riches, or power as an end in itself – which led the Bolsheviks to seize power in Russia in 1917.[10] Lenin was a close student of Marx and Engels. He took voluminous notes on their works, believing that they contained the ideas that could guide a revolutionary socialist party to power. There is an old debate among scholars about whether Lenin was a true follower of Marxist ideas or whether instead he produced a distorted version of them in his drive for power. Whichever may be the case, it is clear that Lenin added a new theory of how to make a workers' revolution which is not found in earlier Marxist writing.

In Russia, ruled by the repressive Tsarist regime, Lenin advocated building a disciplined, secretive party of professional revolutionaries. The Bolsheviks organized their party on a military-like principle which they called "democratic centralism." The central leadership debated policies and made decisions by majority vote among themselves. However, once a policy decision was made, both leaders and rank-and-file members were required to carry it out without further question.

Such a party was the only means, Lenin argued, to survive the Tsarist secret police while spreading the socialist message to the urban working class. To make the revolution, there must be a disciplined party to act as the vanguard, or leader, of the working class in the battle for power. The democratic centralist method of internal party organization, and the vanguard relation between party and working class, proved to be an effective way to build a strong organization under the Tsarist autocracy and to seize power in the chaos that followed the collapse of the Tsarist regime in 1917. But it had important implications for the kind of society that would be built after the revolution.

No one had expected the first attempt to build a socialist state to take place in relatively backward Russia. Marxian theory suggested that socialism would appear first in one of the most economically advanced capitalist countries, such as Britain or Germany. On the eve of World War I, the major cities of western Russia had large factories and a sizeable industrial working class, with about $2\frac{1}{2}$ million workers involved in large-scale manufacturing and mining. However, the urban working class was surrounded by an enormous sea of peasants. More than 80 per cent of the population lived in rural areas and about 75 per cent were engaged in traditional farming.[11] The majority of the peasants were poor and had many grievances against the landowning aristocracy and the Tsarist regime, and as a result they might serve as a temporary ally of the working class in a battle against the old regime. However, most socialists believed that it would not be easy to win over the peasants to socialism, since their ancient desire was to become the proprietor of their own plot of land rather than build a new society based on common property ownership.

In 1917 the discontent of Russia's workers and peasants at the extreme material privations stemming from the world war threatened the Tsarist regime. Bolshevik organizers, along with their more moderate socialist brethren, the Mensheviks, found a receptive audience for socialist ideas among the urban workers. Another party, the Socialist Revolutionaries, organized among the peasants. In March[12] of that year, a series of strikes in the winter capital, Petrograd, led to a spontaneous workers' uprising. When the Petrograd military garrison defied their officers and went over to the workers, the Tsarist regime was toppled.

For the following eight months, power was shared by a new Provisional Government and the "soviets" which sprang up across Russia. The soviets were institutions which represented workers, peasants, soldiers, and sailors.[13] The most influential political groups in the soviets were the three above-mentioned socialist parties. The Provisional Government decided to keep Russia in the war, provoking growing popular discontent and a rapid radicalization of both workers and peasants. Peasants seized land from the landowners, and workers demanded the right to run their factories.

The Bolsheviks, the most radical of the three socialist parties, kept up an incessant call for withdrawal of Russia from the war, workers' control of factories, land for the peasants – and all power to the soviets to enforce those demands. By November the Bolsheviks had won a majority in the Petrograd and Moscow soviets, and hundreds of soviets across Russia passed resolutions calling for a full transfer of power to the soviets.[14] Sensing the opportunity, in November the Bolsheviks organized a seizure of power in the name of the Petrograd soviet. This was soon followed by a similar seizure of power in Moscow. A meeting of a Congress of Soviets from across Russia convened in Petrograd and named a new Bolshevik-dominated government.[15]

Taking power and holding onto it were two different matters. Initially controlling only the main cities, the Bolsheviks faced armed opposition by the supporters of the old regime, who received some troops and supplies from the major Western powers. Despite the Bolsheviks' limited base of support in the countryside, they were able to build a "Red Army" which routed their opponents and won control of most of the former Russian Empire by the end of 1920. In 1922 the new regime created the Union of Soviet Socialist Republics, or Soviet Union for short.[16]

THE FORM OF BOLSHEVIK RULE

From the start, Bolshevik rule took a harsh and authoritarian form. On paper, political power was held by the soviets, which had the form of popularly elected institutions. But in fact all power was held by the Communist Party.[17] The soviets became rubber stamps for policies decided on by the Communist Party leadership. Viewing itself as the vanguard of the working class in whose name it ruled, the Communist Party soon began to outlaw political opposition. At first other left-wing parties were allowed to survive, but after a few years those too were banned. In 1921 the lively and open debate which had taken place among the Communist leadership was proscribed when political factions within the party were banned.[18]

Why did the new Soviet state, contrary to the expectations of most socialists, take such an authoritarian form? Sympathetic observers at first hoped that the authoritarian course of the revolution was a temporary necessity imposed by the requirements of winning the brutal civil war. But after the Red Army emerged victorious, ending the immediate threat of a return of the old regime, the Communists failed to move toward democracy.[19]

Some argue that the thousand years of Russian autocracy, with an absence of any significant democratic tradition, explains the Communist adoption of authoritarian methods of rule in Russia. While this may have been a factor, it cannot be the entire explanation. Traditions do not last forever. The emergence of durable democratic institutions in many previously autocratic societies over the past several centuries attests to the possibility of effectively breaking with a long authoritarian tradition. Democracy in contemporary France, Germany, and Spain are all examples of such a break with historical precedent.

The Leninist form of party, which was so effective at seizing power in the name of the working class in the Russia of 1917, may provide part of the explanation. The democratic centralist party proved well adapted to leading an armed struggle against a repressive but politically weak regime – as evidenced by later Communist victories in China, Yugoslavia, and Vietnam. While such parties were able to mobilize masses of workers, and in some cases peasants, to fight for power, they were not conducive to constructing a democratic state after the old regime had been vanquished. The Bolsheviks, and later Communist parties elsewhere, were compelled to pay close attention to the needs and wishes of their mass base during the period of struggle for power. But once safely in control of the state, the democratic centralist party, with its military-like structure, had a tendency to produce a top-down structure of power in the new state. The principle of setting policies by the top leadership, with the rank and file expected to carry them out without question, was extended from the party to the entire society.

After the civil war had ended in Russia, many Communist leaders, Lenin included, occasionally complained about the increasingly authoritarian behavior of the state which they had created.[20] The seemingly inexorable trend toward authoritarianism may have been partly a result of the uncomfortable social isolation in which the Bolsheviks found themselves after the civil war.[21] The Bolsheviks never had a significant political base in the countryside, where the great majority of the population lived. But the civil war left the new regime with an even narrower base of support than it had in 1917. Much of its urban working-class base had dispersed. Many of the most dedicated socialist workers fought and died in the bloody civil war, while others moved to villages to survive the near-total collapse of Russian industry during and after the civil war. Many other workers left the factories to take positions in the bureaucracy of the new Bolshevik government. The Bolsheviks had seized power to rule in the name of a working class which practically disappeared from under them. The peasant majority, while happy to be rid of their former landlord masters, felt little connection to the urban-based Bolsheviks.

The Bolsheviks faced the problem of how to rule the gigantic country, and build the new socialist system to which they were dedicated, without any discernible social base in society. They solved this problem by substituting their party for a social base. With the disciplined, democratic centralist party as their instrument, they would industrialize the country, and by so doing bring into existence the working class in whose name they ruled.

The authoritarian rule of the Russian Communists divided the world socialist movement. The leadership of most of the established socialist parties of Europe opposed the new Soviet regime and disclaimed any connection to it. Those socialists who thought the Bolshevik transgressions of democracy were justified by the circumstances formed new parties, generally known as Communist parties. This division in the world socialist movement, into "Socialist parties" critical of Moscow and "Communist parties" supportive of Moscow, persisted until the 1991 collapse of the Soviet Union.

SHIFTING ECONOMIC POLICIES IN THE 1920s

More than a decade passed after the revolution before a stable new economic system took shape in Russia. During the civil war period of 1918–20, so-called "War Communism" temporarily prevailed. Industry was nationalized and all production and distribution were geared to the war effort. Under conditions of extreme privation, as blockade and the chaos of war cut off supplies to the major cities, a very centralized system of economic administration was created – as is typical in such wartime conditions.

Victory in the civil war came at the cost of an economy in ruins. After heated debate, in 1921 the Bolsheviks made an abrupt turn in economic policy, adopting what was called the "New Economic Policy," which lasted until 1928. Foreign capitalists were invited to invest in Russia, and private business was encouraged in trade, services, and even industry. In agriculture, the peasants were left free to work their newly-won lands as they wished, selling their produce in the market.

By 1927–28 the economy had largely recovered from the devastation of war and revolution. Again, heated debate took place within the Communist leadership about the next step in economic policy. One faction, associated at first with Leon Trotsky and later with G. Zinoviev and L. Kamenev, favored rapid industrialization and efforts to consolidate the individual peasant agriculture. They feared that free peasant agriculture was a breeding ground for a rural capitalist class, a danger they hoped to head off by converting agriculture to a collective form. The opposing faction, led by Nikolai Bukharin, advocated continuing the New Economic Policy, with a gradual process of industrialization and a more gradual organization of cooperatives for peasants.

The resolution of this debate occurred quite differently from the manner in which the New Economic Policy had been adopted. After Lenin died in 1924, Joseph Stalin, the general secretary of the party, steadily accumulated power in his hands. In a well-known series of maneuvers, Stalin first defeated the advocates of rapid industrialization by siding with Bukharin's gradual development strategy, and then defeated Bukharin and the advocates of the gradualist approach.[22] By the end of the 1920s, Stalin had sufficient personal power to dictate a new economic model.

Having gained full power, Stalin set off on a new course of immediate forced collectivization of agriculture, rapid industrialization, and the complete elimination of private business. Stalin's power was so great that this new course was not even the formal decision of the Communist Party. The first Five Year Plan, which began in 1928, had ambitious targets for industrialization, but it did not foretell the radical remaking of Russia's social and economic structure which was about to take place.[23] The launching of the new model began a year later, in 1929, when Stalin personally initiated the campaign to collectivize by force Russia's millions of peasants.

By the end of the 1920s, a new set of economic and political institutions was either in place or being constructed, and this became 'the Soviet system'. The economic features of this system were to change little during the next 55 years, until the Gorbachev era. The basic political institutions also remained relatively stable over that period, although the locus of political power, and the way in which it was exercised, changed quite significantly after Stalin died in 1953.

THE ECONOMIC STRUCTURE OF THE SOVIET SYSTEM

The most important economic institutions of the new Soviet system were state ownership of the means of production and central economic planning. Nearly the entire productive capital in the Soviet Union was owned by the state. The only significant exception was collective farms, which were considered to be the common property of the members of the farming collective.[24]

The system was coordinated by a highly centralized, hierarchical form of economic planning. The Soviet government, under the guidance of the party leadership, developed five-year and one-year economic plans for the entire country. The five-year plans expressed the intended direction of economic development, while the one-year plans were operative documents carrying the force of law. They specified target outputs for every significant product.

At the top of the planning system was the agency called Gosplan, which had the difficult role of developing an internally consistent economic plan for the vast country. Gosplan used a method called "material balances" to calculate the quantities of productive inputs – steel, concrete, industrial machinery, etc. – that must be produced to make possible the production of the target levels of final goods. At the Gosplan level, the plan specified target outputs of relatively broad product categories.[25] Below Gosplan were government ministries for the major sectors of the economy, which broke down the plan into more narrowly defined product targets for their area of specialization. Actual production took place at enterprises, each of which was under the authority of a particular ministry. At the enterprise level, the plan specified specific quantities of outputs, as well as the inputs to be provided. Gossnab, the supply agency, managed supply relations among enterprises.[26]

Money and finance played a strictly secondary role in the Soviet system. Once an enterprise received its production assignment, the state banking system provided it with the necessary financing to enable it to pay for the labor and material inputs specified in the economic plan. It was the plan's production orders which set economic activity in motion, not the possession of money or credit.

State enterprises tended to be extremely large, both because of a strong belief that giant enterprises were more efficient and the practical consideration that the central planning authorities could more easily deal with a smaller number of giant enterprises than with many small ones. At the enterprise level, single-person management was the ruling principle. Each enterprise had a general director who was given control of the enterprise and was responsible to the higher authorities for its performance. The party secretary and the trade union head for the enterprise also played an active role, but the general director was the ultimate authority.

The Communist Party (CPSU) had an apparatus parallel to the state planning organs. The central committee of the CPSU had departments specializing in the main branches of production, which participated in overseeing the implementation of the plan, as well as its formulation. Party secretaries at the republican, provincial, and local levels were involved in carrying out the plan for their area of jurisdiction, along with the parallel state agencies and enterprises. In each city, the secretary of the party committee would work with the head of the local administration and the general directors of the main enterprises in the city to make sure the plan was fulfilled.

It would not be accurate to say that the Soviet system was entirely based on central economic planning. Markets played a secondary role. Consumer goods were partly distributed through retail stores at which consumers could buy what they wished from among what was available, at prices regulated by the state. However, non-market forms of distribution of consumer goods also played an important role, including the rationing of goods that were in short supply; distribution of goods at special prices to workers, managers, and officials through their workplace; and distribution of high-quality goods to high officials via special stores. Workers were allocated to jobs mainly through a labor market, in which workers chose jobs based on rates of pay and personal preferences.[27] There was also a black market in both producer and consumer goods, as well as an informally tolerated gray market in which enterprises traded goods outside the official plan. But central planning was the main institution for setting economic activity in motion and coordinating it.

The Soviet system included extensive provision of public services to the population. Much of this was done directly by the government. However, a unique feature of this system was the widespread provision of public services directly through the place of employment. Many large enterprises financed and provided day-care centers, clinics, schools, health spas, vacation resorts, and other amenities for employees and their families. In the many single-company towns in the Soviet Union, the dominant enterprise directly financed many of the town's public services.[28]

THE POLITICAL STRUCTURE OF THE SOVIET SYSTEM

Political power was exercised by two parallel bureaucracies in the Soviet Union, those of the state and the Communist Party.[29] On paper the party had a democratic structure. Party members elected delegates to periodic party congresses, which approved the party's policies and selected the central committee, a body of several hundred members in the post-World War II period. The central committee in turn selected a political bureau ("politburo" for short) of one or two dozen members, and a general secretary, to act between meetings of the central committee.[30]

But in reality power flowed from top to bottom, not from the bottom up. The general secretary was the dominant figure in the system, and the politburo, chaired by the general secretary, was the most important body in setting policy on important questions. The central committee had a full-time executive staff known as the "secretariat," which served as the executive arm of the politburo. The central committee became important when a new general secretary had to be chosen, but normally it was dominated by the politburo. Party congresses were infrequently held and exercised no real authority,[31] and individual party members merely carried out the policies set at the top.

The party exercised power in society in several ways. It supervised the work of the government – for example, Gosplan and the industrial ministries reported directly to party bodies about their work. The party also, through its own structures, directly formulated state policies and participated in carrying them out. For example, the party played a central role in developing the economic plans, and as was noted above, its local cadres helped to implement them. The central committee staff was deeply involved in matters of foreign affairs, state security, science, culture, and other policy areas. But the most fundamental source of the party's power was its control over the selection of government, and non-government, officials.

The practice of party control over appointments to important positions was known as the "nomenklatura" system.[32] The top party bodies (the politburo and central committee) determined who would occupy all top posts in the government, the military, the security agencies, the mass media, trade unions, professional organizations, and so forth. Lower-level party bodies named individuals to lower-level positions in state and non-state organizations. Within the party, the highest-level bodies in Moscow controlled appointments to lower-level party bodies and to top party positions in the republics, provinces, and major cities.

The government had a separate structure from that of the party, and it too appeared democratic on paper. The Soviet constitution described a democratic government on the parliamentary model. The members of the soviets were supposed to be selected through free elections. The Supreme Soviet, the top legislative body, named a Council of Ministers which served as the executive and administrative arm of government. The Chairman of the Council of Ministers played the role of prime minister, or head of government.

However, the reality was quite different from a parliamentary form of government. The elections to the soviets were uncontested. The Communist Party determined the nominees for the soviets, as well as selecting the members of the Council of Ministers and the prime minister. The Supreme Soviet, far from being an independent legislature, served as a rubber stamp for proposals prepared by the party hierarchy.

Western specialists on Soviet politics in the post-World War II period debated the exact location of political power within the top institutions of the Soviet system.[33] Some leading state officials sat on the politburo, and nearly all members of the Council of Ministers were also on the party central committee.[34] It is not necessary for our purposes to determine the exact distribution of decision-making between party and state apparatuses. What is not in doubt is that power was concentrated at the top of those two bureaucracies, which interpenetrated one another. The "party–state system" is an apt name for it.[35]

While the basic economic structure of the Soviet system did not change after Stalin died, the nature of political power did. The above description of the Soviet political system describes the form of political power during the Stalin era, but the content was different under Stalin. From 1928 until his death in 1953, Stalin ruled as an all-powerful dictator. It is questionable whether it is even accurate to say that the party held power during that period. Stalin ruled mainly through the secret police, not the party.

Stalin launched the forced collectivization of some 125 million peasants on his own in late 1929. The chaos which resulted from this move led to a terrible famine in which millions died of starvation and disease during 1932–33. In 1936–38 Stalin initiated a series of mass arrests and public political trials which led to the execution of practically all of the original leadership of the Bolshevik party. Between 1935 and 1939 over one million party members perished.[36] As late as 1950 a member of the politburo was executed. In addition to top party leaders, prison and/or execution claimed many ministry officials, enterprise directors, army officers, and cultural figures, as well as ordinary workers and peasants accused of "sabotage." Even officials of the secret police carrying out this terror were periodically subjected to it themselves. All told, some 20 million unnatural deaths resulted from Stalin's methods of rule.[37]

No other major Communist-led revolution produced such a slaughter of its own leadership. Stalin's rule was marked by a turning away from many of the ideological themes which had previously been associated with Bolshevism. Stalin revived Russian nationalism, anti-Semitism, and conservative cultural norms. Earlier legislation favoring workers, women, and national minorities was repealed or ignored. Egalitarianism was condemned. There was a decided shift away from the idea that the masses make history to the view that Stalin, the great leader, was the source of all progress – a cult of the leader which had been completely absent under Lenin.[38]

Stalin's terror-based dictatorship ended with his death in 1953. A few years later Nikita Khrushchev, the new party leader, denounced Stalin's reign of terror. In the post-Stalin period the Soviet political system emerged as one of rule by the general secretary, politburo, secretariat, and central committee, along the lines described above. It remained an authoritarian, top-down system, and political opponents of the system were subject to persecution, exile, or imprisonment. But it was no longer a terroristic dictatorship. Those on the losing end of personal or political disputes within the leadership henceforth were demoted rather than executed.[39]

WHAT WAS THE SOVIET SYSTEM?

What sort of social system was this? Was it socialism, or something else? This question has provoked much debate, and an enormous literature, over the years. Of course, the Soviet leadership and its supporters – at least until Gorbachev – always claimed that the system, whatever imperfections it might have, was the embodiment of Marxian socialism. They claimed it was a workers' state in which the Communist Party was simply the instrument of the working class, interpreting and carrying out its wishes.[40] They viewed state property as property of the people, and economic planning as an instrument by which the people ran their economic affairs.[41]

This view clashes with the Soviet reality. It is apparent that neither the working class nor the Soviet people as a whole had sovereignty in the Soviet system. Power resided at the top of the party–state bureaucracy. From the formulation of the economic plan down to the operation of an individual enterprise, the workers lacked the power to make economic decisions about how the system would operate.

The Soviet system differed radically from capitalism. It bore a superficial similarity to capitalism, in that productive labor was performed by workers who were paid a wage, as in a capitalist system. But many of the distinctive features of capitalism stem from competition among independent owners of capital to make sales in the market, and that was completely absent from the Soviet system. Capitalism's efficiency and dynamism spring from that source, as do the more negative features noted above. While the Soviet system generated a high rate of capital accumulation, that was due to political orders from the top, not the pressure of competition.[42]

The most useful way to understand the Soviet system is as a mixed system, with significant socialist elements, but with non-socialist elements as well. The term "state socialism" seems to best capture this concept, since the role and nature of the state represented the most important non-socialist feature of the Soviet system.[43]

Despite the fact that the working class did not in any meaningful sense control its economic and political destiny in the Soviet system, there were nevertheless significant socialist features of that system. One was state (and cooperative) ownership of virtually the entire means of production. This meant there was no class of property owners who could gain an income simply by virtue of owning property. Legitimate income in the Soviet system came only from work.[44] The Soviet system was the first in history to build a modern industrial society without capitalist ownership of enterprises.

Coordination of the economy by means of planning was another socialist element in the system. Planning did bring some of the economic benefits which socialists had claimed for it, including an absence of periodic recessions or depressions and a very high rate of economic growth (to be explored in the next chapter). Since enterprises were not in competition with one another, there was scope for kinds of cooperation not found under capitalism, such as the sharing of information about technologies and organizational techniques.[45] The economic plan, not the pursuit of profit, set production in motion. While it was the top political authorities' concept of what was needed that drove the plan, it was nevertheless a form of "production for use," rather than for profit.

The full employment that resulted from economic planning was another socialist feature of the system. There was virtually no aggregate unemployment in the Soviet Union after the early 1930s.[46] On the contrary, there was typically an overall labor shortage. Not only was it easy to find a job quickly in the Soviet system, but once on the job there was a high degree of job security. Workers were rarely laid off or fired. This not only meant that workers had a high degree of personal income security, it also meant that, once the Stalin era terror ended, workers enjoyed a significant degree of informal bargaining power on the job. On paper, enterprise managers had all the power, but in practice, with a labor shortage and a tradition of almost never firing workers, managers had to take account of workers' wishes. This resulted in a more relaxed pace of work than is typical of capitalist enterprises. The top economic planners often complained about their limited power to force workers to work harder than they wished.

The extensive array of public services provided for the population was another socialist feature of the Soviet system. These included free education (up through higher education for those who could qualify), inexpensive child care, very low rents on apartments,[47] inexpensive vacations at workers' resorts, free health care, and guaranteed pensions. Socialist parties which have come to power in Western capitalist democracies, such as in Sweden and Norway, have created similar programs of public benefits for the working population, while leaving the capitalist underpinnings of those societies in place. However, in such social-democratic welfare states, capitalist-financed conservative parties, aided by the pressures coming from international competition, continually press for the dismantling or reduction of social programs. No such challenge to social benefits ever arose in the Soviet system, and the programs did not suffer the cutbacks which they have periodically encountered in capitalist welfare states.

While one should not judge the nature of a social system by its official ideology or its mere forms, the official socialist ideology of the Soviet system had a certain impact. Since it was supposed to be a workers' state, the soviets at all levels of the system had significant worker (and peasant) representation on them – an outcome facilitated by party control of who would serve on such bodies.[48] While the soviets had little real power, this did create a certain prestige and dignity for workers – an outcome which, as we shall see below, caused significant resentment among some members of the intelligentsia.

In keeping with socialist values, the distribution of money income was significantly more egalitarian in the Soviet system than in capitalist systems, at least after the Stalin period.[49] A common measure of income inequality used for cross-country studies, called the "decile ratio," measures the ratio of the share of total household income received by the richest decile (10 per cent) of households to that received by the poorest decile. A study by a leading Western specialist found the decile ratio to be 4.5 for the Soviet Union in 1967.[50] This meant that the top decile received 4.5 times as much income as the bottom decile. By contrast, the decile ratio was 15.9 for both the United States and France, which is three and a half times as great as the Soviet ratio.[51] This result is not surprising, given the absence of property income in the Soviet system.[52] However, as is noted below, the relatively egalitarian distribution of money income fails to reflect the disequalizing effects of the special perquisites enjoyed by high-level officials.

NON-SOCIALIST FEATURES OF THE SOVIET SYSTEM

Alongside and intertwined with its socialist features, the Soviet system also had important non-socialist institutions. Some of them were reminiscent of Medieval feudalism, while others resembled capitalist institutions.

The most obvious non-socialist feature of the Soviet system was the monopolization of political power by the party–state elite. In the Stalin era, the form of rule took on a Medieval cast, with a cult of the all-knowing and all-powerful leader worthy of any Medieval monarchy. After Stalin the political system evolved into a more modern oligarchy. Even the milder political system of the post-Stalin era was a repressive one that denied the Soviet population basic civil and political rights and freedoms. Without freedom of speech, freedom to publicize one's views, or freedom to organize political parties, it was not possible for the Soviet people to have much say in the determination of state policies.

The party–state elite sought to control virtually every aspect of public life, including even local social clubs. In a manner reminiscent of the feudal serf's enforced tie to a particular manor, Soviet citizens even lacked freedom of movement. Originating in the social chaos induced by the forced collectivization of the early 1930s, the hated internal passport system tied every citizen to a particular city or town. Moving to a different location without official permission was forbidden.[53]

Just as political power was undemocratic and highly centralized, so too was economic power. Even had the political institutions been democratic, with a free vote of the citizenry electing government officials, the structure of the economy, if unchanged, would have been contrary to the socialist idea of workers controlling their economic life. Economic decision-making was very hierarchical. The most important economic decisions were made at the center and passed down as orders to the subordinate levels. The basic economic role of every actor in the system below the ministry level, from enterprise directors to ordinary workers, was to carry out instructions from above. The demand by the workers of Petrograd and Moscow in 1917 to control their factories, a demand echoed by the Bolsheviks at the time, had been an important aspect of the revolution. But this idea faded after the Bolsheviks came to power, and the one-person management system which characterized the Soviet enterprise was borrowed directly from the capitalist organizational manuals of that era.

Yet the internal relations of Soviet workplaces were not entirely capitalist in form. The long job-tenure of workers and the informal workers' power resulting from the shortage of labor promoted a paternalistic form of management. The large Soviet enterprise, with its stable community of long-tenured employees unable to move elsewhere, providing cafeterias for employees' meals, kindergartens for their children, rest homes for their vacations, and even special distributions of consumer goods, came to resemble a paternalistic feudal manor. Soviet enterprise directors viewed themselves to a significant extent as representatives and protectors of their enterprise and its employees – a pattern that would cause surprising departures from expected capitalist norms of enterprise behavior after the enterprises were privatized in the early 1990s.

The material privileges accorded to the Soviet elite ran counter to the egalitarian ethic of socialism. The relatively egalitarian distribution of money income cited above leaves out the special access to consumer goods that members of the elite possessed. There were special stores, open only to the elite, which carried high-quality products, including Western imports, at low prices. There were even special factories that produced high-quality goods for the elite. Special construction enterprises built fine apartment buildings for the elite. Job perks for top officials included use of luxury automobiles and well-appointed state dachas[54] in the country. Both the special stores and the job perks were carefully graded according to the position of an individual within the hierarchy. This system of privilege was never officially admitted before the perestroika period, because of its obvious clash with the official socialist ideology. However, everyone knew about it.

The best things were not for sale in the Soviet system. Simply having money was not enough to get them. Consumption was attached to one's status and position in the hierarchy. One could view this system of favoring status and position over wealth as semi-feudal. Yet it was an effective motivator for the modern Soviet bureaucracy. Practically the only route to a life of growing privilege was to rise within the elite. Failure to rise within the hierarchical structure of the elite left no alternative means of access to a life of privileged comfort.[55]

The difficulty of determining whether an actual social system is socialist has mainly to do with the problem of the special role of political power in socialism. A capitalist system can coexist with a variety of different forms of state power, including the multi-party democracy of the United States or Great Britain, the lengthy one-party rule of postwar Japan or Italy, the authoritarian state of postwar Spain or South Korea, and the terroristic dictatorship of Nazi Germany. In all of these cases, a capitalist class owned the bulk of the means of production, hired wage workers, and competed to make sales in the market.

Socialism never conceived of workers as owning and controlling the means of production as individuals. The technology which capitalism developed made production a social, not an individual, process. If workers were to own and control the instruments of production, and rise above the competition and rivalry of the capitalist market process, they would have to do so through some kind of public institutions.[56] Thus, if socialism must be based on public property, then the nature of the state, who controls it, the rights of citizens, and the decision-making mechanisms that prevail in both political and economic institutions are all intimately related to the definition of socialism. What arose in the Soviet Union had significant socialist features, but what it lacked most fundamentally was popular sovereignty in both the state and the economy. The people were passive recipients, not active participants, in political and economic life. This was its most important non-socialist feature.

The repressive character of the Soviet system, with its denial of many basic rights to its citizens, has led some analysts to the conclusion that it had little or nothing in common with socialism.[57] This conclusion stems from an unduly pure conception of socialism. Supporters of capitalism may feel uncomfortable that the apartheid regime in South Africa and the Nazi regime in Germany both rested upon a capitalist economic base, yet that does not constitute grounds for claiming that those regimes had nothing in common with capitalism. Similarly, the serious negative features of the Soviet system do not negate the simultaneous presence of important socialist economic institutions in that system. The socialist institutions of the Soviet system made it a very different system from its main rival, modern capitalism.[58]

THE PARTY–STATE ELITE

In order to understand the evolution and demise of the Soviet system, we must have a clear picture of the party–state elite which ran the system. It is widely agreed among specialists that the party–state elite was able to solidify and stabilize after the Stalin era, with its waves of purges and executions, had ended. Yet there is no simple way to demarcate the boundary between this elite and the rest of the Soviet population. It was certainly smaller than the nearly 20 million members of the CPSU, which had party groups in every workplace and community in the country.[59]

The general secretary of the CPSU, the politburo, the secretariat, the Council of Ministers, the central committee – several hundred people – made up the top layer of the elite.[60] This top layer set policies for the country and made the major political and economic decisions, and it had the power to initiate changes in the top leadership. However, it was too small to rule and administer a country of several hundred million people by itself.

The full party–state elite included a much larger group of officials. In the party it included department heads and other key staff of the central committee, the top leaders of the Communist youth organization Komsomol, and the first secretaries of party committees of the Union republics, provinces, and the more important cities. In the government it included high officials in the Union ministries and state committees, the leaders of the Supreme Soviet, and the highest officials of the ministries of the most important Union republics. It included high-level officers in the armed forces and security agencies. Outside the formal government structure, it included the top officials of large enterprises, leading trade union officials, and the heads of the major scientific, educational, cultural, and mass-media institutions.[61] In the postwar (that is, post-World War II) period this numbered about 100,000 people.[62] This represented about one-tenth of one per cent of Soviet households.[63]

What sort of individuals made up this elite? The original leadership of the Bolshevik party had consisted of dedicated revolutionaries. But after taking power and becoming the ruling party, it began to attract, along with those inspired by the prospect of building a new society, others who simply wanted to rise in society and gain prestige, power, and material privilege. At the beginning of 1917 the party had 24,000 members. By the end of that year its membership had swelled to 300,000. In 1928 it had 1.3 million and in 1933 a total of 3 million members.[64]

After Stalin's thorough purging of the party–state elite in the late 1930s, virtually none of the original "old Bolsheviks" remained. Amidst the murderous repressions of the Stalin era, one would expect that few genuine believers in the ideals of socialism would have been attracted to the party and been able to rise into the party–state elite. As the party–state elite stabilized in the postwar period, it had become an entirely different entity from the band of revolutionaries that had seized power in 1917.

Rising into the postwar elite depended on several individual characteristics. Formal education was a prerequisite, and it was made freely available to young people from peasant and worker backgrounds who could qualify.[65] Technical and engineering education became the most common path for those who rose from humble backgrounds into the elite.[66] Personal connections played an important role. Young people made life-long friendships and contacts at school and in the Komsomol which could help propel them upward. Loyalty to superiors was another key factor in promotion in the rigidly hierarchical system. When a person moved up, the most reliable subordinates would move up with him or her. Talent and ability also played a role, particularly in the career path which ascended along the economic administration route. Finally, to rise an individual had to master and repeat the official line – that the goal of social development was to build socialism and communism, that officials should selflessly and tirelessly serve the people, and so forth. While a few actually believed the official line, most did not take it seriously, and believing it was not mandatory as long as it could be effectively voiced on appropriate occasions.

Any group of 100,000 people will include a significant variety of temperaments and personality types. Nevertheless, the Soviet system did tend to select, and produce, a certain type of person for membership in its elite. In its stable phase in the postwar period, the Soviet system produced a ruling group whose members were generally well-educated, ambitious, pragmatic, opportunistic, and materialistic.

The above characteristics of the members of the Soviet elite might sound like a description of the ruling group of any modern social system. However, the situation of the Soviet elite differed from that of the dominant groups in other social systems, past and present, in certain respects. Throughout history, in a variety of different kinds of social systems, the dominant groups have generally consisted of property owners. The ownership of the most valuable kinds of property in a social system, and the need to protect such ownership, tend to forge a strong bond among members of the ruling group, as well as a strong attachment to the system itself. Furthermore, a system of individual property ownership enables members of a ruling group to pass their status along to their offspring through inheritance of property.[67]

The socialist pretensions of the Soviet system prevented its ruling group from acquiring personal wealth.[68] Virtually all valuable property belonged to the state. And it is the consensus of Western specialists that, apart from the very highest officials in the Soviet system, the average members of the Soviet party–state elite were not assured that they could pass on their elite status to their offspring.[69] While the children of the elite had advantages in getting into the best schools and using contacts to get good jobs, one analyst found that most of the children of the top elite and their spouses took jobs in the intelligentsia "but not necessarily over the elite threshold."[70] The most common careers for children of the top elite were in academia, journalism, diplomacy, and foreign trade (they seemed to prize the ability to travel abroad). The Soviet elite was heavily replenished in each generation by individuals from worker or peasant background who gained an education and moved up the hier- archy.[71]

The members of the Soviet party–state elite confronted a paradoxical reality. They were powerful and privileged. They ran one of the world's two superpowers. Yet in many respects they were quite confined. The bar to individual accumulation of wealth, and the uncertainty about passing on ruling elite status to offspring, must have limited the extent to which the Soviet elite conceived of themselves as a class with clearly defined interests in society.[72] It must also have limited the strength of their tie to the system over which they presided. Except for the few at the very top, all of them were entirely subordinated to the next higher level of the bureaucracy and ultimately the party. Retaining their posi- tion, and any hoped-for promotion, depended on approval from higher party bodies. While falling out of favor no longer meant prison or execution, loss of position carried with it loss of material privilege as well as power. These features of their condition under the Soviet system must have rankled members of the elite, especially those who travelled abroad and compared themselves to their Western counterparts. How- ever, they had no choice but to accept the terms of the system if they wished to work within it.

Chapter 3

Growth, stagnation, and the origins of perestroika

In the half-century following its creation in the late 1920s, the Soviet system displayed many weaknesses and problems in its economic performance. These disturbed both Soviet officials and ordinary citizens – and were emphasized by the critics of the system. Yet from 1928 through the mid-1970s, the Soviet economic model was in many respects quite successful in its own terms. The economic successes of the system were the main basis of the political stability which all observers, friend and foe, attributed to it.

However, the performance of the Soviet economy dramatically deteriorated after 1975. This was manifested in a number of ways, most noticeably in a sharp slowdown in the rate of economic growth. We will argue that the rise to power of a new, reformist leadership in 1985 was propelled not only by dissatisfaction with the long-standing problems of the Soviet system, but by the sense of crisis created by this economic slowdown. The nature of the reform program that Gorbachev and his allies proposed, known as "perestroika," emerged from both their understanding of the long-standing problems of the Soviet system and their analysis of the forces that had caused the deterioration in its economic performance.

SOVIET ECONOMIC PERFORMANCE DURING 1928–75

In the early part of this century, when the idea of socialism was still new, Western economists debated whether a centrally planned economy could function at all. The Soviet experience after 1928 settled that debate. Whatever problems the Soviet system may have had, it did not turn out to be unworkable. On the contrary, as the West sank into a decade-long depression after 1929, the Soviet economy began a period of rapid industrialization.

The Soviet leadership concentrated at first on building a base of heavy industry, partly on the foundation of pre-revolutionary industry but much of it created entirely anew.[1] The speed of industrialization in the

1930s is indicated by the pace with which a domestic machine-tool industry was created. Machine tools are critical inputs in virtually all industrial activities. In 1932 the Soviet Union had to import 78 per cent of machine tools installed. By 1936–37 less than 10 per cent were imported, with the remainder domestically produced.[2]

A leading American textbook on the Soviet economy concludes that "By 1937...the USSR had been transformed into an industrial economy."[3] The hallmark of industrialization is the transfer of a country's work force from agriculture into industry. Simon Kuznets, a Nobel Laureate economist and one of the foremost specialists in long-term economic growth, wrote that:

> the rapidity of this shift [out of agriculture] was far greater in the USSR than in the other developed countries...the shift of labor force out of agriculture of the magnitude that occurred in the USSR in the 12 years from 1928 to 1940 took from 30 to 50 years in other countries.[4]

Kuznets adds that "only Japan (on the basis of national product) seems to approximate the speed of industrialization of the USSR."[5]

By the time the Nazi invasion of 1941 brought the Soviet Union into World War II, an industrial base had been built capable of producing all the weapons of that era, from tanks to artillery to warplanes. The war wrought enormous destruction in the Soviet Union – in 1945 industrial output in formerly occupied parts of the Soviet Union, which encompassed the most economically developed areas, was only about 30 per cent of the prewar level. However, economic recovery was swift, and by 1950 prewar levels of industrial output had been surpassed.[6] In the following decades the Soviet economy continued to grow rapidly.

We saw in Chapter 2 that the Soviet economy made some progress in achieving a number of traditional socialist goals, including full employment, a high degree of personal economic security, and a relatively egalitarian distribution of income. But the goal of rapid economic growth and technological progress always held a place of special importance in socialist thinking. Marxian socialists believed an economic system must ultimately be judged by how effective it was at promoting technological progress and raising living standards. They praised capitalism for bringing rapid economic growth, but they believed that one of the most important advantages of socialism was its ability to achieve even faster growth. The ultimate purpose of such rapid growth was seen to be, not an endless increase in the output of consumer goods, but rather the eventual creation of sufficient abundance that everyone's material needs would be met, allowing people to concentrate their energies on more elevated matters than material consumption.

Thus, Soviet leaders regarded the growth performance of the economy as paramount. Only through rapid growth would the superiority of socialism be demonstrated and the final goal of classless communism be reached. The perceived military threat from the capitalist countries reinforced the emphasis on rapid growth, since a strong and growing economy is a necessary basis of military strength in the modern world. Rapid growth would assure both national survival and the future of socialism and communism; failure to grow rapidly would threaten both.

Official Soviet statistics used the concept "net material product" (NMP), rather than the Western "gross national product" (GNP), to measure growth of total economic output. NMP differs from GNP primarily in the exclusion from NMP of most kinds of services, except for those directly related to production of physical goods (such as rail freight transportation). Western specialists believe the official Soviet data on NMP contained serious distortions which exaggerated the rate of economic growth.[7] As a result, Western specialists constructed their own estimates of economic growth in the Soviet Union. The Western estimates, based on the GNP concept, can be used to make comparisons with economic growth in Western capitalist economies.[8] University researchers produced the first such estimates. For the years after 1950, economists at the United States Central Intelligence Agency were the main source of Western estimates of Soviet GNP.[9]

Figure 3.1 provides data on the annual growth rate of real output for the Soviet economy, along with growth data on the US economy for comparison.[10] The official Soviet statistics on NMP show a very rapid rate of growth throughout the period 1928–75. Such high annual growth rates yield enormous increases over time, due to compounding. The 14.9 per cent annual NMP growth rate during 1928–40 translates into more than a 5-fold increase over those twelve years. The 1950–75 annual growth rate of 8.0 per cent mounts up to growth by a factor of nearly seven. For the entire period 1928–75, official Soviet statistics indicate a 60-fold increase in NMP.

Such an enormous increase in output has seemed exaggerated to most outside observers, but even the Western GNP estimates indicate very rapid growth. Except during the decade of war and recovery in the 1940s, Soviet GNP growth was very fast, substantially faster than US GNP growth during the same periods. A contemporaneous comparison of Soviet and US growth has its limitations. The United States industrialized much earlier, in the nineteenth century, and economic growth rates tend to decline after the industrialization process has been completed. Nevertheless, the GNP growth comparison in Figure 3.1 does imply that the Soviet Union was gaining on the United States by the GNP measure during 1928–75. To the untutored eye, the average annual Soviet GNP growth during 1928–75 of 4.5 per cent may not appear to be much faster than the American average of 3.1 per cent. But the Soviet

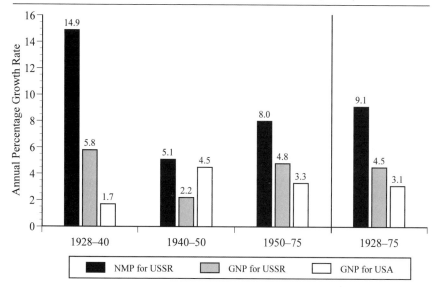

Figure 3.1 Soviet and American economic growth,1928–75
Source: Bergson 1961: 180, 210; Joint Economic Committee 1982: 25, 52–3,1990: 46, 55–6;
US Bureau of the Census 1961: 139; *Economic Report of the President*1985: 234,1988: 250
Note NMP is net material product, GNP is gross national product.

rate implies a nearly 8-fold increase in GNP over that period, compared
to a US increase just over 4-fold. If those trends had continued, the
Soviet GNP would eventually have overtaken and surpassed the US
level.[11] A comparison of the level of GNP between two countries is
fraught with even more problems than a comparison of growth rates.
But, for what it is worth, the CIA estimated that by 1975 the Soviet GNP
was approximately 60 per cent of the US GNP level.[12]

The Soviet system was able to achieve this rapid growth by a number
of means. Central planners controlled the allocation of national output
between current consumption and investment in new capital goods.
They used this control to devote a very large share of output to investment.[13] This meant less consumption at the beginning, but eventually
the resulting rapid growth boosted consumption as well. The large
volume of new machines embodied, over time, increasingly modern
technologies. The Soviet economy did not suffer from periodic business
recessions, the regular occurrence of which reduce long-term economic growth rates in capitalist economies. The absence of unemployment, together with the policy of encouraging every adult to take part
in production, achieved a much higher ratio of employment to population than in Western capitalist countries.[14] The rapid rise in the educational level of the population contributed to making the work force

increasingly productive over time.[15] The rapid employment shift from agriculture to industry contributed to GNP growth, since output per worker is much higher in industry than in agriculture.

Despite the relatively low share of national output devoted to consumption, after World War II consumption began to grow rapidly in the Soviet Union. From 1950 to 1975, real consumption per capita grew at a rate of 3.8 per cent per year, according to Western estimates. This produced a 2.5-fold increase over that period. By comparison, real consumption per capita in the United States grew at a rate of 2.0 per cent per year during those 25 years, for a 1.6-fold increase.[16] One Western specialist on the Soviet economy described the results of rapid consumption growth after 1950 as constituting

> a real revolution in the Soviet standard of living, a revolution that goes beyond the quantitative rise. The estimates do not capture the improved consumption environment and the variety and quality of goods and services that together brought a radical change in the quality of life in the Soviet Union.[17]

In 1960 about one out of two Soviet families owned a radio, one out of ten a television, and one out of twenty-five a refrigerator. By 1985 there was an average of one of each per family.[18]

Soviet planners emphasized industrial might more than consumer goods output. They achieved significant success along this line. By 1975 Soviet output had exceeded the US level in crude and rolled steel, cement, metalcutting and metalforming machines, combines, and tractors. The same was true for some agricultural products, such as wheat, fish, hogs, milk, and cotton.[19]

Soviet society had been radically transformed since the 1920s. A predominantly rural country had become urbanized.[20] The children of peasants were now engaged primarily in non-agricultural employment.[21] A population with little formal education and widespread illiteracy had become well-educated.[22] By the 1980s the Soviet Union had more doctors and hospital beds per capita than the United States.[23] Its successes in science and technology are well known, symbolized by its launching of the first earth satellite in 1957. Its industrial and technological accomplishments were the basis of the rise of Soviet military strength to rough parity with the United States. The Soviet system had engineered the development of a backward, semi-developed nation into one of the world's two superpowers.

The debate over Soviet economic performance

The above description of Soviet economic achievements would have been relatively uncontroversial in the 1980s.[24] But in the 1990s many

Western observers downgraded their view of past Soviet accomplish-ments. This was not the result of new documents emerging from hitherto closed archives. Rather, there was a reaction on the part of many observers something like the following: if the Soviet system col-lapsed so suddenly, it must have been much weaker, economically as well as politically, than had been believed.[25]

In the perestroika years of 1985–91, open criticism became possible in the Soviet Union for the first time since the 1920s. Some dissident Soviet economists published greatly diminished evaluations of past Soviet economic performance. These claims were soon picked up by conservative foundations in the West, and the new Soviet critics were invited to conferences and their claims widely publicized. As Soviet economic problems mounted at the end of the 1980s, followed by the demise of the system in 1991, these new downward re-evaluations of past Soviet economic performance had a great impact on the Western public.

For example, in the 1980s a Soviet economist, Grigory Khanin, issued challenges not only to the official Soviet statistics on past economic growth but to Western estimates as well.[26] His own estimates were well below the official Soviet growth rates, and for some periods below the Western estimates.[27] Khanin's work was widely publicized, with help from the conservative Heritage Foundation of Washington, DC.[28]

Although Khanin's estimates, which were for NMP, are not directly comparable to the CIA's GNP figures, his work spurred a great deal of criticism of the CIA estimates. Critics hinted that the CIA had padded Soviet growth estimates to make the Soviet Union appear to be a more formidable enemy, justifying continued ample funding for the agency. Yet a moment's reflection shows that, while the CIA might have had a motive to exaggerate Soviet military strength, it is not clear in which direction any political influence might have swayed the CIA's economic growth estimates. Exaggerating the growth rate of Soviet GNP would make the Soviet system look more successful, absolutely and relative to the United States, than it actually was, which is hardly an impression one would expect the CIA to wish to foster. Furthermore, faster growth and a larger GNP would make Soviet military spending appear to represent a smaller proportion of Soviet output, making the Soviet Union appear less militaristic.

However, it does not appear that political considerations played any role in the CIA estimates of Soviet growth. In response to all the criti-cisms, in 1991 a panel of five distinguished American academic econom-ists, chaired by Professor James R. Millar, was asked to prepare an outside evaluation of the CIA estimates.[29] The Millar panel found that the CIA's Office of Soviet Analysis "has been professional and appro-priately reasonable and cautious ... we find no indication of systematic misrepresentation."[30] They found CIA estimates of Soviet growth to be based on the best-known methodologies and that the unavoidable uncertainties in the estimates had been carefully explained in CIA reports.[31] By contrast, the Millar panel dismissed Khanin's alternative growth estimates, concluding that "Methodologically, Khanin's approach is naive, and it has not been possible for others to reproduce his results."[32]

Perhaps because many observers had been so ready to believe that Soviet economic accomplishments must have been greatly overstated, the Millar panel's findings had little impact on public perceptions. As one scholar noted several years after the panel had completed its evaluation, "There appears to be a general public impression that the CIA grossly overestimated Soviet economic capability, although explanations differ widely and the impression itself is largely based on hearsay and misinformation."[33] A column in *Newsweek* in 1994 referred to "the monumental miscalculation of the size of the Soviet economy, which the CIA judged to be three times as big as it really was."[34] A year later, even the normally cautious *New York Times* editorialized that "the CIA... grossly overestimated the size of the Soviet economy."[35] Thus, the belief that the CIA greatly overstated Soviet economic performance lived on, despite the absence of any reliable basis for it.

A few specialists have criticized the CIA estimates of Soviet growth from the opposite perspective – that they understated the true growth rate. A study by Michael Boretsky, a Commerce Department economist, took the CIA methodology for estimating Soviet GNP growth and used it to estimate West German and US GNP growth. The resulting estimates were 32 per cent below the official GNP growth rate for West Germany and 13 per cent below the official growth rate for the US.[36] Boretsky's criticism found its way into footnotes in academic survey articles. However, because it ran counter to the prevailing political winds, it made no impression on the broader public perception of the issue.

The total economic output of a nation consists of diverse goods and services. It is impossible to fully capture this concept, or its growth rate over time, by a single number. Any such effort is necessarily a rough estimate, for any nation. But the balance of the evidence shows that CIA economists made a good-faith, large-scale effort to make such estimates, and they are the best ones available for the Western GNP concept. The official Soviet NMP statistics are also relevant, since they embodied the priorities and values of the Soviet system and were the indicators by which the Soviet leadership judged the success of the system. The Western and official Soviet statistics in the end tell the same basic story – that the Soviet economy grew rapidly through the mid-1970s but thereafter ran into serious difficulties.

Problems of the Soviet economy

Rapid growth of output was only one side of Soviet economic performance. The Soviet economy was beset by nagging problems, and recur-
rent minor reforms were undertaken to try to solve them. Nikita
Khrushchev, Stalin's successor, tried reorganizing the planning system,
but the problems did not go away. In the early years of Leonid Brezhnev's long reign, the 1965 Kosygin economic reforms failed to live up to
their promise.

While the quantity of goods produced in the Soviet Union increased
rapidly, their quality was very uneven. Some products were of high
quality, including weapons, aircraft, metals, spacecraft, fuel cells, chem-
icals, and some types of machinery.[37] But many Soviet products,
particularly consumer goods, were of low quality. Furthermore, for both
producer and consumer goods, the particular variety produced was
frequently not suited to the wishes or requirements of customers. The
Soviet economy operated with a perpetual shortage of goods relative to
demand, which allowed producers to readily dispose of whatever they
produced, whether or not it was what the customer really wanted.

Shoppers confronted a retail distribution system that seemed
designed to torment them, rather than cater to their needs. Customers
often had to stand in three separate lines to purchase something – one to
request the item, a second to pay for it, and a third to pick it up.
Availability of goods was never certain, and people had to carry "just-
in-case" bags for the moment when a desired good suddenly appeared
in the stores. Consumer services were insufficiently available and generally of poor quality.

Enterprises typically failed to use inputs efficiently. Fearing that
essential raw materials or components would be unavailable when
needed, enterprises accumulated large, wasteful stockpiles of them.
Some enterprises produced their own components and parts, when they
could have been more efficiently made by a specialized firm, out of fear
that they would be unavailable when needed, or to make sure that
inputs would match their specific requirements. The inflexibility of the
Soviet planning system forced many enterprises to barter goods with
one another on a technically illegal gray market. Investment projects
typically took much longer than planned to complete, leaving a substantial part of Soviet output tied up in unfinished projects.[38] While the
Soviet system had some well-publicized successes with advanced technologies, as a rule new products and new production techniques were
introduced slowly and unevenly. The incentives operating for enterprise
directors made them cautious and hesitant to try things that were new.[39]

The primary focus on increasing production allowed little room for
environmental considerations. While Soviet environmental protection

laws looked good on paper, they were generally ignored by powerful industrial ministries that cared only about boosting production. Environmental costs mounted, but concerned citizens lacked the political freedom to launch the kind of powerful environmental protest movement which developed in Western countries.

Agriculture remained a perennial problem. This was partly due to unfavorable climatic and soil conditions in much of the Soviet Union. But nature was not the only cause. Despite pouring large inputs of labor and capital goods into agriculture in the postwar years, the Soviet authorities had difficulty delivering a high-quality and appealing diet to the citizenry.[40]

Many of the problems of the Soviet economy stemmed from an over-centralized and inflexible planning system, in which too many and too detailed decisions were made by the top authorities in Moscow. The central authorities were unable to create effective incentive mechanisms to ensure that their detailed decisions would be carried out in the manner intended. And the system placed nearly all power in the hands of producers, leaving little for the consumer. Of course, everyone was both producer and consumer, depending on the time of day. Ordinary people benefited from these power relations as workers, as did enterprise directors in their role as providers of goods. But workers paid when they went shopping, as did enterprise managers when they needed inputs.

However, as long as the system produced rapid growth, the problems generated nothing more serious than grumbling and occasional minor reform efforts. When growth suddenly slowed dramatically after the mid-1970s, these long-term problems suddenly loomed much larger.

STAGNATION

It was inevitable that the extremely rapid growth which the Soviet Union achieved in the prewar years would slow over time. Every country which made the transition from agricultural to industrial economy eventually experienced a slowdown in growth. A successful late industrializer can grow very rapidly by borrowing technologies and rapidly moving its labor force into industry, but eventually these possibilities are exhausted.[41]

However, in the mid-1970s the Soviet economy experienced something more dramatic than the inevitable gradual growth slowdown of a late industrializer. At that time, a sharp break occurred in key indices of Soviet economic performance. This break is visible in both Western and official Soviet statistics. Economic growth not only slowed down but dropped to a very low level. This was true not only in comparison to the past Soviet record but relative to the major Western capitalist countries.

(a) NMP for USSR

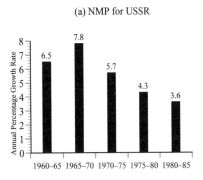

(b) Non-farm Business sector for USSR

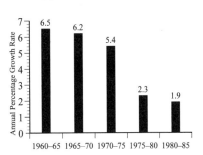

(c) GNP for USSR and GNP for USA

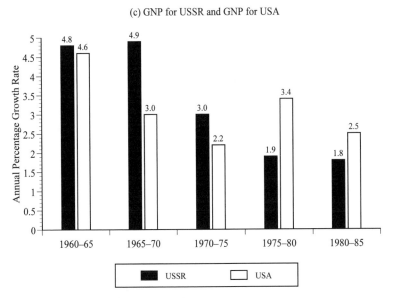

Figure 3.2 Slowdown in total output growth
Source: Joint Economic Committee 1990: 46, 58; Pitzer and Baukol 1991: 53; *Economic Report of the President 1988: 250.*

Figure 3.2 shows growth data for three measures of Soviet output – NMP, GNP, and the output of the nonfarm business sector – with US GNP growth data included for comparison.[42] Growth rates are shown for half-decades, which correspond to successive five-year plan periods. Because of large gyrations in Soviet agricultural output, primarily due to weather variations, NMP and GNP growth rates over five-year periods can be misleading. It happens that in 1970 there was an unusually good harvest (up 14.2 per cent from the preceding year) while 1975 saw an unusually bad harvest (down 12.5 per cent from the preceding year).[43]

Because of this, the 1970 levels of NMP and GNP were inflated, while those for 1975 were reduced, causing the measured growth rate of NMP and GNP during 1970–75 to significantly understate the underlying long-run growth trend of the economy during that half-decade. As a result, the sharp break in growth that occurred in 1975 is not evident in part (a) for NMP or part (c) for GNP. By those two measures, growth appears to decelerate even more in 1970–75 than in 1975–80.

The non-farm business-sector data, in Figure 3.2 part (b), provide a broad measure of Soviet economic growth, with the effect of agriculture removed. This measure clearly shows a sharp downward break after 1975.[44] But the GNP series does contain some useful information. Despite the downward distortion from agricultural performance in the 1970–75 GNP growth rate, the 3.0 per cent rate achieved in that half-decade is quite respectable, and it was well above the US GNP growth rate for the same period. However, as Figure 3.2 part (c) shows, after 1975 Soviet GNP growth fell below the US rate for the first time since the war years and remained below it through 1985.

Figure 3.3 shows more clearly the sharp growth slowdown after 1975. The growth of Soviet industrial production, whether measured by official Soviet statistics or Western estimates, slowed dramatically after 1975. Based on the Western estimates, it fell below the US rate of growth in industrial production during 1975–85.

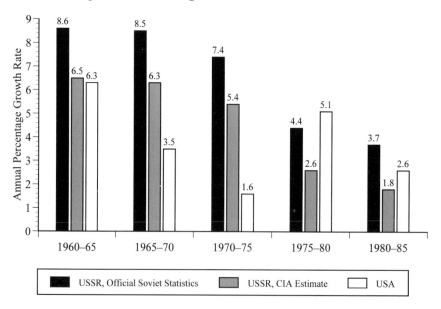

Figure 3.3 Slowdown in industrial production growth
Source: Directorate of Intelligence 1988b: 9; Economic Report of the President 1988: 302.

Rapid growth of economic output can be sustained by a nation over the long run only by raising the output produced per hour of labor.[45] As Figure 3.4 shows, the Soviet economy achieved a relatively rapid rate of growth in output per labor hour through 1975, with an acceleration in 1970–75. Even the lower Western estimate in part (a) of Figure 3.4 finds that industrial output per labor hour grew between 3 and 4 per cent per year during 1960–75. After 1975 industrial labor productivity growth fell drastically – by nearly 50 per cent according to official statistics and by two-thirds based on Western estimates. However, by the labor productivity growth measure, Soviet performance, while losing its previous edge over US performance, did not fall significantly below the (also reduced) US productivity performance of 1975–85. Part (b) of Figure 3.4, which compares labor productivity growth in the non-farm business sector for the two countries, shows little difference in performance between them during 1975–85.

Thus, after 1975 Soviet growth slowed down dramatically, falling to a very low rate, compared either to past performance or the performance of its main rival, the United States.[46] In light of this, it is reasonable to refer to the period 1975–85 as one of "stagnation." However, the reader should keep in mind that, according to these data, the Soviet economy did not actually stop growing during 1975–85. The fact that stagnation showed up in official Soviet statistics, as well as Western estimates, means that the Soviet leadership was well aware of the problem. Given the central role that rapid growth played in the Soviet Union, the slowdown heralded a potential crisis for the Soviet leadership. Suddenly socialism was failing to bring rapid growth. The gap between the Soviet and American economies, rather than progressively narrowing, was now growing wider.

The sudden worsening of Soviet economic performance in the 1970s was not limited to economic growth. There is also evidence that the rate of technological innovation slowed down around the 1970s.[47] While the rate of technological progress had never met the high expectations of the founders of the Soviet system, since 1928 the technological gap with Western capitalism had clearly narrowed, and in a few technologies the Soviet Union reached or surpassed Western levels. The high rate of increase in labor productivity was one reflection of Soviet technological progress. However, around the 1970s it appeared that the technological gap, like the GNP gap, began to widen. Most noticeably, the Soviet Union largely failed to absorb the revolution in communication and information-processing brought by electronics and computers, which was rapidly altering Western capitalist economies from the 1970s.

It is difficult to measure the rate of technological progress of an economy. The sharp slowdown of labor productivity growth in the mid-1970s might be indicative of a slower rate of innovation, but many

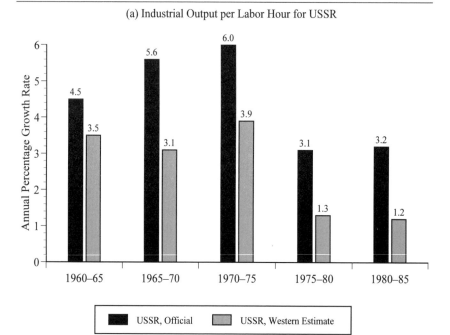

(a) Industrial Output per Labor Hour for USSR

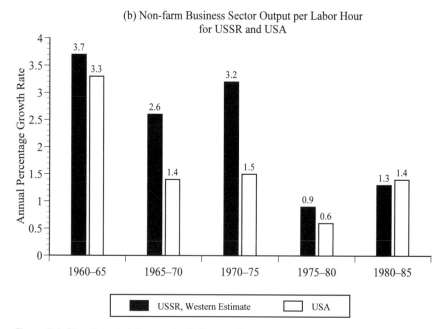

(b) Non-farm Business Sector Output per Labor Hour
for USSR and USA

Figure 3.4 Slowdown in labor productivity growth
Source: Hewett 1988: 52; Directorate of Intelligence 1988b: 63; Pitzer and Baukol 1991: 53;
Economic Report of the President 1988: 300.

other factors besides innovation influence the rate of labor productivity growth.[48] Vladimir Kontorovich did a study of the direct data available on innovations in the Soviet economy, which confirms the casual impression that technological performance worsened in the 1970s. He found steep declines in several measures of the rate of innovation in that decade.[49] Kontorovich's research provides firm evidence that, along with the decline in economic growth, the rate of technological progress also slowed markedly in the 1970s, although the dating of the technological slowdown is difficult to fix with any precision.

As was the case for economic growth, the data do not suggest that technological progress stopped or that technological decline set in. Rather, the rate of technological advance slowed significantly. But it seems clear that, by the mid-1970s, the long trend of a narrowing gap in both economic output and technological level between the Soviet Union and the United States had been reversed.

There is also evidence that, at the same time that economic stagnation set in, the social and political problems of the Soviet system grew more severe. The connection with the economic slowdown, if any, is difficult to prove. But in this period there was a growing sense of alienation and aimlessness among the Soviet people. Corruption and cynicism spread throughout the institutions of Soviet society. Alcoholism was on the rise.[50] And a small, but vocal, dissident political movement was growing.

Why stagnation set in

There is no agreement among Western specialists about what caused the 1970s Soviet stagnation. This is not surprising. American economists still vigorously debate the causes of the Great Depression of the 1930s in the United States, with no agreement yet in sight. It is difficult to pinpoint the main causes of any major economic event, and the 1970s Soviet stagnation is no exception.

By the early 1980s, the Soviet stagnation had been noticed, and a large literature arose seeking to explain it. Among the possible causal factors cited in this literature are the following: (1) increasing difficulty in carrying out central planning effectively; (2) a reduction in labor discipline; (3) a decision by the planning authorities to deliberately reduce the economic growth rate after 1975; (4) bottlenecks that arose in key sectors of the economy, particularly rail transportation and oil production; (5) unfavorable demographic trends; (6) unfavorable weather conditions; (7) indirect effects of the post-1973 growth slowdown in the West; (8) the large Soviet military burden.[51] This list contains four different categories of potential causal factors. Items 1 and 2 involve structural problems of the Soviet system. Items 3 and 4 concern policy errors. Items 5 and 6 involve uncontrollable developments in the Soviet experience. The last two items concern the Soviet Union's relations with the West. We will consider these four categories of potential causes, in reverse order to their appearance in the above list.

The large Soviet military burden does not appear to be a likely cause of the stagnation of the mid-1970s. It is true that, in order to compete with the United States, with its much larger GNP, the Soviet Union had to devote a much larger share of output to the military than did the United States. In 1950, about 17 per cent of Soviet GNP was devoted to defense, according to Western estimates, which was about triple the share spent by the United States at that time. However, during 1950–80 the defense share of Soviet GNP fell slightly, to 16 per cent. While Soviet military spending grew rapidly over that period, the Soviet economy grew slightly faster.[52] Since the military burden did not prevent rapid economic growth during 1950–75, it is unclear why a military burden that had become no larger relative to the economy should have undermined growth after 1975.[53]

It is intriguing that, at almost the exact date of the onset of stagnation in the Soviet Union, the major Western capitalist countries also entered a period of sharply reduced economic growth. Most economists date the Western slowdown to around 1973, although some find evidence of emerging problems as early as 1966.[54] For the United States, Western Europe, and Japan, the period since the early 1970s has been one of much slower economic growth, and much slower growth in labor productivity, than the preceding decades.

By the 1970s the Soviet Union had come to rely on imports from the West for new technologies and for grain in years of poor harvests. As the Western economies became severely depressed in the mid-1970s, many non-Western countries found it more difficult to export to them to earn the hard currency to finance imports from them. However, the most important Soviet export to the West was oil, which experienced huge price increases in 1973–74 and again in 1979. As a result, the Soviet Union faced no shortage of hard currency earnings during the second half of the 1970s. Thus, it would appear that the Western economic slowdown should not have had any significant negative impact on the Soviet economy in the 1970s.[55]

The explanation of the Soviet stagnation must be sought in factors internal to the Soviet Union, not in its relation to the West. Unfavorable demographic trends and weather patterns did cause problems after 1975. The rate of movement of the population from rural to urban areas slowed slightly after 1975. After 1980 the rate of growth of the working-age population as a whole slowed. And the late 1970s had several years of unusually harsh weather. But these factors account at most for only a small part of the slowdown, and in any event there is little a nation can do about bad weather or the inevitable slowdown in urban labor force growth that follows industrialization and urbanization.[56]

Items 3 and 4 on the above list – the deliberate reduction in growth targets and the appearance of bottlenecks in rail transportation and oil production – represent policy errors by Soviet planners. The Tenth and Eleventh Five Year Plans, for 1976–80 and 1981–85, incorporated large reductions in the planned rate of economic growth. Figure 3.5 shows the planned and actual growth rates for "national income utilized" (a concept similar to net material product) and industrial production for five-year plan periods during 1960–85.[57] The planned growth rates of both national income utilized and industrial production were reduced markedly in 1976–80 and again in 1981–85.[58]

The purpose of these planned reductions in growth rate targets was to increase efficiency and product quality by reducing the pressure on managers to concentrate on rapidly increasing the quantity of output.[59] However, actual economic growth rates, particularly for industrial production, fell well below the reduced target levels, as Figure 3.5 shows. The investment growth cutbacks that accompanied the lower planned output growth caused unanticipated bottlenecks in the system, and they may also have contributed to slowing the innovation rate, since many innovations are embodied in new capital equipment. The hoped-for improvements in efficiency and product quality did not materialize. Instead, the lowering of growth targets apparently simply amplified the trend toward slower growth.[60]

Planning mistakes were also made in the key sectors of rail transportation and oil production. Soviet planners had built an excellent rail system, which served as the primary mode of long-distance freight transportation. After the early 1950s, relatively little new investment was allocated to it, but the system worked effectively through tightly controlled central direction by the Railroad Ministry. In contrast to the inefficient use of capital goods in many sectors of the economy, the railroads used their capital stock quite efficiently and achieved a very high intensity of rail use.[61] However, by the mid-1970s the Soviet rail system had reached the limit set by its rail miles, and congestion began to slow deliveries. The failure to make timely investments in expanded rail miles and new sidings had created a serious bottleneck for the Soviet economy.[62] Another serious bottleneck arose in the critical petroleum industry. Soviet planners focused investment on developing existing oil fields rather than exploring for new ones. As a result, by the early 1980s oil production stagnated as existing fields could no longer yield rising production.[63] The rail and oil bottlenecks contributed to the growth slowdown.

If policy mistakes had been the primary cause of the stagnation, it would not have been difficult to remedy. But the stagnation proved very

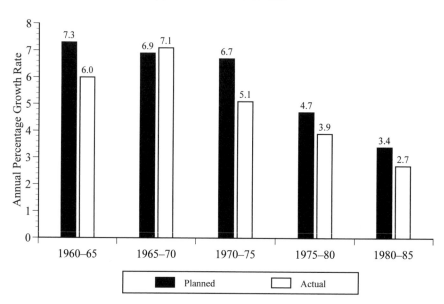

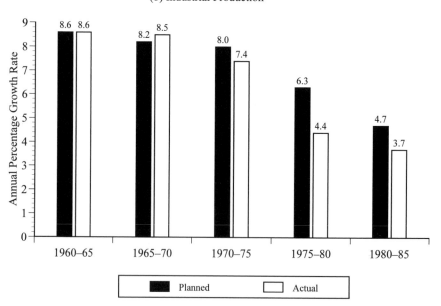

Figure 3.5 Planned and actual economic growth
Source: Official Soviet data from Hewett 1988: 52; Directorate of Intelligence 1988b: 9.

difficult to reverse. The reason is that the most important causes of the stagnation were not simply policy errors. The problems went much deeper. They involved a declining effectiveness of the major institutions of the Soviet system.

To aid in understanding the fundamental problems that arose with Soviet growth performance, it is helpful to place the Soviet growth slow-down in the context of the general historical pattern of long-term growth in industrialized economies. The historical evidence suggests that a long period of rapid growth in a modern economy eventually gives way to a period of stagnation, followed after another lengthy interval by renewed rapid growth. This pattern has been observed for Britain, the United States, Germany, and other countries over the past few centuries.[64] Peri-ods of stagnation in Western capitalist countries have been overcome in the past only after major reforms were carried out in the economic, social, and political institutions of the country.[65]

The process of rapid economic growth and development appears to eventually run out of steam in countries with widely differing economic institutions. The very process of rapid economic growth seems to under-mine the conditions for its maintenance over time. The most telling explanations for periods of stagnation must be sought in the ways in which, paradoxically, success eventually breeds failure.

The stagnation that set in after 1975 in the Soviet Union was due, not so much to the failures of the Soviet system, but to its successes. Nearly fifty years of rapid economic growth and development had changed the economy and society in ways that undermined the continuing effective-ness of the particular configuration of institutions which had generated the rapid growth. Items 1 and 2 on the above list – the declining effec-tiveness of Soviet planning and declining labor discipline – both fit within this way of analyzing the problem.

The particular form of economic planning adopted in the Soviet Union at the end of the 1920s was, as we have seen, very centralized and hierarchical. This type of planning proved very effective at mobilizing resources for the goal of industrializing an agricultural economy. It achieved a very high rate of investment which made possible the rapid creation of a whole set of new industries. It was able to rapidly educate and train the population for industrial work and rapidly shift the popu-lation into better-paying, more-productive urban industrial jobs.

Some analysts believe that the Soviet planning system was effective only at basic industrialization. However, the continuing rapid growth during 1950–75, after industrialization had already been achieved, shows that the system was not so limited. The highly centralized planning system also proved effective at the process of building at least the first stages of a modern urban society, with a reasonably high level of amen-ities and consumer goods for the population. During this stage there was also a relatively simple set of major goals. Soviet central planning proved able to rapidly build urban infrastructure (transportation, communication, power, etc.), construct new housing, and manufacture new consumer goods. For a population that had lived in miserable poverty prior to 1950, the provision of apartments with individual kitchens and indoor plumbing, efficient mass transit, an adequate diet, and a refrigerator and television set for every family produced a great improvement in living standards. This was true despite the low quality, by Western standards, of many of these items.[66]

However, by the 1970s the success of the previous fifty years of rapid growth, achieved on the basis of a highly centralized planning system, had changed the requirements for further economic progress. The Soviet economy had grown much larger and was producing many more products. Urban households that have reached a modest level of consumer comfort have more complex needs. They want a wide variety of consumer goods, and the quality of those products becomes increasingly important. The process of meeting such needs is more complex than the earlier stages of economic development. It cannot be resolved down to the fulfillment of a few central economic goals. The highly centralized planning system, which was so effective at rapidly meeting the simpler goals of the early stages of development, was not flexible enough to be well adapted to this new stage.[67]

Although it is difficult to find hard evidence, the Soviet Union apparently suffered a decline in labor discipline around the 1970s.[68] This may have been a result of the radical change in the character of the Soviet population produced by fifty years of rapid economic transformation. The development process initially was based on an urban work force consisting of people just off the farm, with little formal education. The authoritarian system of managing the labor process in the Soviet Union, based on single-person management and strict hierarchy within enterprises, worked reasonably well with this work force. A combination of strict disciplinary measures, some material incentives, and the promise of a bright communist future served to extract work effort reasonably well from such workers.

By the 1970s the Soviet people had been transformed. The majority were now well-educated, sophisticated, urban-dwellers living at a modest level of comfort. The top-down, authoritarian system, which left the work force with little to do but obey orders, increasingly clashed with the need of the transformed Soviet population for some autonomy and authority of their own. The previously effective system for managing the labor process had lost its effectiveness.[69]

The highly centralized, inflexible form of economic planning and the hierarchical, authoritarian mode of managing the work process had lost their effectiveness. The particular forms of economic planning and management which had been created in the Soviet Union in the late 1920s appeared to have reached the end of their ability to provide rapid economic progress for the Soviet Union. With the end of rapid growth, all of the long-standing problems of the Soviet system appeared more serious. The system clearly required a major renovation.

THE ORIGINS OF GORBACHEV'S PERESTROIKA

No minor reforms, much less a major renovation, were possible during the last years of Leonid Brezhnev's rule. Brezhnev was the longest-serving Soviet leader since Stalin, remaining in office from 1964 until his death in 1982. After the minor economic reforms of the mid-1960s, the Brezhnev era gradually settled into a mode of political stagnation and drift. Top officials were virtually assured of life-time tenure as long as they did not rock the boat. Corruption spread through the system and was tolerated by the leadership.

When Brezhnev died in November 1982, his successor, Yuri Andropov, sought to instill new life in the system. As former head of the KGB, the Soviet intelligence agency, he was well aware of the accumulating problems of the Soviet system. He called for a campaign to root out corruption and increase discipline and efficiency. He authorized experiments with new methods of economic management intended to improve work incentives and hasten technological innovation. Perhaps most importantly, he encouraged a relatively open debate about the economic problems of the system.[70] However, he was already seriously ill with kidney disease when he took office, and he died 15 months later, before any significant changes could be introduced.

The central committee confirmed the elderly Konstantin Chernenko as his replacement in February 1984, in what appeared to be intended as a temporary caretaker role. Although viewed as a Brezhnev-style traditionalist, Chernenko did not terminate the Andropov economic experiments or call off the debate over the economy. Chernenko's rule was even briefer than Andropov's. When he passed away in March 1985, Mikhail Gorbachev replaced him as Soviet leader.

An energetic, hard-working, and gregarious person, Gorbachev had risen very rapidly in the Communist Party hierarchy. After receiving a law degree in Moscow in 1955, he returned to his home province of Stavropol, a rich agricultural region in the north Caucasus. Gorbachev rose through the Stavropol Komsomol and party organization, becoming first secretary of the provincial party committee in 1970. In 1978 he was brought to Moscow to serve as central committee secretary for agriculture. At age 47, he was the youngest member of the Soviet leadership at that time.[71] Two years later he became a full politburo member.

Andropov, himself from Stavropol, apparently was favorably impressed with Gorbachev, and his standing in the leadership rose during Andropov's rule. When Chernenko replaced Andropov, Gorbachev became the heir apparent. Although Gorbachev had climbed the rungs of the party system in a traditional manner, he was seen as a representative of reformist sentiment within the party. Many of Brezhnev's closest associates on the politburo hoped to find a way to block Gorbachev's rise.[72] That they were unable to do so was probably a result of the widespread desire for reform within the broader party leadership. It is believed that, despite uneasiness about Gorbachev on the part of a majority of the holdover politburo, strong support from provincial party secretaries and other central committee members forced the politburo to name Gorbachev as the new leader in 1985.[73]

Gorbachev brought into the leadership with him a varied group of new people. He named Yegor Ligachev, an older man who had spent years as party first secretary in Tomsk, in western Siberia, to be his second-in-command of the party politburo and secretariat. With a reputation for being honest, incorruptible, and hard-working, Ligachev's traditional party style and cautious approach helped garner support for Gorbachev's reforms from within the party apparat.[74] Nikolai Ryzhkov, an able industrial director who had risen to central committee secretary for industry and chief of the economic section under Andropov, became the new chairman of the Council of Ministers.[75] Eduard Shevardnadze, the new Foreign Minister, was pragmatic and flexible.

Alexandr Yakovlev was perhaps the most influential of Gorbachev's close associates.[76] He was named central committee secretary in charge of ideological matters, which included the job of appointing heads of the mass media.[77] Yakovlev's background was in ideology, and he had been the acting head of the central committee propaganda department in the early 1970s. Later he had served as Ambassador to Canada. Unlike the others, Yakovlev was an intellectual who thought about revising and updating Marxist theory.[78]

When Gorbachev took office, the theme of economic reform was already well established. Andropov had called for it and Chernenko had done nothing to discourage it. But there was no indication at first that Gorbachev would soon become the advocate of a radical and thoroughgoing remaking of the Soviet system. Nothing in Gorbachev's background or early speeches gave grounds for expecting such a surprising departure. Western experts at first expected that there would follow merely another episode of modest tinkering with the Soviet economy, along the lines of past Soviet economic reforms under Khrushchev and in the early Brezhnev years.[79]

But the conditions of 1985 were very different from those of 1955, when Khrushchev had consolidated power, or 1965, when Brezhnev agreed to the Kosygin reforms. Past reform efforts had been a response to long-standing economic problems – but to problems within a system that continued to bring rapid growth and significant technological advance. By contrast, in 1985 the Soviet economy had experienced a decade of stagnation, with no end in sight. This stagnation posed a serious danger to the leadership. The well-educated, urban-dwelling population was demanding a better standard of living. They wanted more and better housing, food, and other consumer goods. At the same time, the leadership faced a challenge from the Reagan administration's military buildup. The leadership could not possibly meet these two demands, both of which required more economic resources, in the face of a stagnating economy. Successful economic reform was imperative if a genuine crisis were to be avoided.

No Soviet leader after Stalin possessed absolute power. Yet the CPSU general secretary was a very powerful figure, compared to any Western president or prime minister. While various interest groups within the bureaucracy could resist directives for change from the top, there was no recalcitrant legislature, no opposition parties, and no uncooperative media to thwart the plans of the Soviet leader. If the general secretary became persuaded that major reforms were needed, he appeared to have significant power to carry them out.

As will be explained in more detail in Chapter 5, at first Gorbachev tried relatively minor tinkering with the economy. Within a year of taking office, however, he became convinced that a deeper reform was needed. At a party congress in February 1986, Gorbachev announced that "now the situation is such that it is impossible to simply limit our measures to partial improvements – what is needed is a radical reform."[80]

In Gorbachev's speeches and writings during 1987, there emerged an analysis of the main problems facing the Soviet system, the underlying causes of those problems, and the solutions required.[81] He recited the familiar, long-standing problems of the Soviet economy – poor quality consumer goods, shortages, lack of consumer services, waste of inputs, and so forth. But he particularly stressed the need to reverse the stagnation that had set in. He wrote that "in the latter half of the seventies ... the country began to lose momentum." Economic growth rates fell "to a level close to economic stagnation." He noted that "the gap in production efficiency, output quality and technology, compared to the most developed countries, began to widen." Indeed, he warned that "Perhaps the most alarming thing is that we had begun to lag in scientific–technological development ... And not because of any absence of scientific backing, but mostly because the economy was not responsive to innovation." He complained of "the mounting contradictions in society's development" which, he warned, "were acquiring pre-crisis dimensions."[82]

Gorbachev located the underlying cause of these problems in the particular configuration of economic institutions which had been adopted originally under Stalin. He was critical of the traditional Soviet model, stating that it was based on "methods and forms . . . not always in accord with socialist principles." While noting that for a time it had been economically effective, he argued that it had now begun "to contradict the demands and conditions of economic progress. Its positive potential was exhausted." He concluded that "Historical experience has shown that socialist society is not ensured against the emergence and accumulation of stagnant tendencies and even against major socio-political crises."[83]

Gorbachev stressed two specific flaws in the traditional Soviet model which now rendered it outmoded. One concerned the means of coordination of the various parts of the economic system. This flaw was the "rigid centralism" of the system, with its tradition of "command" from the center. This he held responsible for many of the irrational economic outcomes.[84] The second flaw was the absence of effective work motivation – the problem of lack of work discipline. Gorbachev's belief that these two structural problems caused the stagnation closely parallels our own view presented above.

Based on his analysis of the problems facing the Soviet system and their causes, Gorbachev proposed solutions that entailed a radical restructuring of the Soviet economic mechanism. Scattered through his writings of 1987 are proposals that reflect two principles for reforming the economic system so as to resolve the problems facing the country. One theme was the democratization of Soviet economic institutions. The second was the introduction of elements of a market economy.

The first theme called for the replacement of command planning by a more decentralized and democratic form of planning in order to more effectively coordinate the economy, and it also proposed the replacement of authoritarian single-person management of workplaces by worker self-management to create an effective motivational system. For example, Gorbachev stated that the aim of the reform should be "the transition from an excessively centralized management system relying on orders, to a democratic one." Promising that "We are contemplating democratizing planning," he spells out what that would mean, as follows:

> This means that plan-making – not formal but actual – will begin within enterprises and work collectives. It is they who will be planning the production of their output, on the basis of social needs expressed in target figures and government contracts and on direct economic contract ties with consumers.[85]

There are also many references to self-management and worker participation as the solution to the labor discipline problems. For example, Gorbachev wrote:

The worker must assume the position of a real master in his work-place, collective and society as a whole; this is how to stimulate higher production efficiency ... the interest of working people as masters of production is foremost and represents the most powerful force for sparking social, economic, scientific and technological progress.[86]

Democratization became the central theme of Gorbachev's entire reform program. He argued that the key basis for renewing Soviet society was "extensive development of democracy ... Democratic, and only democratic, forms are capable of giving us a mighty acceleration." He called for "broad democratization of all aspects of society."[87]

A second theme ran through Gorbachev's speeches and writings of 1987 – that the solution to the economic problems of the system lay in an expanded role for market forces, or "commodity–money relations," to use the Soviet term. Gorbachev called for placing enterprises on "full-scale profit-and-loss accounting and self-financing." Producer goods should be allocated by a system of "wholesale trade" based on contracts between enterprises, rather than directly allocated by the economic plan. He noted that "competition is central to activating the motive forces of socialism," adding that "Enterprises must be put in such conditions as to encourage economic competition for the best satisfaction of consumer demands." Such comments suggest that Gorbachev wanted to use a competitive market mechanism to make enterprises display more effi-cient behavior and greater attentiveness to consumer wishes. However, the market was not to replace economic planning, but rather "the advan-tages of planning will be increasingly combined with stimulating factors of the socialist market."[88]

Gorbachev also suggested that the way to improve labor discipline was to ensure that pay was based on productivity. He criticized "the tendency of leveling [of wages]" which "negatively influenced the qual-ity and quantity of work." Instead, "the incomes of working people should be linked to their performance on the job."[89]

Democratic participation and worker self-management on the one hand, and profit incentives, competition, and a system of pay based on performance on the other hand, rest on different methods of eliciting effective economic performance. The former stress solidarity, coopera-tion, and common purpose; the latter emphasize individual calculation of gain and loss. Gorbachev believed the two principles, democracy and market forces, should be combined in the restructured Soviet economy.

Gorbachev made it clear that his aim was to radically reform Soviet socialism, not replace it with capitalism. He wrote that:

we are conducting all of our reforms in accordance with the socialist choice ... We are sure that if we really put into effect the potential of socialism, if we adhere to its basic principles, if we take fully into consideration human interests and use the benefits of a planned economy, socialism can achieve much more than capitalism.

He added that "Socialism and public ownership, on which it is based, hold out virtually unlimited possibilities for progressive economic processes."[90] In 1987 the plan for radical restructuring of the Soviet system included market elements, and even approval for expansion of individual and cooperative property, but it was clearly a plan to produce a reformed and democratized socialism, not its replacement by capitalism. There was no countenance of either private ownership of large-scale productive property or the replacement of planning by free markets in Gorbachev's thinking.

The radical restructuring of Soviet society that Gorbachev would initiate was not limited to the economy. Even before the call for radical economic reform had fully emerged, Gorbachev would begin a new policy known as "glasnost," or openness. This entailed inviting the public and the mass media to openly criticize Soviet society and the leadership. In 1988, a year after Gorbachev's economic plans had been spelled out, the leadership would propose the democratization of Soviet political institutions. These three elements – glasnost, radical economic reform, and democratization of political institutions – made up what came to be known to the world by the Russian term "perestroika," which means "reconstruction." Unbeknownst to Gorbachev at the time, his plan to renovate Soviet socialism and finally bring out its full potential would instead unleash forces that would soon dismantle the Soviet system and usher in an attempt to replace it with Western-style capitalism.

Part II

Perestroika and the demise of the Soviet system

INTRODUCTION TO PART II

Mikhail Gorbachev and his associates sought to transform the undemocratic, highly centralized state socialist system into a new democratic
socialism. By so doing, they expected to finally bring out the long-
suppressed potential of a socialist system. But to democratize an undemocratic system inevitably meant a political battle. It required the
unleashing of a public that had been tightly controlled for generations.
The political process that resulted might take a different direction from
what the reformist leadership intended.

From 1985 through 1991 a political battle of rising intensity engulfed
the Soviet Union. It ended with the defeat and destruction of the Communist Party, the dismantling of the state socialist system, and the
dismemberment of the Soviet nation-state itself. Understanding the
course of this battle – who the main protagonists were and the strengths
and weaknesses of each – is complicated by the one-party Soviet state.
One cannot chart the rise and decline of various competing political
parties.

The battle was fought within the Communist Party. It was fought
within the mass media, as contending views competed for influence. It
was fought in academic journals and conferences, as intellectuals
debated the direction of economic and political reform. It was fought
in electoral campaigns in which most contenders were Communist Party
members and few candidates had a clear program. It was fought in the
new Soviet Congress of People's Deputies and Supreme Soviet, as well
as in new republic-level legislatures. And it was fought in the streets as
mass demonstrations and strikes became regular features of Soviet life.

During the perestroika years an opposition movement gradually
developed in the Soviet Union, and Boris Yeltsin soon emerged as its
undisputed leader. This opposition movement, ill-defined at first, began
to coalesce with greater clarity in 1989 when the first major contested
legislative elections took place. This movement gave birth to several

important organizations, such as the Interregional Group of Deputies and Democratic Russia, but no single organization ever encompassed the opposition movement as a whole.

Precisely what the opposition movement led by Yeltsin stood for was not easy to determine in the early stages of the political battle. Among the main themes it raised were democracy, individual freedom, and economic reform. It was most often identified as a pro-democracy movement. However, that failed to distinguish it from the direction of change which Gorbachev represented. Under Gorbachev's leadership, a significant democratization of the Soviet state took place. As we shall see below, by October 1990 the Soviet Union had created representative legislative institutions, rescinded the Communist Party's constitutional right to rule, adopted a law granting equal status to all political parties, and ended the Communist Party's former monopoly on the news media. The opposition movement played a role in pressing for these reforms, but it continued to remain in opposition to Gorbachev.

What kept Yeltsin and his followers in opposition to Gorbachev until the end was their disagreement with Gorbachev's commitment to reform and democratize socialism, rather than replace it with capitalism. After Yeltsin and his followers came to power in independent Russia at the end of 1991, there were no further dramatic gains in building democratic institutions or guaranteeing individual liberties, beyond what had already been accomplished at the end of the Soviet period.[1] The most significant change after December 1991 was that the government, under the leadership of Yeltsin and the movement he headed, undertook a program intended to rapidly and radically transform Russia's socioeconomic system. The Yeltsin government sought to quickly eliminate the remaining elements of a socialist system and create the basis of a capitalist one.

While Yeltsin and his followers did support democracy and individual liberties, in the end what defined their distinct position in the Soviet political battle was their determination to replace the Soviet system with a capitalist system similar to those in the West. This goal was what distinguished them from both Gorbachev's effort to build democratic socialism and the Old Guard's hope that the state socialist system could be retained with only minor changes. In view of this, it seems appropriate to refer to the movement Yeltsin led as "the pro-capitalist coalition" – "pro-capitalist" because its determination to bring capitalism was its distinguishing feature, and "coalition" because the movement was so loose and undefined organizationally and drew its support from diverse elements within Soviet society. As was noted in Chapter 1, not every active supporter of this movement conceived of the goal as "capitalism." But at the end of the 1980s the movement pressed more and more clearly for a program of privatization of business and free markets, and once it won state power, it set out to build a socioeconomic system that anyone would recognize as capitalist.

Mikhail Gorbachev's reform program of perestroika unwittingly produced conditions that nurtured the growth of the pro-capitalist coalition, which finally emerged as the victor in the battle over the future direction of Soviet society. It won the battle because it was able to assemble, within the changing institutional realities of the Soviet system, the strongest base of support from those parts of society that were active in the struggle over social change. Decisive for the victory of the pro-capitalist coalition was the support it gained from the party–state elite of the Soviet system. In Part II we examine how this process unfolded.

Perestroika had three main parts to it. One was glasnost, the lifting of ideological control and the opening up of cultural life to free discussion and debate. The second was economic reform, the effort to replace the old highly centralized, unresponsive, inefficient economic mechanism by a reformed socialist economy. The third was democratization of Soviet political institutions. Chapters 4 through 6 trace the evolution of each of these components of perestroika. We will see how each aspect of the reform changed Soviet society in ways that encouraged the development and growing political strength of the pro-capitalist coalition. Chapter 7 examines in detail the question of why, and how, a decisive part of the party–state elite ended up giving its support to the pro-capitalist coalition.

The last chapter in this part, Chapter 8, examines the unfolding of the complex political battle in Soviet society during the last years of the Soviet Union. In that chapter we discover how the pro-capitalist coalition was able to defeat its rivals, amidst increasing economic disorder and intensifying nationalist conflicts. We will also see that the breakup of the Soviet state resulted, not simply from the release of nationalist passions, but from the political aims of the pro-capitalist coalition, whose path to power required separating the Russian Republic from the rest of the Soviet Union.

Chapter 4

Glasnost and the intelligentsia

The first significant changes after Gorbachev took power were not in economics but in the realm of culture and individuals' right to freedom of thought. Gorbachev initiated the policy known as glasnost, which entailed lifting the stifling controls on public debate and individual expression of opinion, at the beginning of 1986. The decision to tackle the cultural and political repression of the Soviet system as the first step in his reform agenda may have come from a belief that economic reform could not succeed, or even get an effective start, if the population remained passive and fearful. Perhaps it was hoped that glasnost would arouse the population and stir them into action in support of renovating the Soviet system.

Glasnost had a major impact on the Soviet intelligentsia. By the "intelligentsia" we mean those whose work was to develop and express ideas, knowledge, values, and images – that is, writers, artists, journalists, natural and social scientists, academics, and those in other similar occupations.[1] As the strict party control over their work was lifted, members of the intelligentsia suddenly had a new freedom of expression. At first the intelligentsia's delight with glasnost translated into strong support for Gorbachev and his policies. However, a significant part of the newly freed Soviet intelligentsia would eventually move into opposition to Gorbachev's central goal of building a reformed socialism.

Two months after Gorbachev became general secretary, the banned film *Agoniya* was released, a move interpreted in Moscow as a harbinger of a new freedom. In February 1986 the well-known political prisoner Anatoly Shcharansky was released.[2] The world really took notice when renowned dissident physicist Andrei Sakharov, father of the Soviet H-bomb, was suddenly freed from his exile in Gorky in December 1986 on the personal initiative of Mikhail Gorbachev.

Freeing political prisoners was an important step toward changing the political atmosphere, but even more important was the new freedom granted to the mass media. In March 1986 Gorbachev invited the mass media to criticize the Communist bureaucracy.[3] Soon new editors were appointed to many leading newspapers and magazines. Liberal intellectuals were named to run *Ogonyok, Sovetskaya Kultura, Moscow News, Znamya,* and *Novy Mir.*[4] The state-run television networks began to allow a diversity of views in news reporting.

These initiatives promised an end to decades of strict regimentation and top-down control of social life in the Soviet Union. The result was the rapid emergence of "civil society" – that is, citizen organizations and activities that are outside the sphere of state control.[5] One reason a civil society could appear so rapidly is that one actually had been developing, in semi-underground form, since the liberalizations of the Khrushchev era in the 1950s.[6] The new policy of glasnost permitted this hidden civil society to break out into the open and rapidly develop.

Soviet history, economics, politics, and culture suddenly were opened to an increasingly free examination and debate. Gorbachev hoped that glasnost would permit an open discussion about how best to carry out the reform he was urging. He hoped it would mobilize the social energy to overcome the natural resistance to significant change. But once glasnost stimulated the emergence of civil society, the Soviet leadership lost the power to fully control the debate which it had unleashed. People used their new freedom, not just to do what Gorbachev had wished, but to express a wide variety of views. Some opposed change, more or less openly, insisting that Soviet society had no serious ills. Some called for returning to the Stalinist past. Some looked even further back – monarchist ideas found expression, as did a pre-Bolshevik extreme nationalism.[7] For example, the extreme Russian nationalist, anti-Semitic organization Pamyat surfaced and began holding public demonstrations in Moscow in May 1987.

The Soviet past was subjected to a close and critical examination. Stalin's repressions were condemned with a vigor not seen even in the days of Khrushchev. The leadership began rehabilitating early revolutionary figures who had been executed under Stalin, such as Nikolai Bukharin. Eventually some analysts began to trace the roots of Stalinism to Lenin himself. Others pointed to the Bolshevik seizure of power as the root of the Soviet Union's problems. Some began to criticize socialism and compare it unfavorably to capitalism.

Thus, the full range of positions – reformist, conservative, reactionary, and revolutionary – suddenly burst into the public space. The Soviet Union was a society not accustomed to such an open and wide-ranging debate. New positions were typically expressed tentatively at first, often camouflaged as a debate over how best to carry out perestroika. But as people found that the new freedom was genuine, unofficial positions were expressed more and more boldly over time.

The new freedom of the mass media played a central role in this outpouring of new ideas. Newspapers, magazines, and television gave expression to the diverse views that emerged. A fierce debate developed within the top leadership over whether things were getting out of hand. Those who worried that they were placed major blame on "the liberal media." Some ordinary Soviet citizens were amazed to see attacks on their sacred beliefs in the media, which had formerly been reliable promoters of the official line. This reaction was shared by Yegor Ligachev, Gorbachev's second-in-command of the Communist Party during the first years of perestroika. Ligachev complained that the media were "blackening Soviet history." He periodically warned Gorbachev that the media were falling into the hands of opponents of socialism. And it was true that much of the Soviet media in the late 1980s became increasingly critical of the Soviet social and economic system and increasingly favorable toward Western-style capitalism as a model for the Soviet Union to follow.

In his memoirs, Ligachev blamed Alexandr Yakovlev, whom Gorbachev had named secretary of the central committee in charge of ideological matters, for appointing editors who were hostile to the Communist Party.[8] Yakovlev had the main responsibility for replacing editors in chief of the media. Ligachev suggested, without directly saying so, that Yakovlev had a plan to undermine socialism, naming anti-Communists to key editorial positions to further this plan, while Gorbachev inexplicably turned a blind eye to this process. It is true that Yakovlev eventually, in 1991, resigned as an advisor to Gorbachev and became a critic of socialism.[9] Yet even if Ligachev was right about Yakovlev's intentions during the 1980s, which is doubtful, he was mistaken about why so much of the media came to increasingly promote views opposed to any form of socialism.

The flaw in Ligachev's interpretation is provided, unintentionally, by Ligachev himself, in his own account of one of the most important editorial appointments of 1986 – that of Vitaly Korotich as head of the popular weekly journal *Ogonyok*. Under Korotich's stewardship, *Ogonyok* was transformed into a leading voice for the pro-capitalist movement. Yet Korotich was not named to this position by Yakovlev. It was Ligachev himself who made this particular appointment! Before approving Korotich's appointment, Ligachev read Korotich's recently published book, *Faces of Hatred*. Ligachev found it to be acceptably orthodox, his only complaint being that Korotich was "too much of an extremist when it came to America," expressing "harshly anti-American" views. Yet Korotich was soon guiding *Ogonyok* to a pro-American and pro-capitalist position.[10]

The fundamental reason that so much of the Soviet media grew increasingly critical of the Soviet system, and even of the effort to turn it into a democratic form of socialism, was not any hidden plan of Alexandr Yakovlev to undermine socialism. The real reason the media underwent such a shift was that they were reflecting a vast ideological change in the Soviet intelligentsia. Prior to perestroika, a few Soviet intellectuals had become dissidents, but the great majority served as faithful promoters of the official ideology. For rendering this service, the intelligentsia was provided with a comfortable lifestyle and the means to pursue their work. Approved writers and artists received a salary and access to well-appointed dachas where they could spend time practicing their trade. Natural scientists, supported by the vast Academy of Sciences network of research institutes, did not have to spend their time pursuing foundation grants. Social scientists received stable support for producing Marxist analyses of social and economic problems.

Yet the intelligentsia's actual belief in the official ideology was shallow. Well before perestroika, some would admit their doubts to Western friends. Intellectuals resented the strict adherence to official dogma that was a prerequisite to functioning within the system. The heavy-handedness of the Communist system of oversight of intellectuals clashed with the self-definition of an intellectual as one who independently develops and expresses ideas, knowledge, values, and images. Writers wrote, journalists reported, economists analyzed, scientists theorized, and artists created with full knowledge that someone would judge each product for its ideological correctness. Transgressions would eventually lead to loss of one's job, along with expulsion from the system of privileges, and transgressors would face persecution if the deviation were viewed as sufficiently threatening. The intelligentsia could not help but resent being coerced into a straitjacket defined by party officials who had little knowledge of their specialty.[11]

Glasnost suddenly freed the long-controlled Soviet intelligentsia to express criticisms of the system. They were even invited to do so. They responded with enthusiasm. Their resentment of Communist Party officialdom, which had long suppressed them, propelled them into very sharp criticism. Many of them identified socialism with their former state of subjugation. They were naturally attracted to Western ideas of individual freedom of expression. They wanted a change in the system that would ensure that such freedom would be permanent. The claim of Western ideology that freedom of ideas is inseparable from the free market in goods and services, and the related idea that personal autonomy from the state is secure only in a system of private ownership of the means of production, held great attraction for the intellectuals. Many of them gravitated to such views over the perestroika years, rejecting the socialist reformers' belief that individual freedom could be combined with a socialist system.

Another feature of intellectuals as a social group came into play. In times of social crisis, upheaval, and reform, intellectuals in any society, particularly the younger among them, tend to be the first to be radicalized. As people whose profession is to deal with ideas, theories, and images, to play with them in the mind and consider new and alternative formulations, intellectuals tend to be more open than others to considering radical alternatives to existing institutions and beliefs. In a time when society is undergoing reform and change, many young intellectuals abandon moderate reform for revolutionary ideas. This was well illustrated in the West during the Great Depression of the 1930s, when a large proportion of the intelligentsia flocked to Marxism and Communism, while other sections of society opted for moderate welfare-state reform of capitalism.

A similar process of radicalization gradually began to take place among the Soviet intelligentsia in the decade before perestroika, as the Soviet Union's economic and social problems worsened. Perestroika then greatly accelerated this process of radicalization. But its implications for the Soviet system were much greater than had been the case when similar processes had occurred in the West. While much of the intelligentsia was radicalized in the West in the 1930s, the major media, being the property of wealthy capitalists, were not readily accessible to them. Radicalized writers had to resort to small left-wing presses and journalists to writing columns in the *Daily Worker*. Radicalized screen writers could see their works produced only in carefully circumscribed form, with hints of progressive themes, not unlike the pre-perestroika Soviet movies that carefully danced around the edges of censorship. It is a remarkable fact that, in 1936, in the face of a devastating depression, an increasingly angry and desperate citizenry, and an intelligentsia rapidly giving up on capitalism, nearly every major newspaper in the United States backed Republican Alf Landon for President, finding even Franklin Roosevelt's New Deal reforms to be too radical.

But the newly appointed editors in the Soviet Union of 1986–87 faced no such barriers. At first they couldn't believe their new-found freedom was real. Soon they realized that it was. The top political leadership had actually given editors, journalists, writers, and economists freedom to write as they wished, using the mass media as their vehicle. The newspapers, magazines, television networks, and other media of expression were all effectively state-owned, but the state had granted them substantial independence.

In March of 1988 it briefly looked like this idyll might end, when *Sovetskaya Rossiya* published a letter by neo-Stalinist Nina Andreyeva attacking the media for their "excesses."[12] It was feared that the letter represented official policy, signalling an end to glasnost. But after a long and stormy politburo meeting, pitting Ligachev, who offered conditional support for Andreyeva's letter, against Yakovlev, the politburo decided to prepare an editorial for *Pravda*, the official organ of the CPSU central committee, condemning the Andreyeva letter and reaffirming support for journalistic freedom and independence. The publication of this editorial on 5 April, three weeks after the Andreyeva letter was published, showed that the green light for independent writing and thinking was for real.[13]

This episode was followed a few months later by the first scholarly attack on Lenin to be published in the Soviet Union. Writing in the liberal magazine *Novy Mir*, economic journalist Vasily Selyunin disputed the Gorbachev leadership's view that the distortions in Soviet socialism began with Stalin.[14] Selyunin argued that Stalin's repressions had been prefigured by the harsh methods he attributed to Lenin. This article set off a debate that ended with much of the intelligentsia concluding that Lenin, and the Bolshevik revolution which he led, had been a misfortune for Russia from the start. A new orthodoxy arose in the liberal media which held that pre-revolutionary Russia had been gradually developing into a Western-style capitalist democracy, a development which had been artificially blocked by the Bolshevik seizure of power and the following misguided socialist experiment. The implication was that, if Communist rule could be thrown off, Russia would again return to its pre-revolutionary path of what had come to be called "normal civilization," by which was meant Western-style democratic capitalism.[15]

During 1989–90 belief in any form of socialism was rapidly evaporating among the intelligentsia. Tatyana Zaslavskaya is a leading Russian sociologist who is considered to have played an important role in inspiring Gorbachev to initiate perestroika. Originally she viewed perestroika as a way to reform socialism. But by 1990 her views had shifted. She described "a big seminar" at the Academy of Sciences during 1989–90 on socialism, chaired by vice-president of the Academy Vladimir N. Kudryavtsev. The seminar concluded that the Marxist idea that capitalism must be superseded by socialism and then communism was basically wrong. The participants agreed that there were not really two distinct systems of capitalism and socialism at all and that mature capitalism had "socialist features."[16] One Western Soviet specialist described the new consensus about the desired Soviet future among Soviet scholars as follows: "it would not be based upon public ownership ... would not supersede capitalism and might not even offer an alternative to it."[17]

Thus, members of the Soviet intelligentsia, undergoing a rapid process of radicalization, were given free access to, and even control over, much of the mass media.[18] During 1987–91 the media reflected this radicalization process, as ever more daring and anti-establishment ideas found expression.[19]

One puzzle remains about the conversion of much of the Soviet intelligentsia to a belief in Western-style democratic capitalism. The Soviet system had devoted a lot of resources to creating comfortable conditions for intellectuals. Soviet writers did not have to wait on tables to stay alive while hoping for the first successful novel, nor did academics fear being lost in an academic underworld of part-time, low-paying teaching jobs. Did the Soviet intelligentsia, opting for capitalism and the free market, ignore their material interests in the pursuit of freedom of the mind?

Not at all. Far from believing that state socialism had created good material conditions for them, most Soviet intellectuals believed that their material position was much worse, both absolutely and relatively, than that of their counterparts living in the capitalist West. Although shielded from the insecurities of the market and generally provided with good working conditions, most Soviet intellectuals earned pay that was little better than that of manual workers. This had not been the case several decades earlier. For example, in the early post-World War II period, Soviet scientists had been paid relatively well compared to manual workers, but their relative pay declined over the next decades.[20] Western visitors frequently heard complaints from Moscow intellectuals like the following: "My dacha outside Moscow is right next to one belonging to a truck driver, and mine is no better than his."[21] Soviet intellectuals perceived, correctly, that the material position of successful intellectuals was relatively higher on the scale in Western capitalism than was the case under Soviet state socialism.

Some also looked with favor at the opportunity Western intellectuals had to get rich. The most successful Western writers, artists, and performers could amass personal wealth that was unavailable to individuals in the state socialist system. As contact with the West increased during the 1980s, Soviet intellectuals tended to disproportionately meet the most successful of Western intellectuals, receiving a distorted impression of the living standard of the average of that group.

Whatever role material considerations played in the ideological conversion of the Soviet intelligentsia, these worked to reinforce, rather than to hold back, the other factors propelling them in that direction. One of the great ironies of the rapid rush to free-market capitalism, which began in Russia in 1992, is that among the biggest losers in this process have been the intelligentsia, who were suddenly dumped into the unforgiving world of the free market as the system of state support for intellectual endeavor largely collapsed.

Economists underwent the same process of radicalization during the perestroika years as did the rest of the intelligentsia, but the effects of their radicalization were particularly profound. Perestroika had various dimensions, but the issue of how to reform the economy was the central one. Economists, as the specialists in how the economy worked and how it could be improved, had particular influence in the debate over restructuring the society. Like other members of the Soviet intelligentsia, economists had been required to support the official ideology, including the superiority of socialism over capitalism, the advantages of central planning over the "anarchy of the market," and the benefits of public over private ownership. In the official view, private ownership of the means of production was particularly taboo, since it meant exploitation of workers for the benefit of capitalists.

In the past many Soviet economists had parroted these views without fully, or even partially, believing them. Western "neoclassical" economic thought, which views free markets and private ownership of industry as the only rational way to organize an economic system, achieved significant influence among Soviet economists even before perestroika. Soviet economists taught what they were supposed to teach, and they dutifully published orthodox Marxist–Leninist books and journal articles, but many of them quietly doubted what they were teaching and writing.

In the Soviet system professional economists had not previously been very influential. Real power over economic policy was held by the party politburo, and secondarily by top officials in the economics ministries and state committees. Few of these officials had been academic economists, nor had economists been very influential in those institutions prior to perestroika. Officials responsible for the economy most often had backgrounds as managers or engineers. As in the West, people with such backgrounds did not have a great deal of respect for academic economists, whom they tended to view as out of touch with the real world.

But as glasnost gave rise to an increasingly free debate in society, economists began to promote their views more actively and effectively in public forums. Glasnost set off the same process of radicalization among Soviet economists as it did for other intellectuals, while it freed them to state their true beliefs. Gorbachev seemed to take their views seriously. In the last years of perestroika, the top political leadership kept turning to groups of economists to draw up new plans for reforming the economy. What the economists were thinking now had a significant impact on events.

What the economists were thinking would be very familiar to anyone who knows Western economic thought. While there were exceptions, the great majority of Soviet economists emerged during the later perestroika years as vocal advocates of free markets and private ownership. Like their neoclassical counterparts in the West, most of them shied away from using the term "capitalism," but their advocacy of free markets in place of planning, and private ownership in place of state or worker ownership, was clearly the advocacy of capitalism as it is known in the West.

Many Soviet economists were attracted to an extreme version of Western economic thought known as "free-market economics." This theory is descended from the simplistic view that dominated nineteenth-century British economic thought. It holds that unregulated market forces produce ideal results with respect to economic efficiency, technological progress, economic stability, and distribution of income. This theory practically disappeared among Western academic economists in the decades after the Great Depression of the 1930s. It was replaced by a more balanced view holding that, while market forces should play the major role in the economy, the government had to provide a framework of regulation to prevent such social ills as severe depressions, excessive inequality of income, the development of monopoly power, environmental destruction, and unsafe working conditions. In the 1970s the old free-market doctrine made a comeback in Western academic economics, and since then it has competed for influence with the more interventionist brand of mainstream economic thought.

Free-market economics became very influential in the Soviet economics profession in the late 1980s. While Soviet economists knew first-hand the problems of central planning, they had not experienced the problems of unregulated markets. Perhaps believing that the tales of poverty and unemployment in the West were just Communist propaganda, many of them enthusiastically adopted the free-market creed.[22] Evidence of this turned up in a questionnaire study of Russian and British economists conducted in 1991. Asked whether "the market is the best mechanism to regulate economic life," 95 per cent of the Russian economists surveyed agreed, compared to 66 per cent of the British economists. Fully 100 per cent of the Russian economists thought "private property is a necessary concomitant condition for markets," while 25 per cent of British economists disagreed.[23]

Not all Soviet economists accepted the free-market theory. A small minority continued to believe in the superiority of socialism. A number of influential economists, including Leonid Abalkin, the Director of the prestigious Institute of Economics of the Academy of Sciences, adopted the more balanced view that markets require significant government regulation.[24] But the overwhelming weight of economists' views swung, over the course of the perestroika years, increasingly toward the view that the only salvation for the Soviet economy lay in free markets and privatization.

The growing shift of the Soviet intelligentsia, and particularly the economists, toward support for capitalism was an important factor in the eventual demise of state socialism and the political victory of the pro-capitalist coalition. By 1990, after only five years of glasnost, the intelligentsia had been thoroughly radicalized, and their voices were widely heard in the print and electronic media. Former Soviet prime minister Nikolai Ryzhkov, who served in that post during almost the entire perestroika period, from 1985 to 1990, believed that the Soviet mass media, by the late 1980s, had become "an important force" in opposition to the leadership's effort to stick with its program of reforming Soviet socialism.[25]

The media were very centralized in the Soviet Union, and the radicalized Moscow intellectuals were able to project their views into every corner of the country. Alexander Savitsky, formerly the Communist Party secretary of Magnitogorsk, a steel-producing city at the southern tip of the Ural Mountains, remarked that the constant drumbeat in the television broadcasts and newspapers and magazines from Moscow led "nearly all of the intelligentsia and many workers [in Magnitogorsk] to support Yeltsin and the American model of life."[26]

The intellectuals made their influence felt not only through the mass media, and as advisors to the government, but, as we shall see, in the electoral campaigns and new legislative institutions that developed beginning in 1989. But the voice of the intellectuals is far from the whole story. As the intellectuals argued increasingly openly for capitalism, they could have been struck down by those with the real power in the Soviet system – the party–state elite. Yet they were not. Why they were not is the key to understanding the demise of the Soviet system.

Chapter 5

Economic reform

Three years after perestroika began, the world's media projected dramatic images of economic hardship in the Soviet Union. In 1988–89 severe shortages of basic consumer goods developed, and Soviet citizens had to spend their time in ever-lengthening lines to obtain food and other household necessities. More and more goods were subjected to rationing. Pictures of empty store shelves seemed to portray a system in its death agony.

These images underlie the most common explanation for the demise of the Soviet system. This is the view that the collapse of an unworkable, unreformable economic system was the root cause. According to this interpretation of events, the ultimate unworkability of a socialist economy finally showed itself with unmistakable clarity in the Soviet Union at the end of the 1980s.

Gorbachev and his associates tried to reform the Soviet Union's sputtering economy, but their reform attempts were doomed to failure, it is said, because they stayed within the bounds of a socialist economy. The refusal to give up the institutions of economic planning and public ownership of the means of production prevented any successful economic reform as long as Gorbachev was in charge. Despite the reform efforts under Gorbachev, Soviet economic performance grew worse and the economy "collapsed" or "imploded," as evidenced by the consumer shortages. Because Gorbachev resisted the inevitable demise of socialism, he was ultimately swept aside by Boris Yeltsin and the popular movement which Yelstin led. Yeltsin and his followers triumphed because they understood that adopting a capitalist system was the only viable option.

The above conventional account of the Soviet demise is not convincing. One problem with it is that it rests upon a very simplistic theory of social change. It assumes that an economy can suddenly become "unworkable," at which point a social revolution to replace it with an alternative economic system becomes inevitable. Such a theory is often called a "mechanistic" one, since it draws inspiration from the realm of mechanical devices. An automobile engine can at some well-defined point become unworkable and cease functioning, leaving the hapless owner with no alternative but to replace it with a new engine or even an entire new automobile.

However, the same cannot be said of an economic system. Economic systems, whether socialist, capitalist, or another variety, do not suddenly become unworkable due to their own internally generated problems. An economic system may work well in its own terms at certain times, meeting the expectations which it generates among the population. Such performance tends, of course, to contribute to social and political stability. At other times it may not work so well, producing dissatisfaction. While the term "collapse" is misleading when applied to an economic system, an economy can suffer a drastic contraction, as did most of Western capitalism when the Great Depression of the 1930s struck. In the United States the Great Depression put one-third of the non-farm labor force out of a job by 1933. Yet even then the American economy did not literally stop functioning, and no absolute necessity compelled the adoption of a radically different economic system.

All economic systems have powerful institutions that tend to preserve them in hard times, even in time of severe economic crisis. Whether economic crisis leads to reform or revolution is no simple question. During the 1930s many radical critics of American capitalism fervently believed that the "unworkability" of the system had been amply demonstrated, yet no revolution took place. The Great Depression, severe though it was, led not to revolution but to the reform of capitalism. In the United States the reform process began in 1933, when Franklin Roosevelt took office as President. It was not completed until a few years after World War II, some fifteen years later. By the late 1940s, American capitalism had emerged greatly transformed and poised, as it turned out, for some twenty-five years of the most rapid, and widely shared, economic expansion in its history.

No purely speculative analysis can tell us in advance whether an economic system can, or cannot, be reformed under a given set of circumstances. Most economic systems are surprisingly adaptive, if not perfectly so. The Soviet economic system had undergone minor reforms before perestroika, under Khrushchev in the 1950s and Brezhnev/Kosygin in the 1960s. But in the 1980s the world did not have an opportunity to learn whether Soviet socialism was capable of being reformed so as to surmount the problems it faced at that time. The reason is that, a few years after Gorbachev and his associates introduced their first major economic reforms, the reformers rapidly lost power to a group that can only be called revolutionaries. As we shall argue below, by 1990 the effort to reform the Soviet economic system was replaced by the beginning of the dismantlement of its main institutions.

Table 5.1 Growth rates for Soviet economy during 1980–91 (per cent per year)

| | Western estimates | | Official Soviet data | |
	(1) GNP	(2) Consumption	(3) NMP	(4) Consumption
1980–85	1.8	1.9	3.2	3.2
1986	4.1	1.5	2.3	3.5
1987	1.3	2.2	1.6	3.5
1988	2.1	3.5	4.4	4.2
1989	1.5	2.3	2.5	5.1
1990	−2.4	1.5	−3.9	2
1991	−12.8[a,b]	[N.A.]	[−15[b]]	[−13[b]]

Source: Joint Economic Committee (1990, p. 58), Joint Economic Committee (1993, pp. 14, 17), International Monetary Fund (1992a, pp. 41, 43, 49). Column 2 is growth in aggregate real consumption of goods and services. Column 4 is growth in real private and communal consumption based on Soviet accounting conventions
Notes: a GNP for 1991 is the average of two different estimates (−8.5 per cent and −17 per cent), b Estimate excluding Georgia and the Baltic republics

The conventional explanation of the Soviet demise does not fit the pattern of Soviet economic performance during the perestroika years. The evidence shows that the Soviet economy did not even contract, much less "collapse," as long as the socialist elements of the Soviet system were still in place. Economic restructuring during the perestroika years took place in three stages. In stage 1, during 1985 and 1986, a relatively modest change was implemented. In stage 2, during 1987 through 1989, a more radical reform was carried out, although within the bounds of a socialist economy. The years 1990 and 1991 marked the third stage of economic change. In that period the pro-capitalist coalition gained sufficient political strength to push economic change beyond the bounds of socialist reform. The Soviet economy did not begin to contract until stage 3 – when political means were used to start dismantling the system. This sequence does not conform with the view that the Soviet economy collapsed due to its own internal contradictions.

Table 5.1 presents data on the growth rates of total output and total consumption for the Soviet economy, including both Western estimates (columns 1 and 2) and official Soviet statistics (columns 3 and 4). The accompanying Figure 5.1 compares the performance of these variables during various sub-periods of the perestroika years. The effects of the modest stage 1 policies primarily showed up in the growth rates for 1985–87. The more radical socialist restructuring policies of stage 2 took effect right at the beginning of 1988, with the economic consequences affecting growth rates for the period 1987–89. The growth rates for 1989–91 record Soviet economic performance in stage 3, when socialist institutions were being dismantled. Figure 5.1 shows the growth rates resulting from these three stages of restructuring, as well as comparing the results during the

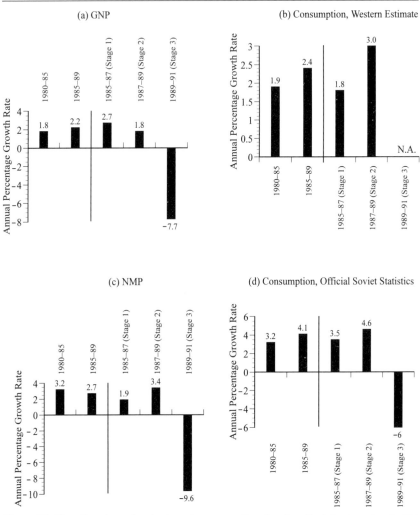

Figure 5.1. Growth rates of output and consumption for the Soviet economy during 1980–91
Source: See Table 5.1.

socialist reform period of stages 1 and 2 together – 1985–89 – with the growth experience of the half-decade preceding perestroika.

Table 5.1 and Figure 5.1 make two important points. First, they show that the Soviet economy continued to expand during 1985–89, the first two stages of perestroika, and that only in 1990 and 1991, when the effects of the stage 3 dismantling of socialist institutions were felt, did the economy begin to contract. Table 5.1 shows that the Soviet economy as a whole experienced positive growth every year during 1985–89. In 1990 total output, measured either by GNP (column 1 of Table 5.1) or

NMP (column 3 of Table 5.1), contracted slightly. Then in 1991 the economy entered a severe depression by any measure. As part (a) of Figure 5.1 illustrates, measured by the Western concept of GNP the Soviet economy actually grew faster during the first two stages of perestroika together (1985–89) than it had in the five years preceding perestroika. Measured by the Soviet net material product concept, shown in part (c), it still grew during 1985–89, although more slowly than in the first half of the 1980s.

The second point, seen most clearly in Figure 5.1 parts (b) and (d), is that total consumption, the variable most directly experienced by the citizenry, grew significantly more rapidly during 1985–89 than in 1980–85, based on either Western or official Soviet estimates. Furthermore, consumption increased significantly faster in stage 2 of reform than it had in stage 1 by either measure.[1] Table 5.1, columns 2 and 4, shows that consumption did not begin to contract until 1991, the last year of the perestroika period.

These data appear to contradict the widely held impression that the perestroika years saw steadily worsening economic performance, particularly with respect to the availability of consumer goods. The average Soviet citizen did experience growing economic problems starting in 1988. People encountered worsening shortages of consumer goods, yet the data show an increasing level of real consumption, until 1991. This paradox has a solution, and the solution, which is discussed below, helps explain why perestroika ultimately led to the demise of the Soviet system.

The economic reforms of perestroika, despite the continuing economic growth which accompanied them as late as 1989, also generated economic dislocations which, with remarkable rapidity, strengthened the political faction that wanted to pass beyond the reform of socialism. The growing political strength of the pro-capitalist coalition, and its ability by 1990 to begin dismantling the key socialist economic institutions of the Soviet system, played a major role in the economic contraction of 1990 and 1991, although it was not the only factor explaining that contraction. Only a few years after it began, the socialist reform effort was pushed aside by a more radical agenda. Let us look at how the economic reforms and their consequences contributed to this development.

POLICY EVOLUTION DURING STAGES 1 AND 2 OF ECONOMIC RESTRUCTURING, 1985–89

Gorbachev's initial economic policies were relatively orthodox. The Five Year Plan for 1986–90 was based on the slogan of "acceleration" (*uskorenie*), an idea attributed to Gorbachev's first close economic advisor, Abel Aganbegyan. The main aim was to reverse the slowdown in Soviet economic growth, doubling the annual GNP growth rate from the slow 2 per cent rate of 1980–85 to a more respectable 4 per cent in 1985–90.

No basic changes in Soviet economic institutions were envisioned yet. The old system of highly centralized planning would be relied on to raise the growth rate. Diagnosing the problem as one of poor worker discipline and outmoded capital equipment, the plan called for tightening worker discipline and stepping up investment to replace and modernize the country's aging capital stock.

One part of this plan was the ill-fated anti-alcohol campaign. Drunkenness was viewed as a major cause of poor worker discipline. To combat this, state production of alcoholic beverages was sharply curtailed. While a slight increase in sobriety may have resulted, this campaign, like the American experiment with Prohibition after World War I, had unforeseen harmful consequences. Illegal private production arose to meet the unsatisfied demand. Private distillers stripped the retail stores of sugar, causing severe shortages. And an estimated 20 billion rubles in tax revenues were lost on alcohol sales during 1986–88.[2] Both consequences were a harbinger of things to come, as later, more radical, reforms would produce more serious consumer goods shortages and budget deficits.

To aid in modernizing the capital stock, twenty-three new scientific–technical research complexes were established in 1986–87 to develop new technologies. The rate of growth in the production of new machines and other capital goods did rise to double the level of the preceding decade (1975–85) during 1985–87.[3] But neither rising machinery production nor attempts at modernization succeeded in making a lasting impact on the performance of the economy. As Table 5.1 shows, GNP growth achieved the new target of 4 per cent in 1986, mainly due to a large improvement in agricultural output that year, but over the following two years it fell to an average of 1.7 per cent per year, a rate essentially equal to that of the pre-perestroika half-decade.

Although Gorbachev had begun with relatively orthodox economic reform measures, he simultaneously extended glasnost to economic policy discussion. A wide-ranging debate on economic reform was encouraged in 1986 as part of glasnost, and this led to the first serious economic reform efforts in the summer of 1987. A meeting of the central committee in late June 1987 approved a document called "Basic Provisions for the Radical Restructuring of Economic Management." A few days later the Supreme Soviet adopted a series of decrees designed to carry out the new policy and also adopted the Law on State Enterprise, the latter to take effect on 1 January 1988.[4]

This package of measures embodied the ideas for reforming the Soviet economy that were discussed in Chapter 3. They were intended to transform the highly centralized form of planning, with its detailed determination of the entire nation's production from the center in Moscow, into something different. Substantial autonomy was to be granted to enterprises. Gosplan, the central planning agency, was to shift its focus to long-term plans and goals, while the economic ministries were to end their day-to-day management of production. Republican, regional, and local soviets were to be granted a larger role in overseeing the economy of their respective areas. Within enterprises, workers were to be given expanded power over decision-making. These reforms embodied the leadership's idea of democratizing and decentralizing the economy, within the framework of public ownership and economic planning.

How were these aims to be carried out? Enterprise autonomy meant abandoning the system of central determination of a detailed plan of outputs and inputs for each enterprise. Instead, the center would issue "non-binding control figures" giving a target for the value of each enterprise's output and for other indicators of enterprise performance. There would also be mandatory "state orders" for part of the enterprise's output, to ease the transition away from the old system of detailed central administration. But, over time, state orders were to gradually shrink as a proportion of output. The remainder of enterprise output would be sold through "wholesale trade." This meant that enterprises would become relatively free to determine what they would produce and to whom they would sell their products. The share of wholesale trade was supposed to rise to 60 per cent by 1990 and still higher thereafter.[5]

While some prices would remain centrally controlled, others would be set by contracts, with growing freedom of pricing over time. Enterprise directors were granted increased power over employee pay, with the hope that this would lead to a closer link between pay and productivity. Enterprises were supposed to become "self-financing," obtaining funds from retained earnings and loans from the state banking system.

The Law on State Enterprise provided for the election of Labor Councils at enterprises. The Councils were to play a role in decisions about pay, discipline, and worker training. Furthermore, key managerial personnel, including the enterprise director, were to be elected by the employees, with the right of removal by vote as well.[6]

The 1987 reform did not eliminate central controls over the economy, but it provided for a progressive loosening of them over a period of a few years. The intention was to gradually replace the strict central controls by a new system of democratized and decentralized planning together with a greater role for market relations. However, the design of this reform turned out to have serious flaws. First, it failed to create new institutions to coordinate the behavior of the newly independent enterprises. The shifting of enterprises from central diktat to relative autonomy over sales, purchases, and financing would require new ways of operating for enterprise managers accustomed to following orders from above. Such new ways of behavior, and the necessary supporting institutions for the new, more decentralized system, do not spring up quickly or automatically. Thus, the rapid shift to greater enterprise autonomy, without adequate preparation, would inevitably entail a good deal of chaos.

Second, granting enterprises more freedom to determine the allocation of enterprise income could potentially produce imbalances in the economy. Short-sighted behavior by enterprises might raise employee incomes beyond the ability of the economy to produce consumer goods. And if revenue were diverted from investment to employee pay and benefits, it would undermine the plans for faster economic growth.

Third, under the old system the central government had never had difficulty obtaining revenues to finance its expenditures. The central government's control over enterprises allowed it to readily collect from them whatever taxes were required. But the new enterprise autonomy meant that now the state would have to shift to a system of taxing semi-autonomous entities to obtain revenue, and no new tax system had been introduced that could effectively collect needed revenues under the new conditions.[7]

CRISIS IN THE CONSUMER MARKET

These three problems exploded on the Soviet economy in 1988–89, bringing a crisis of the consumer market. During those two years the Soviet Union experienced ever-lengthening lines outside stores, the rationing of more and more commodities, and the complete disappearance of many goods from the stores.[8] The growing shortages had a profound impact on the political climate, changing it from one of optimism to one of crisis. This made it much easier for advocates of more radical changes to gain a serious hearing.

Yet if one consults the economic data on household consumption for these years, this crisis is not at all visible. Private household consumption, corrected for inflation, actually increased significantly, growing by 3.9 per cent in 1988 and 5.3 per cent in 1989.[9] How can the worsening consumer goods shortages be reconciled with the growth of actual consumer purchases?

At the time, some Soviet officials blamed diversion of consumer goods by secretive "enemies of perestroika." But the explanation requires no such conspiracies. The simple fact is that, while the quantity of consumer goods available increased, the money incomes of households rose much faster. A growing gap emerged between consumer goods available and money demand for those goods, which, given the controlled prices in the Soviet system, led to a breakdown of the retail distribution system.

Before the 1987 economic reform, central planners had kept a reasonable balance between the growth of household income and the quantity of consumer goods available. After the Law on State Enterprise came into effect in 1988, household income suddenly took off. Although the consumer goods available increased, that increase was far outstripped by the growth in household spending money. Figure 5.2 illustrates this phenomenon.

Nominal household disposable income, which is not corrected for inflation, tells us how much cash Soviet households had to spend on consumption. Real private consumer spending, which is corrected for inflation, is an approximation for the volume of consumer goods available for purchase.[10] From Figure 5.2 we can see that in 1986 and 1987 (as in earlier years) the growth of household disposable income was kept in line with the growth of available consumption goods. The difference between the two was under two percentage points, a difference small enough to be absorbed by the Soviet rate of retail price inflation of 1–2 per cent per year. However, as Figure 5.2 shows, in 1988 and 1989 household income grew at an accelerating pace, far outstripping the real growth in consumer goods available.[11] The growing excess of consumer

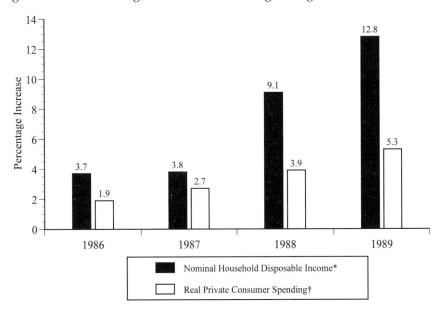

Figure 5.2. Growth of household income and consumption
Source: Official Soviet data cited in International Monetary Fund 1992a: 49, 56.
*Household income after taxes, not corrected for inflation.
†Real consumer spending, excluding communal consumption.

demand over consumer goods available, given the price controls in effect, caused the shortages and disappearance of goods from normal retail channels that was observed in 1988 and 1989. The flaws in the 1987 economic reform explain this mushrooming of consumer buying power. Finding themselves partially freed from central control, enterprises provided big pay increases to their employees.[12]

Another factor behind the worsening shortages was the growing government budget deficit, due to the decline in tax revenues as the 1987 reforms took hold. Figure 5.3 shows the growth of the Soviet budget deficit as a percentage of gross domestic product (GDP).[13] Prior to 1985 the Soviet Union had a negligible budget deficit. A sizeable deficit suddenly arose in 1986–87 when the anti-alcohol campaign drastically reduced state revenues from alcohol sales. In 1988–89 the effects of the 1987 Law on State Enterprise produced a very large deficit.[14] This compounded the problem of excess demand for consumer goods, as state employees were paid partly by means of printing new money.[15]

The 1987 reforms had not freed prices, which largely remained under state control. Hence, the excess money demand did not immediately produce significant inflation: retail prices rose by only 0.6 per cent in 1988 and 2.0 per cent in 1989, according to official statistics.[16] Instead, the gap produced a breakdown in the distribution system for consumer goods. Goods would sell out as soon as they appeared.[17] Consumer goods enterprises, now growing more sensitive to profit considerations, responded to the excess demand by shifting production toward higher-quality, higher-priced items, which carried a higher profit margin. Thus, basic goods that the lower-income part of the population

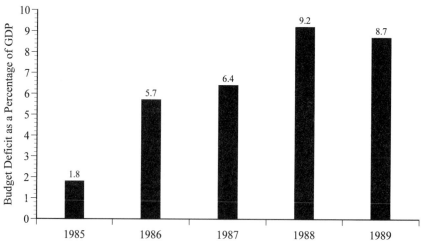

Figure 5.3 The Soviet budget deficit as a percentage of GDP
Source: Joint Economic Committee 1993: 47.

relied on became even harder to find. The sale of goods through "back-door" channels to people with influence, or to those willing to secretly pay above the official price, which had always been a feature of the Soviet system, apparently began to draw off a growing share of consumer goods. The inevitable counterpart to bare store shelves was bulging household stocks; as consumer goods became more and more difficult to find, consumers began to hoard supplies at home.[18] This hoarding behavior, while understandable from the consumer's standpoint, only worsened the shortages at the stores.

While the consumer market was in turmoil in 1988–89, an equally serious, although less noticeable, problem was developing in the economy. Net fixed investment, the amount by which the stock of capital goods increases each year, suddenly began to decline in 1988. That year net investment declined by 7.4 per cent, and in 1989 it fell by 6.7 per cent.[19] This trend threatened the future productive capability of the economy. This unprecedented development was another consequence of the 1987 reforms. With the center no longer dictating a high rate of investment, enterprises were sacrificing the future for the present. The economy as a whole continued to expand in 1988 and 1989, with GNP growing at 2.1 per cent in 1988 and 1.5 per cent in 1989, but the rate was no better than the laggard early 1980s.

RADICALIZATION OF THE DEBATE

The year 1989 marked a critical turning point in the struggle over the direction of the Soviet system. The chaotic consumer market, declining investment, and disappointing GNP growth were bound to have an impact on the debate over the course of economic reform. The effect was to encourage the radicalization of the terms of debate. Two years earlier, in May 1987 a little-known young economist, Larisa Piyasheva, had published a letter in the literary journal *Novy Mir* which openly challenged socialism.[20] She argued that world experience showed that only a market system could bring prosperity, that planning cannot be combined with a market system, and that socialism is incompatible with a market system. This heretical piece was outside the bounds of acceptable opinion at that time. Yet two years later those themes were adopted by a growing chorus of economists, utilizing the liberal mass media to project their views to the public and the policymakers. The economic difficulties of 1989 made many people ready to listen.

The debate over economic reform evolved rapidly, beginning in 1989, and one can chart this evolution through the at-times subtle, yet very important, shifts in the precise terms that came into vogue. The debate centered on two key issues. The first was the extent to which the economy should be guided by economic planning or by market forces. The second was the relative effectiveness and desirability of public or private property in the means of production.

As we saw in Chapter 3, the reform ideas that Gorbachev developed in 1987 called for an economy that would retain economic planning, but with decentralization and a significant role for market forces within the planned framework. This seemed to be the intent of the 1987 Law on State Enterprise. Starting in 1989, this conception was subject to increasingly bold attacks. The original conception was slightly altered when the terms "socialist market economy" and "planned market economy" came into use. These terms implied that the economy should become *primarily* a market economy, with "socialism" or "planning" as a modifier. In 1990 the term "regulated market economy" came into use, which was a further step away from the conception of the economy as a socialist one. It suggests something like the system in such countries as Germany or Japan, where the state actively regulates the market within the framework of a capitalist market system.

The evolution of terminology continued, and next the word "regulated" was dropped by many commentators, leaving the desired goal as simply "a market economy." The final step was the increasingly heard call for a "free-market economy," which arose toward the end of this period. This phrase – misleading though it may be, given the fact that in no major capitalist country are markets allowed to operate entirely freely – completed the transition, within the debate over how to coordinate the economy, from a position of socialist reform to one that entirely rejected the socialist belief that a framework of planning is necessary if an economy is to serve popular needs.

The debate on property underwent a similar evolution, beginning in 1989. At first there were calls for a "mixed economy," that would take account of the small-scale individual and cooperative enterprises which had been approved, beginning in 1986, to exist alongside state enterprises. Initially it had been assumed that individual and cooperative enterprises could make a positive, albeit small, contribution, while state enterprises would continue to predominate. Next came advocacy of "equal status" for all forms of property, a step beyond the original conception. Soon commentators began to discuss the advantages of "joint-stock enterprises," a form of property that has some ambiguity, in that the real nature of the property relation it entails depends on who owns the shares. If public agencies own the majority of shares in a joint-stock corporation, then it may be considered a partially state enterprise. Yet the form of joint-stock companies opens the door to non-state ownership of large enterprises.

By 1990 the view that state ownership of enterprises was the root of the difficulties of the Soviet economy was openly argued in the press. The superiority of private over public ownership was asserted, typically based on the argument that only a private owner will be motivated to effectively manage a business.[21] Calls to "destatize" enterprises began to be heard. The latter term meant removing enterprises from ownership by the Union state, and it might include conversion to ownership by employees or regional or local governments. But soon the evolution reached its conclusion with calls for privatization, which clearly meant the conversion of state enterprises into capitalist firms.

Very rapidly the economic reforms discussed by economists and other policy analysts in the media had evolved from a reform of socialism to what can only be called the advocacy of capitalism. At the start, the talk was of incorporating some market forces within a planned economy, and allowing some small non-state businesses within the context of public ownership of most of the means of production. Now the radical reformers were calling for a free-market economy and privatization of industry.

Many leading economists participated in this evolution of slogans, emboldened by the economic difficulties of 1988–89. One example was Oleg T. Bogomolov, the head of the Institute of the Economics of the World Socialist System. Bogomolov had worked in the central committee under Yuri Andropov in the 1960s, and for twenty years he had been the Soviet Union's official spokesman on economic relations with other socialist countries. He was cautious in the early years of perestroika, but by 1990 he advocated a free-market economy and privatization.[22]

Another example is Stanislav Shatalin. In the mid-1980s he was a follower of the "optimal planning system," an approach that sought to use linear programming techniques to perfect central planning.[23] In 1985 he emerged from relative obscurity to become deputy director of a new research institute, the Institute of Economic Forecasting and Scientific and Technical Progress. After being criticized for advocating price liberalization in 1986, he retreated into a more cautious stance. In 1989 he became head of the Economics Department of the Academy of Sciences. At the end of the 1980s, Shatalin turned against central controls, coming out for free markets and privatization.[24] He headed the task force which produced the famous Five Hundred Day Plan in 1990, which is discussed below.

It was noted in Chapter 4 above that not all of the leading economists travelled this road. Leonid Abalkin, director of the Economics Institute, held to the position of reforming socialism rather than opting for capitalism. In July 1989 Gorbachev named him to the post of deputy prime minister in charge of economic reform. In a 1989 article in the Soviet economic journal *Voprosy Ekonomiki* (Problems of Economics), Abalkin envisioned a significant role for market forces in the Soviet economy, but he criticized the idea of a "free market." Rejecting the market mythology that had come into vogue in Moscow, he approvingly cited the work of Harvard professor and well-known critic of "free markets," John Kenneth Galbraith. Abalkin noted that:

The free market practically does not exist in any country today... Economic life is regulated not only by the 'invisible hand' of the market but also by very visible methods of state control, financial policy, intrafirm planning, and intergovernmental agreements.

Abalkin stuck with the term "socialist market," summing up his view in the following way: "A distinguishing feature of the socialist market is the combination of its mechanism with a quite highly developed system for the planned regulation of economic processes."[25] He stressed the need to develop markets gradually and did not link markets with any need for privatization.

Yet one can detect a defensive tone in Abalkin's argument. He felt the need to cite Western capitalist experience and Western authorities to defend a policy of continuing with socialist reform. He was clearly swimming against a tide.

The economic problems that followed the 1987 reforms undoubtedly helped assure that the newly expressed pro-capitalist ideas would receive a serious hearing. But they do not fully explain the extremely rapid growth in the influence of these ideas during 1989–91. If one did not know the actual evolution of ideas and beliefs in this period, one might suppose that the economic problems would have increased the influence of those who wanted to go back to the old pre-reform, central-ized system. Advocates of that position did indeed argue that the eco-nomic problems showed the dangers of such "radical reforms."

Alternatively, the supporters of the Gorbachev strategy of reforming socialism might have learned, from the economic problems caused by their first serious reform measures, that they had to proceed more care-fully and plan their reforms more comprehensively. The central prob-lems of runaway employee incomes, falling net investment, and declining tax revenues might have been remedied. In 1989 the Soviet state still had the power to impose an effective system of taxation on enterprises. A system of revised enterprise incentives could have been devised to restrain wages and channel funds back into investment.

Yet the main effects of the economic difficulties were seemingly to strengthen the advocates of moving from reform to revolution, while the socialist reformers grew weaker and the advocates of return to old pre-perestroika ways remained marginalized. This outcome cannot be explained solely by the economic problems that developed after 1987.[26]

THE ECONOMIC PROPOSALS OF 1990–91

At first the Soviet leadership resisted the ideas coming from the increas-ingly radicalized economists. Abalkin's first economic plan after being named deputy prime minister in 1989 called for market relations to play a significant economic role but within a framework of economic planning, and with the large enterprises to remain in state hands. In November 1989 Gorbachev and Prime Minister Ryzhkov spoke on television about the dangers of private property. "I do not think the working class will support those authors who want to start making our society capitalist," Gorbachev remarked, adding "No matter what you do with me, I am not going to forsake this position." He allowed for the possibility that "Perhaps later . . . there will develop forms that will resemble small-scale private property," but he opposed large private businesses. Ryzhkov added that "The most important thing is to exclude the possibility of exploitation of man, of hired labor."[27] In February 1990 the central committee of the CPSU adopted a platform that reiterated the call for finding "an organic combination of plan and market methods to regulate economic activity," emphasizing that "Modern production is impossible without a centralized planned management" while simultaneously accepting the need for the "creation of a full-fledged market economy."[28]

But during 1990 the economists' proposals for free markets and private property moved beyond academic conference papers and articles in the mass media. These ideas became the basis of a series of economic reform plans that achieved wide publicity that year. The economic problems of 1988–89 evidently persuaded Gorbachev that another round of economic reform was needed, and in March 1990 he declared that now "perestroika should be radicalized" and economic reform should move faster.[29] He set Deputy Prime Minister Abalkin to work, with a team of 60 economists and lawyers, to devise a new economic plan. They came up with recommendations for speeding up the transition to a market economy. Their plan included gradual freeing of most prices; denationalization of small companies and turning of large companies into joint-stock corporations; and replacement of job guarantees with a system of unemployment compensation. However, some key sectors, including fuel, metals, and transportation, were to remain state-owned and with controlled prices.[30] Although Abalkin had been opposed to a headlong rush to the market in 1989, his proposal of March 1990 was a big step in that direction.

Gorbachev's sudden shifts in position during his years in power have been widely noted. Despite his call for radicalizing perestroika in March 1990, in mid-April Gorbachev balked at the recommendations of Abalkin's team. Gorbachev complained that:

> They want to take a gamble. Let everything be thrown open tomorrow. Let market conditions be put in place everywhere. Let's have free enterprise and give the green light to all forms of ownership, private ownership . . . I cannot support such ideas.[31]

Instead, in May the government adopted a plan for a gradual, five-year transition to a "regulated market economy," prepared under Ryzhkov's direction, with centralized economic controls to remain in force during the transition.[32] In a prescient remark at that time about Gorbachev's hesitance to adopt a radical economic program, Gosplan economist Gennady N. Zoteyev said, "It may be that we need a non-Communist administration. Only such a government can persuade the country to pay the price of introducing a real market."[33]

By the summer of 1990, Gorbachev appeared to be moving toward the economists' recommendations. Speaking at a Communist Party congress in July, he rejected "the monopoly of one form of ownership [state ownership]," calling for "equal economic and political rights" for a diversity of property forms. "Nothing prevents us from beginning to turn state enterprises into joint stock companies," or "putting up . . . stocks, shares and other equities, as well as part of the means of production, for purchase and sale."[34]

In August Gorbachev and Boris Yeltsin, by then the chairman of the Supreme Soviet of the Russian Republic, jointly named a team of economists to come up with a new economic reform plan. It was headed by Gorbachev advisor Stanislav Shatalin, with Yeltsin advisor Grigory Yavlinsky also playing a leading role. In early September the team reported the famous 500 Day Plan, which called for a drastic transformation of the Soviet economy within 500 days – that is about 17 months.[35] While the plan was never implemented, it played a key role in the transition from the stage of reforming socialism to the dismantling of socialist institutions. The flavor of this plan is shown in the following introductory passage:

> As paradoxical as it might seem, the period of 1985–90 was objectively necessary for society to become aware of the hopelessness of the existing socioeconomic system and to elaborate a program of transition to a different development model.

The different "development model" called for was one based on the free market: "Its [the market's] own self-adjustment and self-regulation mechanism takes care of the best possible coordination of activities of all economic subjects, rationalizes the use of labor, material and financial resources, and balances the national economy." They argued that the government should intervene in the market only to improve macroeconomic stability, to avoid excessive inequality of incomes, and promote more even development of different regions. They called for denationalizing and privatizing at least 70 per cent of industrial enterprises within 500 days by turning them into joint-stock corporations, with large foreign investments encouraged. Finally, they called for creating a financial system based on private commercial banks and securities markets.[36]

Thus, this was clearly a blueprint for building a capitalist system as we know it in the West – and quickly. It called for the rapid freeing of many prices, cutbacks in subsidies to enterprises, allowing a substantial number of enterprise bankruptcies, encouraging cheap imports to keep costs down, and advocacy of tight fiscal and monetary policy. While Prime Minister Ryzhkov opposed the 500 Day Plan and devised a more moderate alternative, Gorbachev appeared to approve of it initially. Gorbachev complained that some opponents called the 500 Day Plan "a program leading toward capitalism. It's clear that such accusations have no grounds." He insisted that the plan was consistent with his view that "private property would play a substantial role only in some domains, but only a rather limited role in society as a whole." He emphasized the continuing role for state enterprises, cooperatives, and other collective forms of property, insisting that the plan was consistent with socialism. He remarked, "In essence, we are returning to the slogan, 'Factories and plants to the workers, land to the peasants!' "[37]

Gorbachev was apparently torn between his continuing belief in socialism and the enormous and growing pressure to jettison the socialist features of the system and proceed with building capitalism. The latter was clearly the aim of the 500 Day Plan, as anyone who reads it can readily see.

However, a month later Gorbachev backed away from the 500 Day Plan, although Yeltsin obtained its approval by the parliament of the Russian Republic. In October 1990 Gorbachev submitted a compromise plan to the Soviet parliament, which passed it on 19 October. This compromise plan, known as the "Presidential Plan," retained the goals and broad features of the 500 Day Plan, such as the eventual phasing out of most price controls, the privatization of industry, and the creation of a market-type financial system. It eliminated the 500-day timetable, calling for a more gradual transition.[38] Speaking before the Soviet parliament, Gorbachev insisted that this plan "does not contradict the socialist choice of our people." However, he noted that it would leave "commodity producers free to multiply their property," and it called for "nonparticipation of the state in economic activity' except in such activities as "defense, health care, education, science and culture."[39]

By the end of 1990, the Soviet economy had begun to change dramatically. The 1987 Law on State Enterprise had called for a gradual reduction in the central allocation of products. In 1990 this process was accelerated, and the number of products distributed by Gosplan and Gossnab fell by a factor of fourteen compared to 1987.[40] Central coordination of the economy was melting away.[41]

In June 1991 Grigory Yavlinsky teamed up with a group of Harvard University economists to propose another plan for speeding the transition to free markets and private business. It was tagged as "the Grand Bargain" by the media because it called on the West to provide $100 billion in economic aid to the Soviet Union if the plan was adopted.

Prime Minister Valentin Pavlov, who had replaced Ryzhkov after the latter's heart attack in December 1990, counterposed a more cautious plan. Once again, Gorbachev combined the two into a compromise plan to bring to the upcoming meeting of the Group of Seven leading industrial nations.

On 1 July 1991 the process of dismantling economic planning reached its climax, when the agencies Gosplan and Gossnab were abolished entirely. Gosplan had been in charge of overall coordination of the economy, while Gossnab had managed supply relations among enterprises. Political pressures had led to the abolition of the old coordinating mechanisms of the Soviet economy, and no effective new ones had yet developed in their place. Later that month, Gorbachev startled the world by applying for Soviet membership in the International Monetary Fund and the World Bank, two pillars of world capitalism. The intention to integrate the Soviet economy in the world capitalist system was now clear.

At the beginning of this chapter, it was asserted that during 1990–91 perestroika's original aim of reforming Soviet socialism gave way to the dismantling of socialist economic institutions. We can now see that this was indeed the case. While the 1987 Law on State Enterprise had sought to attain a balance of central and local authority, with market forces operating within a framework of state economic planning, in 1990–91 economic planning was virtually eliminated. The Soviet state banking system, which had previously been part of the state economic planning apparatus, was actively being transformed into a privatized system of commercial banks and securities exchanges. By the end of 1990 a stock exchange had opened in Moscow.

While the early reforms had proposed that small-scale individual and cooperative businesses might coexist with a dominant state-enterprise sector, since the fall of 1990 privatization had become official policy. Although few legitimate privatizations of large enterprises actually occurred before the end of 1991, it was clear that privatization was coming. Enterprise directors now knew their enterprise would soon become private property, but who the new owners would be was anybody's guess.[42]

These rapid economic changes had occurred despite the top leadership's continuing professed belief in socialism. The increasingly influential opposition to socialism had pressed these measures on a reluctant leadership.

ECONOMIC CONTRACTION

Of the basic economic institutions of Soviet state socialism – economic planning and state ownership of the means of production – one had actually been eliminated and the other had been marked for elimination. Yet no new economic institutions had been put in their place. Economic chaos was the inevitable result.[43]

In 1990–91, the Soviet economy moved from a condition of severe problems to one of crisis. For the first time in memory, the Soviet economy actually contracted, with the GNP falling by 2.4 per cent in 1990 and about 13 per cent in 1991 (Table 5.1). Net fixed investment declined at the astounding rate of 21 per cent in 1990 and an estimated 25 per cent in 1991.[44] The money income of the population continued its climb, as did the budget deficit, worsening the already disastrous condition of the consumer market.

The dismantling of the institutions of Soviet socialism bears a major part of the responsibility for the turn from economic disruption amidst continuing economic growth to economic contraction.[45] However, two other factors were also important as causes of the 1990–91 economic crisis – the 1989–90 revolutions in Eastern Europe and the breakdown of economic links among the republics and regions of the Soviet Union.

The main trading partners of the Soviet Union had been its fellow members of Comecon in Eastern Europe. These six countries – Bulgaria, Czechoslovakia, the German Democratic Republic, Hungary, Poland, and Rumania – had accounted for 54.2 per cent of Soviet imports and 48.9 per cent of Soviet exports in 1988.[46] In 1989–90 every ruling Communist Party in the region, outside of the USSR, fell from power. This had a significant effect on the Soviet economy, for two reasons. First, as the socialist economies of Eastern Europe were rapidly dismantled, the ensuing economic disruption led to large declines in economic activity in those countries, reducing their ability to engage in trade with the Soviet Union. Second, the new pro-Western leaderships moved to reorient their nations' trade toward the West.

As a result, in 1990–91 the Soviet Union suddenly found that it was losing its main trading partners. This hit especially hard in 1991, when the value of Soviet imports, in rubles at the official exchange rate, fell by 56.2 per cent, mainly due to the decline in imports from Eastern Europe.[47] The sudden disappearance of a major source of industrial inputs and consumer goods, as well as the major foreign market for Soviet goods, was a serious blow to the economy. On the other hand, the severity of this blow should not be overstated. It was softened by the fact that the Soviet Union, having a large, diversified economy with practically all important natural resources within its borders, was not a heavily trade-dependent country. Its total imports in the late 1980s were only about 7–8 per cent as large as its GNP. Thus, while the approximately 50 per cent drop in foreign trade in 1991 did hurt, it did not represent a large proportion of total Soviet economic activity.

More devastating for the Soviet economy was the growing autonomy of the republics of the Soviet Union during 1990–91. In Chapter 8 we examine the nationalist movements that arose in 1988–89 in a number of Soviet republics. By the summer of 1990 nearly all of the Soviet republics, including the Russian Republic, had declared sovereignty over their territory and natural resources. Since the beginnings of Soviet state socialism, the economy had been built as a highly integrated mechanism. Many products, including critical industrial inputs, were produced by only one or two enterprises for the entire Soviet market. A single factory in Baku was the sole manufacturer of deep-water pumps. One consortium produced all of the Soviet Union's air conditioners. An estimated 80 per cent of the products of the Soviet machinery industry had a single source of supply.[48] Now many of the links in this highly integrated economy began to break down, as traditional supply relations between enterprises located in different republics were disrupted by the autonomy policies pursued by the newly assertive republics. In some cases barter deals had to be arranged between enterprises across republic lines. This process was a major contributing factor to the economic contraction of 1990–91.[49]

PRIVATE BUSINESS EMERGES

We have seen that the economic reforms produced economic chaos which in turn contributed to the undermining of the socialist reform project. There is a second way in which some of the economic reforms – those concerned with property relations – helped weaken the socialist reformers. The gradual easing of the ban on private economic activity presented a problem for the socialist reformers by building a new constituency for the pro-capitalist coalition.

As early as 1985 the new leadership began to take limited steps to allow private business activity by Soviet citizens in the form of individual labor or cooperatives. This was expanded with the Law on Individual Labor Activity in November 1986 and finally the Law on Cooperatives in May 1988. These measures were intended to allow, and encourage, two types of private business activity. One was individual craft or service businesses, from sale of handmade artifacts to repair businesses. The second was cooperative enterprises, in which a group of workers would pool their labor and property to produce goods or services directly for sale to the public. Cooperatives could operate a restaurant, repair business, retail store, wholesale trading company, bank, or small consumer-goods manufacturing business. Cooperative members had to actually work in the business, and capital could not be raised from outsiders, except for state enterprises or other cooperatives. In Marxian lingo, the aim was to permit "independent commodity production," in which an individual or small group produces something for sale, with the producer acting as both owner and laborer. This form is distinguished from the capitalist firm, with its separation between capitalist owner and hired wage-laborer.

The idea behind permitting such small private businesses was the recognition that the state-run economy had been particularly poor at providing the kinds of services and small-scale manufacturing that small businesses typically supply in the West. But the expectation that these new laws would give rise only to genuine cooperatives, as opposed to capitalist firms, turned out to be wrong. The number of cooperatives grew rapidly, and by July 1989 there were an estimated 2.9 million people working in 133,000 cooperatives.[50] Among them were a significant number of firms that were in effect capitalist businesses, in which one or a few owners ran a business employing wage workers. Operating mainly in trade and finance, some of these firms were able to take advantage of the rigidities and controlled prices of the Soviet system to make a great deal of money. Trading firms bought scarce materials and resold them at much higher prices.[51]

The opportunities to make a lot of money in private business improved greatly after a decree was passed by the Council of Ministers in December 1988 called "On the Foreign Trade Activity of State, Cooperative, and Other Enterprises." Previously all foreign trade had been the monopoly of the state. This decree allowed both state and private firms to trade directly with foreign entities. Restrictions on foreign trade remained, one of which was that export and import licenses from the Ministry of Foreign Economic Relations were required for many products.

The decree on foreign trade of 1988 opened an important means to get rich. The Soviet Union's low controlled prices made many Soviet goods, particularly oil and metals, potentially lucrative export items for anyone who could get hold of them. After this decree opened up foreign trade to private firms, import–export companies were formed, in the legal form of cooperatives, which soon began to conduct a partly legal, partly illegal, and very profitable export trade. Over three thousand such firms were formed. Exporting raw materials required a license, but the Ministry of Foreign Economic Relations turned out to be susceptible to bribes. Even Soviet television sets, food, and medicine were exported by these private firms, where a ready market could be found in the Third World.

By 1990–91 a new group of private capitalists had developed and was getting rich mainly through connections with the outside world. They had an interest in supporting the pro-capitalist coalition. Any turn away from the emerging pro-capitalist direction of change, toward either a return to the building of a reformed socialism, or an effort to bring back the pre-perestroika system, would threaten the basis of their lucrative economic endeavors. Proceeding to capitalism was essential to the survival of their new businesses.

Although they quickly became wealthy, even by 1991 this group of private capitalists was not very large, nor did they occupy a very significant position in the Soviet economy. Had this group emerged mainly from the margins of the old system – disgruntled engineers and scientists, energetic and individualistic young misfits, shadow economy operators – its influence would have been limited. But we will show in Chapter 7 that this group did not emerge mainly from such sources, but that from the start members of the party–state elite played the central role in the growth of this new capitalist class.

The course of economic reform in the Soviet Union during 1985–91 was mainly driven by a set of forces that operated within the Soviet system. Yet the Soviet Union was not isolated from the rest of the world, and toward the end of the perestroika period, the major Western powers began to exert a certain limited influence over the course of events. During 1990–91 the Group of Seven leading industrial nations began offering the Soviet Union significant Western aid, making it conditional upon undertaking "serious reforms." This meant adopting and implementing a program of rapid marketization and privatization. The seal of approval of the International Monetary Fund had to be obtained before this aid would be dispensed. In 1991 large sums of foreign aid were dangled in front of the Soviet Union, if the economic changes desired by Western governments were enacted.

Had the Soviet leadership been pursuing its program of the reform of socialism with greater economic success, and with less internal opposition, the Western offers would have had little impact. But given the economic and political conditions in the Soviet Union in 1990–91, these Western offers must have strengthened the hand of those in the USSR who wanted to follow the Western capitalist economic model.

The radicalized intelligentsia plus the wealthy class of newly formed capitalists, backed by the promise of large-scale Western aid, created a significant base of support for the pro-capitalist position. Yet if the bulk of the party–state elite had rejected this position and had opted either for continuing reform of socialism or going back to the old system, it seems almost certain that the outcome would have been different. Certainly the developments would not have been so peaceful. The party–state elite in 1990–91 still controlled the organs of state, including the armed forces. And the International Monetary Fund's promised funds were never large compared to the enormous losses being generated by the economic contraction in the USSR in 1990–91.

Yet a pro-capitalist coalition was able to take power toward the end of 1991, defeating the previously all-powerful Communist Party, and elbowing aside both socialist reformers and would-be restorers of the old regime. To understand how this was possible, we must examine the remarkable changes that took place in Soviet political institutions during the perestroika years.

Chapter 6

Democratization

We have seen that the policy of glasnost began soon after Mikhail Gorbachev became the Soviet leader. Serious economic reform followed not long after, by the middle of 1987. The third part of perestroika, the democratization of political institutions, came last. Although Gorbachev began to emphasize democracy at the start of 1987, it was not until the middle of 1988 that serious plans were laid for significant changes in Soviet political institutions. The actual changes did not occur until 1989.

The democratization of the Soviet Union's political institutions was undoubtedly the riskiest part of Gorbachev's agenda. Free speech could always be qualified or even quashed, and economic reform could always be revised or even reversed – as long as the leadership kept political power in its grip. However, serious democratization of political institutions could potentially weaken the leadership's hold on power, with unforeseeable consequences. Real democratization might open the way for power to pass to groups with different aims from those of Gorbachev and his associates.

Why did Gorbachev take this risky path? It appears that three reasons prodded the leadership forward. First, far from thinking that socialism and democracy were incompatible, Gorbachev and his associates believed that socialism could reach its full potential only through democratization. As we saw in Chapter 3, Gorbachev viewed lack of democracy as having been the greatest obstacle to successful socialist development in the past. He argued that "only through the consistent development of the democratic forms inherent in socialism and through the expansion of self-government can we make progress in production, science and technology, culture and art, and in all social spheres."[1]

Second, the leadership had a more pragmatic reason for pressing forward with democratization in 1988. As resistance mounted to their program of economic and social reform from parts of the bureaucracy, Gorbachev apparently concluded that democratization was the way to break this resistance and prevent perestroika from being stopped in its tracks. Since perestroika would benefit ordinary Soviet citizens, they had to be activated to overcome the resistance to change. Democratization would empower the majority to push aside the resistance to economic and social reform. Furthermore, Gorbachev noted that "democratization is also the main guarantee that the current processes are irreversible."[2]

Third, with the advantage of hindsight, it appears that Gorbachev and his circle came to view democracy as an end in itself. They appeared to view it as an aim nearly equal in importance to their traditional goal of building socialism. "The essence of perestroika lies in the fact that *it unites socialism with democracy*," Gorbachev wrote (italics in original).[3] The good society must be both socialist and democratic. They would soon face the problem of a tension between those two goals, as democratization opened the way for the pro-capitalist coalition to contend for power.

From the start of Gorbachev's rule, references to the need to "perfect socialist democracy" appeared in speeches and programs. However, such phrases had been uttered often before by previous Soviet leaders, without any change following in the Soviet Union's authoritarian political institutions. Then in January 1987, addressing a meeting of the Communist Party central committee, Gorbachev called for the "profound democratization" of Soviet society, referring to this aim as the party's "most urgent task."[4] This meeting had been postponed three times, suggesting significant struggle over the wisdom of the call for democratization which the leadership was to make at the meeting.

The January 1987 central committee meeting set off a debate about how to democratize the Soviet system. Several themes emerged in this debate. One was the need to change the method of selection of the members of powerful political bodies. The leadership proposed competitive elections for both Communist Party and government offices, to replace the old system of appointment from above and single-candidate elections. A second theme was a change in the roles of the main institutions of power, with the official government bodies, particularly the soviets, to become more active and independent, while the Communist Party would withdraw from day-to-day management of public affairs. There was talk about creating a "socialist law-based state" and a system of "checks and balances."

Gorbachev devised a novel strategy for implementing these new democratic ideas. He proposed that a Communist Party conference be held to plan the democratization of Soviet institutions. This proposal was approved by the central committee in June 1987 and the conference was scheduled for the summer of 1988.[5] No party conference had been held in nearly fifty years. With broad representation of the party membership from all over the Soviet Union, and free of the regular party congress's need to handle pressing normal business, a party conference seemed the best instrument to debate and chart a new political structure for the country. It was the Nineteenth Party Conference of June 1988 that would set the Soviet Union on the path to serious democratization.

DEMOCRATIZATION WITHIN THE COMMUNIST PARTY

The process of democratization was to include the Communist Party itself. At the central committee meeting of January 1987, it was proposed that party organizations in workplaces, towns, and cities should select cadres by elections. It was further suggested that the powerful secretaries of party committees at the regional and republican levels be chosen by secret ballot of that level's party committee.[6]

The Nineteenth Party Conference, prodded by Gorbachev, reinforced the call for democratization of the party. In addition to competitive elections for party officials, a limit of two five-year terms would be imposed on party officials, up through the general secretary. Party officials were to be subject to recall, not by their superiors, but by the constituents below who had elected them. Thus, power would flow up from the base, rather than down from the top as it previously had.

However, the plan to turn the Communist Party into a democratic institution was never effectively carried out. A few cases of contested elections to party offices did follow. For example, in Turkmenistan an advocate of safe drinking water narrowly defeated the establishment candidate for a position as a secretary of the republican party central committee in January 1989.[7] In that same month the traditionally secretive Soviet Communist Party central committee began to publish a new journal, *CPSU Central Committee News*, which made available official documents, letters from citizens, and biographies of party and government leaders. In January 1990 the new first secretary of the provincial party committee in Kharkov, in the Ukrainian Republic, was chosen by secret ballot from five candidates. The race was won by the former director of the Kharkov aviation plant, reportedly a non-political technocrat who had never previously held any party office.[8]

However, these examples of democracy and openness in the party were exceptions. Very few party secretaries were chosen in competitive, secret-ballot elections. More than two years after the January 1987 central committee meeting's call for democratization of the party, *Pravda* admitted, in July 1989, that so far no more than one per cent of provincial party secretaries had been selected in that manner.[9] Power continued to flow from the top down in the Communist Party.[10]

It may be that the leadership decided that democratization outside the party – that is, in the governmental institutions – had a higher priority. They may even have feared that real democratization in the party would undermine the leadership's own position within the party at some point, given the traditionalist views of many party members and middle- and lower-level party officials. Indeed, as problems multiplied in Soviet society, and as the Communist Party faced growing opposition in 1989 and 1990, the reformist leadership might well have been voted out of party office had the party actually been democratized. The fact that it remained a top-down institution enabled Gorbachev, as general secretary, to prevent any uprising within the increasingly restive lower ranks of the party from removing him as party leader.

Instead of focusing on reforming the party, Gorbachev and his associates attempted to use the party, undemocratic as it was, to launch the democratization of the larger society. The unquestioned power of the party leader within the party was, at least at the start, an advantage in carrying out this program. As general secretary, Gorbachev could press the politburo to approve his plans for democratization, and he had the power to then gain approval from the party central committee. The only hitch was that, if the plans succeeded, a tension would inevitably develop between a democratizing government and a still unreformed Communist Party claiming the right to lead society.

DEMOCRATIZATION OF THE STATE

The central committee meeting of January 1987 launched the campaign to democratize the Soviet governmental structure. At it Gorbachev called for a change in the elections to the soviets. In practice the members of the soviets ran for office unopposed, with voters' only choice that of voting "yes" or "no." Gorbachev called for a new system of multi-candidate contests for the soviets. A few months later a decree was issued calling for an experiment with competitive elections for some local soviets. In June 1987 the experiment was carried out, as 94,184 deputies were chosen in contested elections for some local soviets, 4 per cent of the total of over 2 million elected deputies. A few prominent people suffered the previously unknown indignity of losing an election.[11]

The growing enthusiasm for democracy even reached the staid and previously docile Supreme Soviet. Officially the highest legislative body in the land, it had always quickly endorsed whatever measures the party leadership put before it. But in the summer of 1987 the deputies unexpectedly criticized and amended a piece of legislation, an act without precedent in recent Soviet history.[12]

However, the old Supreme Soviet was in its twilight hours. The following summer the Nineteenth Party Conference approved a far-reaching reform of the national government, which was given its final form in constitutional amendments and a new electoral law adopted by the Supreme Soviet in December 1988. The old Supreme Soviet was to be replaced by a new two-chamber parliament. A 2,250-member Congress of People's Deputies would be elected, whose members would in turn select a smaller Supreme Soviet from among the deputies, of about 500–550 members, to act as the standing legislature. While 750 members of the new Congress would be chosen by a list of "public organizations," including the Communist Party, the remaining 1,500 would be elected by the population in potentially contestable elections.[13] The Congress would elect a chairman of the Supreme Soviet who would serve as head of state.

Commenting on the upcoming elections to the new Congress of People's Deputies, the Communist Party central committee stated that they would be "unlike all those that had preceded them."[14] This was indeed the case. In March 1989, 89.8 per cent of Soviet voters went to the polls. In three-fourths of the races, two or more candidates vied for the seat. On average there were two candidates running for each seat.

With only one legal political party, the election looked quite different from those in the West. Yet, despite the fact that 80 per cent of the candidates were Communist Party members, many of the seats were hotly contested.[15] Boris Yeltsin, cast out of the national leadership in 1987, won a seat from an all-Moscow district with 89 per cent of the votes. In a contest rich in symbolism, Yeltsin, despite strong opposition from the Moscow party leadership, defeated the establishment candidate, who was director of a factory that manufactured the ZIL limousines favored by top Soviet officials. Many other advocates of faster and more radical reform won election against establishment candidates. In the Baltic republics, candidates supported by unofficial nationalist movements swept the elections to the Congress.

There were various limitations on democracy in the election process, including a nomination procedure that weeded out many would-be candidates. But the public enthusiasm for democracy, at least in the European republics of the Soviet Union, forced local officials to permit many candidacies which they had hoped to block. The biggest departure from usual democratic practice was the reservation of 750 seats for public organizations, a procedure some compared to a sort of Communist House of Lords. But even here the newly released popular pressure produced some surprising outcomes. When the leadership of the Academy of Sciences announced an initial selection of candidates that included only safe, establishment individuals, it set off an uproar among the member scientists. The leaders had to revise their list, and in the end a number of well-known advocates of radical change were elected from the Academy, including the dissident scientist Andrei Sakharov.[16] The Writers' Union also sent several liberal deputies to the Congress.

There is an irony here. The reservation of 750 seats for public organizations was viewed as the most egregious violation of democracy in the organization of the Congress of People's Deputies. At the end of 1989 the

Congress eliminated this procedure entirely for future elections. Yet many of the best-known, and most effective, pro-democracy deputies had been elected via that procedure, and it is uncertain how many of them would have won election had they been required to run in ordinary geographic districts.

Many establishment-backed candidates were defeated in the election. Several high-level military officers lost. The commander of the northern fleet in Murmansk and the military commanders of Moscow and Leningrad fell to civilian challengers, while the commander of Soviet troops in East Germany was defeated by an upstart lieutenant colonel.[17] Many Communist Party officials were defeated, including some who faced no opponent but suffered the indignity of having a majority of voters vote "no." This fate befell Yuri Solovyev, leader of the Leningrad regional party organization and a candidate member of the politburo. Local party leaders fared particularly badly in Moscow, Leningrad, and Kiev.

It is important not to exaggerate the Communist Party officialdom's difficulties in this election. Eighty per cent of the republican and provincial party secretaries who were on the ballot won. Party officials fared especially well in Central Asia, where no provincial first secretary lost. The new Congress of People's Deputies had more party members among its ranks (87 per cent) than had the old Supreme Soviet (71.5 per cent).[18] But as the debate and division that was spreading in Soviet society had also intruded into the ranks of the Communist Party, party membership no longer meant what it once had.

In the Soviet Union's largest and politically most important republic, the Russian Republic, party and government officials did not fare well. One study of a sample of 232 two-person election contests in the Russian Republic (out of a total of 645 publicly elected deputies from Russia) found that 78 per cent of the high officials running in such contests lost, as did 47 per cent of middle-level officials. By contrast, 72 per cent of the intellectuals who ran won their contests.[19]

The new, relatively free elections provided a great opportunity for Soviet intellectuals. With no political parties participating in the election, people ran as individuals. Intellectuals, being typically articulate and knowledgeable, were well positioned to win such elections. As was noted in Chapter 4, by 1989 much of the electronic and print media was dominated by relatively independent editors and journalists who favored radical change. Party and government officials faced a skeptical media, while intellectuals who favored radical change found the media friendly and receptive to their campaigns.

A study of all 645 deputies elected from districts in the Russian Republic (excluding only the deputies chosen by public organizations) shows that intellectuals did indeed fare well in the elections for the Congress of People's Deputies there, coming to make up a sizeable proportion of the body. The study found that intellectuals made up 28 per cent of the 645 elected Russian deputies, party and government officials 21 per cent, workers 16 per cent, industrial managers 14 per cent, farm directors 13 per cent, and farmers 8 per cent. Intellectuals made up 37 per cent of those elected from urban districts.[20]

The Congress began meeting in May 1989. As expected, it elected Mikhail Gorbachev as chairman of the Supreme Soviet (with over 95 per cent of the votes), or "president" as the media called the position. It selected 542 of its deputies to serve in the new Supreme Soviet. The first meetings of the Congress had an enormous impact. For thirteen days they were televised live, to an estimated audience of 200 million Soviet viewers. The interest was so great that millions of people stopped working to watch – one official estimated that industrial output fell by 20 per cent during the live coverage – prompting a switch to evening broadcasts.[21] In contrast to the stage-managed votes of the former Supreme Soviet, what the viewers saw was genuine political debate among the best-known figures in society. No subject was off-limits for the debate. The Soviet intervention in Afghanistan, Stalin's crimes, the military–industrial complex's huge appetite for economic resources, the failure to effectively reform the economy, corruption – all these and more were the subjects of speeches and sharp interchanges among the deputies. Baltic republic delegates demanded independence. Some deputies condemned the Communist Party's role in society. Over it all presided Chairman Gorbachev, often lecturing and admonishing, yet allowing relatively free rein to the debate.

The new Soviet parliament had the power to pass laws, and it did pass some, yet its importance was not mainly as a conventional legislature. Its debates, and the wide coverage on television, produced a political catharsis in the Soviet Union. Suddenly politics was being conducted in the open, was addressing issues people cared about, and was reflecting the real variety of viewpoints found in the society. Not so obvious at the time was that the simple meeting of the Congress was starting a shift in power, away from the Communist Party apparatus. Mikhail Gorbachev, who came to power by virtue of being chosen leader of the party, had now been made president by a semi-democratically elected government body that had no legal connection to the party.

The new Supreme Soviet took its powers seriously. When Prime Minister Nikolai Ryzhkov presented his ministers for approval to the Supreme Soviet in June 1989, he found that what he faced was far from a rubber stamp. Of the 70 ministers he proposed, 11 were rejected either in committee or on the floor and had to be replaced by new nominees. Ryzhkov himself was subjected to some sharp grilling at his own confirmation hearings.[22]

The following year, in 1990, the Soviet republics held even more democratic elections for republican and city soviets. In 1991 the Russian Republic would create executive positions to be filled by direct popular vote, including a new president of the republic and mayors of major cities. These developments, which played a central role in the final battle for power in the Soviet Union, are discussed in Chapter 8.

TRANSFORMATION OF THE ROLE OF THE COMMUNIST PARTY

As we saw in Chapter 2, before Gorbachev's reforms there had been a complex relation between the Communist Party and the administrative organs of the state. The party leader was the most powerful figure in the system. The party leader and his associates in the politburo devised the policies, which the Supreme Soviet approved and the executive branch of the Union state was expected to carry out. This relation was replayed at the lower levels between the republican, provincial, and local party bodies and the corresponding levels of government. The central party leadership gave instructions to local party leaders, which lent cohesion to the manner in which the party intervened in the management of state affairs.

In a large organization, administrative bodies inevitably have some autonomy. A policy prescription can never be so precise as to specify every detail of how the policy is to be carried out, which tends to leave some judgments in the hands of the administrator. And monitoring can never be perfect, permitting some unnoticed actions by those charged with carrying out policies. The party's role as the institution which named people to state positions gave it significant leverage, yet such a role is not necessarily decisive – as King Henry VIII of England once found to his dismay when Thomas Becket, whom he had made the Archbishop of Canterbury, began to serve the interests of the Church rather than the Crown. Once ensconced in a high position in a large organization with its own particular mission, there is a tendency for an official to become an advocate of the interests of that organization.

Because of these problems, in order for the party to exercise real power it had to be involved, at least to some extent, in carrying out policies, as well as devising them. One mechanism for doing this was the inclusion in the politburo of the top officials of the state structure. For example, throughout the 1980s the politburo had always included among its members the chairman and first deputy chairman of the USSR Council of Ministers, the chairman of the Russian Republic's Council of Ministers, the chairman of the KGB, and the ministers of defense and foreign affairs.

As Chapter 2 explained, the party also acted almost as a shadow government and economic management system. The central committee had a large number of committees that paralleled the main functions of the state, covering economic, political, and cultural areas. The secretariat of the central committee oversaw a large party administrative apparatus whose job it was to make sure party policies were implemented. The secretariat itself met regularly and acted to ensure that party policies were actually carried out as intended. Local party secretaries had traditionally been a major force at the local level, solving disputes, arranging compromises, and seeking additional resources from the higher levels of the bureaucracy.

The democratization campaign had to confront the difficult issue of the relation between the party and the state. At its peak in 1989, the party had 19.5 million members, which was less than 7 per cent of the population.[23] Real democratization had to mean a reduction in the party's direct control over society. The position which Gorbachev worked out was to call for the party to focus on playing a political and ideological role in society rather than an administrative one. The pejorative term "command-administrative system" came to be applied to the past practice, and it had been the party which had issued the highest-level commands. In January 1988 an editorial in *Kommunist*, the theoretical journal of the central committee, called for the party to stay out of direct management of public affairs.[24]

Shortly after the Nineteenth Party Conference had designed the new Congress of People's Deputies, Gorbachev forced a major reorganization on the central committee of the Communist Party. In September 1988 the number of departments in the central committee was reduced from twenty to nine, and all of the departments dealing with the economy were abolished, except for that for agriculture. The committee structure of the central committee, which had been the basis of active party intervention in the management of Soviet society, was effectively replaced by a new set of "commissions," on such broad topics as ideology, organization, economics, and international affairs, each commission being headed by a politburo member. At the same time the secretariat stopped holding meetings.

This reorganization had a dramatic effect both on the role of the Communist Party in Soviet life and on the relation between the center and local branches of the party. To a significant extent, it removed the party from the management of the Soviet system. An Italian specialist on Soviet affairs, Rita Di Leo, described this development as "a real earthquake ... This step implied the *de facto* resignation of the Leninist and Stalinist party from its historical role and its claim to govern the fate of the country."[25] Politburo member Yegor Ligachev wrote in his memoirs that this reorganization "automatically buried the secretariat ... The

Party was deprived of an operating staff for its leaders."[26] The secretariat held no meetings for one year, and only sporadic meetings thereafter, until the 28th Party Congress in July 1990 reinstituted them.

Local party leaders found that the center was no longer sending instructions. According to Ligachev, local party bodies were left to make their own decisions without any clear policy from the center. "The center seemed to vanish," he noted. Even on matters as important as how to approach the March 1989 elections to the Congress of People's Deputies, local party branches were left on their own.[27] At the same time, the message that had come from the Nineteenth Party Conference – that the party should no longer intervene in administrative matters in society – left local party officials uncertain what they were expected to do.

The party had been a key coordinating force in the Soviet system. It was local party officials who often solved problems that regularly emerged from the rigid central plan. If a critical economic resource was suddenly in short supply in some locale, a local party official would contact the relevant official in Moscow to fix the problem. Gorbachev was rapidly withdrawing the party from its commanding role in the day-to-day life of society for the purpose of democratizing the system. But in so doing, he was removing an important coordinating force. Furthermore, this step was taken nine months after the Law on State Enterprise went into effect, reducing the extent to which the ministries in Moscow ran and coordinated individual enterprises across the Soviet Union.

The newly reconstituted soviets were supposed to step into the role that had been played by the party for the past seventy years. But it was not clear that they would be able to do so effectively in any short period of time. The newly elected soviets were filled with sharply contending factions and had difficulty taking on any coordinating functions in society. Anatoly Lukyanov, the Chairman of the Supreme Soviet in 1990, made the following comment at the 28th Party Congress:

> Half of our misfortunes of the past two years depend principally, in my opinion, on the fact that the party committees have virtually ceased governing and the soviets have been simply incapable of assuming governing functions...Comrades, there is a power vacuum.[28]

Despite the continuing presence of Article 6 in the Soviet Constitution, which guaranteed the Communist Party the right to direct Soviet society, Gorbachev's reforms were leading to the rapid withdrawal of the party from that role.[29] As the party's direct power over society was slipping away, pressure built to formalize this. In February 1990 an estimated 100,000 people demonstrated in Moscow outside a Communist Party central committee meeting, demanding that the party relinquish its constitutional right to rule. At Gorbachev's urging, the central committee approved the elimination of the party's official ruling status. The following month the Congress of People's Deputies, some 87 per cent of them party members, voted 1,771 to 264, with 74 abstentions, to amend Article 6 of the Soviet Constitution to eliminate the party's constitutional right to rule.[30]

These same two meetings in February and March 1990 that ended formal Communist Party rule also created a new presidential system of executive power. While Gorbachev, as chairman of the Supreme Soviet, had been informally called the "president," now the Congress approved an executive presidency with a good deal of executive power. Checks and balances were included in the system – the president could veto acts of the legislature, which the legislature could override with a two-thirds vote. A Committee of Constitutional Control, appointed by the Congress of People's Deputies, could overrule illegal or unconstitutional acts of soviets and could recommend presidential impeachment. The new position of president would be subject to popular election to a five-year term. However, the Congress allowed the first occupant of this new office, who everyone knew would be Gorbachev, to be chosen instead by the parliament.[31]

The new arrangements included a 16-member "Presidential Council," like a cabinet, which the president would appoint. Gorbachev had now created an entirely new structure to exercise state power, independent of the Communist Party. The Presidential Council looked very much like a replacement for the Communist Party politburo. This appearance was confirmed after the 28th Communist Party Congress in July 1990 when the most important state officials – the prime minister, the ministers of foreign affairs, of defense, and of internal affairs, and the chairman of the KGB – left the politburo for the Presidential Council.[32] Unlike previous politburos, the one elected by the 28th Party Congress, apart from the editor of *Pravda*, consisted entirely of full-time party officials rather than state officials. It included the party chief of each of the fifteen Soviet republics and several secretaries of the central committee of the CPSU.[33] The unmistakable message was that henceforth the politburo would be in charge of the party rather than the country, while the latter role would be undertaken by the new national parliament and presidency.

How did Gorbachev justify these changes in the Soviet state and in the role of the party to his party colleagues, whose institutional right to rule Soviet society was being eliminated? He denied that these moves were a retreat from socialism. On the contrary, they were presented as necessary to make Soviet socialism democratic and finally to fulfill the promise of the October Revolution. At the 28th Party Congress, facing a potential revolt of delegates over the party's eroding power, Gorbachev called for a "renewed communist party" that would "confirm the socialist choice and the communist perspective" and stand for "humane and humanistic ideals in general." To do so, he said "the party has formally relinquished its roles of taking the place of government organizations and of carrying out administration and managerial functions." The party would still seek to lead Soviet society in the building of socialism, but in a new way:

> We believe that [the party's] vanguard role cannot be imposed on society; this role can only be earned through an active struggle for the interests of workers...The CPSU will carry out its policies and will fight to preserve its mandate as a governing party within the framework of the democratic process, and via elections to the legislative bodies in the center and on the periphery.[34]

THE EFFECTS OF DEMOCRATIZATION

Gorbachev and his fellow reformers believed the political reforms would strengthen socialism, not lead to its dismantling. How could they have been so wrong? They never expected that democratization would lead to a rejection of socialism. They had good reason to believe that the Soviet people wanted democracy *and* socialism.[35] Thus, they reasoned that democratizing the system should not pose any threat to the goal of building a real socialist society.

However, the democratizing reforms left Gorbachev in a weak political position for completing the process of reforming socialism, although this was not apparent at first. Gorbachev's original base of support in the population had come from the party–state elite, whose top level had made him the party leader in 1985. Once he became the party leader, the hierarchical structure and traditions of the party made it a powerful instrument for maintaining his base of support in the party–state elite. In addition to assuring a base of support, the party, with its powerful apparatus, had been Gorbachev's organizational means for carrying out his plans.

As a result of his democratizing reforms, by 1990 Gorbachev had risked the loss of his original base of support in the party–state elite and also had destroyed his original apparatus for exercising power in the country. As the old strict discipline of the party dissolved, there was no assurance that the party–state elite would continue to support Gorbachev and his reform plans. Establishing a new base of support in the population would not be easy, in the chaotic and difficult conditions produced by radical economic reform. Furthermore, no effective new means of exercising power had been created to replace the party.[36] As president, Gorbachev had many powers, including command over the armed forces, but he did not intend to rule the country via martial law.

He seemed to expect that the power formerly exercised by the party apparatus would now shift to the soviets, but Gorbachev had limited control over them. He faced a semi-independent USSR Supreme Soviet, and soon also confronted fully independent soviets that emerged at the republic level in the Russian and other republics, as well as in the major cities.

Gorbachev would now have to fight for both a base of support in the population and for means to carry out his policies in the increasingly decentralized structure of power to which his reforms had given birth. In this new and fluid situation, the pro-capitalist coalition had an opportunity to contend for power. As a consequence of the democratization process, Boris Yeltsin was able to become the chief executive of the Russian Republic, first by the ballot of the new Russian parliament and then by popular vote. Near the end of 1991, from his position as elected leader of the Russian Republic, Yeltsin was able to sweep Gorbachev aside, dissolve the Soviet state, and move Russia full speed ahead toward a capitalist future. The democratization of Soviet political institutions, inspired and led by Gorbachev, played a significant role in both his personal departure from the scene and the defeat of his socialist reform project.

But one can easily misconstrue the role that was played by the new democratic political institutions in the demise of the Soviet system. The process by which Yeltsin moved from head of the Russian Republic, which had been a subordinate part of the Soviet Union, to the dominant figure in the Soviet Union as a whole after August 1991, and finally to become the leader of an independent Russian state, was not the direct result of any election. The new free elections played an important role in the final battle for power, but they were only part of the story.

No real social revolution has ever been made exclusively by winning elections, and the revolution that occurred in the Soviet Union during 1990–91 was no exception. In order to win state power, Yeltsin and the pro-capitalist coalition which he led had to do more than win elections in the newly democratized Soviet system. They had to politically defeat Gorbachev and the socialist reformers, as well as the Old Guard seeking to bring back the past. As the president of the USSR, Gorbachev outranked Yeltsin, and the representatives of the Old Guard held high positions in the Soviet state. Crucial to the ultimate victory of Yeltsin and the pro-capitalist coalition in this political maneuvering during 1990–91 was the support they gained from the party–state elite, as it turned away from Gorbachev's program of building a reformed socialism. We next examine the process which produced this surprising shift of allegiance by a decisive part of the Soviet elite.

Chapter 7

The party–state elite and the pro-capitalist coalition

According to the received wisdom, during 1989–91 the democratic majority in the Soviet Union defeated the party–state elite. By their victory they abolished the state socialist system and initiated the attempt to build a capitalist system. On one side was the old elite, fighting to maintain its privileges by trying to save the system upon which those privileges were based. On the other side was the majority of the people who, having come to loathe the old system, threw their support to the political opposition, led by Boris Yeltsin. The opposition won the elections and stared down the tanks of the old regime, finally achieving their goal at the end of 1991.

This interpretation parallels the dominant view about who was fighting whom during the early perestroika years, when the issue was the proposed reform of the old system, rather than its overthrow. According to Tatyana Zaslavskaya, a Russian sociologist who was an influential theorist of Gorbachev's reform program, perestroika was resisted at the start by "probably a majority" of the bureaucracy. She said that the resistance to change was greatest "in the middle levels at the center [in Moscow] and at the top elsewhere."[1] That is, except for some at the very top who had initiated perestroika, the bureaucracy of the Soviet system resisted change. This was the dominant Western view during the perestroika years. As the battle in the Soviet Union intensified in the last few years of the system, the increasingly radical Soviet intellectuals promoted the image of a powerful bureaucracy resisting any change, while forward-looking intellectuals were presented as the true supporters of Gorbachev's perestroika. This view of the battle was then extended to the final defeat of the old system. The party–state elite had resisted and finally had lost.

Now that the dust has settled a bit from the intense battle of 1991, one cannot help but notice a fact that clashes dramatically with this received wisdom. When a ruling group is defeated in revolution, its members are normally sent packing – either into exile or, more summarily, to the next world. The American revolutionaries' victory over Britain in 1783 sent

Tory sympathizers streaming to Canada. The aristocrats and Tsarist officials of the old Russian Empire fled to Paris in 1917. Where are the supposed victims of the recent Russian revolution? By and large, they remain where they were – in high-level positions in the successor states to the Soviet Union. Two years after the Soviet demise, fully eleven of the fifteen ex-Soviet republics were headed by former top Communists. Five of them had once served in the Soviet Communist Party's politburo. How can we square the preponderance of former members of the Soviet elite in influential positions in post-Soviet society with the received wisdom that the old party–state elite was defeated?

Zaslavskaya was probably right in claiming that, in the early years of perestroika, many individuals in the middle and lower levels of the traditionally conservative party–state elite had difficulty accepting the changes advocated by the new leadership. But the real dynamics began to change around 1987, and the above-described received wisdom about the nature of the battle soon became outdated. For understanding the final outcome of the battle, the received wisdom is misleading. The evidence indicates that a decisive part of the party–state elite rapidly switched from doubt to enthusiastic support for the most radical change of all – replacing state socialism with capitalism.

WHY MEMBERS OF THE PARTY–STATE ELITE CAME TO SUPPORT CAPITALISM

Why would members of the party–state elite back the pro-capitalist coalition? What about their ideological commitment to socialism, a commitment they had all been required to profess in the past? Such professions were meaningless for most members of this group. As we observed in Chapter 2, the great majority of the Soviet elite were highly pragmatic rather than ideological in their approach. They joined the Communist Party because it was necessary to advance their careers. They were motivated, not by a dedication to an ideology, but by the pursuit of material privilege and power. By joining the party and advancing into the elite, they could indeed gain at least some of both. This attitude toward the party was well expressed in a remark by a long-time Soviet official in July 1991, when he was asked whether he was a member of the Communist Party: "Of course I am a member of the Communist Party – but I am not a communist!"[2]

The careerists who made up the great majority of the Soviet party–state elite in the 1980s had never previously had an opportunity to consider alternative future directions for Soviet society. The regimented system had permitted no questioning of the official goal of building socialism. But once perestroika opened up the society to discussion and debate about the future, and different views found a hearing in the media, the members of this elite suddenly found they had to confront this issue.

Consider the three main alternative futures that were contending with one another at the end of the 1980s. Gorbachev and his allies wanted to democratize and decentralize the socialist system. Workers were supposed to become the masters of their enterprises, and the public would have political sovereignty over the state. This direction of change threatened to reduce the power and material privileges of the party–state elite. They would be under pressure to become real servants of the public, answerable to the public, instead of acting as their bosses. Those engaged in economic management, whether in a Moscow ministry or at the head of a large enterprise, might have to give up the role of haughty boss toward those below them, learning to work by persuasion and compromise rather than diktat. This program would not have required much change in the formal ideological position of the party–state elite – after all, the official rhetoric had always proclaimed a workers' state with more democracy than in the West – but it would have meant a big reduction in what most of them really cared about: material privilege and power.

Some members of the party–state elite did believe in the ideals of socialism and stuck with them through the demise of the system. Gorbachev's writings, speeches, and actions during 1985–91 suggest that he never gave up on the idea of democratic socialism. In October 1992 former prime minister Nikolai Ryzhkov insisted that he still supported a "socialist market economy." He remarked that the original program of perestroika had involved 'no departure from socialism." He argued that "change in the economic mechanism within socialist property relations to make them more efficient" had been the right goal.[3] Yegor Ligachev's recently published memoirs struck even unfriendly reviewers as the testimony of a genuine believer in the ideals of socialism.[4] Those members of the party–state elite who believed in socialism responded avidly to the call to reform and democratize Soviet socialism. But ultimately they turned out to be very few in number.

The second major position favored a return to the old system, with only minor changes. The Communist Party would continue to rule by command, the economy would continue to be run from Moscow, and political life would go back to the Brezhnev days of regimentation. Why did the party–state elite not staunchly back this position – as the received wisdom claims it did?

Most of the party–state elite had become convinced that the old system needed major renovation. The system had been working less and less effectively since the mid-1970s. The elite did not want to preside over a system that would continue to decline. Eventually they would be unable to maintain their rule if the decline could not be arrested. The party–

state elite felt pressure to throw its support behind change. What became clear during the course of the perestroika period was that there was more than one possible direction of change. The democratic socialist direction was contrary to the self-interest of the elite. But that was not the case with the third, previously unthinkable alternative – a transition to capitalism.

The claim that the party–state elite of the Soviet system opted for capitalism seems at first glance implausible. Would the Catholic Church hierarchy suddenly convert to atheism? Would the US Chamber of Commerce call for the nationalization of private business? Would the Quakers offer a man of the year award to Rambo? Yet the Soviet party–state elite ended up embracing the ideological enemy against which they had always rhetorically battled. When one examines this shift, one finds that it is not only plausible but eminently logical.

The members of the party–state did have significant material privileges that flowed to them by virtue of their membership in that elite. They had high salaries relative to the average. Through their jobs they had the use of luxury automobiles. They had preferred access to better housing. They could obtain better-quality food, drink, and other consumer goods through special arrangements for the elite. Through their connections they could secure places for their children in the best schools.

Yet, despite the material benefits accruing to the elite, those benefits paled by comparison to the material advantages enjoyed by their counterparts in the elite of the Western capitalist countries. As we saw in Chapter 2, the Soviet system had a much smaller gap between the top and bottom of the income distribution than do capitalist systems. The general director of a large Soviet enterprise was paid about 4 times as much as the average industrial wage. By contrast, the average American corporate chief executive officer's pay is nearly 150 times that of the average factory worker.[5]

The incomes of the very top members of the Soviet elite were never published, but Vitaly Korotich, editor of *Ogonyok* and a sharp critic of the Soviet elite, claimed in 1989 that politburo members had an income of 1,200–1,500 rubles a month, and that top generals received the highest pay – about 2,000 rubles a month. The average industrial wage in the Soviet Union at that time was about 250 rubles a month.[6] Thus, the very top salaries under the Soviet system were up to 8 times the average industrial wage. In the United States in 1993 the average industrial wage was about $25,000 per year. A salary 8 times larger than that would be $200,000 a year. The top members of the American elite make more than that sum each week.[7]

Top members of the old Soviet elite had comfortable housing, but it did not compare to the private homes of high-level American business or government officials. President Gorbachev himself occupied a rather ordinary-looking four-family apartment building in the Lenin Hills, along with the Shevardnadze family, a Soviet general, and one other unidentified family. In his retirement former prime minister Nikolai Ryzhkov had a pleasant country home outside of Moscow, comparable to what a moderately successful doctor or lawyer might own in the United States, but it cannot be compared to the estates possessed by those at the pinnacle of wealth and power in any capitalist society.

For those at the middle and lower levels of the Soviet elite, the material rewards were remarkably modest, considering that the Soviet Union was one of the world's two great superpowers. American expert on Soviet politics Jerry F. Hough described their conditions as follows:

> Soviet administrative salaries are very low in comparative terms, and living conditions are poor. The first secretary of the Minsk *gorkom* [city party committee] lives in a two-bedroom apartment with his wife, married daughter, and her husband, while the top construction official in Leningrad lives in a one-bedroom apartment with his wife.[8]

Not only was the material living standard of members of the Soviet elite much lower than that of their counterparts in the West, but, as was noted in Chapter 2, a much larger proportion of that living standard came from perquisites associated with the individual's position. Many of the luxury goods available to the elite – high-quality automobiles, large vacation homes, etc. – were job perquisites, not personal property. In the officially socialist USSR, it was not possible to accumulate substantial personal wealth through legitimate means. Individuals who did so had to worry about discovery and prosecution, as did happen from time to time. While business and government leaders in the West have valuable perquisites associated with their jobs, they also are able to acquire substantial personal wealth (with government leaders typically doing so before they enter government, in professional or business careers).

When a member of the American or British elite loses a job, the person's private wealth protects the family's consumption level. But the privileged status of members of the Soviet elite depended on job position. Even high-level members of the elite were fearful of incurring the displeasure of their superiors, knowing that loss of one's position meant not only foregoing the power and prestige associated with the position but also the living standard that accompanied it. And there would be few material possessions to pass on to one's children.

In the course of the 1980s more and more information about the West flowed into the USSR. Movies from Western countries were shown and travel increased greatly. Members of the Soviet elite became aware of the glaring gap between the way they lived and the lifestyle of their counterparts in the capitalist West. Jerry Hough, the Soviet expert cited above, after remarking about the modest conditions of the Soviet elite, went on to note that "Officials of such organizational–administrative ability would do much better in a Western European system, and they now know it." Hough suggested that this fact might make the Soviet system vulnerable to revolution; "Regimes often fall when too many members of an old elite finally decide that it is not worth fighting and give up."[9]

However, if the party–state elite could do better under capitalism, and if they knew it, why would they merely give up defending the system? This pragmatic, self-seeking group had every reason to switch its allegiance and support the replacement of socialism by capitalism. A shift to capitalism would permit them to own the means of production, not just manage them. They would be able to legitimately accumulate personal wealth. They could assure their children's future, not just through contacts and influence, but through direct transfer of wealth.[10]

The only barrier to such a switch of allegiance was ideological. Those who believed in the ideals of socialism indeed could not easily make this switch. As the Soviet system met its end in the second half of 1991, some true believers committed suicide or ended up in the hospital from the stress of losing the system to which they had devoted their lives.[11] But this was a small minority. Most of the pragmatic members of this group had little more difficulty with a sharp shift in ideology than they had had with earlier ideological shifts.

Two generations earlier, in 1939, the Soviet elite had switched overnight from opposition to German fascism to criticism of British imperialist ambitions, after the Stalin–Hitler Pact was signed. The German invasion of the Soviet Union two years later was followed by an immediate switch back to anti-fascism. That and other earlier sharp ideological turns had been dictated from the top of the Soviet hierarchy. At the end of the 1980s, as the discipline of the Communist Party was collapsing amidst the growing political cross-currents, the members of the party–state elite had to decide for themselves. They proved just as capable of negotiating a sharp turn on their own, to follow their own perceived self-interest, as had their predecessors shifted to preserve their position upon orders from above.

A study of the ideology of the Soviet elite, conducted by an American Soviet specialist in June 1991, provides empirical evidence that by that time a large majority of the elite had shifted to support for capitalism. Participants in the study took part in focus group discussions, which were recorded and analyzed. Figure 7.1 presents the findings of this study.[12] The sample of the Moscow elite for this study included some individuals whom we would probably classify as intelligentsia rather than party–state elite, and the study was not based on a random sample.[13] Nevertheless, it provides a striking picture of the near-disappearance of support for any version of socialism within the upper reaches of Soviet society. Only 12.3 per cent of the sample were classified as "Democratic Socialist," who supported the effort to reform and democratize socialism.[14] Less than 10 per cent were classified as "Communist" or "Nationalist," which corresponds to our category of Old Guard supporters of the pre-perestroika Soviet system.[15] As we shall see in Chapter 8, public opinion surveys taken at the very same time showed that, unlike for the elite, within the population as a whole socialism remained popular while only a minority came to favor capitalism.

How can this process of the elite abandoning its own system be observed? Beginning as early as 1987, many members of the party–state elite left their positions to become capitalists – that is, they built, or went to work for, new private businesses. As part of this process, various institutions of the state socialist economic system were quietly, and sometimes surreptitiously at first, converted by their controllers into private, profit-making businesses. This began to take place several years before privatization became official policy. Another facet of this process was the shift by members of the party–state elite, during 1989–91, from support of Gorbachev to support for Yeltsin. With this switch, they typically announced their disillusionment with socialism and Marxism and their new belief that private property and free markets were the only future for Russia.

COMMUNISTS BECOME CAPITALISTS

During the period of Gorbachev's rule, Soviet legislation banning private business activity was gradually loosened. It was noted in Chapter 5

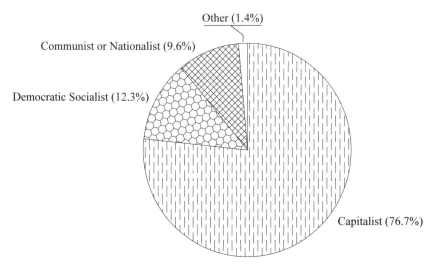

Figure 7.1. Ideological position of a sample of the Moscow elite, June 1991
Source: Kullberg 1994: 940–6.

that the 1988 Law on Cooperatives set off a rapid growth of small private businesses, as thousands of new small firms were created. Some of the new private firms were cooperatives in form only, being in reality capitalist enterprises. By 1990 the state's oversight was rapidly diminishing, and capitalist enterprises could operate more and more openly. Official privatization of state firms did not begin until after the demise of the Soviet Union at the end of 1991, but some state entities began moving out of their accustomed roles well before that.[16]

Who created the growing stream of new capitalist firms? Some were technical specialists – scientists, engineers, technicians, inventors – who were frustrated by the constraints of the state-run system. Siberian native Valery Neverov is an example of the scientist-turned-capitalist. After completing a postgraduate course at the Moscow Institute of Metallurgy, he went to work as a lecturer in physics at Tyumen University, in the oil-rich Tyumen region. He patented several new inventions in the field of oil and gas production, including new kinds of gauges and monitoring devices. In 1986 he set up a small cooperative, initially affiliated with the university, to pursue development and implementation of new technologies in oil and gas. In 1990, using the contacts he had built up supplying his devices to Tyumen's oil and gas industry, he shifted to trading oil. By 1991 his venture had become the joint-stock company Hermes and Company, with capital of fifty million rubles, operating banks, stock and commodity exchanges, and trading companies in various Russian cities.[17]

Mikhail Gura also came from a background in science, having worked as an engineer in radio communications and acoustics in a military-related research center. In 1987 he left the state sector to form a small audio and video recording cooperative, financed by a low-interest loan of 80,000 rubles from a state agency. Gura's scientific background did not deter him from exporting the antlers of reindeer and antelopes, to be used as a folk medicine that is very potent financially for its distributors, if not medically potent. Within a few years he transformed the tiny coop into the Ort International consortium, a multinational firm engaged in export–import business, ruble credit cards for wealthy Russian travellers, and many other activities.[18]

After the Soviet demise, the Russian media advertised and promoted the scientist-to-entrepreneur image. But such cases are a distinct minority, and when inspected closely, it usually turns out that the scientists and engineers who succeeded on a large scale in private business had more going for them than simply their technical know-how. Valery Neverov's big success came from seizing the opportunity to profit from trading valuable Siberian oil in the Soviet Union's primitive markets, not from his inventions. Mikhail Gura's business, launched with public funds, soon left behind its original recording business for the high-profit world of trade and finance.

Success in business in the last years of the Soviet Union required not technical knowledge but connections and an ability to quickly seize opportunities when they arose. Connections were necessary because the rules for private business remained murky, and powerful friends in positions of authority were needed to allow a private entrepreneur to stay in business. Connections were also the only way to get financing, given the absence of private banks or legitimate wealthy private investors.

The opportunities that suddenly presented themselves in the Soviet Union of 1987–91 were not primarily in the production of useful goods. To do that, an entrepreneur would have to compete with giant subsidized state enterprises which sold at low controlled prices. The big potential profits were in two areas. One was trade, both domestic and international. With growing shortages and controlled prices, a sharp operator could buy up goods from state enterprises and resell them in the Soviet Union at much higher market prices. A still larger profit could be made by getting hold of cheap Soviet raw materials and quietly exporting them at world market prices.

The other high-profit opportunity was in financial speculation. As markets gradually developed in raw materials and currencies, sharp operators began to make fortunes investing in Soviet gold or molybdenum, and in dollars or yen, selling them after their value inevitably rose in the worsening Soviet economy.

Technical expertise was not what was needed for business success. It is not surprising that the new private businessmen came largely from the group that had the best connections and could clearly see the growing opportunities in trade and finance – the party–state elite.

A Moscow researcher studied the origins of private businessmen in Moscow in 1993. Based on a random sample of 267 non-state enterprises, he found only 25.8 per cent were run by someone from a "professional" background, the category that included scientists and engineers. More than two-thirds – 68.1 per cent – were headed by a former manager of a state enterprise.[19] However, because this study was based on a random sample drawn from the total population of private firms in Moscow, most of the sample firms were small or medium-size. One would expect scientists and engineers to be even less prominent as founders of big private firms – and the evidence suggests that is the case.

Russian sociologist Olga Kryshtanovskaya studied the Soviet, and then the Russian, elite for many years. A team of researchers under her direction investigated Russia's most influential entrepreneurs during 1992–93. From their research they compiled a list of the hundred top businessmen, based on the criterion of the size of the capital they controlled. The researchers interviewed all hundred of them, as well as doing documentary research.

Figure 7.2 presents Kryshtanovskaya's findings about the origins of the hundred top private businessmen. Four of the categories in Figure 7.2 – Komsomol, industrialists, bankers, and elite families – represent parts of the party–state elite, and together they cover 62 per cent of the group. Scientists were only 15 per cent, and another 5 per cent were what Kryshtanovskaya called "nuggets"[20] – self-made persons of iconoclastic bent who had not fit in under the old system and had, long before perestroika, tried to work on their own in violation of the official rules and norms of state socialism. Another 18 per cent came from miscellaneous other backgrounds (including criminals, the unemployed, etc.).

The youth branch of the Communist Party, Komsomol, was an important gestation place for the new business class. Every upwardly mobile young person in the Soviet Union joined Komsomol, and friendships and contacts formed there were invaluable for ascending the ladder of the Soviet bureaucracy. The term "youth" must not be interpreted too strictly – activists could stay involved until their early 40s. Among Komsomol's many activities was the organization of various civic projects based on volunteer labor. In Komsomol a person made contacts while learning organizational skills.

The word "idealism" is commonly preceded by the modifier "youthful," and, indeed, youth organizations are often infused with idealism. Komsomol had been no exception in the early days after the Russian Revolution. But as careerism replaced idealism among the elders of the

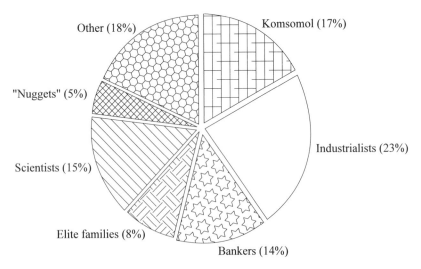

Figure 7.2. Origins of the top one hundred Russian businessmen, 1992–93
Source: Kryshtanovskaya: 1994b.

Soviet elite, the same process took place in Komsomol, perhaps to an even greater extent. Vadim Birykov, publisher of the Russian monthly magazine *Delovie Lyudi* (Business People), remarked that Komsomol activists "did not believe in Marxism–Leninism", that "they were ready for anything."[21] In the mid-1980s, when perestroika began creating new opportunities, Komsomol became a remarkable launching pad for capitalist initiatives.

Viktor I. Mironenko was first secretary of Komsomol from July 1986 until April 1990. The importance of Komsomol in the Soviet structure is indicated by the fact that Mironenko, as Komsomol head, also was a member of the CPSU central committee and of the Presidium of the USSR Supreme Soviet, and he attended some politburo meetings. In 1992 Mironenko thought the very "notion of socialism is debatable." What society needs, he argued, was a "normal economy," the term that became the Soviet euphemism for a capitalist system. He cited approvingly Solzhenitsin's concept of the Russian Revolution as a flaming wheel that must eventually fall over and burn out, adding that he hoped it had fully burned out. He offered high praise for the former British Conservative prime minister Margaret Thatcher. Such views might be expected from a college Young Republican, yet this was the former head of the Communist Youth League of the USSR![22]

Kryshtanovskaya found that 17 per cent of Russia's top businessmen entered private business from the Komsomol apparatus. She also found that this was one of the earliest elite sources of businessmen. The businessmen from Komsomol, along with the scientists, entered private business in the "first wave" during 1987–89, with the maximum number making the plunge in 1988. Over half of these young Communist businessmen started their business ventures initially out of the offices of a Komsomol institute called the Center for the Scientific and Technical Creativity of Youth.[23]

The largest contingent of former elite businessmen, 23 per cent of the total, were previously "industrialists." Of these, slightly over half (56 per cent) came from the industrial ministries and state committees of the USSR or the Russian Republic and another quarter (26 per cent) were directors of large state industrial enterprises. They entered private business during 1989–91, with the largest number in 1990.

Another 14 per cent of the top businessmen came from the USSR state banks. Members of this group either set up new private commercial banks or managed to privatize a part of the existing state banking system under their control. Like the industrialists, they entered private business during 1989–91, with the greatest number, 51 per cent of the total, doing so in 1990.

The final elite category is members of elite families, who were 8 per cent of the total. These were children of high-ranking members of the party–state elite, usually connected with international activities – for example, officials of the Ministry of Foreign Affairs. These are individuals who graduated from the most prestigious institutions of higher education and who knew a good deal about the outside world through their family travels and foreign acquaintances. They entered business early, most of them in 1987.

The process of movement from the old party–state elite to private business can be better understood by looking at some individual examples. We will look briefly at the stories of individuals who made this switch from a variety of locations in the old structure: Komsomol, the industrial ministries and enterprises, the state banking system, the Foreign Ministry, elite families, and even the Soviet cabinet.

Komsomol

Menatep Bank is one of the largest, most influential private businesses to have emerged from Komsomol. Appropriately enough, the head office of Menatep is located a short walk from the former Old Square offices of Komsomol and the CPSU central committee. Tough-looking guards are stationed every ten yards along its corridors. People sometimes refer to Menatep as "the Komsomol bank," a name that accurately reflects the bank's origins. In an interview Menatep president Mikhail Khodorkovsky explained the bank's evolution from a Komsomol project to one of Russia's ten largest private banks.[24]

In 1987 Khodorkovsky was a Komsomol apparatchik, having graduated from the Mendeleev Chemical Institute the previous year. He participated in setting up the Center for Scientific and Technical Creativity of Youth in Komsomol, which he described as an investment company. In 1988 he and his associates organized a bank, with three official founders: the Scientific and Technical Creativity of Youth Center of Komsomol, the State Committee for Science and Technology (part of the Soviet state's central planning apparatus), and Zhilsotsbank (a part of the state banking system).[25] Khodorkovsky had no personal capital; the funds came from the founding institutions. Thus, party and state money launched the bank.

Initially the Menatep Bank was officially municipal property, owned by a district of Moscow, with profits going to the bank's labor collective. It was profitable, and the profits were used to buy out the three founding agencies. In 1990 it was reorganized as a joint-stock corporation, and by 1994 it had assets of about $1 billion.

Menatep's major activity is financial trading, which means buying and selling financial assets with an eye to capital gains. It also makes loans and investments, although these are risky in the unstable economic climate of Russia. Menatep has a third business – private banking, through which it manages the funds of some 2,000 individual clients. Private banking clients are normally very wealthy individuals, and some observers claim many of Menatep's wealthy clients are organized crime figures, although this claim is impossible to verify.

When asked about the origins of Russia's new bankers and business-men, Khodorkovsky estimated that "90 per cent of the prosperous peo-ple in business originated in the old nomenklatura structures and those close to them." He remarked that the old system of selecting cadres was "not so bad," in that it allowed people with talent and energy to rise. To him it seemed natural that the talented, energetic people in Komsomol would emerge as successful businessmen. He did not waste time on the irony that the pursuit of financial gain by him and his associates, and many more like him, helped fuel a revolution-from-the-top that over-turned the Soviet system.

Other private businesses emerged from Komsomol in those years. One was the Most Bank, another of Russia's major private banks, which was backed by the Mayor and City Council of Moscow in addition to Komsomol.[26] The Finist Bank was founded with 700 million rubles from Komsomol; its board chairman, Alexander Shcherbakov, was formerly an official of the Komsomol central committee. Vladislav Sedlenek runs a private employment agency that originally emerged from Komsomol in 1987 with a boost from the 20,000 rubles Komsomol provided for his venture. Fittingly, the Union of Young Entrepreneurs, an organization that seeks to represent the interests of younger capitalists, is directed by former Komsomol secretary Sergei Potapenko.[27]

Industrialists

Yuri Edelman came from a different part of the old elite.[28] After study-ing mechanical engineering and economics in school, Edelman rose rapidly in the machine-tool industry, a favored industry under the Soviet system. Starting as a mechanic in a machine-tool factory in Kras-nodar in 1975, he followed a common upward path to chief engineer, deputy general manager, and then general manager of his enterprise by 1984. In 1987 the Minister of Industry offered him the job of assistant general manager of Krasnodar's Machine Tool Building Association, a position Edelman described as equivalent to deputy department head in a ministry. He noted that, despite his high rank, his salary of 400 rubles per month was "not high."

Krasnodar was far from Moscow. When Edelman heard that the gen-eral director of a Moscow machine-tool factory was retiring, he sought and won the job. A man of strong convictions and independent ideas regarding how to manage a factory, Edelman took advantage of the loosening ties of the Soviet system in 1990, turning his enterprise into an employee-owned business and breaking free of ministry authority. Two years later he converted the successful business into a joint-stock corporation, getting 31 per cent of the shares for himself. With no personal capital to start with, Edelman had turned himself into a successful capitalist, although by 1993 Russia's intensifying economic chaos was making it very difficult to make a profit in any manufacturing business.

People from higher positions than Edelman's in the Soviet economic management hierarchy were able to enter the world of private business still more lucratively. Vagit Alekperov, a deputy minister in the Ministry of Oil and Gas, became president of the holding company Luke Oil, which became one of Russia's major oil companies. When Alekperov left the Oil and Gas Ministry, he brought his former boss at the ministry along as an advisor and consultant. According to Kryshtanovskaya, many of the top people in the former central economic management apparatus shifted to lucrative careers as consultants to the new private businesses. Another example is Nikolai Baibakov, head of Gosplan from 1965 to 1985, who became a consultant to the very successful joint-stock company Gazprom – the head of which was ranked number 8 on a list of the 50 most influential private businessmen in Russia in June 1994.[29]

Many of the new capitalists emerged from the top officialdom of the Soviet Union's industrial enterprises. V. V. Kadannikov, the director of the huge Soviet automotive manufacturer AvtoVAZ, began turning the enterprise into his private property in 1990.[30] He ranked number 10 on the list of most influential Russian businessmen mentioned above and is believed to be one of the wealthiest individuals in Russia.

A similar process took place in smaller state enterprises. Vladimir S. directed a Soviet management training enterprise, which had been set up by several hundred state enterprises from all over the USSR to provide specialized training for their managerial employees. By the summer of 1991 it had become a private business, with Vladimir S. as its sole owner. At that time it had branches in 50 cities across the USSR.[31] The vast economic changes had made management training a big business, and this enterprise, based on Vladimir S.'s wide network of connections, was one of relatively few that has been able to continue operating successfully in several of the successor states of the Soviet Union.

Some former heads of state enterprises became capitalists by starting a new business rather than privatizing their old one. Nikolai Lisai was formerly the head of a combine of six large military enterprises, with a total work force of 75,000. He left in 1991, along with several colleagues, to start a private computer software business. After initial attempts to sell to manufacturing enterprises, he found success in supplying software to Russia's new private banks. As he remarked, "They have all the money, and they are just looking for ways to spend it."[32]

Bankers

New capitalists also emerged from the Soviet state banking system and the Finance Ministry. Sergei S. Rodionov was a department head in the Ministry of Finance who became president of Imperial Bank.[33] Rodionov was ranked number 9 among the most influential private businessmen on the above-mentioned list. In 1989 Vadim V. Parkevich, who had worked for 25 years in the state banking system administration, became chairman of the Stankinbank Interbranch Commercial Bank in Moscow. That same year, Anatoly I. Vasyukov left his position as a department manager at the Leningrad regional office of the USSR Stroybank to become chairman of St Petersburg Astrobank, a private commercial bank.[34]

Many state banks were privatized under the control of their managers. Promstroybank was formerly the largest state bank in the Soviet Union. In 1991 several of the bank's managers left to head new private banks. However, the president of Promstroybank, Yakov Dubenetsky, stayed on and turned the bank into a joint-stock company. In 1994 Dubenetsky remarked that "It seems to me illogical that when the economy is ailing and chaos is all around, banks are flourishing."[35] Promstroybank is among those that have managed to flourish, earning Dubenetsky a ranking of 21 on the list of most influential Russian businessmen.[36]

Sergei Yegorov is another former state bank official who succeeded under the new system. Yegorov, who was also a member of the central committee staff of the CPSU for ten years, now heads the Association of Russian Banks, an organization whose members are Russia's wealthy and influential private banks. Another former state bank official, V.V. Vinogradov, now heads Inkombank and ranked number 1 on the list of most influential Russian businessmen.[37]

Capitalists from other parts of the old system

Since the idea of capitalism was a foreign import, it is perhaps not surprising that many new capitalists came out of the Soviet Union's Foreign Ministry. Vadim Biryukov formerly worked in the press department of the Foreign Ministry. In 1990 he was approached by Robert Hersant, president of Socpresse, publisher of the French magazine *Figaro*, about setting up a new magazine that would write about the economic changes in the USSR and East–West economic relations. Biryukov agreed, and the glossy monthly *Business in the USSR* was born, with Biryukov as editor-in-chief and the highest management official (the top officer was from the French publishing firm). When the USSR disintegrated, the name was changed to *Delovie Lyudi* (Business People).

The financing for this venture came not just from Socpresse but also from the old Soviet state publishing house, Progress Publishers. While Progress Publishers had previously been known for turning out countless copies of Lenin's *Collected Works*, the joint venture with Socpresse was not the only private business initiative in which Progress Publishers participated. In July 1991 it joined with *Reader's Digest* to launch a Russian edition of that magazine, with participation also by the CPSU printing house First Model Printers and the Soviet state book distribution monopoly International Books.[38]

Kryshtanovskaya found younger members of families from the top of the Soviet elite to be a significant presence among the new private capitalists. Anatoly Lukyanov, the chairman of the last Soviet Congress of People's Deputies, remarked that many of the younger members of top Communist families appeared to have come to believe enthusiastically in private ownership of business.[39] One example is Vladimir Sterligov, a grandson of the deceased Mikhail Suslov. Suslov was the ideology chief of the CPSU in the 1950s and 1960s. He was one of the most powerful Soviet leaders of the Brezhnev era, the chief guardian of Marxist–Leninist orthodoxy. His grandson Vladimir worked at *Pravda*, the CPSU central committee's official newspaper, in the late 1980s. In July 1991 Vladimir turned up as an officer at a private commercial bank. Even one of Brezhnev's granddaughters, Vika, became a businesswoman prior to the demise of the USSR.[40]

The movement from party–state elite to private business during the perestroika years did not, for the most part, directly involve individuals from the very top of the Soviet political leadership. Most of them remained in politics. But a few, such as Vladimir I. Shcherbakov, did make this transition. Shcherbakov rose from a management position at the Togliatti automobile complex to work in the automobile ministry in Moscow in the early 1980s. After 1985 he moved up to an important state committee and then to deputy head of a department in the Council of Ministers. By 1990 he had been made a member of the central committee of the CPSU. In March 1991 he was named a deputy prime minister and two months later first deputy prime minister of the USSR.[41] For forty-eight hours, following the collapse of the coup attempt of August 1991, he was the acting prime minister.

In November 1991, shortly before the Soviet state disintegrated, Shcherbakov founded a private business called International Fund for the Assistance of Privatization and Foreign Investment, or "Interprivatizatsia" in the Russian acronym. Past Soviet leaders had, on occasion, moved to seize control of a neighboring state. But when former high-level Soviet leader Shcherbakov emerged in the news in the spring of 1994, it was for attempting to pull off a hostile corporate takeover, as he led a consortium of big Russian private banks and industrial firms in an effort to acquire control of the then Greek-owned newspaper *Pravda* (originally the newspaper of the CPSU central committee). By that time Shcherbakov was reputed to be one of the richest men in Russia.[42]

When Karl Marx wrote of new social relations developing in the womb of the old society, he was presenting his view that socialist relations would grow directly out of the development of capitalism. Yet that image seems to fit quite accurately the process through which capitalist relations emerged from the Soviet state socialist system. Not only did individuals from practically every part of the old party–state elite turn themselves into capitalists,[43] but many of the institutions of the Soviet order helped this process along. Komsomol was only the most widely noticed of these. Soviet publishing houses launched capitalist publications. State banks whose role had been to passively and conservatively provide financing to accompany the state economic plan evolved into private commercial banks that plunged into the rough and tumble of high-risk speculative investment, gaining great wealth for the bankers. Industrial enterprises that had passively turned out products according to the state plan, with limited pay differences between managers and workers, became mines of private profit for directors-turned-owners.

It was not only in Moscow and Leningrad that capitalism was emerging from the institutions of Soviet state socialism. A remarkable instance of institutional enthusiasm for capitalism within the old system took place in the provincial city of Perm during 1991. Unlike in Moscow and Leningrad, in Perm the Communist Party officialdom had managed to fend off the electoral challenge from opposition forces in the local elections of 1990. But the victorious local Perm elite proceeded to vigorously embrace the transition to capitalism. In January of 1991, the Perm provincial Communist Party committee set up a commercial firm which rented out party property, including a party hotel, and established a car-rental business, with individual party leaders as shareholders. Pleased with the results, a written proposal was circulated by the party committee which called for a corporation to be formed to take over all the most profitable enterprises in the city, with the shares to be distributed among the top officials of the party and the city soviet.[44]

COMMUNISTS BECOME PRO-CAPITALIST POLITICIANS

The process of creation of a new capitalist class out of the party–state elite had its counterpart in the political arena. The opposition political movement in the Soviet Union was initially based among dissidents and the intelligentsia. But in the later part of the perestroika period, members of the party–state elite began to align themselves with the opposition. By 1991 a significant number of individuals from the old elite had become political leaders in the growing pro-capitalist coalition.

Some of the prominent opposition political figures were from a dissident background, such as Father Gleb Yakunin, a leader of the Democratic Russia movement that formed in 1990. Anatoly Sobchak, an opposition figure who was elected mayor of Leningrad in 1990, had worked as a law professor and lawyer and had not been a member of the Soviet party–state elite. But many of the most important political figures in the opposition came from the party–state elite.

Kryshtanovskaya's research team studied the new political leadership of independent Russia. They found that 75 per cent of the leadership circle around President Yeltsin came from the former Soviet elite. In Yeltsin's government, as distinguished from his presidential administration, 74 per cent were from the Soviet elite.[45] The Gleb Yakunins and Anatoly Sobchaks were in a distinct minority among the political leaders of the new Russia.

As with the examples of Communists turned capitalists, it is helpful to look at a few cases of Communist officials who became pro-capitalist politicians. Besides the well-known case of Boris Yeltsin, many other individuals from the party–state elite followed this path during the last years of perestroika. One example is Yuri Afanasiev.

Afanasiev was a historian by training. His doctoral dissertation carried the orthodox Marxist–Leninist title, "Contemporary French Bourgeois Historiography of the Great October Socialist Revolution." He worked in the Komsomol apparat, where he rose to the position of secretary of the party committee of the Higher Komsomol School. He served as deputy chief of the Culture Department of the central committee in the mid-1970s. During 1985–87 he headed a department at *Kommunist*, the theoretical journal of the central committee of the CPSU. In 1987 he was named rector of the Moscow Historical-Archival Institute.[46]

In the late 1980s Afanasiev emerged as one of the most important opposition political figures. After winning election to the Soviet Congress of People's Deputies in 1989, he was a cofounder, along with Boris Yeltsin and Andrei Sakharov, of the Interregional Group of Deputies. The Interregional Group of Deputies was the first effective opposition organization, forcing the Communist Party leadership to deal with an organized opposition force inside an institution of state power. In 1990 Afanasiev was a leading figure in the founding of the Democratic Russia movement, which attempted to bring together the various opposition groups and individuals.

Ivan S. Silayev joined the opposition from a different part of the old elite. Silayev rose through the aviation industry, an important part of the military–industrial complex. After heading an aviation concern in Gorky, he moved to the Ministry of Aviation in Moscow in 1974, rising to the position of minister in 1981 and joining the central committee that same year. In 1985 Gorbachev named him deputy chairman of the Council of Ministers, a position he served in until 1990.

Silayev's sudden jump to the opposition came in June 1990. Boris Yeltsin had just overcome the Communist Party leadership's resistance and narrowly won election as chairman of the Russian Republic's new parliament, in effect making Yeltsin the Russian Republic's chief executive. For the position of prime minister of the Russian Republic, Yeltsin chose not a dissident intellectual but Communist leader Ivan Silayev. Silayev left the Communist Party in early 1991, and in July he was a cofounder of another opposition organization, the Movement for Democratic Reform. After the coup attempt of August 1991, Yeltsin, who was now taking power from Gorbachev, named Silayev to head a new committee set up to oversee the entire Soviet economy.

Reflecting on his personal evolution in October 1990, Silayev said, "I myself am completely different from the person I was in the '70s." He added, "We favor the privatization of property...We favor private property of both land and industrial enterprises." This top official of the state socialist system had become an advocate of private property and free markets – that is, of capitalism.[47]

While Silayev was an economic manager who rose primarily within the state wing of the party–state elite, Arkady Volsky climbed up the ladder of the Communist Party's parallel apparatus for overseeing the economy. In 1969 Volsky went to work for the central committee's department of machine-building, rising to the head of the department in 1985. In 1988 he was named as a spokesman for the central committee. In 1989 he rose beyond his industrial specialty to be named the Soviet Government's Special Representative in Nagorno-Karabakh, where he tried to resolve the bitter ethnic war that had broken out there.[48]

Volsky did not openly go over to the opposition until the attempted coup of 1991, when he collected money and brought it to the besieged White House [seat of the Russian Republic parliament] for Yeltsin.[49] Volsky reportedly organized businessmen to condemn the coup attempt and also provided "essential communications support to the White House at critical junctures during the crisis."[50] Thereafter he openly sided with Yeltsin against Gorbachev. In the post-coup period he was named to the committee Silayev headed to oversee the Soviet economy.[51]

Yegor T. Gaidar comes from an old elite Soviet family. His grandfather, Arkady Gaidar, was a civil war hero who later became a famous author of children's books. Yegor Gaidar was trained as an economist, and in the mid-1980s he was an orthodox supporter of central planning.[52] During 1987–90 Gaidar was a department head at *Kommunist*, the theoretical journal of the central committee, and then at the party central committee's newspaper *Pravda*.

During the period when Gaidar worked at *Kommunist* and *Pravda*, his views began to change rapidly. He and his associates reportedly began reading the books of conservative American economist Milton Friedman and the speeches of Margaret Thatcher. He was looking for an alternative ideology, and he found one in the free-market, laissez-faire theories of conservative American and British economists.[53] In the fall of 1991 Yeltsin named Gaidar to be the Russian Republic's deputy prime minister for the economy. Gaidar became the key developer of the "shock therapy" strategy for rapidly converting the Russian economy to capitalism, which is discussed in Chapter 9.

CONCLUDING OBSERVATIONS

Beginning around 1987 the Soviet party–state elite was giving birth to a new class of capitalists and to new capitalist institutions, growing up in and around the old institutions of state socialism. The example of individuals who made the dramatic shift from state or party official to private business illustrates the opportunities that perestroika opened for members of the party–state elite to turn themselves into wealthy capitalists. While most members of the elite did not personally make this shift during 1987–91, they could not help observing those of their associates who did – and noticing the growing wealth and power they attained. To the pragmatic careerists who made up the majority of the elite, the lesson was not lost – that the dismantling of state socialism and a green light for privatization and free markets would be very much in their interests, allowing them to follow in the path of their more agile and fast-moving colleagues. A decisive part of the group that had run the old system, and had been its primary beneficiaries, decided their interests were no longer served by that system. Capitalism appeared as a superior alternative, from their point of view.

Members of the elite played various roles in this process. Those who worked in the central economic management apparatus, or as officials of state enterprises or banks, faced the best opportunities from a transition to capitalism. The adoption of a policy of privatization of state assets would put them in the best position to become the new owners. Others, who worked in one of the regulatory agencies of the state, found that they could tap into the wealth of the new businessmen by soliciting or accepting payoffs. State officials generally looked forward to a big improvement in their material welfare as, in their imagination, a conversion to capitalism would allow them to rise to the living standards of Western elites. Growing numbers of officials jumped onto Yeltsin's coattails, hoping to become part of the political leadership of the new and financially more rewarding order.

Potentially the least favored among the elite were the members of the Communist Party apparatus – those who had spent their careers working in the party wing of the party–state system. It appeared that the Communist Party as an institution would have no role to play in running the new capitalist system, even if it survived as a political party. So, as the party's power began to ebb during 1990–91, many party apparatchiks shifted from the party to the state, obtaining jobs as state officials or enterprise directors. Their long years of intimate contact with their state counterparts made such transitions easy to arrange.[54]

The conventional wisdom, when it does not simply ignore the conversion of many Soviet officials to support for capitalism, provides a different interpretation of this phenomenon from the one offered here. It is claimed that Soviet officials, seeing the old system collapse around them, finally had to admit that capitalism was the only viable system, and, making the best of an unwanted situation, they sought to fit themselves into the new order. However, this interpretation does not fit the time pattern of events in the last years of the Soviet Union. The abandonment of the state socialist system by the party–state elite began too soon to fit in with the conventional interpretation. We have seen that as early as 1987 members of the party–state elite began to turn themselves into capitalists. By 1989 this process was in full flower. The desertion of the state socialist system by the party–state elite did not happen *because of* the demise of the old system. The reverse is true – the demise of the system occurred because the party–state elite deserted it.

Once the old system was buried, after Russia became independent at the end of 1991, some additional members of the party–state elite, who had resisted capitalism when it had not yet arrived, finally grudgingly adjusted to the new situation, as the conventional interpretation suggests. Former prime minister Nikolai Ryzhkov spent five years trying to make perestroika work, finally retiring after a heart attack in 1990. In 1992, when the authors interviewed him, he still held to his life-long belief in socialism and regretted the failure of the reform effort he had helped lead. But 18 months later even he faced the reality of Russia in 1994, accepting an offer to head one of Russia's major private banks, Tveruniversalbank.[55] But the eager support for the pro-capitalist coalition given by a decisive part of the party–state elite during 1987–91 was a different matter.

The party–state elite was not the only actor on the Soviet political stage. When they supported the pro-capitalist coalition, they endowed it with the ability to win power, but they were not the only supporters of this coalition, nor were they first. Members of the Soviet intelligentsia were the earliest and the most vocal contingent in this coalition. One part of the intelligentsia, the economists, played such an important role in the pro-capitalist coalition that they deserve to be singled out. The conversion of most Soviet economists to a pro-capitalist position had a great impact on the course of events. As the economic reforms legalized private business activity, some shadow economy operators, who had bought and sold goods, and run various illegal rackets, around the edges of the centrally planned economy, emerged into the sunlight as wealthy businessmen. They were natural supporters of the pro-capitalist coalition.[56] Those new business people who were from legitimate but non-elite occupations – scientists and technicians, doctors and dentists, even a few workers and farmers – also wanted to expand the opportunities for private business activity. The entire new group of private business people, whatever their background, provided a financial base for the pro-capitalist coalition.

The pro-capitalist coalition thus drew its support from four main groups – intellectuals, economists, private business people from non-elite backgrounds, and the party–state elite.[57] While the intellectuals' arguments, the economists' advice, and the businessmen's money all contributed to the strength of the pro-capitalist coalition, it was the party–state elite's strategic position in the system that would prove decisive.[58]

Chapter 8

The struggle for power

We have seen that glasnost, economic reform, and political democratization unexpectedly led to the growth of a pro-capitalist coalition in the former Soviet Union. Glasnost placed members of the intelligentsia, who were undergoing a process of radicalization, in charge of much of the Soviet mass media. Economic reform began to create serious dislocations in 1988–89, and when leading Soviet economists were asked to propose solutions, they recommended rapid marketization and privatization of the economy which, they argued, offered the only path out of the crisis. Economic reform also legalized non-state business enterprises, leading to the emergence of a wealthy private business class. A major part of the party–state elite of the Soviet system itself began to abandon its allegiance to Soviet socialism, gravitating toward Western-style capitalism. Out of this process there emerged an opposition movement, the pro-capitalist coalition, drawing support from the intelligentsia, economists, private business owners, and a growing section of the party–state elite.

The political democratization of the Soviet system shifted power from the Communist Party to new state institutions, whose leaders were to be selected via democratic elections. This created an opportunity for opponents of the Soviet system to openly contend for power. However, the pro-capitalist coalition did not simply walk into power. As it assembled during 1989–91 and Boris Yeltsin emerged as its leader, it had to fight a complex political battle to achieve its ends. To gain power, it had to defeat both the socialist reformers led by Gorbachev and the Old Guard advocates of a return to the pre-perestroika Soviet system. In this chapter we trace the most important dimensions of this political battle, showing how the pro-capitalist coalition was able to defeat its adversaries and win state power.

The full story of this political battle would require an entire book in itself. Here we will consider four developments that were, in our view, the most central in determining the final outcome. The first of these was Yeltsin's rise to power within the Russian Republic of the Soviet Union during 1990–91. The second was the wave of strikes by miners in 1989–91, which had the effect of strengthening the pro-capitalist coalition. The third was the powerful tide of nationalism that swept the Soviet Union in its last years, which Yeltsin and his allies were able to turn to their advantage. Finally, we will examine the failed coup of August 1991, the collapse of which rapidly shifted power from Gorbachev and the Soviet government to the leaders of the fifteen Soviet republics. By the end of 1991, the Soviet Union was gone, and in its place were fifteen new states – the fifteen former republics which had constituted the Soviet Union – and in most of them the leadership was now committed to building a capitalist system. In the account that follows, it will become clear that the rapid, relatively peaceful demise of the Soviet system, and the associated disintegration of the Soviet state, can be explained by the course of the pro-capitalist coalition's successful battle for state power.

YELTSIN'S RISE TO POWER IN THE RUSSIAN REPUBLIC

After serving for a decade as first secretary of the Sverdlovsk regional Communist Party committee, in April 1985 Boris Yeltsin moved to Moscow to head the construction department of the central committee. A few months later he was named to run the capital city's Communist Party organization. In 1986 he became a candidate member of the politburo.

Yeltsin's falling out with Gorbachev began at a central committee meeting in October 1987 when Yeltsin delivered a sharp denunciation of what he viewed as the slow pace of perestroika. Yeltsin was soon removed from his Moscow party post and from the politburo.[1] At the Nineteenth Party Conference in June 1988, Yeltsin delivered a humiliating plea, in front of the television cameras, asking the Communist Party leadership to rehabilitate him, a plea which they rejected. While denied re-admission into the top leadership, he remained a member of the central committee and a high-level state official.

Prior to perestroika, such a demotion would have ended a person's political career. But by 1989 the advance of Soviet democratic reforms gave Yeltsin a chance to stage a comeback, against the wishes of the party leadership. In March 1989 he was elected to the new Soviet Congress of People's Deputies, where he became a leader of the rapidly coalescing opposition movement. The following year he was elected to the newly reformed parliament of the Russian Republic, which named him its chairman. Later that year Yeltsin dramatically resigned from the CPSU, and in June 1991 was elected president of the Russian Republic by popular vote.

Yeltsin had a complex appeal to the Russian public.[2] He was a populist politician who railed against the unjust privileges of the party elite. Yeltsin's name surfaced in the Western press as early as 1986 when, at a

Communist Party congress, he denounced "special perquisites for leading officials" and "gross corruption in Uzbekistan."[3] As head of the
Moscow party organization, he enjoyed walking the streets and meeting
ordinary people. Yeltsin's attacks on privilege were very popular with
ordinary people, given the widespread resentment toward the special
perquisites of the Soviet elite.

Yeltsin also strongly supported democratization. It was, after all,
democratization that enabled him to rise from the presumed politically
dead. In February 1989, one month before the elections to the Soviet
Congress of People's Deputies, Yeltsin issued a call for the elections to
be truly open and democratic.[4] Democratization had great appeal to the
Russian public, particularly among urban residents.

Yeltsin played upon a certain kind of Russian national feeling. Many
ethnic Russians looked down on the non-Slavic nationalities of the
Soviet Union, viewing them as backward and foreign. Some viewed the
Central Asian and Caucasian republics as a burden on Russia and as
beneficiaries of subsidies and privileged treatment within the Soviet
system. Yeltsin's call for greater authority and autonomy for Russia
within the Soviet Union appealed to these sentiments.[5]

However, Yeltsin was best known for his advocacy of faster economic
reform. He blamed conservative forces in the Communist Party and
state bureaucracy for obstructing economic reform. At first Yeltsin was
vague about what kind of economic reform he favored, but as the
economists began to press for free markets in 1989–90, he fastened on
market reform as his economic program.

Yeltsin's advocacy of market reform was key to his ability to appeal
simultaneously to ordinary people and the party–state elite. As we have
seen, a greater reliance on markets had been part of Gorbachev's socialist reform program since 1987. There was widespread support for "market reform" in Russia, although it meant different things to different
people. The economists promised that market reform would end the
long lines and severe shortages that had plagued the country. But market reform also had another meaning to ordinary citizens, who resented
the special stores and other special distribution mechanisms available to
the elite. The term "market economy" came to mean to ordinary people
a system in which everyone would be able to shop in the same stores
and gain access to the same goods. "Market reform" would allow the
masses to buy the best available goods. To the average Soviet citizen,
this sounded like a step toward actually fulfilling the egalitarian ideals
which were supposed to characterize a socialist system.

To the party–state elite, a market economy meant something very
different. They had not been forced to wait in the long lines that afflicted
ordinary citizens. But their privileged access to consumer goods came at
a high price – continuing dependence on the favor of one's superiors. To

the party–state elite, market reform meant liberation from a system which made privileges entirely dependent on one's position in the hierarchy. Once freed from party strictures against accumulation of personal wealth, they expected to have more secure access to the best consumer goods that money could buy.

Yeltsin's combined message of populism, democracy, Russian nationalism, and market reform had broad appeal in Russian society at the end of the 1980s. Added to these substantive themes was Yeltsin's symbolic role as the best-known opponent of the faltering Communist Party leadership. While at first Gorbachev's reform program enjoyed great popularity and raised people's hopes, the economic chaos that emerged in 1988–89 caused the leadership's standing to take a nose-dive. Boris Yeltsin had stood up to the Communist Party leadership, been cast out, and was now fighting his way back to prominence. This image of Yeltsin appealed to many Russians.

In Chapter 6 we described Yeltsin's runaway victory in the March 1989 election for an all-Moscow seat in the Soviet Congress of People's Deputies. Yeltsin was able to play a prominent role in the Soviet Congress, but his power there was strictly limited. The Russian Republic may have been the largest one, but it had only half of the Soviet population. Yeltsin had little support among delegates from some of the other republics, in which loyalty to the Communist Party leadership remained strong. Gorbachev was able to retain effective control of the Soviet Congress. Yeltsin's limited support in the Congress was clearly illustrated when the Congress selected deputies for the smaller standing Soviet legislature, the Supreme Soviet. Yeltsin was not among those chosen in the secret ballot by Congress delegates. His supporters in the Congress and the liberal Moscow media raised a vigorous complaint, and Gorbachev agreed to an arrangement that allowed Yeltsin to be added to the Supreme Soviet.[6]

Thus, Yeltsin had to depend on the goodwill of his arch-rival, Gorbachev, to even gain a place in the Union-wide Supreme Soviet. There seemed to be no road to power open to him within the Soviet parliament. Yeltsin realized that his best route to power lay through the Russian Republic rather than the Union-level governmental structure. Elections were planned in the Russian Republic for March 1990. The voters would elect deputies to a reformed Russian Republic parliament,[7] as well as new city soviets across Russia. The 1990 election for the Russian parliament was to be even more democratic than the previous year's Union-wide election. No seats in the new Russian Republic parliament would be reserved for the Communist Party or other "public organizations." All of the deputies would be chosen in competitive elections. Yeltsin decided to run for election to the new Russian Republic parliament in March 1990 from his home base of Sverdlovsk.

Yeltsin was a well-known and popular figure in Russia by 1990 and he did not need much help to win election to the Russian Republic parliament. However, he aimed not just at winning a seat but gaining the chairmanship of the parliament, which would make him the chief executive of the giant Russian Republic.[8] To accomplish this, he needed more than personal popularity with the voters.

In the first half of 1990, nearly all of the main contenders in Soviet politics, Yeltsin included, were still members of the Communist Party. But at the beginning of that year, an organized political force arose outside the party which played an important role in the elections and in Yeltsin's climb to power. The Democratic Russia electoral alliance formed in January 1990, growing out of earlier election groupings in Moscow.[9] Democratic Russia organized a slate of candidates for the March 1990 elections for the Moscow city soviet, as well as supporting candidates for the Russian Republic parliament and the soviets of other Russian cities.

Democratic Russia was a real movement from below, led mainly by liberal intellectuals. It stressed many of the same themes as did Yeltsin, such as democracy and market reform. Like Yeltsin, it focused on the Communist Party leadership as its adversary, although at first many of its leaders and supporters remained in the party. Even more than Yeltsin, Democratic Russia emphasized Russian autonomy.[10]

Democratic Russia proved very effective at campaigning in Moscow and some other major cities. Candidates that it supported won 57 per cent of the seats on the Moscow city soviet and 60 per cent in Leningrad in the March 1990 election. But in the races for the Russian Republic parliament, its candidates won only between 20 and 30 per cent of the contests across Russia.[11]

Yeltsin was not formally affiliated with Democratic Russia and had even initially opposed its formation.[12] Its leaders were from the Moscow intelligentsia, while Yeltsin came from a very different background, having spent his formative years as a provincial party boss. Yeltsin was from the party–state elite, despite his opposition to the party leadership. Yeltsin and Democratic Russia had a wary relationship, which symbolized the uneasy tie between two key parts of the developing pro-capitalist coalition, the intelligentsia and the growing section of the party–state elite that was in the process of entirely rejecting the system. Democratic Russia needed a powerful national figure with appeal beyond the big-city intelligentsia and professional classes. And Yeltsin needed the effective organizational support which Democratic Russia could provide.

Democratic Russia did not limit its work to elections. It also became adept at organizing mass demonstrations in Moscow. In February 1990 it brought some 100,000 demonstrators to the Kremlin walls to demand democracy, while the Communist Party central committee was meeting to debate the fate of Article 6 of the Soviet Constitution, which had guaranteed the Communist Party's political monopoly.[13] The ability to mobilize large numbers of Moscow residents would prove important in the battle over Russia's future.

When the newly elected Russian Republic parliament assembled, Yeltsin launched his campaign for the chairmanship. Democratic Russia threw its support to him, yet it did not have nearly enough deputies to prevail on its own. However, Yeltsin could draw on the support of deputies from the party–state elite who were moving into opposition to the system. A few days before the vote, Gorbachev warned the deputies of the Russian Republic parliament that Yeltsin was abandoning socialism, but this failed to sway the majority.[14] It took four ballots, but eventually, on 29 May 1990, Yeltsin was elected chairman by the slim margin of four votes.[15]

Yeltsin maintained his distance from Democratic Russia. He did not name any activists from Democratic Russia to positions in the Russian Council of Ministers or include any of them in his group of close personal advisors.[16] As chairman of the Russian Republic's parliament and effectively the chief executive of the giant republic, Yeltsin now had a powerful institutional position from which to challenge Gorbachev and the leadership of the Soviet system. Two months later, in July 1990, Yeltsin dramatically resigned from the CPSU. A potential situation of dual power was emerging in the Soviet Union, reminiscent of the 1917 Russian Revolution, although the legal authority of the head of the Russian Republic was limited.

In February 1991 Yeltsin successfully pressed the Soviet leadership to grant him an opportunity to address the nation on television. In his televised speech, he sharply attacked Gorbachev, accusing him of harboring dictatorial ambitions, and he demanded Gorbachev's immediate resignation.[17] In response, several hundred outraged deputies in the Russian Republic parliament demanded an emergency meeting of the parliament[18] to remove Yeltsin from its chairmanship.

As the March 1991 meeting approached, Gorbachev banned public demonstrations in Moscow during the parliamentary sessions. Defying the ban, Democratic Russia organized a pro-Yeltsin demonstration of some 100,000 Muscovites.[19] Backing down from his threats, Gorbachev ordered the troops that had been brought into Moscow not to intervene. The tide was clearly running with Yeltsin. At the parliamentary session, many members of the Communist caucus broke away and voted for Yeltsin.[20] The parliament, rather than removing him from the chairmanship, granted Yeltsin additional powers. It also scheduled a popular election for the new post of president of the Russian Republic for June 1991.[21]

In the campaign for Russian Republic president, Yeltsin stressed the same themes that had served him well before. He placed the greatest stress on the need for faster market reform, an effective demand as the Soviet economy descended into chaos and depression during 1991. He promised to defend the "sovereignty" of the Russian Republic. He used his position as chairman of the Russian Republic parliament to adopt the stance of a statesman, rising above the political fray.[22] He chose as his vice-presidential running mate a popular military figure and veteran of the Afghan war, Alexandr Rutskoi. The Yeltsin campaign's ambiguous relation to the Communist Party was indicated by his running mate Rutskoi's position as a leader of a group called "Communists for Democracy."[23]

Yeltsin had to rely on Democratic Russia to organize his campaign. Democratic Russia activists did the major part of the legwork, staffing campaign headquarters and distributing literature all over Russia.[24] Yeltsin won 57.3 per cent of the votes, with the remainder divided between five other candidates, all of whom had stressed either more gradual economic reform or militant nationalist themes.[25] Democratic Russia leaders Gavriil Popov and Anatoly Sobchak won the mayoral races in Moscow and Leningrad, respectively.

Yeltsin's victory in the Russian presidential election cannot be interpreted as an endorsement by the majority of Russia voters of the capitalist transformation which Yeltsin would soon bring to Russia. Yeltsin rose to the presidency of the Russian Republic without ever publicly indicating any such intention on his part. In fact, he and his closest associates never used the word "capitalism" in public. Nikolai Ryzhkov, the Soviet prime minister from 1985 to 1990 and Yeltsin's leading opponent in the June 1991 presidential race, later complained that Yeltsin and his associates "kept their views secret" concerning the vast socioeconomic changes they planned.[26] While some intellectuals, and particularly some of the economists, did openly advocate capitalism, Yeltsin and his associates did not do so in public.[27]

There were good reasons for this failure to explain exactly how the opposition leaders planned to change the system. While the party–state elite and the urban intelligentsia had come to favor capitalism by June 1991, the electorate as a whole apparently had quite different views. Polling evidence showed little support for free-market capitalism among the Russian population as a whole at that time. The Times Mirror Center, based in the United States, conducted a large-scale public opinion survey in the European part of Russia in May 1991 – just one month before Yeltsin was elected president of Russia. The pollsters interviewed 1,123 people, asking them a long list of questions about their political and social views. Among the most revealing was the answer to a question about the type of social system the person wanted; the responses are shown in Figure 8.1.

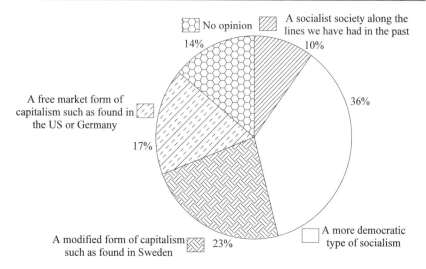

Figure 8.1 Public opinion survey in European Russia on desired form of society, May 1991
Source: 'The Pulse of Europe: A Survey of Political and Social Values and Attitudes' 1991:
50.

The responses show a large plurality supporting democratic socialism. A total of 46 per cent favored alternatives identified as some type of socialism; if those with no opinion are excluded, a majority of 54 per cent of the remaining respondents wanted socialism. Another 23 per cent of the respondents chose the Swedish model, a highly egalitarian social-democratic system that has a degree of workers' rights, social benefits, and personal economic security unequalled in any other Western country. Less than one-fifth said that they favored the type of relatively unregulated capitalism which the Russian pro-capitalist coalition, led by Boris Yeltsin, was to pursue with unwavering determination once it achieved state power. If the poll had not disproportionately sampled residents of Moscow and St Petersburg,[28] the results would undoubtedly have been even less favorable to the capitalist future.[29] Some other polls taken in 1991 found even less support for capitalism.[30]

The responses to other questions in the poll showed very limited public support for privatization of industry, which was to become a centerpiece of the Yeltsin government's policies. Only 3 per cent of the respondents favored privatization for heavy industry, 9 per cent for banks, and 20 per cent for consumer-goods manufacturing. Fully 81 per cent believed the state should guarantee food and shelter to every citizen. At the same time, only 30 per cent viewed the Communist Party favorably, while 60 per cent viewed it unfavorably.[31] The results of this poll portray a large majority that wanted some form of socialism or social democracy but that disapproved of the way the Communist Party had run the country.

Yeltsin and his associates understood that a large majority of the Russian public were unfavorable toward the prospect of free-market capitalism. But the majority responded very well to criticism of the Communist Party leadership and to appeals for faster market reform, democratization, and greater autonomy for the Russian Republic.[32] Yeltsin's election campaign won strong support not only from intellectuals but from ordinary workers, from women, and from elderly pensioners. Only among army troops and in certain Russian regions did Yeltsin's vote fall below that of any one of his rivals.[33] However, one group within the Russian population was overwhelmingly in accord with the direction that Yeltsin would ultimately lead – the party–state elite. As the study of elite opinion cited in Chapter 7 showed, while the general public did not support an attempt to build capitalism, a large majority of the party–state elite favored just such a course.

Winning the presidency of the Russian Republic, together with control of that republic's parliament, provided Yeltsin with a launching pad for his campaign for state power. However, these accomplishments did not yet amount to actual state power for Yeltsin and the pro-capitalist coalition. The Russian Republic had no army of its own. It was not a sovereign state. It was one of fifteen constituent republics of the Soviet Union. The chief executive of the Russian Republic had no more legal or constitutional power to transform its socioeconomic system than would a governor of California to abolish capitalism within that state. The ultimate victory of the pro-capitalist coalition depended on additional changes and developments in the Soviet Union.

THE MINERS' STRIKES

While strikes were not technically illegal in the Soviet Union, the regime had never permitted them in practice. Beginning in 1989 the Soviet Union saw its first episode of mass labor unrest since the 1920s. Various groups of workers engaged in strikes and demonstrations during 1989–91, but only the coal miners held a series of large-scale, devastating strikes with an impact great enough to affect the broader Soviet political battle. The first miners' strike wave took place in July 1989, followed by a one-day strike in October of that year. A second major miners' strike took place in March–April 1991.

Some 2.2 million people worked in the Soviet coal industry, which supplied 20 per cent of Soviet energy needs.[34] Although they received relatively high wages, the miners had many accumulated grievances, including poor housing conditions and lack of social infrastructure. The freer atmosphere of perestroika emboldened them to press their grievances. Miners also felt threatened by some aspects of peres-troika. Coal prices had always been kept low, and miners feared the closure of money-losing mines under the new policy of self-financing for enterprises. The consumer goods shortages of 1988–89 were very severe in the coal regions. A key precipitating factor in the 1989 strike was said to be the sudden disappearance of soap from stores in mining districts.

The July 1989 strike began in the Kuzbass mining district of western Siberia, where some 100,000 miners walked out.[35] The strike quickly spread to the Donbass region in the Ukraine and to Vorkuta in the far north of Russia. The striking miners called for improvements in pay, working conditions, and local amenities, but their demands were not limited to economic issues. Some of the striking groups of miners demanded independence from the ministries in Moscow, with the power to set coal prices to be transferred to the mining enterprises.[36] Others directly challenged Communist Party rule and called for the repeal of Article 6 of the Constitution.

The Soviet authorities made concessions on the miners' economic demands, and the July 1989 strike subsided. However, the miners con-tinued to organize, seeking to build an independent trade union in the face of the official union's failure to effectively represent them. In March and April 1991, a new strike wave broke out, again in the above three mining regions. This time the strikes appeared to focus more on political demands, including a call for the resignation of the Soviet government. The strike in Kuzbass ended when Yeltsin promised on 1 May to trans-fer control of the Russian mines from Soviet jurisdiction to that of the Russian Republic.[37]

While the miners' strikes did not bring down the Soviet government, they contributed to that end in significant ways. They caused severe economic disruption, contributing to a sense that order was breaking down and that things were spinning out of control. The strikes contrib-uted to undermining the legitimacy and authority of the Soviet govern-ment. While the government could readily dismiss the opposition it faced from intellectuals as coming from a privileged section of society, now it was facing bitter and militant opposition from the very working class which it claimed to represent.

Not only did the miners oppose Gorbachev, the Communist Party, and the Soviet government, their leaders gradually moved into an alli-ance with Yeltsin and Democratic Russia during 1990–91.[38] This may seem surprising. Mine workers in most parts of the world have not been known for their sympathy for liberal intellectuals or for capitalism. Yet there was a logic to the miner–Yeltsin alliance. The official miners' trade union, which had done little to represent the miners' interests, was controlled by the Communist Party. This turned many of the miners against the party and made them ready to listen to Yeltsin, the leading critic of the party leadership.

Seeing the Soviet government and its ministries as the source of their oppressive conditions, the leaders of the miners' strikes found the call for a market economy very appealing. To them it held out the promise of independence from the ministries. Yeltsin actively solicited the support of the miners' leaders, promising them that, upon coming under the jurisdiction of the Russian Republic, the mines would be granted substantial autonomy.[39] This illustrates the manner in which the ambiguous demand for a market economy could unite downtrodden miners with elite groups aiming to gain ownership of the Soviet Union's state-owned wealth.

The miners' strike of March–April 1991 came at the best possible moment for Yeltsin. This was the very time of Yeltsin's confrontation with Gorbachev and the Communist faction of the Russian Republic parliament described above. The miners' strike added to the pressure generated by the large Democratic Russia demonstration in Moscow, helping Yeltsin to maintain his control of the parliament and continue his march toward the Russian presidency.

NATIONALISM[40]

The USSR was organized as a federation of fifteen republics. Table 8.1 lists the fifteen republics, in order of population. The three Slavic republics – Russia, Ukraine, and Byelorussia – contained 72.6 per cent of the Soviet population. The five Central Asian republics – Uzbekistan, Kazakhstan, Tadzhikistan, Kirgizstan, and Turkmenistan – had 17.6 per cent of the population. Thus, the Slavic and the Central Asian republics together had 90.2 per cent of the population, as well as 97.6 per cent of the Soviet land area. The three republics located in the Caucasian mountains – Azerbaijan, Georgia, and Armenia – had 5.5 per cent of the Soviet population, the three Baltic republics – Lithuania, Latvia, and Estonia – 2.8 per cent, and Moldavia, bordering Rumania, had 1.5 per cent. Ethnic Russians were scattered across the other fourteen republics, and in some of them they were a large proportion of the republican population.[41]

Strong nationalist movements arose in some Soviet republics in the late 1980s, and the final destruction of the Soviet state in 1991 followed a wave of independence declarations by the republics. This led some analysts to attribute the demise of the Soviet system primarily to the powerful force of nationalism. According to this view, once Gorbachev democratized the Soviet system, the long-oppressed nationalities of the Soviet Union were bound to demand their independence. The end result, so it is argued, could only have been the demise of the Soviet system.

Table 8.1 Republics of the USSR, 1991

Republic	Population (millions)	Republic	Population (millions)
Russian SFSR	148.5	Kirgiz SSR	4.4
Ukrainian SSR	51.9	Moldavian SSR	4.4
Uzbek SSR	20.7	Lithuanian SSR	3.7
Kazakh SSR	16.8	Turkmen SSR	3.7
Byelorussian SSR	10.3	Armenian SSR	3.4
Azerbaijan SSR	7.1	Latvian SSR	2.7
Georgian SSR	5.5	Estonian SSR	1.6
Tadzhik SSR	5.4	USSR total	290.1

Source: *Narodnoe khoziaistvo SSSR* (1991, p. 67)

This explanation fails to account for the most important feature of the Soviet demise: the abandonment of the pre-existing socioeconomic system in Russia and in most of the other newly independent states that emerged from the Soviet Union. While nationalism played an important role in the Soviet demise, the above view is too simple. A perceptive analyst of Soviet history suggested that "it was not...the exit of the nationalities...[that] caused the downfall," but rather "It was the decline and de facto downfall of the regime that gave them the chance to leave."[42] We shall argue that this is closer to the truth than the view that nationalism inevitably sealed the fate of the Soviet system.

Most specialists in nationalism hold the view that, contrary to the popular impression, nationalism is not an age-old force in human society but rather is a relatively recent phenomenon which has only appeared in the world within the last two centuries.[43] While ethnic, racial, religious, tribal, and regional identities go back thousands of years, the nation-state, with its associated ideas of national identity, national loyalty, and the right of every nationality to its own state, are modern developments. It was the capitalist era that gave birth to nationalism. Capitalist industrialization pulled people out of isolated rural communities into large cities, introduced means of mass communication, and tied large regions together in economic interdependence via market relations. All of these processes led people to move beyond their earlier clan, ethnic, religious, or local identities to adopt a larger national one.

As historian Ronald Suny has pointed out, it is misleading to view the Soviet Union as a system which simply established domination over pre-existing, well-defined national groups.[44] The Soviet system, and the rapid economic and social development which it brought, was a key cause of the development of national identity among various groups within the Soviet Union. After the civil war of 1918–20 left the Bolsheviks in control of a huge area with diverse populations, they created the

Soviet state as a federation of republics, each of which was defined as having a national identity.[45] While some Soviet republics were based on groups which had once had an independent state, such as Georgia, others, such as Azerbaijan and Byelorussia, had never been independent states.[46] Ukraine had been part of Russia since 1654. The Kazakhs had been nomadic tribespeople. The people of the Central Asian republics had a stronger identity as Muslims than as any national group.

The cities in some Soviet republics had originally been largely populated by other nationalities. For example, in Byelorussia most of the urban population had originally been Jewish, Russian, or Polish.[47] Baku, the capital of Azerbaijan, was dominated by Russians and Armenians prior to the revolution. The Ukrainian people had been almost all peasants, while landowners and officials were Russian or Polish and merchants Jewish.[48] But the decades of Soviet development changed that, at least in many of the Soviet republics.

For much of the Soviet period, the development of the languages and cultures of minority nationalities was actively promoted, within certain limits. Each republic had many of the trappings of a national state (although without real political sovereignty), with its own political and cultural institutions. As rapid economic development brought urbanization, mass literacy, and mass communication, national identity tended to grow in many of the republics. At the same time, the domination of the Soviet system by Russians, the rigid rule from Moscow, and the pressure on the upwardly mobile among minority nationalities to become "Russified," created national resentments that festered under the surface. When the Stalinist terror ended after his death, nationalist movements gradually began to develop in some of the republics, particularly in the three Baltic republics, which had the experience of statehood during the interwar period, before being absorbed by the Soviet Union in 1940.

When Gorbachev instituted glasnost and democratization, these largely underground nationalist movements were able to come out into the open. But the nationalist movements took different forms in different Soviet republics, and there was no inevitability that they would lead to the destruction of the Soviet state. In a few of the republics – the Baltic states and Georgia – the memory of independent statehood was strong and the drive for independence very powerful. But those constituted a tiny part of the Soviet Union, with few of its natural resources. For the rest, the situation was more complicated and the outcome was far from predetermined.

The national strife of the perestroika period began in 1988, not with an anti-Moscow movement, but in the form of violent conflict between two neighboring republics. Armenia and Azerbaijan fought over control of Nagorno-Karabakh, a predominantly Armenian enclave within the Republic of Azerbaijan. The Soviet authorities sent troops to re-establish order but were unable to find a solution acceptable to both sides in the conflict. That same year the nationalist Estonian Front began agitating for greater autonomy for that Baltic republic.

The following year mass-based nationalist movements arose around the fringes of the Soviet Union: in all three Baltic republics and in Georgia. The democratic reforms of 1989 provided an opportunity for the long-standing underground nationalist movements in those republics to operate openly and seek support from voters. A key event occurred in April 1989 when Soviet troops were sent to quell nationalist demonstrations in Tbilisi, Georgia, and a bloody battle ensued. This generated a wave of opposition to the use of force by the central government, an opposition which was reflected among deputies in the new Soviet parliament and in the mass media. This reaction – known as the "Tbilisi syndrome" – made it difficult for the government to again contemplate a full-scale military response to rebellious republics.

During 1989 the rebellious republics – the Baltics, Georgia, and now Armenia[49] – demanded, with growing boldness, first autonomy and then sovereignty within the Soviet Union.[50] In November 1989 the Soviet parliament granted autonomy to the Baltic republics, but this failed to satisfy them. The republican elections of March 1990 produced majorities for the nationalists in the Baltic republics, and their new legislatures now took the further step of declaring independence from the Soviet Union.[51]

It is clear that only the use of force by Moscow could have kept the Baltic republics within the Soviet Union. The democratic reforms Gorbachev had introduced seemed to preclude that route. The Soviet constitution formally guaranteed the right of any republic to secede from the Union. Gorbachev did not challenge the Baltic republics' right to do so, although he urged them not to; the battle was over what procedures would have to be followed to make a decision on possible Baltic secession.[52] Secession by the Baltic republics would in itself not have been crippling to the Soviet Union, given that they represented only 2.8 per cent of the Soviet population and had no important natural resources, and also in light of the unsavory origins of their incorporation into the Soviet Union as a result of the infamous Stalin–Hitler pact of 1939.[53]

Then in June 1990 an entirely new element was injected into the nationalist conflict, when the Russian Republic passed its own sovereignty resolution. Russia had always occupied a paradoxical position in the Soviet system. Russians were the dominant national group. They constituted about half of the Soviet population, and moreover they were disproportionally represented in the Union party and state institutions. Ethnic Russians also occupied high positions in the party and government organs in all of the other republics. The rebellious republics on the periphery of the Soviet Union were, to a significant extent, rebelling against what they saw as domination by Russians.

Despite all of these ways in which Russians dominated the Soviet Union, at the same time Russian nationalism was in certain respects held in check by the Soviet system. Lenin had always worried that "Great Russian chauvinism" might threaten the unity of the Soviet state, and the organization of the Soviet system reflected that fear. Unlike the other fourteen republics, the Russian Republic did not have its own separate Communist Party organization. It also was the only republic without a separate Academy of Sciences, trade union council, Komsomol, or KGB. In the effort to build a Union-wide identity for the Soviet people, the sense of nationhood of Russians had been suppressed to some extent.

As nationalist movements around the Soviet periphery grew bolder in their demands for autonomy or even independence, Russians' sense of national grievance also grew. This presented an opportunity to Yeltsin and the pro-capitalist coalition. Yeltsin stressed Russian national grievances, often pointing to the fact that, within the USSR, only Russia and Turkmenistan produced a greater value of goods than they consumed.[54] One month after Yeltsin became chairman of the Russian parliament, Democratic Russia proposed a piece of legislation that would declare Russia to be a sovereign entity, with control of its own natural resources, and with precedence for its own republican laws over those of the Soviet Union.[55] Yeltsin recognized in this proposal a way to finally outmaneuver Gorbachev and the entire Union government. Although no basis for such a law could be found in the Soviet constitution, Yeltsin prevailed upon the Russian Republic parliament to pass the sovereignty measure on 8 June 1990, by a vote of 544 to 271.[56]

While the Russian Republic had no legal means to enforce the new measure, its passage had an immediate and profound effect on the other republics, transforming the nature of the nationalist impulses coursing through the republics. However much ethnic Russians might have dominated the Soviet system, the structure of the Union at least provided some safeguards and powers, as well as significant economic benefits, to the non-Russian republics. For example, Russia's plentiful raw materials had been provided cheaply throughout the Soviet Union. Now the Russian Republic was asserting its right to control its own natural resources and their disposition.

The leaderships of the republics which had previously been relatively quiet now immediately passed sovereignty resolutions. By August 1990 sovereignty resolutions had been passed by Uzbekistan, Moldavia, Ukraine, Turkmenistan, and Tadzhikistan. By October even loyal Kazakhstan followed suit as well. In several of these republics no mass-based nationalist movement had even appeared, but the Communist leaders in these republics were positioning themselves to hold on to power if Yeltsin proved able to actually abolish the Union state.

Ukrainian leader Leonid Kravchuk's maneuvers illustrate the process set off by the Russian Republic's move toward sovereignty. Kravchuk had been the secretary for ideology of the Ukrainian Communist Party, specializing in combating Ukrainian nationalism and promoting socialist internationalism as the antidote. In late 1989 a nationalist movement arose in Ukraine, based mainly in the western portion of the republic.[57] As the central government in Moscow began to weaken, and as the momentum toward capitalism grew in strength, Kravchuk, who as a top Communist had risen to the chairmanship of the Ukrainian Supreme Soviet in July 1990, now sought a new basis for maintaining his high position in the power structure of the Ukraine. Shedding his Communist and Soviet identity, and discarding his lecture notes on socialist internationalism, Kravchuk transformed himself into a Ukrainian nationalist. He utilized this new identity to stay in power through the breakup of the Soviet Union.[58]

Yeltsin took further steps to pursue the goal of Russian sovereignty and the promise it held to carry out a capitalist transformation. In September 1990 a team of economic advisors had proposed the 500 Day Plan of rapid marketization and privatization, discussed in Chapter 5. While Gorbachev ultimately withdrew the plan, on 11 September 1990 Yeltsin pushed it through the Russian Republic parliament.[59] Yeltsin did not yet have the power to carry out the 500 Day Plan in Russia, and its passage was in that sense symbolic. But it added to the economic chaos that was now engulfing the Soviet Union. The Soviet Union and its largest republic had now passed conflicting laws on economic restructuring, including the future of property relations. The highly interdependent Soviet economic mechanism began to break down under the impact of this battle for authority. Economic links between enterprises across republican boundaries began to be interrupted.

In December 1990 Yeltsin launched a still bolder strike at the central government. Taxes collected in the Russian Republic had supplied about half of the Soviet government's budget revenues. On 27 December Yeltsin pushed a measure through the Russian Republic parliament to provide less than one-tenth of the tax revenues due to the central government for its 1991 budget.[60] This threatened the very existence of the central government, and it contributed to the mushrooming deficit and rising inflationary pressure which engulfed the Soviet Union in 1991.

After Russia's sovereignty declaration and the resulting string of similar resolutions by the other republics, Gorbachev decided that, if the Soviet Union were to survive, it would have to be reconstituted on a new basis that would allow more autonomy for the republics. He began a process of negotiating a new Union treaty. To build support for this goal, Gorbachev planned a referendum on preserving the Union, believing that the disintegration process did not reflect the wishes of the majority of the Soviet people.

The referendum took place on 17 March 1991, in all of the Soviet republics except the three Baltic republics and Armenia, Georgia, and Moldavia; 147 million people voted and 76.4 per cent approved the preservation of the Union.[61] The voters in each of the nine participating republics overwhelmingly approved the measure.[62] Gorbachev could claim strong popular support for maintaining a reconstituted federative state. The Soviet economy was a highly interdependent mechanism, and everyone knew there would be enormous material costs to disintegration. In the poorer republics many people believed they benefited economically from the Union relationship. Most Russians did not look forward to seeing their state shrink to half its former population, leaving 25 million ethnic Russians, nearly one-fifth of the total, scattered as minorities across what they feared would become separate countries.[63] Many people did want more authority for their republican institutions, but the referendum of March 1991 found that only a small minority in the nine participating republics wanted their republic to become an independent state.

However, despite popular sentiment to the contrary, there remained a powerful force pushing toward disintegration of the Union. Gorbachev and the renewed Union state represented not just the preservation of the Union but also the maintenance of some kind of socialist system. Gorbachev was the key figure holding the republics together, and he refused to give up on his aim of reforming socialism rather than replacing it with capitalism. Yeltsin and his associates were determined to eliminate socialism,[64] and Gorbachev stood in the way. While the nationalist movements that arose in many of the republics were genuine expressions of popular feelings, had it not been for the determination of the pro-capitalist coalition to abolish the socialist system and open a path to capitalism, it is doubtful that the nationalist movements would have destroyed the Union.

The event which set in motion the round of sovereignty declarations was, as we have seen, Russia's own sovereignty declaration of June 1990. This was not motivated by a nationalist desire for independence from an alien power – Russia had more than independence, it had a dominant position over an entire multinational state. It was Yeltsin and the pro-capitalist coalition's plans for socioeconomic change, which were blocked by Gorbachev and the Union state, which motivated the key act, from which followed a process that ultimately tore the Union apart.

THE COUP ATTEMPT OF AUGUST 1991 AND ITS AFTERMATH

The final defeat of Gorbachev, the socialist reform project, and the Union state was dealt by the attempted coup of August 1991 and its aftermath. The failed coup strengthened Yeltsin and the pro-capitalist coalition. It propelled all of the Union republics, most of which had not previously sought independence, onto a path toward that very goal.

On 19 August, with Gorbachev on vacation in the Crimea, eight top leaders of the Soviet government formed an emergency committee which announced that Gorbachev had been relieved of his duties. Quietly placing Gorbachev under house arrest, they imposed a state of emergency in parts of the Soviet Union. Boris Yeltsin and the Russian Republic parliamentary leadership boldly defied the coup. Within a few days the coup collapsed and Gorbachev returned to Moscow. However, power now shifted decisively from Gorbachev and the Union government to Yeltsin. Four months later the Soviet state was abolished and Russia emerged as an independent state, as did the fourteen other republics.

During the spring, summer, and early fall of 1990, Gorbachev and his socialist reform project were not faring well. Boris Yeltsin was growing more and more powerful. Yeltsin and his supporters were demanding that the Soviet Union adopt the 500 Day Plan, which would spell the end of socialism. The Union government's power was steadily eroding. The economy was sinking into chaos.

In response to these adverse developments, in October 1990 Gorbachev shifted his political alliances. As we saw in Chapter 5, in October Gorbachev came out in opposition to the 500 Day Plan. Seemingly abandoning his more liberal advisors, such as Yakovlev and Shevardnadze, he shifted toward individuals who appeared to be more traditional supporters of socialist institutions, preserving the Union, and maintaining social order.[65] In December 1990 he named Boris Pugo as interior minister and Gennady Yanaev as vice-president. When Prime Minister Ryzhkov had a heart attack in December 1990, Gorbachev replaced him with Valentin Pavlov. All three new appointees were viewed as "hardliners." Foreign Minister Shevardnadze responded by resigning and warning of impending dictatorship. On 10 January 1991 Gorbachev warned the Lithuanian parliament that he might impose presidential rule in the republic, charging that Lithuania was moving toward "restoration of the bourgeois order."[66] Soon thereafter Interior Ministry troops seized buildings in Lithuania and Latvia, actions that Gorbachev neither clearly supported nor denounced.

In early March 1991 Gorbachev lashed out at the gathering pro-capitalist forces. He attacked the "democrats" as "a typical right-wing opposition" and accused them of advocating 'the capitalization of society."[67] However, as we have seen, in the month of March 1991 Gorbachev's situation weakened further. A second wave of miners' strikes undermined the legitimacy of his rule. The attempt to remove Yeltsin as chairman of the Russian parliament backfired, leaving Yeltsin's position strengthened. The sole bright spot for Gorbachev was the passage of the Union referendum that month. Realizing that he was losing the battle with Yeltsin, in April 1991 Gorbachev again switched tactics, this time moving toward a more accommodative stance toward Yeltsin.

Now in a position of strength, yet perhaps mindful of the public endorsement of the Union in the March referendum, Yeltsin offered to negotiate with Gorbachev and the other republic heads to draft a new Union treaty. Gorbachev accepted, and the "9 plus 1" negotiations began.[68] On 23 April 1991 the leaders of the nine republics signed an agreement calling for legislative approval of a new Union treaty, which would grant substantial rights to the republics while preserving some sort of union among them.[69] Yeltsin then dropped his former harsh criticism of Gorbachev.

Gorbachev now shifted from attacking "democrats" to warning against "hardliners." In July 1991 he pushed a new, liberal Communist Party draft program through a central committee meeting, angering party traditionalists.[70] Later that month the Union treaty negotiations reached agreement on the specifics of a new treaty. Armenia, one of the six non-participants, announced that it wanted to rejoin the negotiations. The signing of the new treaty was set for 20 August 1991.

The immediate cause of the coup attempt of August 1991 was the impending signing of the Union treaty. It appears that the coup planners began meeting only two days before the coup was announced.[71] They viewed the Union treaty as the final abolition of the Union state. The coup leaders included practically all of the top officials of Gorbachev's administration, except for Gorbachev himself. Among the participants were Vice-President Yanaev, Prime Minister Pavlov, KGB head Vladimir Kryuchkov, Defense Minister Dmitry Yazov, Commander in Chief of Soviet ground forces General Valentin Varennikov, and even Gorbachev's chief of staff Valery Boldin.

In addition to preserving a strong central government, the coup leaders also indicated that they would halt the slide toward capitalism. They decried "the blossoming of profiteering" and insisted that "People should decide what social system should exist, but attempts are being made to deprive them of this right." They called for the protection of the right to work, education, health care, and housing for working people. However, they made no reference to the Communist Party.[72] They acted in the name of the government, not the party. All of the coup leaders were officials of the government, rather than the party.

In the coup leaders' official statement, as well as in their remarks at a press conference on the first day of the coup, they sought to assure the Soviet public that they would preserve at least some of the reforms that had been introduced under Gorbachev. They claimed to support economic diversity, including a role for "private enterprise." One of the coup leaders, Alexander Tizyakov, head of an association of state enterprises, insisted that "the policy of reforms toward a market economy will not be reversed." Vice-President Yanaev assured reporters that "the policy that was initiated back in 1985 by Mikhail Gorbachev will be continued."[73]

However, whatever image the coup leaders may have sought to project, the coup attempt was understood in the Soviet Union as a last attempt to resurrect the old, pre-perestroika system. Since they had pushed aside the leading advocate of a reformed and democratized socialism, President Gorbachev, they could not plausibly claim Gorbachev's reform mantle. The strong representation of top security and military officials in the leadership of the coup reinforced the impression that this was an attempt to bring back the old regime.

The events that followed the coup leaders' attempted seizure of power clearly show the balance of forces that existed among the supporters of the three main contending directions of development for the Soviet Union in August 1991. The advocates of going back to the old system had made their decisive move, yet it found little support, either in the population at large or within the party–state elite. While in most of the Soviet Union, outside of Moscow and St Petersburg, the coup met little active opposition at first, neither did it stir any active support. The leaders of the Soviet Union's second and fourth largest republics, Ukraine's Leonid Kravchuk and Kazakhstan's Nursultan Nazarbaev, adopted wait-and-see attitudes. As soon as active and determined opposition appeared in Moscow, and the coup leaders' hesitance to take strong action became apparent, the coup quickly collapsed. The complete failure of the coup to rally the party–state elite to the cause of bringing back the old system was the final confirmation of its mass defection from the system.

The active supporters of a reformed and democratized socialism, despite the evidence that such a direction of change was the most popular of all among the people at large, nevertheless found themselves as marginalized as the supporters of the old regime. Gorbachev's reform efforts had never succeeded in passing beyond an initiative from the top. It had failed to stir into action the masses of ordinary working people in whose name the reforms had been undertaken. They remained passive observers. With Gorbachev under house arrest, there was no surge of opposition to the coup planners from that quarter.

However, Yeltsin and the pro-capitalist coalition immediately opposed the coup from their stronghold in the nation's capital. Standing

atop an armored truck, Yeltsin called the coup an illegal act and threatened retribution for its architects.[74] He called for a general strike in
opposition to the coup.[75] A crowd quickly gathered around the "White
House," the building that housed Russia's parliament, and a few military units arrived which offered to protect the parliament. The crowd
defending the "White House" was initially estimated at only about
20,000, far below the size of earlier Moscow demonstrations.[76] This
appeared to be the final confrontation over what system would prevail
in the country. Russian Republic vice-president Alexandr Rutskoi told
the crowd that "Either we shall live like the rest of the world, or we shall
continue to call ourselves 'the socialist choice' and 'the Communist
prospect', and live like pigs."[77] Former top Gorbachev aide Alexandr
Yakovlev and former foreign minister Shevardnadze, who had left Gorbachev's camp, joined the crowd at the White House.[78] A Russian businessman claimed that some of Russia's new capitalists joined the fray,
with securities brokers helping to organize the demonstration outside
the White House on 19 August.[79] The situation of dual power that had
existed in embryo since Yeltsin's May 1990 selection as chairman of the
Russian Republic parliament had now emerged as a reality. The Old
Guard had seized the helm of the Union state, while Yeltsin and the pro-
capitalist coalition defiantly defended the Russian Republic. Gorbachev
and the socialist reformers were essentially absent from the confrontation.

In the face of defiance by Yeltsin and his supporters, the coup leaders
failed to take any decisive action. They did not arrest Yeltsin at the start
of the coup, nor did they mount an attack on the parliament building
where he was holed up. They did not even take control of all communications in the country, allowing opponents to start organizing against
them. Some observers attributed these lapses to incompetence. However, it is difficult to believe that a group of the top leaders of the
government, military, and security apparatus of the Soviet superpower
could be totally incapable of the relatively simple organizational tasks
that would have been required to make the coup effective.

It appears that the coup leaders quickly realized that they had little
active support within the party–state elite. It is even likely that they were
at least dimly aware of this before they acted, yet they may have felt
they could not give up without at least some move to stop the dismantling of the system. They apparently hoped that either Gorbachev would
join them, lending their action legitimacy, or that the Congress of People's Deputies would meet and approve their action. Their problem was
not a lack of competence but the absence of any active political support
beyond their small circle. As they realized how isolated they were, they
simply gave up. Pugo committed suicide, and the rest passively submitted to arrest.

As the coup collapsed, Gorbachev was released from house arrest in the Crimea and returned to Moscow to assume control – or so he expected. He condemned the coup organizers, and he thanked Yeltsin and the Russian Republic deputies for standing up to the coup. He also pointedly reaffirmed his commitment to socialism and promised to purge the Communist Party of "reactionary forces."[80]

However, the rapid collapse of the attempted coup had demonstrated how weak the support was within the party–state elite for either the Old Guard or Gorbachev's socialist reform project. Yeltsin and his allies, having vanquished the Old Guard, now realized that they could push Gorbachev – and the Union – aside as well. With no more legal basis than the coup leaders had possessed, Yeltsin signed a decree transferring the ownership of all property on Russian territory to the Russian Republic. He lowered the Soviet flag and raised the traditional Russian flag. He suspended the Communist Party and its newspapers within Russia.[81] Within a few days, Gorbachev was forced to resign as Communist Party leader and to call on the party central committee to dissolve itself. Soon thereafter, Yeltsin forced Gorbachev to disband the Soviet Congress of People's Deputies and transfer central authority to the republic presidents and an appointed legislative council.[82] In actuality, nothing was left of the Union government except one person, President Gorbachev.

Gorbachev spent the next few months trying in vain to preserve some kind of union of the republics. But as Yeltsin rapidly took control of Soviet assets and institutions, there was no longer any union to which they could belong. Not wanting to be part of an openly Russian empire, one by one the republics declared independence, as a genuine desire to leave the Union now gripped nearly all of the republics.[83] Those republican leaders who had retained the role of Communist Party boss followed the Russian lead, banning the Communist Party on their territory and adopting a nationalist identity. For example, in Uzbekistan President Islam Karimov simply changed the name of the Communist Party to the Popular Democratic Party, which acquired all of the assets of the former Communist Party of Uzbekistan and was headed by the same Islam Karimov.[84]

Yeltsin finally buried the remaining efforts to stitch together a new Union in early December. He took over the finances of the Kremlin bureaucracies. Then he joined with the heads of the two other Slavic republics, Ukraine and Byelorussia, to announce the final dissolution of the Soviet Union and the formation of a loose "Commonwealth of Independent States," open to all of the former Soviet republics but with no role for Soviet president Gorbachev. On 25 December 1991 Gorbachev resigned as Soviet president, and on the 31st the Soviet Union formally ceased to exist.

REVOLUTION FROM ABOVE

The Soviet system was swept away in a process that involved little actual violence or bloodshed. An entire socioeconomic system was dismantled, and one of the two most powerful nation-states in the world dismembered, in a relatively peaceful manner, while the world gasped in disbelief. This process undoubtedly qualifies as a revolution, although a revolution of a special type.

Many times in history socioeconomic systems have been swept away by revolutions from below. In such a classical revolution, the underprivileged victims of a social system rise up, defeat the old ruling group, overthrow the system by which that ruling group had ruled, and begin the difficult task of building a new system to replace the old. The French Revolution is the prototype of such a historical event in the modern world, and the Russian Revolution of 1917 is a twentieth-century example.

While the state socialist system in the Soviet Union was overturned by a revolution of sorts, it was nothing like the classical type. The demise of this system issued from a very different social process. It was a revolution from above. A decisive part of the old ruling group tore itself loose from its prior allegiance and turned on the system through which it had ruled. The party–state elite had allies in this revolution – every revolution involves alliances of groups and classes. The pro-capitalist coalition also drew support from the intelligentsia, economists, and the new class of private business owners – all of which were privileged groups within Soviet society, in prestige or material wealth. The intelligentsia and economists in particular played critical roles in the revolutionary process, as we have seen.[85] However, the party–state elite was the decisive actor in that coalition. It supplied the leading figures in the Russian Republic government that emerged as the dual power representative of the pro-capitalist coalition. The new capitalist class was emerging predominantly from the party–state elite. And it was the party–state elite's support for the transition to capitalism that in the end disarmed and defeated the other two factions.

It is difficult to find a recent historical event that closely resembles the Russian Revolution of 1991. The 1868 Meiji Restoration in Japan bears some resemblance to it. This was a seizure of power by a group within the feudal ruling class of Japan, following Japan's humiliation by the superior military might of the Western powers. The new rulers were determined to replace Japan's feudal system with the dynamic capitalism found in the West. They abolished the key institutions of the old system, including class privileges and the feudal landholding system. They laid the basis for capitalist development by using the state to build railroads and telegraph lines and undertake the construction of new industries.[86]

However, the Meiji Restoration had important differences from the Soviet elite's rejection of state socialism in favor of capitalism. A dissident group within the feudal elite of Japan, made up of a mixture of samurai, courtiers, and big feudal landowners, had to fight a two-year war to win power during 1866–68, which contrasts to the essentially peaceful transition in the Soviet Union. And Japan made such a radical turn in response to military and political humiliation by outside powers, whereas the Soviet Union was one of the world's two superpowers, free from any serious threat of military conquest.

The uniqueness of the Soviet demise stems from the peculiar nature of the state socialist system. Other powerful social systems in history had ruling groups which owned the productive assets of the system and more or less openly operated them for the benefit of the dominant group. State socialism was different in this respect. Its ruling group did not own the means of production, and its legitimacy rested entirely on the claim that it ran the system to serve ordinary people. This ruling group was tied to its own system only by historical, cultural, and sentimental bonds, which proved weak when confronted with material self-interest.

We have seen that a number of purely conjunctural, accidental factors played a role in the Soviet demise. The poor design of Gorbachev's economic reforms was one such factor. Another was the peculiar multinational structure of the Soviet state, which fostered the very nationalism it sought to tame. Still another was the personal ambition and special talents of one person, Boris Yeltsin.

Had the Soviet Union not been a multinational state based on many different national republics – as, for example, the other giant Communist Party-ruled state, China, is not – then the demise of its socioeconomic system might not have involved a disintegration of its state. The disintegration of the Soviet state was a by-product of the location within the Russian Republic of the core of the pro-capitalist coalition which arose in the perestroika years, and the accidental fact that the surest road to power for that coalition required taking the Soviet state apart.[87]

The various accidental factors involved in the Soviet demise occurred within a systematic process which took place during 1985–91. That was the process of unleashing the Soviet party–state elite from the strict, hierarchical discipline under which it had existed since the formation of the Soviet system, an unleashing which Gorbachev's democratic reform process required. Once unleashed, the party–state elite quickly realized it had nothing to gain from the preservation of the existing socioeconomic system, while it had everything to gain from its dismantling.

However, elites do not always get their way. In the spring of 1991 the majority of the Soviet people had expressed, in public opinion polls and a referendum, their opposition to living under capitalism and their desire to retain a Union state. But polls and referenda do not typically determine the direction of great social transformations. Whatever views the average person may have held about the desired future for the country, the Soviet system had bred a passivity into ordinary Soviet citizens, and no tradition of active political involvement had survived among them. Despite Gorbachev's talk about perestroika as a "revolution," he was never able to mobilize the ordinary people whom 70 years of hierarchical rule by the Communist Party had taught to stay out of politics and be distrustful of the leadership. Gorbachev's style of operation was one of bureaucratic maneuver, not mass mobilization. His effort to reform and democratize socialism through the instrument of the Communist Party, with its long history of top-down, bureaucratic misrule, probably made it impossible to mobilize ordinary people in active support of the reformed socialism he preached, however much his goals may have appealed to them.

This left the party–state elite, along with its allies among the intelligentsia, in a position to determine the fate of the Soviet system in 1991. Once these structural features of the Soviet system are understood, the surprising end to which perestroika led, and the surprising rapidity and peacefulness of the denouement, no longer appear surprising.

As the Soviet Union disintegrated, Yeltsin and the pro-capitalist coalition now appeared to be free to abolish the remaining state socialist institutions and begin in earnest the task of building capitalism in Russia. However, unbeknownst to the triumphant new leadership of Russia, enormous obstacles awaited them on their chosen path.

Part III

Aftermath of the Soviet demise

INTRODUCTION TO PART III

When the Soviet Union ceased to exist on 31 December 1991, Russia emerged as the largest and most influential successor state.[1] Russia has approximately three-fourths of the former Soviet Union's land mass and half of its population. It succeeded the Soviet Union as the largest nation in the world in land area, possessing over 70 per cent more territory than the world's second largest nation. Russia possesses most of the valuable raw materials and much of the industrial base of the former Soviet Union. By agreement, it will be the only nuclear power among the Soviet successor states. No one questioned it when Russia assumed the former Soviet Union's seat on the United Nations Security Council.

The fourteen other Soviet successor states are not unimportant. Ukraine has 52 million people, some of the best agricultural land in the former Soviet Union, and a significant industrial base. Kazakhstan is the second largest successor state after Russia in land area. It is four times the size of Texas and has abundant mineral resources. But Russia dominates the region of the former Soviet Union. The future of that region depends to a large extent on what happens in Russia. The final chapter of the demise of the former Soviet system will be written primarily in Russia.

Russia's years of independence have seen daunting economic difficulties, accompanied by sharp political strife and unexpected political reversals. The political conflict reached a crescendo when President Yeltsin ordered the shelling of the parliament in October 1993. The lull that followed was short-lived. Two months later the voters filled the new parliament with a majority of Yeltsin opponents, and the president–parliament conflict began anew. The December 1993 election marked the resurrection of the Communist Party from its seemingly final burial two years earlier. After two more years of economic hardship, along with a brutal war in Chechnya, in December 1995 the Communist Party emerged as the leading political force in the newly elected parliament, and a Communist return to power in Russia seemed a real possibility.

The years of political strife have tended to erase the memory of the relatively tranquil mood that prevailed when Russia first became independent at the end of 1991. The remarkable fact about the first days of independent Russia was the political unity of its elite. Yeltsin and his followers controlled all of the important institutions in the country, and initially they faced virtually no significant political opposition. Yeltsin was the popularly elected president. The parliament, particularly its Congress of People's Deputies, held a great deal of power under the constitution which Russia inherited from its former status as a republic of the Soviet Union. But Yeltsin's hand-picked successor, Ruslan Khasbulatov, was chairman of the parliament. Khasbulatov had earlier stood by Yeltsin in defending the White House against the abortive coup of August 1991. This was the same parliament which had, in 1990, chosen Yeltsin as its chairman. Two months before Russia's independence, on 1 November 1991, this parliament had overwhelmingly voted to grant President Yeltsin the power to rule by decree in the area of economic reform.[2] The third branch of Russia's federal government, the constitutional court, was also run by Yeltsin supporters.

The unity of the power structures in Russia at that time derived from widespread agreement within Russia's elite about the direction of economic and political change. They wanted to sweep away the remaining features of the Soviet state socialist system and replace it with democratic capitalism, more or less on the Western model.[3] This is just what Yeltsin was seeking to do. The Communist Party as an organization had been banned, and most of its former cadres were now jockeying for position in the new order. Enterprise directors were worried about how successful their individual firms would be in the new market conditions, but they could not help but be tantalized by the prospect of becoming the owner of a privatized enterprise – as some had already prematurely become through "spontaneous" privatization, as we saw in Chapter 7.

Opposition did exist in the country, but at the end of 1991 it was scattered and marginalized. Some individual Communists rejected the new political direction, but they could muster little support, as the small size of their forlorn demonstrations indicated. Anti-Western nationalists worried over the shrunken size of the new country and its strongly pro-Western orientation, but they had little power. Unrepentant Communists and nationalists were found in the parliament, but together they made up a small minority of the deputies at the start of 1992.

However, by the middle of 1992 increasingly sharp conflicts began to course through Russian politics. The conflicts arose primarily from the particular policy adopted by the Yeltsin government for building a market economy, a policy known popularly as "shock therapy," or "neoliberalism."[4] This policy soon produced effects in Russia which stirred up sharp and ever-growing divisions in the society. Formerly close allies turned into bitter opponents, and President Yeltsin became locked in conflict with the parliament, which had previously been his main base of support. In October 1993 the conflict became a violent one, as Yeltsin used armed force to dissolve the parliament. But this failed to resolve the conflict, which took new forms after October 1993 as the opposition grew more radical.

In addition to shock therapy, Yeltsin's autocratic style of rule has been a second source of political conflict in Russia. Some of his friends ended up enemies, not because of any fundamental disagreement about the best future for Russia, but in reaction to being personally frozen out of a share of the power in the new system. Yet ultimately Yeltsin's increasingly anti-democratic methods are not explained primarily by his personal past as a provincial Communist Party boss. Rather, they are a logical accompaniment to the strategy of economic change he adopted.

In Part III we examine the process of economic and political transformation which took place in Russia after it gained independence upon the disintegration of the Soviet Union. Chapter 9 explains what shock therapy is and how it came to be adopted in Russia. Chapter 10 examines how Russia's economy and people have fared under shock therapy and explains why that policy has not performed as its advocates had promised. Chapter 11 shows how the effects of shock therapy gave rise to sharp, and changing, political conflicts in Russia, producing a growing trend toward authoritarian rule by President Yeltsin and also a rebirth of the Communist Party. Chapter 11 also considers possible future economic and political directions for Russia. The particular strategy that the Russian leadership adopted for building a capitalist market system – shock therapy – not only generates sharp political conflicts, but it threatens to undermine the very aims which the Russian leadership had hoped to achieve. As a result, whether Russia will succeed in building a system that is either capitalist or democratic remains in doubt. Finally, Chapter 12 considers the lessons that can be drawn for the future of socialism from the Soviet experience, from the demise of the Soviet system, and from its aftermath.

Chapter 9

Shock therapy

The shock therapy strategy of economic transformation, which independent Russia adopted, is often identified with a trilogy of specific economic policies: liberalization (that is, freeing) of prices, stabilization of the economy through monetary and fiscal policies,[1] and privatization of state enterprises. But shock therapy is actually broader than that. Shock therapy's name derives partly from one of its most important features: the call for a very rapid transformation of the economy. The huge job of transforming the state socialist system into a capitalist market system was to be carried out as rapidly as possible – within a few years. An entire set of radically new policies were to be introduced simultaneously rather than in sequence.[2]

Advocates of this approach used vivid imagery to promote it, such as the adage, "You can't leap across a chasm in two jumps."[3] Adages aside, several arguments were given for moving rapidly to transform the economy. Moving slowly would require a lengthy period in which the system would be a hybrid of the old state socialist system and the new capitalist market economy. Such a hybrid, it was asserted, cannot work well. Second, it was claimed that history shows gradual transitions do not work, as evidenced by the failed efforts during 1985–91 to gradually reform the Soviet economy. Third, moving rapidly was held to be necessary in order to make the process of transformation irreversible as soon as possible. This was motivated by a fear that the advocates and beneficiaries of the old system might soon mount an effective effort to turn the clock back.

A second feature of the shock therapy strategy, in addition to the emphasis on a rapid transition, is the very limited role assigned to the government in actually creating the new capitalist market system. The government's basic contribution was to abolish the old central planning system, privatize its assets, and draft a new legal framework appropriate to markets and private property. It was left to private initiative to create the new market relations and restructure existing businesses, with little government guidance or regulation of the process. This feature of shock therapy is based on the belief, advocated by free-market economic theorists, that a market economy will spring up more or less automatically if the state simply gets out of the way. A market economy is viewed as the "natural" or "normal" state of the economy in human society, which fails to exist only when state actions prevent it from operating. Furthermore, many Western economists believe that state guidance or regulation of markets is more likely to do harm than good.

Along with the calls for rapid transition and limited government management of the process, shock therapy proposes a specific set of economic policies for the transition period. While the above-mentioned trilogy of liberalization, stabilization, and privatization are important elements in this set of measures, the entire list is longer than that. The main specific measures proposed by shock therapy are the following:[4]

1 Liberalization of prices
2 Macroeconomic stabilization
   (a) Reduction of government spending to achieve a balanced budget
   (b) Strict limits on the growth of money and credit
3 Privatization of state enterprises
4 Abolition of the remaining elements of central allocation of resources
5 Removal of barriers to free international trade and investment

The first item on the list, price liberalization, meant the freeing from state control of both retail and wholesale prices, leaving their determination to the interaction of supply and demand in markets. This was also supposed to include a very special and important price – the ruble's exchange rate against other national currencies. The government was to give up controlling the exchange value of the ruble, allowing it to "float," as the expression goes, meaning that its value would be determined by supply and demand in a free currency market.[5]

Item 2 in the list, macroeconomic stabilization, was aimed at curtailing inflation. It had two main parts, one involving the government budget and the second the money and credit policy of the central bank. A large deficit had opened up in the federal budget during the last years of the Soviet Union, and this was to be quickly eliminated. Large reductions were called for in virtually every category of public spending, including military spending, subsidies to state enterprises, social programs, education, and public investment. The second part of stabilization policy called for the central bank to sharply reduce the growth of money and credit. The banking system obtained funds to lend largely from the central bank, so the central bank was in a position to directly restrict credit availability to enterprises simply by curtailing its loans to the banks.

Item 3, the privatization plank, called for immediately turning small enterprises into private businesses. While it was recognized that medium-size and large enterprises could not be privatized as rapidly, shock therapy called for immediate "denationalization" and "commercialization" of such firms. This meant their conversion from state property into joint-stock corporations and their redirection from plan-fulfillment, as under the old system, to profit-seeking. At first the state might be the major shareholder, but as soon as possible the state's shares were to be transferred to private holders, thus completing the privatization process. Privatization was to include the banking system as well as the non-financial sector, with the exception of the central bank.

Item 4 is the elimination of the remaining elements of central planning in the economy. While the system of central planning had been largely dismantled by the end of 1991, a few elements of government coordination of the economy remained. The most important of these was a system of state orders, requiring enterprises to produce for the state a given quantity of output. Such remnants of central planning were to be discontinued, leaving market forces as the sole mechanism of coordination for the economy.

Item 5 called for a policy of free trade and capital movement to replace the state-controlled system of the former Soviet Union. Exports and imports of goods and services were to be freed from quantitative restrictions and excessively high tariffs. Foreign investment was to be encouraged, and Russian enterprises and individuals were to be free to invest abroad if they chose. Free trade and investment would be facilitated by achieving a fully convertible ruble, meaning that anyone holding rubles, whether Russians or foreigners, would be free to exchange them for foreign currencies at market-determined rates.

Shock therapy stands in stark contrast to the economic approach of perestroika in every respect. Perestroika sought to reform the Soviet socialist economy, and it attempted to do so in a gradual manner using the state to manage the reform. Despite the common use of the term "economic reform" to describe the shock therapy strategy of independent Russia, it is not at all a strategy of reform in the usual sense of that term. It is a strategy of revolution, in a double sense.

Shock therapy is revolutionary in its goal of replacing the socialist economy with a capitalist market system. But it is also revolutionary in its means, in that the replacement of the old system by the new is to take place as rapidly as possible, with immediate abolition of the old system and immediate creation of the new. No elements of the old system were to be allowed to persist for a time, nor did the plan call for utilizing parts of the old system to help construct the new one.

HOW SHOCK THERAPY WAS SUPPOSED TO WORK

The rationale for immediate price liberalization is based on the economic theory found in any traditional Western economics textbook. According to this theory, free prices – that is, prices set by supply and demand – are the key to economic efficiency and the maximization of consumer welfare. Free prices in a market system act as signals, indicating both how much consumers value a product and how much of society's scarce resources are required to produce it.

Price liberalization in Russia was believed to be the means for overcoming the inefficiencies and lack of attention to consumer wishes which afflicted the old state-run economy. With prices freed from state control, the prices of goods consumers wanted would rise rapidly, making their production more profitable and spurring enterprises to produce more of them. This is known as the "supply response" to a price rise. Unwanted goods would experience price declines and their production would decline or cease altogether. At the same time, with free pricing of productive inputs, enterprises could calculate the true costs of alternative ways of producing a product, and they would have an incentive to select the cheapest method.

However, according to this theory, free pricing could not work without two other changes. Central allocation of resources restricted enterprises' freedom to respond to price signals, and so it had to be fully eliminated for the market to work properly. Second, state-owned enterprises might fail to respond properly to price signals. Enterprise directors might care more about their own job perquisites than the profits of the enterprise. They might prefer the comfort of doing things the way they had always done them to the risks of change in response to market signals. Privatization was deemed necessary to place the control of enterprises in the hands of private owners, whose sole motivation would be maximizing the profits of the business. As the former state enterprises lost their access to state subsidies, those unwilling or unable to respond to consumer wishes would go bankrupt, leaving the field for those prepared to follow the dictates of consumers.

Macroeconomic stabilization policies were called for to counter the inflation which everyone knew would be released when price controls were lifted. As we saw in Chapter 5, the money income of the Soviet population far outpaced the consumer goods available, at state-controlled prices, in the last years of the Soviet Union. As a result, consumers had accumulated very large savings by the end of 1991.[6] Government budget deficits during those years had also pumped money into the hands of the population. This so-called "monetary overhang," together with the current income of the population, was bound to produce a large jump in prices if they were suddenly freed from state control.

The stabilization plan had two parts, budget balance and monetary stringency, but they had the same purpose: to sharply reduce the expansion of money and credit. The Russian budget deficit was financed by printing money, so cutting public spending to eliminate the deficit would remove that source of monetary expansion. If the central bank would then resist the pressure from banks and enterprises for excessive credit, according to this view, the inflation could be quickly choked off.

The belief that the inflation should, and could, be defeated by monetary means was largely inspired by the influential economic theory known as Monetarism.[7] The most influential Western advisors in Russia, such as Professor Jeffrey Sachs of Harvard University, have been strongly influenced by Monetarism. Monetarists believe that the only way to bring inflation under control is through stringent monetary policy. They also claim that such a policy, if carried out correctly, has only a brief and limited negative impact on the level of production in the economy.

The removal of barriers to free international trade and investment was intended to further improve the efficiency of the Russian economy. Freely imported goods were supposed to put competitive pressure on Russian enterprises, forcing them to become more efficient.[8] Removing barriers to capital movement would encourage foreign investment in Russia which, it was believed, would bring much-needed expertise, technology, and financing. Making the ruble a fully convertible currency would encourage imports of both goods and capital, by assuring importers and foreign investors that the revenues they earned in Russia could be freely converted from rubles to foreign currencies.

Thus, all of the elements of shock therapy, except for the stabilization policy, had the aim of stirring the Russian economy into action. They were intended to improve efficiency, increase production of desired goods, and raise the satisfaction of Russian consumers. The budget-cutting and monetary stringency were intended to bring inflation under control. The complete package promised to quickly transform the economic system which Russia inherited from the Soviet era into a prosperous, modern, capitalist market system.

HOW RUSSIA CAME TO ADOPT SHOCK THERAPY

The pro-capitalist coalition which developed in the Soviet Union during 1989–91 was determined to bring capitalism to the country. But no one was sure exactly how to do it. Should it be done gradually, or would a rapid transformation be better?

Advocates of a gradual approach suffered from the obstacle that Gorbachev's perestroika was a gradualist strategy for reforming socialism, at least as far as economic restructuring was concerned. Yeltsin and his close associates did not talk openly about building capitalism; instead, calling for faster reform became an important way to distinguish themselves from Gorbachev. As we saw in Chapter 5, by 1991 the

Soviet economy was rapidly contracting, under the impact of the dismantling of central planning and the weakening of interrepublican economic ties. The idea that some drastic action had to be taken quickly acquired great influence under these conditions.

That still left the problem of exactly what drastic action should be taken. At this point Western economic thought began to play an important role. Harvard professor Jeffrey Sachs had begun advising the new post-Communist government of Poland in 1989. A few years earlier Sachs had developed a set of policies to resolve Bolivia's inflation and foreign debt-repayment crisis, and he adapted those same policies for Poland. Thus shock therapy was born. In 1990 shock therapy was applied in Poland and was widely publicized as the best way to make the transition from state socialism to capitalism. The International Monetary Fund began to promote shock therapy as the right solution for the problems of Eastern Europe. Although Hungary was trying a more gradual transition strategy at the same time, it was the Polish experiment which had a significant impact on the economists close to Yeltsin.

Shock therapy is essentially an application of free-market and Monetarist economic theories to the problem of transforming a state socialist into a capitalist system. We noted in Chapter 4 the attraction many Soviet economists felt at the end of the 1980s not only to Western economic ideas but to the conservative, free-market version of them. Thus, it is not surprising that the Russian economists who were close to Yeltsin found the shock therapy strategy appealing.

As the Soviet central government progressively weakened after the failed coup of August 1991, Yeltsin faced the opportunity, not just to criticize Gorbachev's economic policies, but to chart a new course for Russia. In the fall of 1991 Yeltsin's aide Gennady Burbulis introduced economist Yegor T. Gaidar to Yeltsin. Burbulis and Gaidar shared a background as orthodox Communists, before converting to liberal democratic ideology. Burbulis had been a teacher of Marxism–Leninism. As noted in Chapter 7, Gaidar had been an editor at both *Kommunist* and *Pravda*, although he was not among the most prominent economists in Moscow.

While other leading liberal economists in the Soviet Union, such as Grigory Yavlinsky, were hoping to preserve the Union in some form, Gaidar favored a strategy of Russia going it alone. He indicated to Yeltsin his belief that Russia could, and should, develop its own plan for economic transformation, independent of the rest of the Soviet Union. This appealed to Yeltsin and Burbulis. Yeltsin made the youthful Gaidar his main economic advisor.[9] It is believed that Gaidar wrote the famous speech Yeltsin made to the Russian Congress of People's Deputies on 28 October 1991.[10]

Yeltsin made two important points in that speech. First, he argued that Russia should follow an independent course of economic transformation, which signalled that he did not intend to work toward preserving the Union. Second, he outlined a set of economic measures that amounted to an endorsement of shock therapy for Russia. He called for freeing all prices by the end of the year, privatization of both industry and land, large reductions in state spending, and a tough monetary policy. He stressed the need to move quickly on these measures.[11]

Yeltsin promised quick results from these bold new policies. Defending the call for immediate price deregulation in his speech to the Congress, he stated:

> To make a switch to market prices in one motion is a severe, forced, but necessary measure...Everyone will find life harder for approximately six months. Then prices will fall and goods will begin to fill the market. By the autumn of 1992, as I promised before the [June 1991 presidential] elections, the economy will have stabilized and people's lives will gradually get better.[12]

If Gaidar did indeed write the speech, it appears that he accepted the optimistic view of Western shock therapy advocates that any negative effects from the stringent monetary and budget policies would be brief.

Some of Yeltsin's supporters may have harbored doubts about how well shock therapy would work. But it had come highly recommended by Western economists and the prestigious International Monetary Fund. It was assumed that Western economists know the most about capitalism, including how to build it. Thus, the deputies to the Russian Congress put aside any doubts they may have had and approved Yeltsin's economic plan by a lopsided vote of 876 to 16, as well as overwhelmingly voting him the power to make economic changes by decree.[13] This vote demonstrates the implausibility of the later popular view that the Russian parliament of 1992–93 was dominated by hard-line Communists and nationalists. Why would hard-line Communists and nationalists vote not only for a capitalist future but for a Western-inspired plan intended to get there as rapidly as possible?

Some nationalists later complained that the Western powers, operating through the International Monetary Fund (IMF), had forced shock therapy on Russia. While a succession of IMF visiting teams of Western economists had indeed supported shock therapy for Russia, it is clear that they did not have to twist any arms. Russia's shock therapy program was designed under the direction of Yeltsin's own economic advisor, Yegor Gaidar, with little opposition at the time from other liberal Russian economists. Parliamentary speaker Ruslan Khasbulatov, who later became a leading opponent of Yeltsin's policies, apparently had no qualms about shock therapy at first. In October 1991 the IMF managing director, Michel Camdessus, met with Khasbulatov in Moscow to discuss economic policy. Khasbulatov, himself a professional economist, with a reputation as a strong-willed person not known to feign agreement, reportedly expressed strong support for Camdessus's shock therapy approach, including the controversial tough monetary and fiscal policies.[14] Later, in 1994, Khasbulatov even claimed that he had had to persuade an initially reluctant Yeltsin to support privatization, a key component of shock therapy.[15]

When the IMF held a series of meetings with Gaidar and other Russian government leaders in the fall of 1991, they found the Russians already enthusiastically in support of shock therapy. At the first meeting with an IMF visiting team of Western economists in early November 1991, Gaidar laid out his proposal for rapid liberalization, stabilization, and privatization. The meeting was a meeting of minds, not a tug-of-war.[16]

Some differences did develop between the IMF and the Russian leadership during the following months, but they were over the details of implementation of shock therapy, not the policy itself. For example, Gaidar refused, over IMF objections, to include oil in the price liberalization of 2 January 1992. Gaidar reportedly agreed that freeing all prices was desirable but warned that, if oil prices were freed immediately, political pressures would force the government to provide enormous subsidies for agriculture and urban households to cover the greatly increased cost of tractor fuel and home heating oil, which would break the stabilization objectives of the shock therapy program.[17]

THE IMPLEMENTATION OF SHOCK THERAPY

The easiest part of the shock therapy program to implement was price liberalization. Originally promised before the end of 1991, it was postponed to 2 January 1992, the first working day after the formal dissolution of the USSR. Around Christmas Day preceding that date, Russian economics minister Andrei Nechaev expressed concern to an IMF visiting team of economic specialists that prices might double, or go up by even more, in the first month of free pricing. Thomas Wolf, an American economist and member of the IMF team, reportedly reassured him, predicting that prices should rise by only 70 per cent in January.[18]

On 2 January, all across Russia state controls were removed from 80 per cent of wholesale prices and 90 per cent of retail prices.[19] The price jump that followed far exceeded the IMF specialists' predictions. In one month retail prices rose by a factor of 3.5, while producer prices jumped nearly 5-fold.[20]

In February 1992 the Russian government and central bank, working with IMF specialists, issued a policy statement called the Memorandum of Economic Policies, which embodied the entire shock therapy program. It envisioned freeing nearly all remaining controlled prices, achieving a zero budget deficit by year-end (later reduced to a deficit of 5 per cent of GDP),[21] a sharp reduction of subsidies to enterprises, tight credit, commercialization followed by privatization of state enterprises, elimination of state orders, and commitment to a convertible ruble. The following month the IMF endorsed the Memorandum, and the next day US President George Bush and German Chancellor Helmut Kohl announced a $24 billion aid package for Russia.[22] At the end of April, Russia was formally admitted to membership in the IMF. The Russian shock therapy experiment was now under way.

When an economic policy fails to perform as advertised, a debate inevitably arises as to whether the policy in question was ever really strictly followed. Advocates typically argue that the policy has worked better than most people realize while simultaneously complaining that the policy was never really followed. Such a debate surrounded shock therapy in the years following January 1992.

While shock therapy was not followed to the letter in the pristine form in which it emerged from economic theorists' pens, the Russian government made a determined effort to pursue the basic outlines of that program. For the first six months of 1992, the program was followed quite rigorously. This generated enormous economic and political pressures which led to later modifications in the program. But, despite some departures from the original targets, Russia's economic policy conformed, in its essentials, to the shock therapy prescriptions from 1992 through the time this is written (the end of 1995).[23]

Despite many calls for reinstituting price controls on some goods, this did not happen. Instead, more and more such controls were lifted over time, leaving fuel as the only major exception. The system of state orders, which was the last important element of central allocation of resources, was discontinued in 1992.

Government spending was slashed by some 40 per cent in real terms in the first quarter of 1992, realizing a budget surplus of 0.9 per cent of gross domestic product for that quarter by one measure.[24] For the year as a whole, government spending fell to 38.7 per cent of GDP in 1992, from its estimated rate of 47.9 per cent of GDP in 1991, as Figure 9.1 shows. During 1993–94 spending remained at about 35 per cent of GDP, falling even further in the first half of 1995. By 1993 Russia's public spending as a share of GDP was comparable to the figure for the United States of 34.5 per cent for that year.[25]

In the last years of the Soviet Union, tax revenues fell sharply. As Figure 9.1 shows, the Russian government was unable to significantly increase tax revenues relative to GDP, and after 1993 they even fell below the level of 1991, the chaotic last year of the Soviet Union. As a

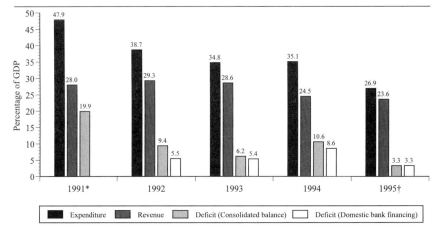

Figure 9.1 Russian government expenditure, revenue, and budget deficit (percentage of gross domestic product)
Source: International Monetary Fund 1992b, p. 70; 1995b, pp. 5, 21.
*Estimated.
†Estimated, for first six months of 1995.

result, despite the large spending reductions achieved by the government, it was not able to fully eliminate the budget deficit after the first quarter of 1992.

Measuring the budget deficit is a tricky business. Several different measures are published, each based on a different definition of the deficit. The deficit based on the consolidated balance, which is the difference between the expenditure and revenue flows for the consolidated budget, is not the best measure for judging the effectiveness of deficit reduction as part of the shock therapy strategy. Rather, the most appropriate measure for this purpose is the deficit based on domestic bank financing. Both measures of the deficit are shown in Figure 9.1. The aim of cutting the budget deficit as part of the shock therapy strategy is to reduce the growth in the money supply, and it is the deficit based on domestic bank financing that indicates the effect of a budget deficit on the money in circulation.

In 1992 and 1993 the deficit based on domestic bank financing was very close to the IMF's revised target of 5 per cent of GDP, as Figure 9.1 shows. The deficit rose to 8.6 per cent of GDP in 1994, due almost entirely to falling tax revenues rather than rising spending. In the first half of 1995 the IMF target was fully met. Thus, the Russian government did follow the shock therapy plan of sharply reducing its spending, and it more or less achieved the IMF deficit target for the first two years. After lapsing somewhat in 1994, it got back on course in 1995.

One of the methods used to achieve these large reductions in government spending has been the policy of refusing to spend as much as the legislature appropriates or even to fulfill the spending commitments which the executives branch itself has made. The treasury simply refuses to spend more than the revenues received plus any additional financing available. This policy, which was codified in a presidential edict on 21 December 1993, has caused a severe problem for enterprises and other institutions in Russia which receive payments from the federal treasury.[26]

The Russian central bank's monetary policy was extremely strict at first. While consumer prices rose by 520 per cent during the first three months of 1992, the money supply was allowed to rise by only 32 per cent.[27] The real value of the money supply had been reduced by 79 per cent in three months. The economic consequences of this remarkably tight monetary policy will be discussed in Chapter 10. These consequences generated political pressures which led to some policy easing. During the second half of 1992, money grew faster than prices. Nevertheless, as Figure 9.2 shows, for all of 1992 consumer prices rose at an average monthly rate of 31.2 per cent, while the money supply rose at only 17.7 per cent per month. For each year shown in Figure 9.2 the money supply grew more slowly than prices.[28] In the conditions of rapid inflation that Russia experienced, this is the best indicator that monetary policy was tight, as the shock therapy program demanded.[29]

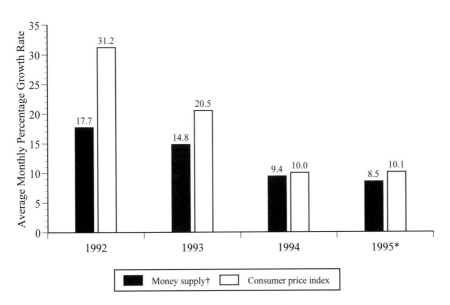

Figure 9.2 Growth in the money supply and consumer prices
Source: International Monetary Fund 1993: 88,100; 1995a: 73, 98; 1995b: 8, 26.
*First six months of 1995.
†Ruble broad money.

Thus, in both branches of stabilization policy, fiscal and monetary policy, the shock therapy prescriptions were followed reasonably closely.

Privatization moved more quickly than had been expected. Most small state enterprises were privatized quickly during 1992. In the second half of 1992, the government began turning medium-size and large state enterprises into joint-stock corporations. In late 1992 and early 1993, 148 million privatization vouchers were distributed to the population, to be used to purchase shares in the newly created corporations. However, only about 18 per cent of the corporate shares were sold through open voucher share auctions.[30] As of 1 July 1994, 74 per cent of the privatizations of joint-stock corporations had taken place through employee purchase.[31] By mid 1994 about two-thirds of state and municipal enterprises had been privatized by one method or another.[32]

The legal form of Russian enterprises was thus rapidly shifted from state to private ownership. According to official statistics, by year-end 1994 non-state enterprises accounted for 78.5 per cent of industrial output and 69.9 per cent of industrial employment.[33] While the government has continued to provide various subsidies to enterprises, the amount has fallen steadily, going from 23.9 per cent of GDP in 1992 to 10.0 per cent in 1993.[34]

Russia followed the shock therapy prescription in the most important areas of foreign trade and investment policy. Russia liberalized its import regime in January 1992 and even temporarily eliminated all import tariffs. Tariffs were imposed after July of that year, but there were no import quotas and almost no licensing restrictions for imports. The IMF happily remarked that Russia's "import regime has been almost completely free of restrictions."[35] The Russian government has sought to welcome foreign investment, although significant obstacles remained.[36] The system of government-controlled multiple exchange rates for the ruble gave way to a single market-determined rate by July 1992 and current-account convertibility of the ruble was achieved by November of that year.[37]

Russian exports have been subject to licensing restrictions, quotas, and centralized export procedures. While shock therapy called for all-round free trade, unrestricted imports were stressed much more than exports. In any event, export restrictions have had limited effects in practice, because of weak enforcement by the government. This is even more true with respect to capital export by Russians; while there have been restrictions, they have been widely evaded.

The shock therapy strategy has been in force in independent Russia for four years, as of this writing. This is a long enough interval to allow an assessment of how it has worked. To this we now turn.

Chapter 10

The results of shock therapy

Shock therapy was applied in Russia for the four years following 2 January 1992. It was supposed to bring about a rapid transformation of the Russian economy, building an efficient, technologically progressive, consumer-oriented, prosperous capitalist market system. What has actually happened over this period? Has shock therapy worked in the manner that its advocates had predicted? Who has gained and who has lost from this policy?

Free pricing was supposed to encourage increased output – the expected "supply response." An International Monetary Fund report in April 1992 saw "evidence of a supply response to the price liberalization" in the appearance of small-scale street traders in Moscow, many of whom were offering household possessions for sale to make ends meet.[1] Store shelves in Moscow and St Petersburg did rapidly fill up with a wide variety of goods for sale, a development cited with approval by the Western media. However, this did not result from any upturn in production. The only increase in supply came from an influx of previously unavailable imported goods. The sudden surplus in the markets was due, not to increased supply, but to a drastic drop in consumer purchasing power as rising prices placed many goods beyond the reach of most households.[2]

Rather than a positive supply response following the price liberalization, the official data on economic output show that the reverse happened. Russia experienced a severe four-year-long decline in production after shock therapy was introduced, a decline that still had not ended as of the end of 1995.

Figure 10.1 shows the decline in several indicators of overall economic activity in Russia during 1990–95. Macroeconomic data are problematic in any country, having many problems of interpretation.[3] However, they do provide some indication of the direction and magnitude of economic growth or decline.[4] While Russia's economy was already contracting in 1991, the decline accelerated after shock therapy began in January 1992, as the data in Figure 10.1 show. The rate of decline, measured by gross

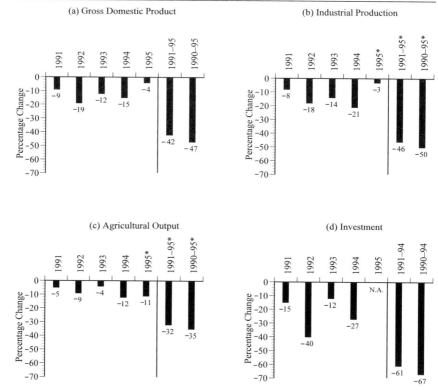

Figure 10.1 Percentage change in macroeconomic indicators for Russia
Source: Statisticheskoe obozrenie 1995: No. 4, p. 9; International Monetary Fund 1993: 85, 1995b: 1; OECD 1/1995: 94, 2/1995: 102; OMRI Daily Digest, No. 12, Part I, 17 January 1996.
* Through first six months of 1995.

domestic product (GDP) or industrial production, moderated slightly in 1993 and then accelerated again in 1994. In 1995 the declines in GDP and industrial production continued, although at significantly slower rates. During the four years following the introduction of shock therapy, GDP fell by 42 per cent and industrial production by 46 per cent. By comparison, in the United States the four-year economic contraction in 1929–33, which brought the American economy to the low point of the Great Depression, entailed a decline in gross national product of 30 per cent.[5] By this measure, the Russian depression since shock therapy was introduced has been 40 per cent more severe than America's worst economic crisis ever.

Figure 10.1 shows that agricultural output also declined steadily, although generally not as rapidly as did GDP or industrial production.

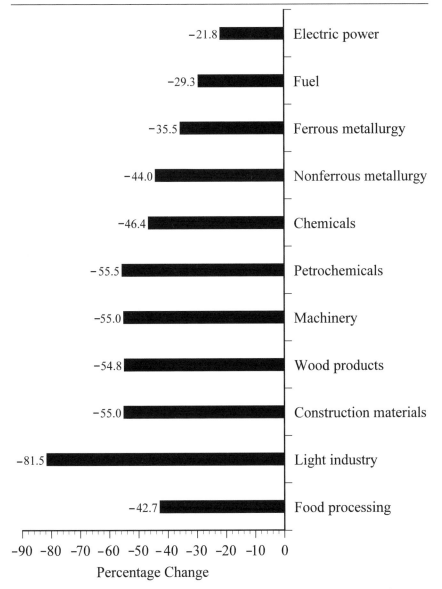

Figure 10.2 Percentage change in real gross industrial output by sector, 1991–95*
Source: International Monetary Fund 1995b: 2.
*Through first six months of 1995.

Investment suffered a near-total collapse, falling by two-thirds during 1990–94. This threatens a bleak future for Russian industry.

Aggregate output data give only a rough approximation of the condition of a national economy, since a single number cannot fully capture the performance of an entire economy. Such aggregate data can some-times hide widely divergent trends in different sectors. Because of this, it is useful to supplement aggregate data by looking at trends for indi-vidual economic sectors and individual products. Tables 10.1 and 10.2 and Figures 10.2 and 10.3 show that the severe depression portrayed by the aggregate data in Figure 10.1 is no statistical mirage.

Table 10.1 and Figure 10.2 show the output performance of the eleven sectors of Russian industrial production. As Figure 10.2 shows, during the shock therapy period from 1992 through 1995 all of the sectors experienced large declines in output.[6] Only electric power and fuel declined by less than one-third. Light industry – which includes textiles, clothing, and leather goods – suffered the worst decline of the group.[7] As Table 10.1 shows, in 1995 the four metal and chemical sectors finally began to grow and fuel nearly stopped declining.

Table 10.1 Percentage change in real gross industrial output by sector (minus sign means rate of decrease)

Sector	1991	1992	1993	1994	1995[a]
Electric power	0.3	− 4.7	− 5.3	− 8.8	− 5.0
Fuel	− 6.0	− 7.0	− 15.0	− 10.0	− 0.6
Ferrous metallurgy	− 7.4	− 16.4	− 16.6	− 17.4	+ 12.0
Nonferrous metallurgy	− 8.7	− 25.4	− 18.1	− 9.0	+ 0.8
Chemicals	− 8.3	− 22.6	− 19.9	− 20.0	+ 8.0
Petrochemicals	− 3.0	− 19.4	− 24.9	− 35.0	+ 13.0
Machinery	− 10.0	− 16.2	− 16.6	− 33.0	− 4.0
Wood products	− 9.0	− 14.6	− 18.7	− 30.0	− 7.0
Construction materials	− 2.4	− 20.4	− 17.6	− 27.0	− 6.0
Light industry	− 9.0	− 30.0	− 23.4	− 46.0	− 36.0
Food processing	− 9.5	− 16.4	− 9.2	− 17.0	− 9.0

Source: International Monetary Fund (1995b, p. 2)
Note: a First six months of 1995

The data available on individual industrial products do not show a single major product for which output rose over the period 1991–95.[8] Figure 10.3 shows the percentage decline in the physical quantity of output of a sample of producer and consumer products, arranged from smallest to largest percentage decline over the four-year period. Note that the two food products in Figure 10.3, vegetable oil and flour, which are consumer necessities, show declines of over 40 per cent. Only for natural gas has the decline been modest, at 7 per cent. Table 10.2 shows that only in the fourth year of shock therapy, 1995, did some of the products in the sample show increases in output (natural gas, steel, mineral fertilizer, paper, and chemical fibers and threads).

The price inflation unleashed by shock therapy was not only faster than had been predicted but also much more difficult to contain. Before

Table 10.2 Output volumes for selected products

Product	1991	1992	1993	1994	1995[a]
Natural gas (billions of cubic meters)	643.4	641.0	618.5	561.1	600.0
Passenger cars (thousands)	1,030	963	956	799	785
Steel (million tons)	77.0	66.9	58.1	48.8	51.6
Petroleum (million tons)	462.3	399.3	353.5	312.7	306.8
Mineral fertilizer (million tons)	15.0	12.3	10.0	7.5	8.9
Paper (thousand tons)	4,765	3,604	2,882	2,214	2,775
Vegetable oil (thousand tons)	1,165	994	1,137	793	678
Flour (million tons)	20.5	20.4	17.2	12.7	11.6
Cement (million tons)	77.5	61.7	52.2	37.2	36.9
Refrigerators and freezers (thousands)	3,710	3,184	3,485	2,626	1,764
Chemical fibers and threads (thousand tons)	529	474	349	197	220
Washing machines (thousands)	5,541	4,289	3,863	2,100	1,325
Cotton textiles (million square meters)	5,295	3,294	2,324	1,508	1,225
Television sets (thousands)	4,439	3,672	3,975	2,161	979
Tractors (thousands)	178	137	89	29	22

Source: International Monetary Fund (1995a, p. 66), *Statisticheskoe obozrenie* (1994, Nov.–Dec., pp. 13–22; 1995, No. 4, pp. 13–22; 1995, No. 12, pp. 12–20)
Note: a Estimate based on first eleven months of 1995

1991 there was little open inflation in the Soviet economy. Soviet consumer price inflation was less than 2 per cent per year in the 1980s and 5.6 per cent in 1990.[9] Figure 10.4 shows the inflation performance since 1990.[10] As central planning was dismantled during 1991, the authorities allowed consumer prices to rise in several steps, going up by a total of 160 per cent during that year, or 8.3 per cent per month. After most prices were freed in January 1992, consumer prices rose by 2,500 per cent over the course of 1992 (31.2 per cent per month). Inflation gradually slowed over the following three years, but in the last three months of 1995 consumer prices were still rising at 4.1 per cent per month, or 63 per cent on an annual basis.[11]

By the end of 1995, consumer prices had risen by a factor of 1,411 compared to year-end 1991 and by a factor of 3,668 compared to year-end 1990. A ride on the metro, Moscow's subway system, which cost 5 kopeks (0.05 rubles) in 1991 had risen to 400 rubles by June of 1995. A kilogram of beef rose from 2 rubles in Moscow shops in January 1991 to 3,187 rubles in June 1994.[12] While, except for January 1992, Russia kept below the traditional hyperinflation demarcation of 50 per cent per month, the persistent rapid inflation undermined the hopes for economic recovery, as we shall argue below.

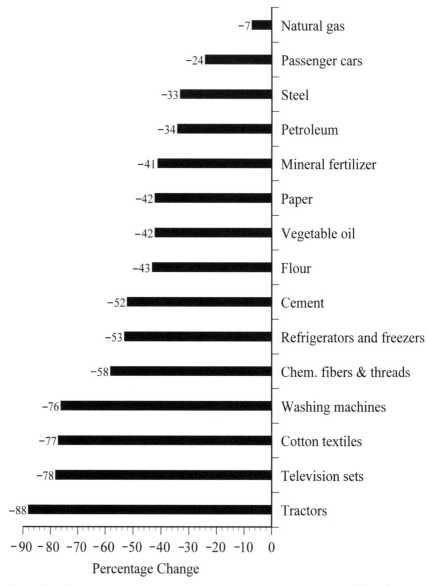

Figure 10.3 Percentage change in output volumes for selected products, 1991–95
Source: See Table 10.2.

The combination of depression and rapid inflation sharply decreased the real incomes of Russian wage earners and pensioners.[13] In the face of rapid price increases, the ruble rate of pay of Russian workers also rose. The average monthly wage and salary earnings in Russia rose from 297

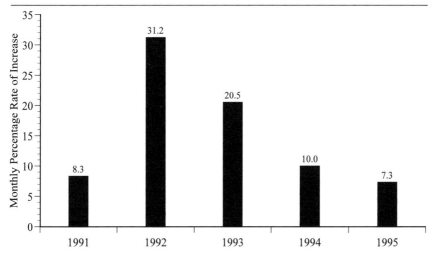

Figure 10.4 Average rate of consumer price increase per month during 1991–95
Source: OECD 1/1995: 92, 2/1995: 100; *Statisticheskoe obozrenie* 1995: No. 12, p. 44; OMRI
Daily Digest, No.4, Part I, 5 January 1996.

rubles in 1990 to 595,000 rubles by October 1995.[14] While a 2,000-fold rise
in ruble earnings over five years may sound impressive, it was not
enough to keep pace with rising consumer prices. As a result, real

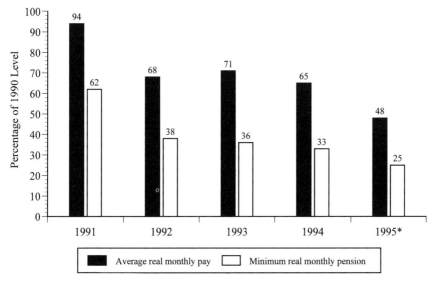

Figure 10.5 Real pay and pensions (base year 1990 = 100)
Source: International Monetary Fund 1993: 88, 91, 1995a: 73, 78; *Statisticheskoe obozrenie* 1995: No. 4, pp. 45, 59, 61, 1995: No. 12, pp. 44, 60, 62.
* For monthly pay, January through October 1995; for pensions, January through September 1995.

(inflation-corrected) earnings fell over this period. Indeed, this was virtually inevitable given the sharp decline in GDP and industrial production, since falling real output generates falling average real income for those producing it.

As Figure 10.5 shows, in 1992 average real pay fell to 68 per cent of its 1990 level, climbed slightly in 1993, and then fell to 48 per cent of the 1990 level by 1995. The actual decline in real pay was probably greater than these figures suggest, because during 1992–95 it became increasingly common for employees of large enterprises and other institutions, including state employees, to be paid late – sometimes with a delay of many months – or to be paid only a fraction of the official wage. In March 1995 unpaid back-wages in industry, agriculture, and construction alone amounted to an estimated 5.3 trillion rubles, which was about 22 per cent of the total wage and salary bill of Russia that month.[15]

Pensioners experienced even larger declines in real income than did wage earners. The minimum pension fell steadily, reaching 25 per cent of its 1990 level in 1995. The average real pension (not shown in Figure 10.5) also fell more steeply than real pay, declining to 43 per cent of its 1990 level in the first 9 months of 1995.[16]

By early 1995 the real earnings of the average Russian worker had fallen by more than 50 per cent. Many people survived by buying only what is absolutely necessary – food, primarily. Many Russian urban residents spent their weekends cultivating potatoes and other vegetables at their small dacha outside the city, to survive the collapse of their money income. Rents and utilities remained relatively inexpensive. Purchases of clothing were postponed as long as possible, and new household durables became out of reach for the average Russian family.

One would have thought that the huge decline in production would bring massive unemployment, yet this did not happen. The official unemployment rate, which counts only those who register as unemployed, had reached a mere 3.0 per cent of the labor force in June 1995. Goskomstat, the Russian government statistical agency, also publishes a broader estimate of unemployment, which includes those who are unemployed but fail to register. This latter estimate reached 7.7 per cent by June 1995.[17] Even the higher figure is surprisingly low, given the scope of the production collapse. An unemployment rate of 7.7 per cent in the US would signal only a moderate recession. One might have expected the 47 per cent drop in GDP since 1990 to produce a decline in employment of a nearly similar magnitude, which would mean an unemployment rate of 30 to 40 per cent, but this has not happened.

While most Russians have suffered a large drop in their living standard, they have not experienced the massive unemployment which had been widely feared. The reason is that Russian enterprises, despite the privatization of most of them, have not behaved like traditional capitalist businesses. Although demand for their products has collapsed, enterprise directors have laid off few workers. Traditional practices do not die easily, and the long tradition of paternalism toward employees has made Russian enterprises reluctant to cut costs by slashing the work force. Enterprises have kept workers on the payrolls, and continued to pay them (often with a delay), despite the absence of much work for them to do.

In 1992, the first year of shock therapy, many Russian enterprises responded to the sharp drop in sales, not by laying off workers, but rather by simply "producing for the warehouse," as the expression goes. Many observers reported factory warehouses bulging with unsold goods that year. The national product accounts confirm such casual observations – in 1992 increases in inventories amounted to a remarkable 16 per cent of GDP.[18] By contrast, in the United States, increases in inventories are typically a fraction of 1 per cent of GDP. This phenomenon shows up most dramatically for certain individual products. For example, in 1992, while only 400,000 passenger automobiles were sold in Russia, 1 million were produced. That same year factories produced 3.2 million refrigerators and freezers despite selling only 1.1 million.[19]

Not everyone fared badly in the new Russia. As income was redistributed by the rapid inflation, there were gainers as well as losers. A CBS News poll conducted in Russia in May 1995 found that, while 66 per cent of the respondents said they were worse off than they had been before perestroika began, 16 per cent said they were better off.[20] The top officers of some of the new Russian banks became very wealthy. One study reported that, of the 50 richest and most influential members of the Russian business elite, 25 were bankers.[21] Others grew rich through gaining ownership of privatized raw materials firms and automotive enterprises, or by investment in real estate and housing construction. Some politicians are reputed to have become very wealthy, including two successive mayors of Moscow, Gavriil Popov and Yuri Luzhkov.[22] In addition to the new rich, a middle class arose in the main cities, based on professional and managerial jobs in banks and foreign firms, as well as the sale of various specialized services, such as language interpreting and computer consulting, for both Russian and foreign businesses.

The new rich appear to have achieved their status primarily through acquiring pre-existing valuable assets and by buying and selling currencies, stocks, real estate, precious metals, and raw materials. With few exceptions, the new Russian banks have mainly been engaged in trading securities and other assets, rather than acting as intermediaries steering capital to productive activities as Western banks do.[23] As Figure 10.1 showed, little productive investment has taken place in Russia since 1990.

It is widely believed that the new rich have sent large sums of money abroad for safe-keeping. Estimates of the capital flight during 1992–94 range from the $50 billion claimed by the central bank of Russia to as much as $100 billion.[24] Even at the low-end figure, this capital flight exceeds the combined inflow of Western direct investment and official aid during those years, which totalled $19.4 billion.[25] Rather than producing the desired capital inflow, shock therapy has, on balance, prompted a capital outflow from Russia.

A growing gap emerged between the majority, whose living standards dropped rapidly, and the minority who have done well under shock therapy. Figure 10.6 shows the distribution of income among Russian households in 1995, with US income distribution included for comparison. The figure shows the percentage of total income received by the poorest 20 per cent of households through to the richest 20 per cent. The former Soviet system had produced a relatively egalitarian distribution of money income. After only a few years of building a capitalist market system, Russia achieved an income distribution roughly comparable to that of the post-Reagan United States.[26] The top 20 per cent of households in Russia actually had a larger share of total income than in the United States, as did the bottom 20 per cent; the three middle quintiles in Russia had less than their American counterparts.

Another measure of income inequality, the decile ratio, measures the ratio of income received by the top 10 per cent of households to that of

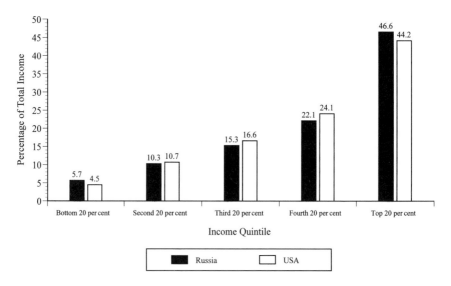

Figure 10.6 Distribution of money income of households in Russia and the USA.
Source: Statisticheskoe obozrenie 1995: No. 12, p. 59; US Census Bureau 1993: p. 463.
The data for Russia are for the first eleven months of 1995 and for the USA for 1991.

the bottom 10 per cent. A study cited in Chapter 2 found that ratio to be 4.5 to 1 for the former Soviet Union in 1967; in 1995 it had reached 13.5 to 1 in Russia.[27]

Some wage and salary earners have done better than others under shock therapy. Figure 10.7 shows changes in the relative wage from 1989 to 1994 in sectors of the economy that experienced unusually large changes, up or down, relative to the economy-wide average wage. Scientists, whose pay had been 20 per cent above the economy-wide average in 1989, experienced a drop in relative pay of about one-third by 1994, while the pay of financial services employees more than doubled relative to the average over the period. Talented young people in Russia now dream about becoming bankers, not scientists, whose low salaries make it difficult for them to make ends meet. Agricultural employees, whose pay was previously just below the average, sank to only half the average rate of pay. The minimum wage fell by two-thirds relative to the average pay, indicating a great drop in the living standards of the lowest-paid workers.

While the private income of the average household dropped sharply, so too did the level of public services. Vacation resorts and summer camps previously available and affordable for average Russians converted themselves into spas for the wealthy. The quality and availability of health care declined sharply as the government subsidy was slashed. In response, many clinics and hospitals reconfigured themselves to provide fee-for-service medicine, while young doctors sought to emigrate.

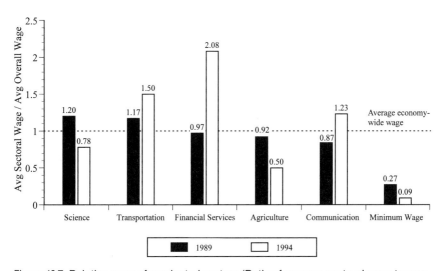

Figure 10.7 Relative wages for selected sectors (Ratio of average sectoral wage to average economy-wide wage)
Source: International Monetary Fund 1995b: p. 14.

Public health services also declined. As a consequence, there have been epidemics of diseases rarely seen in Russia in the past. In the summer of 1993 a cholera epidemic hit southern Russia, and 15,210 cases of diphtheria were recorded in Russia in 1993.[28]

Russian science, one of the most impressive achievements of the old regime, has suffered along with the economy. Research institutes had their budgets slashed and were told to find projects that could be self-supporting. Some of Russia's world-class research scientists have had to spend their summers, not working on their research, but tutoring American high-school students in order to keep groceries on the table.[29] Others have left science to take accounting jobs at banks, responding to the financial incentives suggested by Figure 10.7. In a unique science version of cheap foreign labor, American corporations have hired top-flight Russian scientists to work for them in Russia, at wages that are a small fraction of what they would pay US researchers.[30]

Organized crime in Russia is a favorite media topic.[31] From a serious but peripheral phenomenon in the former Soviet Union, it has emerged as a major force in Russia, although just how powerful it is, no one is certain.[32] A report prepared for President Yeltsin in 1994 found that 70 to 80 per cent of private banks and businesses in major cities were forced to make payments of 10 to 20 per cent of their revenues to organized crime.[33] The head of the Russian Interior Ministry's organized crime section estimated that 20 per cent of Russian bank loans are actually payments to "mafia" organizations.[34]

The mob is certainly visible in Russia and very violent. Organized crime-style slayings, with automatic weapons or bombs, occur frequently. Gang-style violence killed 120 bank employees, including 15 directors, in 1993, and bank offices were subjected to 780 arsons and explosions that year.[35] This moved Sergei Yegorov, president of the Association of Russian Banks, to write a letter to President Yeltsin complaining that "all of society and new financial and entrepreneurial institutions have become the target of well-organized, well-equipped bandits."[36] At least two members of the Russian parliament were murdered during 1994–95, with organized crime believed to be responsible.[37] Any observant shopper at a Moscow street market can spot the suited, tough-looking "mafia" enforcers who patrol the market, discouraging price-cutting and collecting payments from merchants.

Organized crime groups have shown few scruples in the pursuit of valuable assets. It has been reported that some residents of well-located Moscow apartments have been murdered in scams aimed at obtaining ownership of the recently privatized apartments.[38] The power of the mob is suggested by the police practice of wearing masks when arresting organized crime figures.[39] The mob bosses feel no need to hide their identities, but the forces of law and order apparently fear retribution.

Table 10.3 Vital statistics of Russia

Year	Births per thousand of population	Deaths per thousand of population	Natural increase or decrease
1980	15.9	11.0	4.9
1985	16.6	11.3	5.3
1986	17.2	10.4	6.8
1987	17.2	10.5	6.7
1988	16.0	10.7	5.3
1989	14.6	10.7	3.9
1990	13.4	11.2	2.2
1991	12.1	11.4	0.7
1992	10.7	12.2	−1.5
1993	9.4	14.5	−5.1
1994	9.5	15.5	−6.0
1995[a]	9.5	15.0	−5.5

Source: Rossiiskii statisticheskii ezhegodnik (1994, p. 43), Statisticheskoe obozrenie (1995, No. 12, p. 5)

Note: a First ten months of 1995

Any society in which the police rather than the criminals must hide their identities has a serious organized crime problem.

Corruption, the twin of organized crime, has been flourishing in Russia. A large, but unknown, proportion of Russia's raw material exports are believed to be illegal, with payoffs to officials to overlook the lack of an export license. Lenient border guards turned Russia's border with Latvia into a sieve, and, as a result, Latvia managed to export 238,000 tons of nonferrous metals in 1992, although it produces none.[40] Military planes have been found transporting minerals for pay. An academic study of private businesses in Moscow in 1993 found 80 per cent reported that bribes were required to do business.[41] One Moscow businessman, who requested anonymity, told the authors in June 1995 that he was able to obtain a 30 to 40 per cent discount from state-owned suppliers of building materials in exchange for bribes.

Shock therapy has turned Russia from a distorted caricature of the socialism which Marx conceived into an equally distorted caricature of the capitalism which Adam Smith described. There are private businesses, banks, and even stock markets. Yet the outcome so far has been nothing like the new efficient, growing, technologically progressive economy that had been promised.

Perhaps the most troubling statistics in Russia are demographic. Table 10.3 shows Russia's birth rate, death rate, and resulting rate of natural population increase per thousand of population. A variety of factors can cause either the birth or death rate in a country to rise or fall, among them such innocuous factors as changes in the age structure of the population or increased availability of birth-control devices. But the sudden break in both birth and death rates in Russia is clearly due to the vast social and economic changes.

The birth rate, which had been rising in the first half of the 1980s, declined in 1988. Then in 1989, the first year in which the nature of Russia's future course of development was suddenly in doubt, the birth rate fell below the 1980 level. It fell steadily during 1989–93, declining by 36 per cent over that period. It may be that Russians grew so unsure of their future that fewer and fewer were willing to take on the responsibility of having children.

The death rate declined significantly in 1986, then gradually rose back to approximately the 1985 level by 1991. In 1991–94, the first three years of shock therapy, it grew very rapidly, rising by 36 per cent, before registering a small decline in 1995. While demographers do not agree about the causes of this remarkable rise in the death rate during 1991–94, it is unlikely to be a coincidence that it took place during a period in which the majority of the population experienced a sharp decline in real income while funding for both public and private health care dropped. Added to these factors was stress from the disappearance of the world with which the Russian people had been familiar.

The falling birth rate and rising death rate eroded the sizeable natural population increase which Russia had experienced in the postwar Soviet period. In 1992 the population began to decline. By 1994 the rate of decline had shot up to 6.0 per thousand. Such population decline normally occurs only as a result of major wars, epidemics, or famines. The negative population trend particularly affected males. From 1990 to 1994 male life expectancy in Russia fell from 65.5 years to 57.3 years. The latter figure is lower than that for India, Egypt, or Bolivia, and is below that of any other country which reports to the World Health Organization.[42]

WHY SHOCK THERAPY DID NOT WORK AS PREDICTED

There is no evidence that the application of shock therapy is transforming the Russian economy into an efficient, technologically progressive, consumer-oriented, prosperous capitalist market system. The immediate effects have been plummeting production, rapid inflation, impoverishment of the majority, increased inequality, declining public services, growing crime and corruption, and demographic collapse. Over the longer run, Russia is in danger of being deindustrialized, becoming a raw-material-exporting country dependent on imports for obtaining manufactured goods.

It is not surprising that shock therapy failed to produce the benefits promised by its advocates. With hindsight, one can clearly see the various problems with shock therapy, and many of them were apparent to some analysts even before the policy had been introduced.[43] As the effects of shock therapy became known, in Eastern and Central Europe as well as the former Soviet Union, a sizeable literature arose critical of shock therapy.[44]

The disappointing results which followed the introduction of shock therapy in Russia can be explained in a variety of ways. In what follows, we will first discuss the unexpected effects of each of the policy elements of shock therapy, showing how these policies produced the set of economic problems which Russia experienced during 1992–95. This will be followed by a critique of the claim that the best way to transform the former Soviet system was to do so rapidly and with a limited role for the government. Last, we present a case that the basic conception of economic transformation on which shock therapy is based has such serious flaws that, apart from the short-run problems it has engendered, it cannot lead to a successful transition to an industrialized capitalist market system over the long run in Russia.

The problems with the shock therapy strategy in Russia are ultimately of two sorts. First, it failed to take account of the structure of the pre-existing socioeconomic system which Russia inherited from the Soviet days, and as a result it produced very different outcomes from what had been expected. Second, the economic theories underlying shock therapy have serious internal flaws, which render this strategy of doubtful effectiveness regardless of the pre-existing economic system in any place where it might be applied. The latter line of criticism involves relatively technical debates among economists. In what follows we will stress problems of the first sort – the mismatch between shock therapy and the inherited institutional framework – although some reference will also be made to problems with the underlying theory of shock therapy.

THE INDIVIDUAL COMPONENTS OF SHOCK THERAPY

On p. 162 we listed five main components of shock therapy: price liberalization, macroeconomic stabilization, privatization, abolition of central allocation of resources, and free trade and investment. None of these policies worked in practice in the manner expected. The rapid elimination of the remaining elements of central allocation of resources, rather than allowing market forces to take over, left the economy with no system of coordination at all. The result was economic chaos and declining production. As was noted in Chapter 5 above, the partial dismantling of central allocation during 1990–91, before market relations had developed, was a major cause of the economic contraction in those years. The elimination of the remaining elements of central allocation in 1992 provided one more harmful shock to the already contracting economy, as enterprises had to struggle to create new supply and marketing relations amidst the economic chaos.

Price liberalization, inflation, and the missing "supply response"

Price liberalization, the centerpiece of shock therapy, produced an inflation much more severe and long-lasting than had been predicted. The enormous initial burst of inflation, resulting from the shortage of goods relative to the large monetary savings of the population, had secondary effects which embedded inflation in the Russian economy in a manner that is difficult to root out. As consumer prices leaped up by a factor of three and a half in January 1992, workers mobilized to gain wage increases to chase the galloping cost of living. The rising prices drove the newly freed ruble's value down relative to foreign currencies, sharply raising the ruble cost of imported inputs. Thus, enterprises, after initially raising prices, found their costs sharply rising, as labor, domestic non-labor inputs, and imported inputs all became more expensive.[45] The cost squeeze led enterprises to raise prices again, introducing Russians to a stubborn cost–price spiral.

The inflation was made worse by the highly monopolized economy which Russia inherited from the Soviet days. Russia's giant enterprises faced little competition and did not fear entry into their markets by new rival firms any time soon. Hence, when prices were suddenly freed, Russia's monopolistic enterprises raised prices without restraint.

While Russia experienced the bad side of price liberalization, namely inflation, the good side – the supply response to rising prices – did not materialize. Rising prices were supposed to lead to increased production. Only unwanted goods, whose prices were supposed to fall, were expected to experience production declines. But instead, as we have seen, the output of virtually all goods plummeted together.

Shock therapy caused production to decline throughout the economy by causing a sharp contraction of demand for the goods produced in Russia. As John Maynard Keynes taught the world, the three main components of total demand are consumer demand, investment demand (mainly spending by businesses for plant and equipment), and government spending.[46] Shock therapy, both directly and indirectly, caused all three of the main components of total demand to decline rapidly.

Slightly less than half of Russia's national output had traditionally been sold to households in the form of consumer goods.[47] The sudden price liberalization of January 1992 drove the average real wage down by 28 per cent that year.[48] Most households could afford to buy only absolute necessities, and consumer demand plummeted as a consequence.[49]

The rapid inflation unleashed by price liberalization created a poor investment environment which also worked against any positive supply response. Rapid inflation caused people and institutions that had money on hand to exchange their rapidly depreciating rubles for assets that were expected to hold their real value, particularly foreign currencies, real estate, and minerals. As those with money to invest poured it into such assets, their prices were driven up rapidly. This created opportunities for very high profits from speculation – that is, from buying whatever has a relatively rapidly rising price and reselling it later. Those positioned to do so made quick fortunes. By contrast, investing in the production of ordinary goods and services could not gain such large and quick returns. Russian investors responded to the profit motive, but it did not lead them into much productive investment. Productive investment – that is, the building of new plants or buying of new machinery – appeared to be a poor investment, compared to speculation in currencies and minerals.

Thus, the rapid inflation produced by price liberalization drove down the first two components of total demand, household consumption and business investment. This made a severe depression unavoidable, unless government spending grew by enough to make up for declining private spending.

Macroeconomic stabilization

The anti-inflation policy component of shock therapy required just the reverse of growing state spending. Government spending was supposed to be drastically reduced as part of the shock therapy program – and we saw in Chapter 9 that it was indeed sharply reduced in 1992. With all three major components of aggregate demand falling rapidly, a depression naturally followed. Shock therapy's tight monetary policy worked in the same direction, by making it difficult for enterprises that might want to invest in plant and machinery to obtain funds for that purpose.[50]

To make matters worse, shock therapy's tight fiscal and monetary policies failed to accomplish the intended aim of quickly stopping inflation. Although such policies do tend to dampen inflation over time, one that is roaring ahead with the momentum of the Russian inflation of 1992 is very difficult to stop with the blunt instrument of tight monetary policy. This is particularly so when the inflation takes on a cost–price spiral character and is accompanied by economic contraction.[51] The three months of very tight monetary (and fiscal) policy in the first quarter of 1992 did slow the inflation, but it did so by exerting a severe squeeze on Russian industry.[52]

As Figure 9.2 showed, prices raced far ahead of the money in circulation in 1992, particularly in the early part of the year. By the summer of

1992, enterprises' working capital had fallen far behind the amount needed to stay in operation at the greatly increased prices. That is, they did not have the funds to pay their workers or pay for non-labor inputs, and the central bank's tight monetary policy was preventing them from obtaining the needed funds. Production threatened to grind to a halt.

It is widely believed that political pressure from desperate enterprise directors at that time played a major role in the ousting of central bank president Georgy Matyushkin. In mid-July 1992, Matyushkin was replaced by Victor V. Gerashchenko, who was more sympathetic to the financial needs of Russian industry.[53] Matyushkin's replacement by Gerashchenko was followed by the easing of monetary policy.

As monetary and fiscal policy vacillated between less tight and more tight over the shock therapy years, the inflation rate varied with it. As we saw above, the trend in inflation during 1992–95 was downward, but it had still not been conquered by the end of 1995. The oft-heard claim that, if the Russian government had only been tougher, the policy would have stopped inflation, is both true and misleading. If some imaginary Russian government, unconcerned with, and unaffected by, a rapidly declining economy had rigidly pursued super-tight policies long enough – two years, perhaps – inflation could indeed have been stopped. However, the cost would have been intolerable to any actual government that was at all responsive to its citizens and their economic plight.

Shock therapy's tight public spending and monetary policies carry serious long-term costs for Russia's economy. Scarce and expensive credit have presented a major obstacle to the much-needed modernization of Russian industry. Many Russian enterprises could succeed in domestic, and world, markets, if they could obtain the financing they need to upgrade product quality and develop an effective marketing system. Tight money makes it difficult, if not impossible, to make such improvements.[54]

Government spending cutbacks also damage long-run economic welfare. Russia needs upgraded and expanded systems of transportation, communication, and power, but state spending has been slashed in those areas. The large cuts in support for science undermine Russia's future technological potential. Cuts in education and health-care spending, in addition to their human costs, are reducing the quality of Russia's work force.

The problems of privatization

The Russian government succeeded in privatizing most of Russia's enterprises, but this policy has not brought the expected benefits for the economy. During the several years which it necessarily took to privatize the larger enterprises, they were left with little incentive for economically rational behavior. Once shock therapy was announced, it was known that the big state enterprises making up much of the economy would soon belong to a private owner – but to whom, no one knew. This left little incentive to invest for the future of the enterprise, since it was unknown who would reap the benefits of investment – apart from the workers, who had little influence. This was one more factor driving the collapse of investment.

It is not clear that rapid privatization was necessary to ensure that enterprises would respond to market signals. Restructuring Russia's enterprises, rather than quickly privatizing them, would have been a wiser policy.[55] In many industrialized capitalist countries, a sizeable portion of industry is state-owned. Government-appointed managers have been able to respond quite effectively to market signals in the many successful state enterprises in Canada, France, and Germany.

Handing over industry to private owners does not assure that it will be operated efficiently. There are many factors that determine the effectiveness of an economy; the relative importance of the form of ownership was exaggerated by the shock therapy advocates. One careful study of the effects of the form of enterprise ownership on economic success in the Russian context concluded that it is much less important than the external environment in which enterprises must function.[56] We are not suggesting that it would have been easy to get Russian state enterprises to respond effectively to market signals while keeping them as state firms. However, privatizing them does not solve this problem, since the main obstacles to rational firm behavior lie in the economic environment of the enterprise, not its ownership form.

The policy of rapid privatization imposed high costs on Russian society. Russia had no pre-existing legitimate wealthy class of people who could buy large state enterprises. Under such conditions, it was inevitable that a hasty attempt to place Russia's economic wealth in private hands would end up turning much of it over to well-placed members of the old elite, who had the best connections to those making the privatization decisions.[57] This process deprived Russia's new property ownership structure of legitimacy in the eyes of the population.

Privatization, taken together with the other components of shock therapy, has been the major cause of the rapid expansion of organized crime and corruption. Besides members of the old elite, the other group in society well positioned to gain control of the newly privatized state assets was organized crime. The so-called "mafias" had both substantial funds to invest and the ability to use strong-arm tactics to gain control of enterprises through illicit means. Price liberalization impoverished the majority of the population, including the state employees who were in charge of managing valuable economic assets prior to privatization.

Even the more honest among them suddenly found they could survive only by accepting bribes. Drastic cutbacks in state spending weakened the forces of law and order, while price liberalization deprived them of a living wage; they too become increasingly receptive to offers of bribes. It is not surprising that this set of policies propelled organized crime and corruption to such prominent roles in Russian life.

The limited impact of free trade and investment

Under the new policies of relatively free trade, foreign products quickly displaced many domestic ones in the main cities, as large Western corporations moved in with their superior financial and marketing muscle.[58] While this may have provided some incentive for Russian industry to produce more efficiently, the peculiar nature of the Russian market has limited such effects. The new rich and new middle class are the main market for the import surge. They prefer foreign products and do not object to the high prices most imports carry. The majority of Russians, who have been left with very limited purchasing power, can buy some imported food or small luxuries, but they are largely forced to rely on cheaper domestic goods. Thus, the new imports exert less of the competitive pressure for product improvement or price restraint than had been expected.

Most of Russia's industry cannot yet compete with Western products on an equal footing. Given this problem, turning the country open to relatively free importation is not a wise policy. It is certainly not the policy which today's leading industrial nations – the United States, Germany, Japan – followed in the earlier period when they themselves faced superior foreign competition. All used forms of trade protection to nurture domestic industry, until they became able to compete effectively without such supports.[59]

Russia's declaration of welcome for foreign investment has failed to attract much of it. Besides some investments in oil and other raw materials, and for marketing Western consumer products in Russia, little has been forthcoming.[60] The continuing legal and bureaucratic obstacles faced by foreign investors are undoubtedly part of the reason. But even had these problems been solved, the conditions created by shock therapy did not make Russia an attractive location for the kind of foreign investment that was desired. Rapid inflation, falling production, declining real incomes, and expanding crime and corruption have created an environment that is very unstable, both economically and politically. Foreign investors will not make large long-term investments in any country suffering such conditions. Only quick-profit investments are appealing under such conditions, but what Russia needs is investments in the long-run development of its economy.

RAPID TRANSFORMATION AND THE HANDS-OFF APPROACH

Shock therapy is not just the set of five policies listed on p. 162. It also includes the prescription that the economic transition take place very rapidly and with limited state direction of the process. Three arguments were given for a rapid transition: (1) that a hybrid of the old and the new system could not work; (2) that history shows gradual transitions do not work; and (3) that rapid transition was necessary to prevent a reversion to the old system. None of these arguments is persuasive.

A gradual transition to a capitalist market system would indeed mean a more or less lengthy period in which the system would be a hybrid of the old and the new systems. But far from hybrid economic systems being unworkable, they are typical of real-life economies. No actual economy is a pure form of only one type of economic relation. Modern capitalist systems have major elements of other economic systems within them. A great deal of economic activity in Western Europe and North America is carried out by entities other than capitalist firms for aims other than profit, including the activities of national and local governments, non-profit institutions (hospitals, schools, research institutes, religious organizations), and households. China, which formerly had an economic system similar to that of the Soviet Union, now possesses a private, market-oriented sector about equal in size to the planned, state-owned sector – and this hybrid system, whatever its problems, has had one of the fastest economic growth rates of any major economy over the past fifteen years.

History shows that gradual economic transitions can indeed work. Capitalism first arose in Britain very gradually over a period of centuries. Later transitions to capitalism took less time, but even twentieth-century transitions to capitalism, such as those of South Korea and Indonesia, have taken decades. The building of a highly centralized type of system, such as state socialism, can be attempted rapidly, although even in that case it is a costly method of transition. But a capitalist market system, being relatively decentralized with many independent centers of decision-making and action, necessarily takes a significant period of time to develop.

The belief that a rapid transition was necessary to prevent the old Soviet elite from regrouping and stopping the process was based on a false premise – that the party–state elite was opposed to building capitalism. The great majority of that elite favored capitalism. Ironically, it is the costs and failures of shock therapy that threaten to abort the transition to capitalism.

Shock therapy's laissez-faire approach to transforming the economic system is unrealistic. Some historians believe that capitalism developed in Britain with little state help, although even that is disputed. But there is no dispute that later transitions to capitalism received major support from the power of government. In the United States the federal and state governments played a critical role in fostering capitalist development in the early and mid-nineteenth century. Government subsidized and built canals and railroads, educated the labor force, and protected manufacturers from superior foreign competition.[61]

But the state role was relatively limited then compared to the cases of successful market systems that developed in the late nineteenth and twentieth centuries. In Japan, and later in South Korea, the government played a very active role, encouraging the development of technologically advanced industries and providing subsidies, investment guidance, and a well-educated labor force. In South Korea the government prevented capital from leaving the country, ensuring its domestic reinvestment.[62] Activist governments have guided and regulated the market, steered credit to key sectors, provided subsidies to important industries, forced the restructuring of lagging industries, and used public ownership for certain key industries. Such methods, rather than running counter to developing a market economy, seem to be essential to the success of that process today. Even if Russia were prepared to wait for the several centuries which it required for capitalism to develop in Britain, it is unlikely that, in the face of powerful industrialized capitalist economies as competitors, Russia could ever achieve an industrialized capitalist economy without an activist state to guide its development.

THE BASIC FLAWS IN SHOCK THERAPY

The designers of shock therapy showed a deficient understanding of the process by which a capitalist system develops.[63] They also paid little attention to the features of the pre-existing economic system in Russia, which was to be transformed.[64] As a result, they operated with a conception of the transition which, apart from the particular problems considered above, was fundamentally flawed. These flaws make it unlikely that, even if the serious short-run problems that shock therapy has caused could be overcome, this strategy could attain the long-run goal of building an efficient and effective capitalist market system in Russia.

The shock therapists' basic conception of the transition was to take the existing productive entities of the Russian economy and, by privatizing them and freeing them from state control and support, to transform them into normally-functioning capitalist enterprises. But economic institutions such as productive enterprises are not isolated entities. They develop and function within a particular socioeconomic system. The belief that the giant state enterprises of Russia could, with relative speed and ease, be turned into normal capitalist firms ignores the symbiosis between individual units of production and the economic system as a whole.

With only a few exceptions, Russia's enterprises had been built from the ground up within the Soviet state socialist system.[65] These enterprises developed with a structure and set of traditions that were appropriate to functioning within the Soviet state socialist system. Several features of the Soviet system, and the enterprises within it, render the shock therapy strategy of transforming those enterprises into normal capitalist firms a problematic one.

First, the state socialist system was a very centralized one in which outputs, inputs, and production processes were closely specified for enterprises all across the Soviet Union from the center in Moscow. Given this coordination system, there was a logic to building very large enterprises with only one or two sources producing each major product. The typical enterprise, particularly those that made producer goods, were much larger than Western firms. Had they been operating in a market context, they would have possessed enormous monopoly power.[66]

Second, the system was based on a very high degree of vertical integration. Each enterprise would receive a given input from the same, typically single source year after year. In a sense, the individual enterprises were not really separate, independent entities like capitalist firms. They were more similar to the subsidiaries of a single capitalist firm – except that Soviet enterprises had even less autonomy from the central planner than the typical subsidiary of a large capitalist firm has from its parent company. It would be only a small exaggeration to say that there was really only one enterprise in the Soviet Union. It was a vast, interconnected, integrated production machine.

Third, the "company town" pattern that developed under this system was different from what one finds in a capitalist market system. Many towns and cities in Russia are dominated by a single enterprise, or a few enterprises. The chief enterprise in the city provides not only employment but most of the social services for the city.

Fourth, the top managers of large enterprises were, to a significant extent, paternalistic protectors of the employees of the enterprises, and often of the citizens of the city or town as well. A manager's career was not advanced by keeping wages down, firing redundant workers, or suggesting the plant move to another location. Soviet managers had to balance demands from above for good performance with the need to protect employees' interests.

Fifth, since the system worked by direct allocations of goods and services from one enterprise to another, the financial side of the system remained very underdeveloped and largely passive. Financing was automatically provided for planned activities and played no independent role in directing production.

These five features of the state socialist system help explain the poor prospects for long-term success of the shock therapy transition strategy. The monopolistic structure of the economy bequeathed by state social-ism creates a severe problem for the plan to turn enterprises into private, autonomous entities. The expected benefits of competitive markets – minimizing costs, quick response to consumer wishes, and rapid intro-duction of new technologies – are unlikely to materialize in a system characterized by monopolistic rather than competitive markets. Privatiz-ing the large enterprises simply turns them from public into private monopolies. Because the economic concentration is largely based on monopolistic plants or plant complexes, rather than multi-firm enter-prises, there is no easy way to restructure the existing productive units to make them competitive.

By cutting enterprises off from cheap credits and state subsidies, it was hoped that market forces would drive firms that were inefficient or produced unwanted products out of business, while rewarding those that effectively met consumer wishes. But the vertical integration and company-town structure of the inherited Russian economy make this an unworkable means of achieving efficiency. If one inefficient producer goes bankrupt, it will drag down many other enterprises, efficient or inefficient, that depend on it for either supplies or markets.[67] And down with the bankrupt enterprises go the towns and cities dependent on them for employment, tax revenues, and public services.

A scheme of market-determined bankruptcy, given this economic structure, is not appropriate. The pressure to keep the pipeline of credits and subsidies open, even if at a reduced rate of flow, was very difficult to resist. The state has little choice but to keep enterprises afloat through direct subsidies and cheap credit. This suggests that it is not possible to turn enterprises into autonomous entities as the privatization program envisions, as well as rendering tight monetary and fiscal policy ineffect-ive as a means to rein in the inflation.

As we saw above, the paternalistic role of enterprise managers pro-duced an unexpected response to the collapse in demand in 1992. While capitalist managers would have drastically cut their work forces, Rus-sian managers were unwilling to do so, even maintaining production well above what was justified by demand. If the now privatized Russian enterprises do bring in new managers who are prepared to drastically prune work forces and increase the pace of work to the capitalist stand-ard, it would be likely to set off sharp conflicts at the workplace. Russian workers are accustomed to the old paternalistic relations, and they would be likely to respond to such a drastic change in their treatment at work with a fight that would interfere with economic recovery.

Amidst the declining economy, enterprise managers have cast around for ways to make their enterprises healthy. Many that were left making products no longer needed, whether military equipment or exports to former trading partners, have come up with good ideas for new products. Others produce goods of enduring demand but must upgrade capital equipment and build a marketing capacity. Yet all of this would require a lot of capital, which the underdeveloped Russian financial system is unable to provide.[68] However bright the future prospects might be for a tractor plant, or an optics plant ready to shift from military to civilian products, little capital is available for restructuring.

Shock therapy's underlying conception of capitalist transition is inconsistent with the economic system which Russia inherited from Soviet state socialism. This transition does not start from a blank slate but from a pre-existing system. It may be that the only effective way to build a capitalist market system out of a state socialist system is to mimic capitalism's original process of development, which took place at the edges of, and in the interstices of, a pre-existing economic system. Capitalist economic activity did not begin in Europe by converting large feudal manors into capitalist corporations. The remnants of feudalism – peasant and artisan production – kept supplying the basic goods society needed, while capitalist forms gradually developed and, over time, supplanted the earlier forms.

The analogue of this process suitable to the current conditions of the Russian economy would require retaining large enterprises in state hands, under central control, with low controlled prices, while encouraging the formation of new non-state, market-oriented enterprises. Such an approach might be called a "two-sector strategy" in that it seeks to develop a new private market sector alongside the old state sector, rather than converting the state sector into a private market sector. By keeping state-produced inputs cheap and providing low-cost credit for start-up enterprises, favorable conditions could be created for starting new consumer-goods firms.[69] This is the strategy China has successfully followed since the late 1970s.

Apart from a policy of relatively free trade and investment, China did not apply any of the key features of shock therapy in its effort to convert its economy to a market system. There was virtually no privatization – state enterprises were kept under state ownership and control. There was no sudden price liberalization – state enterprises continued to sell at controlled prices. Central planning was retained for the state sector of the economy. Rather than slashing state spending, various levels of government poured funds into improving China's basic economic infrastructure of transportation, communication, and power. Rather than tight monetary policy, ample credit was provided for expansion and modernization. The state has sought to gradually develop a market economy over a period of decades, and the state has actively guided the process.

The development of a market economy in China, which began in the late 1970s, took place *de novo*, outside the state sector; China encouraged the creation of new non-state enterprises while providing a stable and supportive economic environment for one to develop. The non-state sector grew at the remarkable rate of 17.6 per cent per year during 1978–90.[70] By 1994 over half of China's industrial output came from the non-state sector.[71]

The Chinese experience with this very different development model is not all positive. It has produced environmental degradation, periodic bouts of moderate inflation, and growing inequality of income. There is reportedly widespread resentment of members of politically well-connected families who have used their connections to become rich through business endeavors. And in the political realm, there have been no moves toward democracy or respect for individual rights in China.

But in contrast to Russia's shock therapy approach, the Chinese model has produced very rapid economic growth and rising living standards for most of the population.[72] Many Russians are chagrined to read about Russian nationals who travel to China, once its more backward junior partner, to find employment in restaurants and nightclubs there. A key difference between the Russian and Chinese strategies for building a market system is that China's strategy was designed by Chinese leaders who, whatever their faults, paid close attention to the features of their pre-existing economic system and understood the advantages of a gradual, state-managed economic transition.[73]

Despite the economic success of the Chinese strategy, it is not surprising that, when the Soviet Union disintegrated, Russia did not follow a similar strategy. A gradual, state-directed approach ran counter to the neoliberal ideas that had become dominant among Yeltsin's advisors. The Chinese strategy appeared to be linked to continuing rule by a Communist Party, while Russia had abolished Communist rule. However, as we shall see in Chapter 11, the economic problems produced by shock therapy soon made some influential Russians begin to consider whether the quite different Chinese approach might have some useful lessons for Russia.

Shock therapy has had a sharply different impact on different groups in the Russian population. A small minority grew rich, a somewhat larger minority improved their economic position somewhat, while a significant majority became worse off. Even for the groups that made up the original pro-capitalist coalition, the effects of shock therapy have been uneven. Some members of the former party–state elite grew rich, while others saw their state salaries melt away under the impact of inflation. Some enterprise directors in the raw-materials and metal-processing sectors were able to gain ownership of valuable enterprises, while managers in other sectors of the economy struggled to keep their enterprises from collapsing. The intelligentsia enjoyed their newly won intellectual freedom, but many of them suffered a significant cut in their living standard and were alienated by the extreme commercialization of society.

The disequalizing impact of shock therapy would not have caused so much social unrest if the policy had delivered the overall economic benefits that its advocates had promised – that is, if the costs to the economy as a whole had been mild, or at least brief, followed quickly by economic expansion and improved efficiency. A growing gulf between rich and poor is less destabilizing if it is accompanied by general economic progress and a rising living standard for the majority. But the combination of a growing gap between the lucky few and the unfortunate majority, plus rapid decline for the economy as a whole, represents a sure prescription for political instability.

The enormous costs that shock therapy has imposed threaten to undermine the entire process of transition to capitalism in Russia. The irony of the situation is difficult to miss. The victorious pro-capitalist coalition had swept to power in Russia at the end of 1991. It had totally vanquished its opponents. It had strong support from the Western powers. It appeared that nothing stood in the way of returning Russia to the capitalist fold, from which it had strayed nearly 75 years earlier – nothing, that is, except an economic policy so flawed that, after a mere twelve months of its implementation, the political climate began to change radically. Soon Moscow, long the center of anti-Communist jokes, was circulating a new type of joke, which went as follows: "What has one year of capitalism in Russia done that 70 years of Communism were unable to accomplish?" The answer: "It has made Communism look good." The bitter truth of that joke for millions of ordinary Russians makes the future direction of Russia highly uncertain.

Chapter 11

Russia's political evolution

Russia has been the scene of unrelenting political conflict since six months after its emergence as an independent state. This conflict has been driven by the direct and indirect consequences of the decision to build a capitalist system in Russia, and particularly by the adoption of shock therapy to achieve that aim. The interpretation of the Soviet demise presented in Part II above, and particularly the role of the party–state elite in that process, helps explain the course of Russian politics since 1991. This chapter examines several important developments in Russia from this perspective: (1) the emergence of the so-called centrist opposition and the Yeltsin government's response to it; (2) the shift over time in the balance of power within the opposition from centrists to Communists; (3) the trend toward an increasingly authoritarian regime in Russia. Perhaps the most remarkable development in these years has been the re-emergence of the Communist Party as a serious contender for power. We conclude the chapter with a consideration of possible future courses of economic and political development in Russia.

THE CENTRIST OPPOSITION

As we observed in the introduction to Part III, initially the plan for shock therapy in Russia faced no significant opposition. In November 1991 the Russian Congress of People's Deputies had, by overwhelming votes, approved Yeltsin's economic strategy and granted him special powers to implement it. However, as Deputy Prime Minister Gaidar and his group of Western-oriented liberal economists began to work out the specific plans for price liberalization and sharp cutbacks in state spending and credits, some officials began to worry. In December 1991 Vice-President Alexandr Rutskoi delivered a sharp criticism of the youthful, inexperienced Gaidar and his team, ridiculing them as "small boys in pink shorts and yellow boots."[1]

When prices were freed on 2 January 1992, Russians were shocked by the enormous price jumps and the corresponding collapse of their buying power. Two weeks later parliamentary chairman Ruslan Khas-bulatov criticized the government for "uncontrolled, anarchic, nonregu-lated price increases," adding that the manner in which the initial reforms were carried out was "completely unwise and far from realistic." Yet at this time Khasbulatov's criticism did not venture beyond the framework of shock therapy, complaining that the government had failed to achieve a true liberalization of prices.[2]

Despite these early criticisms, shock therapy enjoyed a honeymoon of sorts for the first three months of 1992.[3] But by April many of Russia's enterprise directors had begun to worry about the long-term effects of shock therapy on their industries. In June a new organization called Civic Union was formed, under the leadership of Arkady Volsky.[4] Volsky had close contacts with many enterprise directors, and Civic Union became known as the representative of the enterprise directors' concerns about the direction of economic policy. It became the most influential organization in a new "centrist" opposition to the govern-ment's economic policy, so called because it positioned itself between supporters of shock therapy and the marginalized Communist and nationalist opposition.

The centrist opposition did not oppose the goal of building a capitalist market system. They objected to shock therapy as the means to reach that goal. They argued that shock therapy was destroying Russian industry and impoverishing its people. They called instead for a gradu-alist strategy which would retain a strong role for the state in stabilizing the economy, directing the transition process, and protecting people's living standards.

Civic Union economists developed a series of alternative economic plans which resembled the Chinese strategy in many respects.[5] They called for reintroduction of state orders to reverse the collapse of indus-trial production; state support for large enterprises to help them restruc-ture to become more competitive; gradual rather than rapid privatization, with emphasis on conversion to ownership by managers and workers; greater state support for pensioners and low-wage workers; and wage–price controls rather than tight monetary policy to stop inflation.[6]

During 1992 the centrists attracted a great deal of media attention, both in Russia and the West. As Russia experienced rapid inflation, declining production, and falling real incomes for the majority during that year, support for the centrist position grew in the parliament. By the eve of an important meeting of the Congress of People's Deputies in December 1992, the centrists had become a powerful bloc in the Con-gress, claiming the support of about 40 per cent of the deputies. Support for the Communist and nationalist positions had also grown, to about 30 per cent between them, while the supporters of shock therapy had shrunk to about 20 per cent of the deputies.[7] By the end of 1992, parliamentary chairman Khasbulatov had moved to a centrist position. He sought to use the two main opposition blocs, the centrists and the Communists and nationalists, which together were a large majority of the parliament, to pressure Yeltsin into changing the government's economic policy along the lines proposed by the centrists.

The rise of the centrist opposition reflected a division in the previously united pro-capitalist coalition. While most of the party–state elite had supported the building of capitalism, there had never been any certainty among them about the best way to do so. Once shock therapy began to impose heavy costs on Russian industry, a major part of that previously united coalition – particularly the enterprise directors most worried by the industrial decline – began to challenge, not the goal of capitalism, but the means that had been adopted for building it.

It also appears that there was an ideological component to the division which the centrist opposition represented. Kullberg's study of the ideology of the Moscow elite in June 1991, reported in Chapter 7, found over three-fourths of them to favor capitalism. However, she also found that the pro-capitalist majority broke down into two different groups, which she called "Westernizers" and "Moderate Reformers." The former favored both very rapid building of capitalism and very close emulation of specific Western institutions. The latter, while also wanting a capitalist system, expressed more caution about the speed at which the transition should be made, as well as believing that some attention had to be paid to the specific features of Russian history in designing a transition to capitalism.[8] Kullberg found that only one-fourth of the pro-capitalists in her sample were Westernizers, while the remaining three-fourths were Moderate Reformers. The Yeltsin government was dominated by an ideological minority group within the pro-capitalist elite, and it is not surprising that a split emerged once the policy of rapid change began generating high economic costs.[9]

President Yeltsin's response to the centrist opposition

President Yeltsin's response to the growth of the centrist opposition had several facets. First, he and Gaidar condemned the new centrist proposals, as well as those making them. The centrists were characterized as stalking horses for a return to the Soviet past, a view which was quickly taken up by the Western media. They lumped the centrists together with the Communist and nationalist opposition, viewing them as working together to bring back the old Soviet system. This was a serious misrepresentation of the centrist position. The Civic Union program supported continuing privatization and marketization. They did not oppose a capitalist future for Russia. Their disagreement with Yeltsin and Gaidar was about means, not ends.

While denouncing the centrists' views, Yeltsin brought a series of industrial managers and centrist political figures into the government during 1992–94. In early June 1992 Yeltsin named three former industrial managers, who were viewed favorably in Civic Union circles, to high positions in the government. Vladimir Shumeiko, former director of a large measuring instrument factory in Krasnodar, was named a first deputy prime minister; and Viktor Chernomyrdin and Georgi Khiza were named deputy prime ministers. In July 1992 Yeltsin named to the post of central bank president Viktor V. Gerashchenko, who appeared to be sympathetic to the centrist critique of shock therapy. In December of that year, facing growing pressure from the parliament, Yeltsin dismissed Acting Prime Minister Gaidar and replaced him with Chernomyrdin.

Chernomyrdin's appointment as prime minister was overwhelmingly approved by the centrist-dominated Congress of People's Deputies. His background as a manager, and then minister, in the Soviet gas industry, rather than as an academic economist, pleased the centrists. Chernomyrdin expressed support for a market economy, but "without impoverishing our people...No reform will work if we destroy industry completely...We should...pay serious attention to production."[10] These were the very themes that the centrists had been stressing.

In September 1993 Gaidar returned to the government as first deputy prime minister in charge of the economy, as Yeltsin's confrontation with the parliament was escalating toward the October armed confrontation. But in January 1994, following an opposition victory in the December 1993 parliamentary elections, Yeltsin again shuffled his government in favor of former industrial managers who appeared sympathetic to the centrist position. Gaidar again left the government, along with Finance Minister Boris Fyodorov, who had been a leading proponent of strict adherence to the shock therapy guidelines.[11] Former Soviet minister of metallurgy Oleg Soskovets was named first deputy prime minister. It appeared that the only leading shock therapy advocate left in a top post was Deputy Prime Minister Anatoly Chubais, the chief architect of the privatization program.

Chernomyrdin, who had served as prime minister since December 1992, appeared to emerge with greatly enhanced power in January 1994. On 20 January Chernomyrdin gave a widely publicized speech that seemed to signal a sharp change in policy. He announced that "The period of market romanticism is over." While stating that "Russia will not return to the past" and is not "turning away from a market economy," he observed that "the mechanical transfer of Western economic methods to Russian soil has done more harm than good." He promised an activist policy to combat the collapse in production and living standards.[12]

Some changes did occur in government policies over these years. In the area of foreign policy, Yeltsin shifted toward a more nationalist rhetoric, following a strong showing by nationalists in the December 1993 parliamentary elections. Yeltsin became much more critical of the proposed extension of NATO membership to Eastern European nations. He became less willing to automatically assent to Western political demands.

Minor adjustments in the government's economic policy took place after mid-1992, as was noted in Chapter 9.[13] But despite the major personnel shifts and the talk of new policies, no significant move away from the shock therapy strategy is discernible during 1992–95. Neither after Chernomyrdin first became prime minister in December 1992, nor after Chernomyrdin's hand was apparently greatly strengthened in January 1994, was shock therapy significantly modified, much less abandoned. No big changes were forthcoming in either monetary or fiscal policy. No expansion of public investment or support for industry took place. No wage–price controls were introduced. The government continued to refuse to pay much of its own debt to enterprises. No expansion of social protection programs was instituted to help workers or pensioners. And rather than slowing privatization, in 1994, despite Chernomyrdin's dramatic speech seemingly criticizing shock therapy, a major part of the medium-size and large state enterprises were privatized. By the end of 1994, Gaidar and Fyodorov had concluded that Chernomyrdin, whom they had once viewed as a deadly enemy of capitalist economic transformation, was not so bad after all.

Why did the Russian government stick with shock therapy?

Why, despite the changes in personnel in Yeltsin's government, did shock therapy remain in place? One possible explanation is that Yeltsin retained the real power. While the parliament possessed significant potential power during 1992–93 under the old constitution, Yeltsin managed to retain control of economic policy-making.[14] After the parliament was dissolved in October 1993, Yeltsin ruled unchallenged for a few months, until a new constitution was approved and a new parliament elected in December. As will be explained below, the new constitution gave nearly all of the real power to the office of the president.

Thus, it may be that Yeltsin responded to public pressure for a change in economic policy by making purely cosmetic changes in the cabinet and making minor changes in rhetoric, while preventing Chernomyrdin from making any substantive change in economic policy. This may be part of the explanation, but it still requires an answer to the question, why did Yeltsin want to stick with shock therapy, in the face of the economic problems it was causing and its growing unpopularity?

A second interpretation explains the continuity of economic policy by claiming that no workable alternative policy existed. While some advocates of shock therapy, such as Jeffrey Sachs and Anders Åslund, insisted that it worked quite well, other advocates admitted that it caused many problems, but insist that any alternative would have been worse. Thus, so this argument goes, once entrusted with governing, the new cabinet, being realistic, had no choice but to continue with shock therapy.

But the centrist critics insisted that an alternative gradual transition policy was possible and would entail far lower social costs. Such an alterative has been followed, with much success, in China, although whether a similar policy would work in Russia cannot be known for certain.[15] The fact that, despite the personnel changes and the promises of new policies, none has even been tried, suggests that the Chernomyrdin government either did not really want to make such changes or was prevented from doing so by Yeltsin.

Although Yeltsin appears to have no deeply held economic views of his own, it was his early adoption of the strategy of rapid transition to capitalism that originally propelled him into power. Despite its negative effects for the majority of Russia's people, and the danger it poses for the future of Russian industry, shock therapy has greatly benefited a small but influential part of the population, which has a strong interest in the continuation of the policy. Bankers have made fortunes from speculation in the conditions created by shock therapy.[16] Exporters of raw materials have done likewise. Both legal and illegal operators in the milieu created by shock therapy fear that the conditions for their further enrichment might disappear if Russia shifted to a more gradual, state-managed course of economic development. Furthermore, the major Western powers, particularly the United States, have been willing to overlook almost any transgression, as long as Yeltsin has held steadfastly to the shock therapy approach.

Thus, it is not surprising that Yeltsin has refused to abandon shock therapy, despite the problems it has caused. To abandon it would alienate the new rich and the Western powers, both of which have been key supporters of Yeltsin.[17] But why have industrial managers with links to the centrist coalition agreed to serve, and remain, in a government whose policies they had publicly opposed?

The enterprise directors, whose opposition to shock therapy formed the basis of the centrist challenge, appeared to grow increasingly divided over time. Whenever centrist leaders convened large meetings of enterprise directors during 1992, they found far from unified opposition to shock therapy among those who attended.[18] It was noted in Chapter 10 that shock therapy did not affect all enterprise directors in the same manner. The oil and gas, minerals, and metal sectors of Russian industry, though harmed in the short run by shock therapy, still faced promising futures. And even for industrial managers in sectors whose futures looked bleak, there was still the appeal of rapid privatization. As privatization proceeded during 1993 and 1994, and enterprise directors found that outside takeovers were rare and instead the old managers were becoming the new independent masters of industry, the opposition of many of them appeared to wane.[19]

Yeltsin followed an effective strategy, when bringing industrialists into the government, of choosing individuals from those sections of Russian industry which were not doing so badly under shock therapy. While the great bulk of Russian industry declined severely, a few sectors declined to a lesser degree.[20] The output of natural gas, Chernomyrdin's home base, fell by only 7 per cent during 1991–95,[21] and Chernomyrdin's family is reputed to have become very wealthy from the privatization of Gazprom, the natural gas monopoly.[22] First Deputy Prime Minister Oleg Soskovets came from the steel industry, some parts of which have done relatively well by selling inexpensive, good-quality steel in foreign markets.[23]

The influence of the centrist opposition was always based more on the powerful institutional position of its main political base, in the directorships of large enterprises, than on widespread support from ordinary voters. The elections of December 1993 and December 1995 showed the centrists to be quite weak at the polls (discussed below). Yeltsin found it possible to win over some leading centrist figures by offering them the comforts and power of government positions. Even Arkady Volsky ended up in the Yeltsin government.[24]

THE SHIFTING POLITICAL OPPOSITION

Russian politics gave birth to a very large number of political parties, movements, and coalitions. Their political positions have covered every imaginable viewpoint. However, most Russian political organizations have been small, and many of them faded away soon after their appearance.

Three main political groupings arose during 1992. One was the supporters of Yeltsin and Gaidar, a grouping that was often called "radical reformers" or "democrats" in the media. The centrists, described above, were the second main grouping. The third major grouping was a coalition of Communists and nationalists.

At first the centrists appeared to be the strongest part of the political opposition. The Communists were widely viewed as discredited by the failures of the old regime, and few analysts thought they had any political future. Their demonstrations were attended largely by elderly people angry at the demise of the Soviet Union. They were further weakened by the splintering of the once-unified Communist Party. The Russian branch of the CPSU had been banned in Russia, and several different parties vied for the political mantle of socialism.[25] Several nationalist organizations also became active although, like the Communists, they were regarded as politically marginal.[26]

Although Communists and nationalists had traditionally been adversaries, in 1992 many individuals and groups from the two camps began to hold joint demonstrations, and an alliance formed. Despite their many differences, they were united in their opposition to the pro-Western policies of the Yeltsin government, the collapse of Russia's industrial base under the impact of shock therapy, and the loss of superpower status.[27] This coalition, which took a variety of organizational forms over time, was referred to by their opponents as the "red–brown" alliance.

In February 1993, following the lifting of the ban on the former Communist Party in Russia, it was revived under the name Communist Party of the Russian Federation (CPRF). Led by Gennady Zyuganov, it quickly became the dominant left-wing organization, claiming the allegiance of most former members of the CPSU in Russia who wanted to belong to a Communist party. In the course of 1993 the CPRF moved away from the alliance with the nationalists and toward a more traditionally left-wing position, with a mixture of moderate Russian patriotism and socialist appeals.[28] The CPRF soon emerged as by far the largest political party in Russia, claiming hundreds of thousands of members spread across every region of the country.

The first year of shock therapy had propelled the centrists into the leading role in the political opposition, with the Communists and nationalists decidedly the junior partners. But after one more year of shock therapy, the roles of the two main parts of the opposition reversed. It may be that the centrists never had as large a popular base among the voters as many analysts had thought. It appears that, as the years of a rapidly declining economy wore on, the population came to look increasingly favorably on the more radical wing of the opposition. When the first parliamentary elections were held in independent Russia on 12 December 1993, the centrists were edged aside by resurgent Communists and nationalists. Two years later, on 17 December 1995, the centrists declined further while the Communists emerged as the dominant political force in the parliament.

A very large number of parties ran in the 1995 elections, but in both elections there were five main groupings. One was pro-government parties, which supported the shock therapy economic policies and the pro-Western foreign policies of the Yeltsin government. A single major party represented this position in the 1993 election, Gaidar's Russia's Choice, while in the 1995 election a second pro-government party, Our Home is Russia, led by Prime Minister Chernomyrdin, was also on the ballot. A second grouping represented the centrist position. In the 1993 election the Democratic Party of Russia and the Women's Party had centrist programs; by the 1995 election the Congress of Russian Communities had emerged as the most publicized centrist party.

A third position, between the pro-government and centrist parties, was occupied by Grigory Yavlinsky and his followers in both elections. Yavlinsky's "Yabloko" party criticized various aspects of the government's policies but was more cautious than the centrists about proposing clear alternatives.[29] The CPRF was the main Communist party, but there were other parties closely allied to it in both elections. The Agrarian Party was widely viewed as the rural branch of the CPRF, and Power to the People was formed in 1995 by well-known individuals close to the CPRF, including former Soviet prime minister Nikolai Ryzhkov. In both elections Vladimir Zhirinovsky's misnamed Liberal Democratic Party offered an extreme nationalist, anti-Western position to the electorate.

In both elections half of the 450 seats in the lower house of the new parliament, called the duma, were filled based on votes for political parties.[30] The other 225 seats were filled by geographical constituency elections, which could be contested by members of a party or independents. Figure 11.1 shows how each of these five groupings fared in the two elections, with part (a) showing the results of the vote for political parties and part (b) showing the allocation of the total 450 duma seats among the five groupings.[31]

Before the 1993 election the media had predicted a victory for Gaidar's Russia's Choice party. However, it won only 15.4 per cent of the party vote and 16.9 per cent of the duma seats. The surprise victor was the extreme nationalist Zhirinovsky, whose Liberal Democratic Party confounded the predictions and won 22.8 of the party vote. Zhirinovsky had enlivened the campaign with a string of outrageously belligerent statements and been rewarded with the largest vote.[32] The CPRF and their Agrarian Party allies also did well, winning 12.4 per cent and 7.9 per cent of the party vote respectively, for a total of 20.3 per cent. The centrist parties did not perform as well as had been expected, winning only 13.6 per cent of the party vote and 9.3 per cent of the duma seats. Yavlinsky's party won a small but respectable following.[33]

The new duma was dominated by opponents of the government, but the Communists and nationalists had emerged as the strongest forces within the opposition, with the centrists decidedly weaker. However, the alliances were complex and shifting. Despite Zhirinovsky's bombastic rhetoric, his party often supported the government on budget issues, and Zhirinovsky was one of the few duma supporters of the military campaign in Chechnya that Yeltsin launched in December 1994.

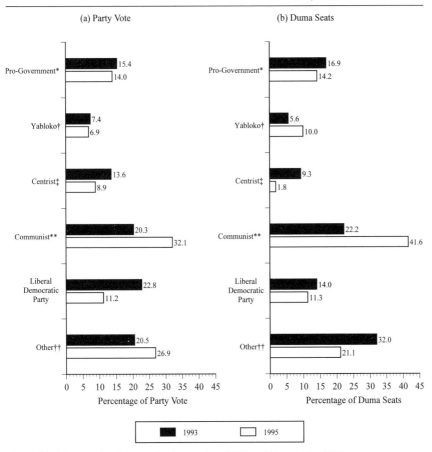

Figure 11.1 Duma election results, December 1993 and December 1995
Source: Central Election Commission (for 1995, preliminary final report dated 29 December 1995).
* For 1993 Russia's Choice; for 1995 Our Home is Russia and Democratic Choice of Russia.
† For 1993 Yavlinsky–Boldyrev–Lukin bloc; for 1995, Yabloko.
‡ For 1993, Democratic Party and Women of Russia; for 1995, Congress of Russian Communities and Women of Russia.
** For 1993, CPRF and Agrarian Party; for 1995, CPRF, Agrarian Party, Communists–Working Russia, and Power to the People.
†† For party vote, other parties; for duma seats, other parties and independents.

In 1995 President Yeltsin instructed his prime minister, Viktor Chernomyrdin, to build a new pro-government party, Our Home is Russia. Thus, in the December 1995 election Russians had two major pro-government parties to choose between, Gaidar's Democratic Choice of Russia and Chernomyrdin's new party.[34] As the election approached, with Yeltsin's popularity suffering from the economic decline and the war in Chechnya, the media this time predicted a strong showing for the new centrist party, the Congress of Russian Communities, led by Yuri Skokov. It won the endorsement of the popular Russian general Alexander Lebed, who was often mentioned as a possible presidential contender.

In the December 1995 campaign Our Home is Russia spent money freely on television advertising, Zhirinovsky came up with new outrageous utterances, and the media kept referring to the likely strong showing of the centrist Congress of Russian Communities. The Communists spent little money, relying mainly on their large organization to spread their message. The result was a big victory for the CPRF, which by itself won 22.3 per cent of the party vote and 34.9 per cent of the seats. As Figure 11.1 shows, combined with its two close allies and a more radical Communist group, the Communists won nearly a third of the party vote and just over 40 per cent of the duma seats. When official duma fractions formed after the election, the CPRF fraction, together with the allied fractions formed by the Agrarian Party and Power to the People, gathered in 221 deputies, just five short of a majority of the 450 deputies.[35]

In 1995 only four parties gained enough votes to pass the 5 per cent benchmark for winning duma seats from the party vote – the CPRF (22.3 per cent), the Liberal Democratic Party (11.2 per cent), Our Home is Russia (10.1 per cent), and Yabloko (6.9 per cent). Gaidar's Democratic Choice won only 3.9 per cent of the party vote. No centrist party passed the 5 per cent threshold.

The centrist parties practically disappeared in the new duma, gaining less than 2 per cent of the seats. As Figure 11.1 shows, the two pro-government parties together won fewer party votes and fewer seats in 1995 than Russia's Choice alone had won in 1993. Zhirinovsky's Liberal Democratic Party did not disappear, as some had hoped, but its party vote dropped sharply from its 1993 level. Yavlinsky's party, which had bitterly criticized Yeltsin on Chechnya, emerged somewhat stronger in the duma than it had been before. But the Communists had become the strongest force in Russian politics, well positioned for the presidential race scheduled for June 1996.

Four years of shock therapy had divided the previously unified Russian elite and driven down the living standards of the majority of the Russian population. These developments, along with the other effects of shock therapy described in Chapter 10, led a large share of the electorate to vote for the Communists, whom they had so decisively rejected only five years before.

THE TREND TO AUTHORITARIAN GOVERNMENT

The creation of new democratic institutions in the last years of the Soviet Union played a critical role in the overthrow of that system. The attempted coup of August 1991 was defeated by an elected president of Russia, Boris Yeltsin, and the leaders of the elected Russian parliament. These democratic institutions gave political legitimacy to the opponents of the coup. The defense of the parliament's home, the Russian White House, became the symbol of the defeat of the old order by the new. It proclaimed the victory of democracy over authoritarian rule.

Just over two years later, in September 1993, the same Russian parliament, with the same deputies who had been in office two years earlier, was ordered dissolved by the executive branch of government – but this time it was Boris Yeltsin who ordered the dissolution. The next month tanks attacked the White House, and this was followed by the arrest of the deputies who had resisted the parliament's dissolution. Once again an assault on the White House became a symbol of a changed direction of political evolution – but this second time it symbolized a drift back toward authoritarian government.

Russia's political evolution during 1992 to 1995, despite some zigzag-ging, followed a course of constriction of the role of democratic institu-tions at the national and local levels and a movement of political power toward the Kremlin, the traditional seat of centralized authority in both Tsarist and Communist times. This process began in 1992, as soon as the effects of shock therapy divided the previously unified Russian elite and sparked the growth of a significant opposition movement.

By the middle of 1992 the Russian parliament was reflecting the growing public concern with the effects of shock therapy – a role that one expects an elected legislature to play in a democratic system. The parliament had accorded President Yeltsin limited power to rule by decree, which he had used to carry out shock therapy. Yeltsin's 1991 election as president in a vote of the entire Russian electorate gave him a great deal of legitimacy.[36] But the constitution also granted the parlia-ment significant power. Its larger body, the Congress of People's Dep-uties, was in many respects the supreme branch of government under the constitution. The Congress had the right to amend the constitution and even to abolish the office of president. It could, less drastically, rescind the limited right to rule by decree which it had extended to Yeltsin in November 1991.

During the second half of 1992 the conflict between parliament and president, primarily over economic policy, grew increasingly sharp. Yeltsin began to charge that the parliament itself was an obstacle to economic reform. He floated the idea of a referendum to decide which should be supreme, the president or the Congress of People's Deputies. The battle between president and parliament came to a head at the December 1992 meeting of the Congress of People's Deputies. With Yeltsin's emergency powers due to expire, the stakes were high. After a measure to transfer authority over key government appointments from the president to the parliament failed by a single vote, a compromise was struck. The Congress allowed Yeltsin to keep his decree-making powers for the time being, and a popular referendum on constitutional questions which Yeltsin wanted was scheduled for April 1993. In exchange, Yeltsin agreed to replace Gaidar by Chernomyrdin as prime minister.

But with no change in economic policy following the cabinet shuffle, and with the continuing decline of Russian industry, relations between president and parliament deteriorated again. In March 1993 Yeltsin suddenly announced a "special order of rule" that seemed to imply the dissolution of the parliament, but he quickly backed away from it in the face of widespread criticism, as well as uncertainty about what the armed forces would do in a confrontation between president and parliament. In response to Yeltsin's action, an emergency session of the Congress met that same month. It removed some of Yeltsin's powers and came within 72 votes (out of some 1,000 deputies) of impeaching the president. In the corridor after the failed impeachment vote, Sergei Baburin, a leading nationalist deputy, remarked that the Congress had just "committed suicide," a judgment that would be proved right six months later.[37]

After March 1993 relations between Yeltsin and the parliament deteriorated further. There were disputes over many issues, including foreign policy and constitutional questions as well as economic policy. A committee of the parliament was preparing a new draft constitution based on a parliamentary form of government such as the British have, while Yeltsin and his supporters favored a strong presidential republic. The parliamentary majority wanted changes in policy and it sought to defend its constitutional right to play a major role in governing, while Yeltsin regarded its assertiveness as intolerable.

The April 1993 referendum, which Yeltsin had originally wanted to deal with constitutional questions, instead became a popularity contest between president and parliament. There were four questions on the ballot, asking voters to state whether they (1) had "confidence" in the president; (2) "approve of the socioeconomic policies" of the government; (3) wanted early elections for president; (4) wanted early elections for parliament. Yeltsin seemed to believe the referendum could solve his problem with the parliament.

Yeltsin was confident he could win in the referendum. He had significant power over the media, which he used aggressively to campaign for a vote of "da, da, nyet, da," which was made into a jingle that dominated the airwaves. He sought to persuade people that the hardships associated with the economic changes were due to the parliament's obstruction of his plans, and that if the stalemate could be broken, the reforms would work. Polls showed that, despite a decline over time in Yeltsin's popularity, he still retained significant personal popularity at that time, deriving from his leadership of the battle against the CPSU and his resistance to the attempted coup of August 1991. The bitterly divided and unruly parliament was decidedly less popular with the public.

Table 11.1 shows the referendum results. All four referendum questions gained a plurality of "yes" votes, although the turnout was not high enough to make the votes on questions 3 or 4 binding. The president's position won on three of the questions; only on question 3 (early presidential elections) did he lose.

Yeltsin claimed the results as a victory, but they were not as clearcut as he suggested. While on questions 1 and 2 Yeltsin found strong support in Moscow and St Petersburg, where most of the beneficiaries of the new order live, support was much weaker elsewhere in Russia. Yeltsin lost on both questions 1 and 2 in over half of Russia's regions.[38] The referendum showed a public sharply divided in its view of the president and his economic policy.

Perhaps the outcome of the referendum persuaded Yeltsin that he could move decisively to end the stalemate. He had no constitutional means to rid himself of the parliament or bring it under his control. After the traditional August vacation period ended, Yeltsin acted. On 2 September 1993 he suspended Vice-President Rutskoi, using as a pretext corruption charges that a Yeltsin-appointed commission had levelled against him.[39] On 18 September he named Gaidar the first deputy prime minister in charge of the economy. And on 21 September he announced the dissolution of the parliament, stating that elections would be held on 12 December to select a new parliament and ratify a new constitution.

The story of the confrontation between president and parliament that followed has been told effectively elsewhere.[40] The confrontation ended on 4 October 1993 with tanks firing on the White House, home of the parliament, followed by the arrest of the deputies who had refused to leave the building. Yeltsin had triumphed.

Table 11.1 Results of the referendum of 25 April 1993

Question	Percentage yes	Percentage no	Percentage spoiled ballots
1 Confidence in president	58.7	39.2	2.1
2 Socioeconomic policies of president/government	53.0	44.6	2.4
3 Early elections for president	49.5	47.1	3.4
4 Early elections for parliament	67.2	30.1	2.7

Source: Sakwa (1993, p. 428)

While it is agreed that Yeltsin had no legal or constitutional grounds for his actions, he defended them as the only way to resolve the stalemate and finally defeat the remaining forces of Bolshevism in Russia. Western governments, including the Clinton administration, supported him, arguing that the Russian parliament represented the last gasp of the old Soviet regime while Yeltsin represented democracy and economic reform.

The predominance of centrist forces in the parliament in 1992–93 makes this interpretation of events difficult to sustain. The red–brown coalition had the support of a distinct minority of the deputies. The parliament's opposition to Yeltsin did not arise from a desire to bring back the old regime. The parliament was reflecting the growing discontent among much of the population with the effects of shock therapy. The largest bloc in the parliamentary opposition in 1992–93 wanted a different, more gradual means to build a capitalist market system, and their aim was to press Yeltsin into shifting policy in that direction. Yeltsin violated the constitution and crushed the first genuinely democratic parliament that Russia had ever had in order to sweep aside criticism of his policies – a criticism which, as the April referendum showed, reflected the views of a substantial part of the population.[41]

In the two months following the dissolution of the parliament, Yeltsin had nearly absolute power in Russia. He suspended the constitutional court, leaving his office as the sole source of political authority at the federal level. He suspended local and regional legislatures, many of which had opposed his dissolution of the parliament. He removed regional administrators who had opposed him and named pliant replacements. He forced the leader of Russia's trade union federation, Igor Klochkov, to step down, and he warned the federation to stay out of politics if it wanted to survive. He banned 18 Communist and nationalist organizations and closed 15 newspapers.[42]

In this atmosphere of near-total presidential power, Yeltsin abandoned the previous effort to work out a new constitution for Russia through a process of widespread discussion, debate, and compromise. Instead, a small circle of his close advisors wrote a new draft constitution for Russia, with no public input in the process. The draft constitution was to be voted up or down in the December 1993 election.

While previously Yeltsin had called for a constitution creating a democratic republic with a strong presidency, on the French or US model, the new draft constitution was quite different. It created a presidential system, with a very weak, largely advisory legislature, unlike any system found in countries considered to be democratic. The lower house of the new legislature was even named the "duma," which recalled the powerless body created under the Tsarist regime before the revolution.

The new constitution accorded the president the right to issue binding decrees, as long as they did not conflict with constitutional provisions or laws passed by the legislature.[43] But the new legislature (the Federal Assembly) would not find it easy to pass any laws, which had to be supported, not just by a majority of those present and voting in each house of the legislature – the normal procedure in democratic legislative bodies – but by a majority of the total membership in each house. This novel twist had the effect of making it very difficult to pass laws, leaving the field open for presidential decrees.

Similarly, overturning a presidential veto required a vote of two-thirds of the total membership, not just of those present and voting. This made the overturn of vetoes practically impossible, unless the legislature were nearly unanimous in its sentiment. The only significant power accorded to the new parliament was the passage of a budget. A particularly novel provision stated that, if the lower house passed a vote of no confidence in the government twice, then, rather than the government resigning, the president could dissolve the parliament.

Thus, the outcome of Yeltsin's victory over the Congress of People's Deputies, embodied in the new draft constitution, was an authoritarian presidential regime with few democratic features. To be adopted under the rules set by Yeltsin, the new constitution had to be approved by a majority of those voting in the December 1993 elections, with at least 50 per cent of the eligible electorate turning out to vote. Either a negative vote or a low turnout would have left the new constitution in limbo.

On 25 December 1993 the government announced that the constitution had been approved by 58.4 per cent of the voters, with a 54.8 per cent turnout.[44] However, there was a strong appearance of electoral fraud. As results trickled in after election day, the Central Election Commission kept reducing the official figure for the eligible electorate.[45] It is widely believed in Russia that the turnout was actually below 50 per cent.

Most of the opposition parties, both centrist and Communist, had denounced the proposed new constitution as undemocratic. Even many moderate critics and some traditional supporters of Yeltsin had expressed concern. Ironically, only one major opposition party had called for approval of the new constitution during the election – Zhirinovsky's Liberal Democratic Party. Zhirinovsky fully supported a dictatorial presidential regime, intending to be the one to fill the presidency eventually.

Given Yeltsin's monopoly of power in the months preceding the December 1993 election – and the government's domination of the mass media, particularly television – it is remarkable that the opposition was able to win such an overwhelming victory in the parliamentary vote. It appears that between the referendum vote of April and the parliamentary vote of December, public support for the policies of Yeltsin and

Gaidar had fallen off significantly. But under the new constitution, the popular rejection of those policies had little effect. The new parliament had little power to change the government's policies.

This became evident when Yeltsin decided in December 1994 to use armed force to quell the republic of Chechnya's assertion of independence from Russia. While few Russians favored allowing Chechnya to leave the Russian Federation, there was little public support for Yeltsin's military action against the breakaway republic.[46] This was reflected in the parliament, where opposition was expressed not only by centrist and Communist deputies, and many nationalists, but also those who had previously been Yeltsin's core supporters. Former prime minister Gaidar sharply condemned the assault, effectively breaking relations with Yeltsin.[47] But the parliamentary opposition had little impact on events. By contrast, when Yeltsin had declared a state of emergency in Chechnya in November 1991, opposition from the former parliament had compelled him to quickly rescind it.[48]

Yeltsin's decision to take military action in Chechnya bypassed not only the parliament but Prime Minister Chernomyrdin and his cabinet. Instead, Yeltsin made the decision through a presidential body, the National Security Council, in which the so-called "power ministers" (the heads of internal security and foreign intelligence and the Minister of Defense) were believed to exercise great influence.[49] Some liken this body to a new "politburo," holding secret meetings which make key decisions affecting the fate of Russia. As the war in Chechnya dragged on, claiming many lives and destroying the main cities in Chechnya, Yeltsin's popularity sank to single digits in the public opinion surveys.[50] Yeltsin appeared less and less frequently in public.[51]

The presidential apparatus has grown steadily more powerful since Russia's independence. Alexander Korzhakov, a former KGB agent who heads the armed security guard for the president, has been widely reported to have become one of President Yeltsin's most influential advisors.[52] On 2 December 1994 a unit of the presidential guard attacked the headquarters of the Most financial group, beating up the head of Most's security force. The Most group controls NTV, the independent television network in Russia, which has run critical and satirical shows about the Yeltsin government. Russian media people regarded this attack as a threat to those who would criticize the government.[53]

Why democracy has ebbed in Russia

One might explain the trend toward authoritarian government in Russia by the weight of Russia's past. Russia had a thousand years of autocracy, under the tsars and the Communist Party. Yet Russia's people appeared to reject this heritage decisively during 1985–91. Independent

Russia began its life in 1992 with young but apparently healthy and promising democratic institutions. Citing history does not suffice as an explanation, since history does not consist entirely of continuity. Some of today's industrial democracies, such as France and Germany, had long authoritarian traditions in the past. One must explain what specific pressures have been moving Russia back toward its pre-1985 political traditions.

In the West it is commonly believed that capitalism and democracy are inseparably linked. There is indeed a case that can be made for such a linkage. Historically, modern parliamentary democracy developed in Europe along with modern capitalism. One can argue that the institutions of private property and free labor that are the basis of capitalism, and a political system of free elections and individual civil rights, have worked effectively together in Western Europe, North America, and some other parts of the world for a long period of time.[54] But this linkage is not an absolute one. Capitalism has prospered in some countries with authoritarian states, such as Singapore, South Korea, Brazil, and Chile. Contemporary Russia seems to be a place in which capitalism and democracy do not go together.

Democratization in the Soviet Union and Russia first emerged in the 1980s, not from capitalist development, but from Gorbachev's socialist reform project. Institutions that were genuinely democratic, albeit imperfect, developed in the Soviet Union during 1989–91. Democracy was seen by Gorbachev and his associates as the missing element in Soviet socialism, the absence of which had prevented socialism from reaching its true potential. Democratization was pursued, not just as an end in itself, but as a means to build a socialism that would finally fulfill the promise that had attracted so many people to the socialist cause over the years – the promise of a society in which the people would exercise sovereignty not just in the state but in the economy as well.

The defeat of Gorbachev and the ascendancy of Yeltsin marked a shift from the reform of socialism to the building of capitalism. This was a sharp turn in the economic agenda. Now the aim was to privatize state assets and relinquish collective responsibility for the individual's welfare. Productive property was to be rapidly transferred from public ownership to ownership by a new class of wealthy capitalists. While Yeltsin supported democracy as he rose to power, once he had achieved power, democracy increasingly came into conflict with his central project of building capitalism – and particularly with the effort to build capitalism by means of shock therapy.

Since 1992 this clash has become ever more apparent. The Russian parliament of 1990–93, which had institutional power rivalling that of the president, and which reflected the reactions of diverse groups in the population that were harmed by shock therapy, became an obstacle to the process of rapidly building capitalism – and Yeltsin swept it aside. Any institution which permitted the expression of popular power became an impediment to the economic transformation that the leadership was trying to effect. Democracy would grant the majority the potential power to stop the process of their dispossession and impoverishment. While a democratic state may be consistent with a mature and established capitalism, it poses severe problems for the process of rapidly building capitalism in a formerly state socialist society such as that of Russia.

This explains why Yeltsin, despite a probably genuine desire to reproduce in Russia the democratic as well as the capitalist institutions of the West, has been driven to progressively restrict the democratic elements in the new Russian system. Some Russian intellectuals openly discuss this problem and offer support for what they refer to as the "Pinochet" option, which symbolizes for them the use of an unhindered authoritarian state power to impose a rapid transition to capitalism.[55] The present course of Russian development does not encourage hope for a democratic future in that country.

WHERE IS RUSSIA HEADING?

Predicting the future direction of social development in any country or region is a hazardous business. The future always keeps surprises in store for us. Nevertheless, the analysis offered here of the process which has taken place in the Soviet Union and Russia does have implications for the possible future course of development in Russia. From the vantage point of the end of 1995, there appear to be five possible directions Russia might take over the next decade or so.

Russia might continue on its present course, despite the destruction it is wreaking on the country's industrial potential and the suffering it is causing for the majority of its people. As we argued above, the logic of the present course is to turn Russia into primarily a producer and exporter of raw materials, dependent on imported manufactured goods. The Third-Worldization of Russia would produce an economy that is inconsistent with the socioeconomic structure inherited from the Soviet days. Such an economy would provide great wealth for a small part of the population – those who are owners of, or hold high positions in, enterprises in the raw-materials sector, as well as in other sectors which provide financial, marketing, and other services to it. Others would prosper working for companies that import foreign manufactured goods.

Such a system would have no need for a large well-educated class. It would not need a large scientific and cultural establishment, nor would it need large numbers of engineers and technicians. It would also be unable to support a mass of well-paid industrial workers. Russia's current population decline would fit the limited labor requirements of such a system. Much of the population would end up unemployed, competing for the insufficient supply of service jobs available in the system. Large numbers of people would probably be forced to emigrate.

In this scenario, one would expect the Russian state to continue evolving in an undemocratic, authoritarian direction. Free elections, and a legislature with any real power, would obstruct this path of development. If the shock therapy, or "neoliberal," path continues, then rigged elections, or even their formal abolition, might replace the relatively open democracy which Russia experienced for a few years. A Russian Pinochet may indeed be needed to preside over this process.

Three alternative courses of development would each involve a more active state role in the economy. They are the neofascist, the state capitalist, and the socialist directions of development. The neofascist road would entail the coming to power of an extreme nationalist such as Vladimir Zhirinovsky. The social base for such a development is present in the demoralized and impoverished part of the Russian population. People have been disoriented by the sudden loss of an entire way of life. Everything familiar is gone, and everything they had believed in has been discredited. From a great power, they have been reduced to a weak appendage of the West. Such a process produces a psychological reaction that begins with self-hate – a phenomenon highly visible in the Russia of 1992, when everyone seemed to worship all things foreign and disdain anything Russian. But self-hate tends to give way to anger and the search for a scapegoat. In Russia the traditional scapegoats are Jews and Freemasons first, and the West second. Zhirinovsky's sizeable votes in 1993 and 1995 were an expression of this reaction. He denounced foreign influence. He demanded a warm-water port on the Indian Ocean for Russia. The more outrageously he twitted the world community, the more popular he seemed to become in Russia.

The coming to power of a neofascist could take place through elections, or through a seizure of power by a section of the military – much of which apparently voted for Zhirinovsky in the 1993 elections.[56] The neofascist appeal is political and cultural, devoid of any clear economic program. A neofascist in power would be likely to seek to extend Russia's borders to at least encompass areas of high concentration of ethnic Russians, in Belarus, Ukraine, and Kazakhstan. It would be likely to pour funds into remilitarizing the Russian economy, which might well reverse the economic decline, as occurred in Nazi Germany in the 1930s. While probably permitting the new private owners of industry to keep their wealth, it would undoubtedly exert significant state control over industry. And it would probably subject Russia to a new gulag, with repression of political dissidents and ethnic minorities. The danger of a new world war would be a very real one, as a neofascist Russia sought to exert its power and redress its perceived grievances on the world stage.

An alternative direction would shift from shock therapy to the centrist vision of reaching capitalism through strong state guidance and support of economic transformation. The base of support for such a state capitalist direction of development is found in those groups in Russian society that favor capitalist development but want Russia to become a technically advanced manufacturing nation, rather than an exporter of raw materials. Much of the enterprise directors corps, in both public and private enterprises, may still favor such a course. Some of the new private banks, having reached a size and wealth that permits them to look into Russia's future, may now favor this course – since to be a banker in Japan or Germany is more attractive than to be a banker in Mexico or Colombia.[57] Some more moderate military officers, who understand the perils of neofascism, may, along with their troops, support this direction as the best way to rebuild a strong Russia, with a strong industrial base for its armed forces and a renewed respect for the military within society.

Although the main centrist parties which espouse such a road have not been very popular with voters in the past, they could conceivably come to power through elections as part of a coalition, perhaps with the apparently more popular moderate nationalists as allies. Alternatively, a shift from shock therapy to the state capitalist approach might emerge if Yeltsin died in office (his health problems are well known) and a process of political deal-making and jockeying among elite groups produced a new government devoted to this approach. One could even imagine, under such circumstances, the nimble Prime Minister Chernomyrdin, Yeltsin's constitutional successor, presiding over such a shift in policy – although he may be too tied to shock therapy to make such a switch. One could also imagine a military coup by moderate officers leading to a new state capitalist regime.

However such a regime might emerge, it would be likely to rule through a moderately authoritarian system, perhaps similar to the current constitutional setup. The main base of support for this approach consists of elite groups – enterprise directors, bankers, military officers – that are unlikely to place a high value on democracy as compared to order and a strong state. And the commitment to completing the establishment of capitalism in Russia would mean continuing sacrifices for ordinary people (large-scale layoffs, plant closings, low wages) that would make too much democracy inconvenient.

Such a state capitalist regime would probably seek friendly, if more arm's-length, relations with the West. After a period of criticism and complaint by the Western powers, they would probably have no choice but to accept such a new Russia.

A fourth possibility is a return to a socialist direction of development for Russia. A few years ago such a prospect seemed unimaginable. It appeared that socialism of any sort had been so thoroughly discredited by the Soviet experience and the failure of perestroika that it had been removed from the political agenda in Russia for the foreseeable future. But the years of shock therapy may have changed this situation.

In several Eastern and Central European countries, the popular reaction to shock therapy propelled reformed Communist parties back into office by means of election victories, in Lithuania in 1992, in Poland in 1993, and in Hungary in 1994. The same dynamic revived the fortunes of the Communist Party of the Russian Federation. As we saw above, the CPRF, together with its close allies, won over 40 per cent of the duma seats in the December 1995 election. CPRF leader Gennady Zyuganov is viewed as a leading contender for the presidency in the elections scheduled for June 1996.

The social base for a possible return to power by a coalition of parties professing a belief in socialism is the mass of workers, both industrial and agricultural, and retirees, who have suffered the brunt of shock therapy. Much of the older generation is nostalgic for a socialism which they did not like very much when they had it but now sorely miss. Those from all parts of the social spectrum who never lost a belief in the official socialist ideology of the old system would support this direction. A section of the military, which was the most heavily indoctrinated group in Soviet society, and not one with much natural affinity for either markets or private property, might support a return to socialism. It is possible that the Communists might come to power in Russia through elections. Alternatively, a failed attempt at a seizure of power by a neofascist group, or the cancellation of a scheduled election, could set off a process that brought the Communists back into power.

What a return to power by the Communists would mean is difficult to predict. If one takes the published program and public statements of the leaders of the CPRF at face value, they would seek to stop the current attempt to bring capitalism to Russia and return to the path of building a democratic socialist system. This would mean a second attempt to build an economic system, based mainly on public property and some combination of economic planning and market forces, which would be both economically effective and consistent with a democratic form of government.[58]

However, a return to power by the Communists would not necessarily be followed by a rejection of capitalist development and a renewed attempt to build democratic socialism in Russia. No such radical shift in economic strategy followed the coming to power of reformed

Communists in Poland or Hungary.[59] Some leaders of the CPRF insist that they would not follow the very moderate example of the Polish or Hungarian reformed Communists.[60] But even the most genuine of intentions would not matter if the political mood in Russia remained as apathetic and cynical as it has so far been since 1992. People may come out to vote for the Communists, but it appears that most Russians are not prepared to become actively involved in political affairs.

The previous attempt in Russia to build democratic socialism, led by Gorbachev, ultimately failed because the natural base for such a project, the Soviet working people, never became actively involved or empowered, and elite interests determined the outcome. Even if a Communist-led government in Russia came to power and set out to build democratic socialism, if it failed to draw large numbers of ordinary people into active participation in political life, it would not be able to realize that goal.[61] The pressure from members of the Russian elite to be allowed to hold onto their new property would be difficult to resist, particularly given the old personal links from Soviet days between many of the new rich and the CPRF leadership. The Western industrial nations and the international financial institutions they control would undoubtedly exert pressure on a Russian Communist government to continue on the road to capitalism. Without an activated base, the result might be a variant of the state capitalist path, with greater protections for workers and pensioners than would be the case with centrists in charge. There are some within the leadership of the main left parties in Russia who are more nationalist and statist than democratic socialist and who might welcome such a direction of development in the end.

The Western reaction to a Communist-led government in Russia would be likely to depend on which course that government took. If it sought to reverse the transition to capitalism entirely, the response from the West would probably be very hostile, and a new Cold War might result. On the other hand, a CPRF-led government would probably eventually be accepted by the West if it followed a state capitalist path of development.

Despite significant nostalgia in Russia for the stability of the pre-perestroika Soviet era,[62] a return to that past does not seem possible. There is no leadership with any influence which calls for heading in that direction. The most influential Communist organizations reject it. The great majority of the former elite of the old system were unwilling to defend it the last time around, and they have even less reason to seek its return after its demise. The only possibility of a future anything like the old system for Russia would come through the neo-fascist option, which would seek to recreate a version of the political features of the former Soviet system but without its central economic features.

A fifth possibility for the Russian future would entail a progressive breakdown of the Russian state and society. Russia occupies a huge and diverse land mass, some regions of which are inhabited primarily by non-Russian ethnic groups. This diverse society was held together as a state during the Soviet days by the state socialist system, which tied the country together in a web of economic and political interdependence. That system is gone.

A large, multinational state can also be held together by an effective capitalist market system, which can tie together a nation through the economic interdependencies generated by market relations. But if the attempt to build an effective capitalist system continues to fail in Russia, the pressures for regional autonomy, already strong, will probably increase, encompassing not just non-Russian ethnic regions in Russia but even regions of predominantly ethnic Russian population. This could lead to a breakdown of the Russian state into a large number of new smaller states, with a diversity of economic and political courses of development among them. Old-style empires have not survived in the modern world, and if Russia cannot build an effective system, be it capitalist or socialist, then fragmentation and disintegration seem to be the likely future for it.

Whichever path Russia follows, it seems that capitalism and democracy are not compatible in that country in the near future. Neither continuing shock therapy nor the state capitalist path promises much public participation in political life. It appears that only a turn away from capitalism, back to the socialist reform project that first injected genuine democratic reform into Russian life, is likely to resume progress toward a democratic Russia.

Chapter 12

Lessons for the future of socialism

Since capitalism arose and became the dominant socioeconomic system in the world several centuries ago, the only comprehensive challenge to that system has come from socialism. Capitalism has been criticized by liberal Christian philosophers and by fundamentalist Islamic thinkers, by anarchists and by opponents of modern technology. However, only its socialist critics proposed a well-defined and comprehensive alternative socioeconomic system for the contemporary era.

From its beginnings among European intellectuals and working-class activists in the early nineteenth century, socialism grew to a world-wide movement. The source of its appeal has been the vision of a system which would surpass capitalism in its area of greatest success – the rapid development of human productive power – while promising an end to the inequality, insecurity, and exploitation which capitalism, in the view of its critics, could never transcend. The idea of an economically effective social system, based on the principles of cooperation, social justice, and democracy, motivated millions of people, from every race and ethnic group, to support and work for socialism. Socialism was supposed to be not just an improvement but a new stage of human development. It promised not only material comfort for all, but the emergence of ordinary people as the masters of society.

The Russian Revolution, and the Soviet system which it created, gave rise to the first large-scale attempt to build this new society. The Soviet system was based on some of the key institutions long associated with the idea of socialism, including public enterprise, economic planning, and production for use. Yet, as we have seen, the resulting social system bore only a slight resemblance to the picture that socialists had previously painted. It had features antithetical to the original vision of socialism, including a repressive state ruled by a small, privileged elite; a highly centralized political and economic system; rigorous controls over people's daily life; and authoritarian work relations little different from those of capitalist enterprises. When Communist Party reformers, led by Mikhail Gorbachev, sought to reform the system by eliminating its repressive and non-socialist features, the result was not the system's transformation into the promised democratic socialism. Instead, the system quickly met its demise, replaced by the current effort to rejoin world capitalism.

Despite the fact that the Soviet system departed markedly from the original conception of a socialist society, its 75 years of experience hold important lessons for the future of socialism in the world. However, just what lessons are drawn depends on how one interprets the Soviet experience. Of particular importance is the interpretation of the process by which the Soviet system met its end. A central claim of this book is that the interpretations of the Soviet demise which have been dominant in the West, in both academic writing and the popular media, are unconvincing. We have offered an alternative interpretation which, we believe, rests upon strong support from the historical record and also has the virtue of explaining why the Soviet demise was so sudden and relatively peaceful. This dispute does not just involve the past. The dominant interpretations of the Soviet demise point to one set of lessons for the future of socialism. Our interpretation suggests quite different lessons.

In what follows we consider first the popular view that socialism has been finally buried by the Soviet demise. This conclusion rests upon an interpretation of the Soviet demise which we believe to be faulty. Then we consider what, in our view, are the main lessons for the future of socialism that should be learned from the Soviet experience, including learning from the manner in which the system met its end.

SOCIALISM BURIED?

Many analysts have concluded that the sudden demise of the Soviet system was the final proof that socialism is an economically non-viable system. This conclusion naturally follows from the influential interpretation of the Soviet demise which points to the internal contradictions of a socialist economy as its cause. According to this view, the performance of the Soviet economy steadily worsened until it "collapsed" or "disintegrated" at the end of the 1980s. This left no alternative for the people of the former Soviet Union but to seek to replace it with the only economic system which history had shown to be effective – capitalism. Thus, the world should forget about impossible utopias based on equality and cooperation. According to this view, the Soviet demise has proven the impracticality of an egalitarian alternative to capitalism in the modern world.

Western advocates of unfettered free-market economies seized upon the Soviet demise as proof that, not only was Soviet-style socialism not a viable alternative to capitalism, but any form of state intervention in the economy had now been shown to be a path to economic ruin. With renewed vigor they have attacked state regulation of market activity, state provision of public services, and public-welfare programs. All of these are characterized as "socialistic" threats to the dynamism of unfettered free-market capitalism.

The traditional supporters of an active, interventionist role for the state in a capitalist economy – trade unions, centrist and social-democratic political parties, poor people's organizations, environmental movements, and so forth – have continued to battle against the free-market advocates. However, the Soviet demise has tended to strengthen the supporters of unregulated markets in this battle. The widespread belief that the Soviet demise has demonstrated the perils of state intervention in the economy has left the defenders of such intervention very much on the defensive. It also appears that, once the demise of the Soviet system eliminated the fear that those on the bottom might be attracted to "Communism," the propertied classes in the West have been less inclined to tolerate welfare-state programs.

However, the conclusion that the Soviet demise demonstrated the economic non-viability of socialism rests on the untenable view that the Soviet economy collapsed due to its internal contradictions. The evidence shows, as presented above in Chapter 5, that the Soviet economy began to contract only after the process of dismantling the key institutions of Soviet socialism was well under way, in 1990–91. Although the Soviet economy performed poorly during 1975–89, output did not decline during those years, and it even continued to slowly grow through to the end of that period. It was the abolition of central planning in 1990–91, along with the announcement of coming privatization of state assets, that, along with other factors discussed in the above chapter, first set off an economic contraction. The Soviet planned economy did not "collapse"; it was dismantled through political means.

An alternative version of the "socialism is buried" view claims, not that the Soviet demise demonstrated that socialism is entirely unworkable, but rather that it showed socialism to be inferior to capitalism in economic performance and hence not a viable alternative to it. But that conclusion rests upon a selective interpretation of the relevant history. The best available evidence shows that Soviet state socialism, despite its many flaws, produced rapid economic progress from 1928 through to the mid-1970s – that is, for nearly 50 years. As we have seen, the Soviet system accomplished one of the most rapid industrialization processes in world history, and for several decades after industrialization had been completed it continued to bring very rapid economic growth – more rapid than that of the United States. It is true that after 1975 Soviet economic performance was indeed inferior to that of the leading capitalist economies in the most important respects. Yet that no more demonstrated that capitalism is in general superior to socialism than did the Soviet Union's superior growth record during 1928–75 prove the economic superiority of socialism.

It is perhaps the absence of convincing support for the "socialism is buried" conclusion in the historical record that has inspired the effort to rewrite the record of Soviet growth, which was discussed in Chapter 3. To make the "socialism is buried" case really convincing, it is not enough that the Soviet system disappeared. The decades of rapid Soviet growth must also be abolished.

Still another version of the "socialism is buried" position is based on the claim that the Soviet economy had sunk into a stagnation from which it could not recover, because it was unreformable. It is clear that, for vigorous economic progress to have resumed in the Soviet Union, a thorough renovation of Soviet state socialism was required. No major changes were actually made in the Soviet economy during the first three years of perestroika, 1985–87. The Law on State Enterprise, the first real attempt at economic restructuring, took effect on 1 January 1988.

As Chapter 5 showed, the two years following the introduction of the Law on State Enterprise saw serious economic problems. The freeing of state enterprises from decades of detailed control from the center led to rapidly rising money incomes of the population, which in turn produced severe shortages as consumer demand far outpaced production. The state's power to obtain revenues was greatly eroded by the economic changes, and a growing budget deficit emerged. There was rising, although suppressed, inflationary pressure. Despite these serious problems, total output, and even total consumption, continued to grow, although at a low rate.

The economic problems unleashed by Gorbachev's effort at restructuring in 1988 show that the policies had serious failings. It was to be expected that an effort to radically transform a 60-year-old economic system would not proceed smoothly. But we cannot determine from the historical record whether adjustments in those policies could have achieved the goal of democratic socialism at which the leadership was aiming. Other developments soon intervened. By June of 1990 the Russian Republic, under Yeltsin's leadership, had declared its sovereignty, followed in September by the issuing of the 500 Day Plan. The dismantling of central coordination of the Soviet economy was under way, and the prospect of privatization of state enterprises loomed ahead. The agenda of the pro-capitalist coalition was pushing aside that of the socialist reformers. The attempt to radically restructure Soviet state socialism into democratic socialism actually only lasted about two and a half years. This was too short a time to determine whether the economic restructuring might have succeeded, had political conditions permitted it to continue.[1]

Consider the experience of the post-1991 effort to transform the Russian economy to a capitalist one. We saw in Chapter 10 that this effort was followed by four years of rapid decline in production and the living standards of the majority, as well as very rapid inflation. This does not support a favorable conclusion regarding the particular set of policies, embodied in the shock therapy approach, that have been the basis of this attempted transition to capitalism. But it does not demonstrate that a transition to capitalism in Russia is impossible, if the right policies were adopted. As was the case with Gorbachev's attempted transition to democratic socialism, political factors will determine whether the effort to build capitalism will continue in Russia, by the same means as before or by an alternative set of methods, or whether instead a new direction of economic change will emerge.

Finally, some believe that the Soviet effort to build democratic socialism was bound to fail because that system is not a viable one. However, it is difficult to see how such a claim could be based upon any lesson from the Soviet demise, since the attempt to build such a system in the Soviet Union was halted so soon after it had begun. The potential viability of democratic socialism cannot be finally determined by the events of recent history. Yet the Soviet demise may have some lessons that are relevant to the question of what a democratic socialist system might look like, even if it cannot settle the question of such a system's viability.

LESSONS OF THE SOVIET EXPERIENCE

The Soviet system had three main interrelated flaws. First, contrary to its pretensions to being a workers' state, it was run by a privileged elite. Second, the state through which the elite ruled was an authoritarian one, denying civil rights and liberties to the population. Third, both political and economic institutions were very centralized and hierarchical, with all important decisions made in the center by a small group of top officials, while the rest of the population was supposed to simply carry out their orders.

The many long-standing problems of the Soviet economy stemmed largely from these features of the Soviet system. The concentration of economic decision-making in a country of more than 200 million people at the very center of the system made it very inflexible and inefficient, leading to the wasteful use of resources. Enterprises tended to ignore the needs and wishes of their customers, because the latter had no power in this system – enterprise directors had to worry mainly about pleasing their superiors in the hierarchy. Work incentives were of limited effectiveness, since workers neither feared unemployment nor felt they had a stake in the hierarchically structured production system. Despite the demand for faster technological innovation from the top leadership, the caution and conservatism bred by this hierarchical system created an inhospitable climate for it. The terrible record of environmental degradation was one more consequence of the disempowerment of the population, who had no means to press for taking environmental effects into account. Overall, the Soviet system had no institutions through which the people – in their roles as consumers, producers, and members of communities – could participate in making decisions regarding production and distribution. It had the form of economic planning, but it lacked this crucial substance of it.

Despite these failings, we have seen that the Soviet economy managed to bring very rapid growth for many decades. However, although it continued to produce some economic growth down to the end, in its last fifteen years the system suffered a serious deterioration in its economic performance. We argued above in Chapter 3 that the most important cause of that deterioration was the declining effectiveness over time of the highly centralized form of planning and the hierarchical form of work organization that characterized the system.

The Soviet system met its end, not because the economy stopped working, but because a political coalition arose and gained power which was dedicated to replacing it with capitalism. The same three features of the Soviet system cited above – rule by a privileged elite, an authoritarian state, and the centralization and hierarchy of the system – ultimately account for the rise and success of the pro-capitalist coalition. The party–state elite, concluding that capitalism would bring greater and more secure individual privileges for them, set about dismantling the system. The repressive character of the system had turned against it many of its citizens, particularly the intelligentsia, whose craft suffered the most severely from the repressiveness of state socialism. The intelligentsia became an invaluable ally of the party–state elite in the project of bringing capitalism to the Soviet Union. The centralized, hierarchical character of the Soviet system depoliticized and made passive the ordinary citizens who might have otherwise responded to the call to democratize socialism, leaving the pro-capitalist coalition facing no effective opposition in the end.

This interpretation of the Soviet experience does not suggest that socialism is unworkable or inferior to capitalism. The real lessons of the Soviet experience have to do with what form socialism must take in the future, if it is to overcome the problems of the Soviet version of it. For this purpose we can draw on the lessons of the Soviet system's longstanding economic weaknesses, its serious bout of stagnation after 1975, and the manner in which it met its end.

Three major lessons follow from the three main defects of the Soviet system identified above. First, a viable socialist system must include a democratic state, with respect for individual civil liberties. Second, centralization and hierarchy must be replaced by alternative institutions. Third, socialism must have institutions that forestall the development of a privileged and dominant elite.

There is no longer any controversy about the requirement that socialism must be a democratic system. It is impossible for the people to be sovereign in the economy, as socialism requires, if they are not sovereign with respect to the state. This is the only one of the above three goals on which Gorbachev made significant progress during the perestroika period. Gorbachev ultimately sought to secure a democratic state by means of a system of free elections with competing parties and candidates, and to ensure individual rights by guaranteeing them in law and enforcing them through an independent judiciary. These new Soviet political institutions resembled those found in capitalist democracies. However, political institutions vary considerably among capitalist democracies. Exactly what type of democratic institutions would prove most suitable for a democratic socialist system cannot be known in advance. But the historical record shows that rule by a single party, claiming to represent the entire population, cannot serve as an instrument of democracy.[2] Whatever effectiveness a disciplined democratic centralist party may possess at seizing power in an autocratic state, history has demonstrated that the resulting single-party rule does not lead to building a form of socialism that is viable over the long run.

The best way to design a socialist economy that is decentralized and non-hierarchical is a controversial matter. There are two main schools of thought on this among Western socialists. One believes that the best way to incorporate decentralized, non-hierarchical institutions in a socialist framework is through assigning a major role to competitive market forces. They deny that a competitive market system can only function in a capitalist framework. They argue that the socialist critique of capitalism really involves values rather than specific economic institutions, such as market relations or central planning, and that what really counts is that the core socialist values of economic justice, solidarity, and democracy be built into the new system.[3] These values cannot be realized within a capitalist system, because of its large differences in income and wealth, its individualist ethic, and the threat to genuine democracy posed by the political power of great wealth. However, they are held to be attainable through market socialism.

The idea of market socialism goes back at least to the 1930s, and the demise of the Soviet system has led to renewed interest in this approach.[4] The current generation of market socialists propose a system in which profit-seeking enterprises would compete with one another in markets but the ownership of the enterprises would depart from the traditional capitalist form. Enterprise ownership may be vested in a government entity, in enterprise employees, or distributed to the public in a way intended to assure a relatively equal allocation of shareholdings among the population.[5] In each of these versions, it is intended that the typical enterprise would not have access to state subsidies but must succeed in competition for customers' favor to survive.

Market socialists argue that such a system would attain the efficiency and technological progressivity of a capitalist market system but without its problems. By eliminating the capitalist type of private ownership of enterprises, exploitation of workers would be eliminated, along with a major source of the large differences in wealth and income that characterize capitalism. However, market socialists do not support an unregulated market system but rather see a need for significant state intervention in the market. They reject the claim, made by free-market theorists, that allocation of resources entirely by unregulated markets will maximize society's well-being. Under market socialism, the state would redistribute income to reduce market-based inequalities and provide a social safety net for those who cannot gain sufficient income through market activity.[6] The state would regulate market activity to prevent monopolization, environmental damage, or unsafe jobs or products. It would use fiscal and monetary policy to avoid high unemployment or inflation. In some versions the state would also play some role in guiding investment and the long-run pattern of economic development. With no class of wealthy capitalists to oppose state intervention in the market, it is argued that such intervention would be both more successful and more durable.

Market socialism can be seen as one possible solution to the problems created by the excessive centralization and hierarchical relations of the Soviet model. It would replace centralization by decentralization, as economic decisions would be made by managers of many competing enterprises, rather than central planners. In its most common version, it would also replace the hierarchical work relations inside the enterprise, which characterize both state socialism and capitalism, by worker control.[7]

A second school of thought supports an alternative approach known as democratic, or participatory, planning.[8] In this approach, the centralized, hierarchical form of planning of the Soviet model would be replaced by a decentralized, participatory form of planning. Every economic decision would be made at the most decentralized level that is consistent with its scope. Local and regional planning bodies would play a prominent role in economic planning, leaving to a central planning body only those aspects of economic activity which absolutely require coordination at the center.[9] All planning bodies would be democratically constituted, with representatives chosen by all the relevant constituencies that are affected by the planning decisions to be made.

Unlike the hierarchical form of planning that characterized the Soviet system, democratic planning would rely on negotiation and compromise to develop and implement economic plans and to resolve the conflicting interests that exist with respect to economic activity. Within a planning body, this process of negotiation and compromise would apply to the interaction of representatives of different constituencies. It would also underlie the relations among planning bodies at the central, regional, and local levels. Enterprises would also be structured so as to provide a voice in their decisions to all of the groups affected by enterprise actions. Workers would have the primary authority to make decisions within an enterprise, but on its board would also sit representatives of customers and the local community, as well as employee representatives.

Advocates of democratic planning argue that this approach would avoid the problems that competitive markets generate, such as business cycles, unemployment, inequality, and a tendency to destroy the natural environment. They also stress that the active participation of the population in such a planning system would empower ordinary people, arguing that this would best embody the socialist vision of popular control over economic and social development.

As we have seen, Gorbachev's plan for transforming the Soviet economy contained elements of both of these approaches. Indeed, it is difficult to imagine how a large-scale, interdependent economic system could possibly function fully satisfactorily without some elements of both public regulation and market forces. A future democratic socialism would have to incorporate both kinds of institutions. The knotty problems involve how to combine these two different institutional means for achieving a decentralized, non-hierarchical form of socialism.

The third requirement for a socialist system is that it should not tend to produce a privileged and dominant elite. The kind of oligarchic political elite that ruled the Soviet system would be excluded by a democratic state, as well as the absence of centralized, hierarchical planning. But the presence of a democratic state does not by itself assure that a different kind of privileged elite could not arise to dominate the system.

Under capitalism, the class that owns the means of production has a great deal of economic power. Its economic power translates into political power, making capitalism a system dominated by an economic elite. The exclusion of concentrated private ownership of the means of production under democratic socialism would prevent that source of elite domination. If ownership of capital is held only by some combination of state agencies and enterprise employees, no separate owning class would exist. Those market socialist schemes which would allow indirect ownership of capital by citizens usually include provisions that would prevent accumulation of such ownership in the possession of a minority of private owners.

Whether a socialist system, having a democratic state and some combination of democratic planning and market forces, would be able to avoid domination by an elite, cannot be foretold with certainty. A central lesson of the Soviet experience is that a ruling elite can arise from a group which the institutions of a socialist system allow to accumulate privileges and power over time. A small band of idealistic revolutionaries gave birth to a privileged ruling elite in the Soviet Union.

There exist two possible sources from which a new ruling elite might arise under democratic socialism. Market forces inevitably generate significant inequalities in income and wealth, and those whose particular talents and proclivities are most rewarded in a market system would tend to rise to high positions within the economy. They might emerge as a self-conscious economic elite that would eventually come to dominate the system. They might even at some point seek to eliminate the bar to accumulation of productive assets by individuals.

The mechanism of democratic planning harbors a second potential source of the formation of a privileged and powerful elite under democratic socialism. Not everyone is equally endowed with the particular skills and motivations that lead to successful performance on participatory planning and management boards. Some are very good at it and enjoy it, while other have less skill and motivation for such activity. A class of managers and planners might develop who would come to dominate the management and planning boards of the system. If they found ways to secure their institutional position, and used it to accumulate privileges and power, they might tend to evolve into a political elite somewhat like that of state socialism.

No institutions can absolutely guarantee against the development of a privileged ruling elite in a large-scale interdependent society. The main safeguards against such an outcome in a democratic socialist system would appear to be a broad dispersal of ownership and income along with a widespread willingness of the population to participate in the process of managing and planning. Only strong development of the values of egalitarianism and participation among the population would ultimately guard against a new elite arising and eventually establishing a new form of elite rule over the majority. But in this regard democratic socialism would have a great advantage over both capitalism and state socialism, whose basic institutions guarantee domination by a privileged elite.

This leaves many questions unanswered. Would a democratic socialist system be economically workable? How would it perform in the areas in which Soviet state socialism was found wanting? Would it utilize resources efficiently? Would it cater effectively to consumer needs and wants? Would it provide effective work incentives? Would it promote rapid development of new products and processes? Would it guard against destruction of the natural environment? Would its collective decision-making processes be consistent with individual freedom?

Could it match and surpass the rival system of capitalism on these, and other, dimensions?

Such questions are of great importance to the future of socialism. We believe that democratic socialism has the potential to overcome the problems of the flawed and now defunct Soviet version, and that the answer to the above questions about its potential can be answered in the affirmative. However, to make a case for this position would take us beyond the lessons of the Soviet experience, which is the proper focus of this book.

The Soviet experience showed that a system based on state property and economic planning can function and that it can bring an uneven economic progress for a certain period of time. But the main lessons of this experience are negative ones. We have learned what aspects of a socialist system should be avoided because, besides violating the original socialist ideal, in the end they only served to undermine the economic performance and political viability of the system. We now know more than was known in 1917, before any attempt to build a socialist system had taken place. But we remain without any positive historical model of a successful democratic socialism.

However, although capitalism has changed significantly over the past two centuries, the conditions which originally inspired the search for an alternative to it have, in the main, not passed away. In recent decades, the process that had formerly brought undeniable material improvements for millions of people in the industrialized capitalist nations has seemed to shift into reverse. In most of the industrialized capitalist countries, while a minority has rapidly increased its wealth, the majority have been experiencing some combination of declining incomes, growing job insecurity, disappearing social safety nets, rising urban poverty and violence, declining public services, domination of more and more spheres of life by commercial criteria, and a worsening environmental crisis. In the newly developing capitalism of the former state socialist countries, conditions are even worse, as they are in much of what used to be called the Third World nations of Africa, Asia, and Latin America. It is such conditions that are likely to promote new efforts to bring into being a democratic socialist system. As long as such conditions continue, the absence of any positive historical model of a successful democratic socialism is unlikely to deter future attempts to create a socialist system, any more than the absence of a previous historical model deterred the first attempt in 1917.

To interpret the demise of state socialism as the end of the socialist challenge to capitalism is premature. The Soviet system was only the first attempt to build a large-scale egalitarian, cooperative alternative to capitalism. That the first such attempt, built under very unfavorable conditions, eventually met its demise after some achievements and many flaws, large and small, is not surprising. What failed was a distorted version of socialism, not socialism *per se*. After all, capitalism first arose, prematurely as it turned out, in the fourteenth century in a few northern Italian city-states. That first emergence of capitalism did not survive, and only several centuries later did the new system establish itself firmly elsewhere in Europe.[10] The most important lesson of the experience, and the demise, of the Soviet attempt to build socialism is that we are not at the end of the socialist challenge to capitalism but rather still at the beginning.

Appendix

LIST OF PEOPLE INTERVIEWED IN THE FORMER SOVIET UNION/RUSSIA

Note: Affiliated institutions listed below are located in Moscow, unless otherwise noted.

Abalkin, Leonid, Director, Institute of Economics, and former Soviet Deputy Prime Minister for Economic Reform

Aliev, Alexander, head, Economics Department, Magnitogorsk City Administration

Arbatov, Georgy, Director, Institute of USA and Canada Studies

Ashin, Gennady, political scientist, Institute for Culture, Education, and Political Science

Biryukov, Vadim, Editor in Chief and Deputy Director General, *Delovie lyudi* (Business People)

Borovoi, Konstantin, businessman and political leader

Buzgalin, Alexander, Professor, Economics Department, Moscow State University

Demchuk, Mikhail, former Deputy Chairman, Council of Ministers, Republic of Byelorussia

Edelman, Yuri, President and General Director, "Mzds & Al-Stankoross" Joint-Stock Company

Faminsky, Vladimir, department head, *Voprosy ekonomiki* (Problems of Economics)

Foglizzo, John, former representative of the International Monetary Fund in Moscow

Gordon, Leonid, labor specialist

Helmer, John, Australian journalist based in Moscow

Isaev, A., labor editor at Moscow Federation of Trade Unions

Kagarlitsky, Boris, author, former deputy on Moscow City Soviet

Keremetsky, Jacob, Institute of USA and Canada Studies

Khasbulatov, Ruslan, former Chairman of the Russian Supreme Soviet

Khodorkovsky, Mikhail, President of the Board, Menatep Bank

Klepach, Andrei, economist at the Institute of Economic Forecasting

Koryagina, Tatyana, economist

Kotovsky, Grigory, head, Department of Indian and South Asian History, Institute of Oriental Studies

Kryshtanovskaya, Olga, head, Department of Elite Studies, Institute of Sociology

Lachinov, Dmitry, Union of the Entrepreneurs and Industrialists of Russia

Lloyd, John, Moscow Correspondent, *Financial Times* of London

Lukyanov, Anatoly, former Chairman of USSR Supreme Soviet

Merzlikin, Konstantin, President and Board Chairman, Russian International Money and Stock Exchange

Miliukov, Anatoly, former Chairman of Expert Analytical Service, Russian Supreme Soviet; Vice-Chairman, Mosbisznesbank

Mironenko, Viktor, former First Secretary of USSR Komsomol

Mironov, Alexander, President, Moven Co.

Nagaitsev, Mikhail, Vice-President, Moscow Federation of Trade Unions

Nosov, Sergei, director of a division of Magnitogorsk Metallurgical Works

Osinkin, Yevgeny, Vice-President, Moscow Federation of Trade Unions

Plekhanov, Sergei, Institute of USA and Canada Studies

Polokov, Michael, businessman

Radaev, Vadim, Department of Economic Sociology and Labor Economics, Institute of Economics

Rakitskaya, Galina, economist

Ryzhkov, Nikolai, former Soviet Prime Minister

Saveliev, Nikolai, staff of Communist Party of the Russian Federation

Savitsky, Alexander, former First Secretary of Magnitogorsk Communist Party Committee

Sergeyev, Alexei, economist, Russian Communist Workers Party

Shadrina, Irina, leader of Sobor

Shmakov, Mikhail, President, Federation of Independent Trade Unions of Russia

Skokov, Yuri, Congress of Russian Communities

Slavin, Boris, head of department, *Pravda*

Sukhotin, Yuri, Institute of Economics and Mathematics

Titkin, Alexander, former Minister of Industry, Russia

Vartazarova, Ludmila, Co-president, Socialist Party of Working People

Volsky, Arkady, former leader of Civic Union and Chairman, International Congress of Industrialists and Entrepreneurs

Voronin, Yuri, central committee, Communist Party of the Russian Federation, and former Deputy Chairman, Russian Supreme Soviet

Yablokov, Alexey V., Counsellor for Ecology and Health to the President of Russia

Zaslavskaya, Tatyana, sociologist

Notes

1 INTRODUCTION

1 The "Union of Soviet Socialist Republics", or "Soviet Union" for short, was not actually formed until 1922, five years after the revolution (Riasanovsky, 1977, p. 540). Prior to 1922 the new regime was usually referred to as 'Soviet Russia'.

2 *Narodnoe khoziaistvo SSSR* (1981, p. 7; 1982, p. 41; 1987, p. 409), *Compendium of Social Statistics and Indicators* (1988, pp. 395–8), *Statistical Abstract of the United States* (1985, pp. 843, 845).

3 See Chapter 3 below.

4 One of the first to use the concept "state socialism" was David Lane. See Lane (1970, p. 273).

5 A strong version of this view is presented by Malia (1994), who writes that "it had always been only a question of time before the internal contradictions of the impossible undertaking of 'building socialism' worked themselves out... to the brusque implosion... of the system" (p. 496). Ticktin (1992) also views the Soviet economic system as inevitably doomed to collapse, although he does not consider it a socialist system. Ellman and Kontorovich (1992b) offer a weaker version of this view, arguing that, while the Soviet planned economy did not collapse, it was "probably not viable over the long run" and was also probably not reformable (pp. 13, 27).

6 The classical presentation of this view is found in Mises (1935 [1920]).

7 The record of Soviet economic growth has become highly disputed, a matter which is discussed in Chapter 3.

8 In Chapter 12 we also criticize the weaker versions of this explanation, which point to poor economic performance, and the impossibility of reform, rather than outright economic collapse.

9 Karklins (1994, p. 42) concludes that "the breakdown of the old system was propelled by an accelerating revolution from below." In an insightful analysis, Reddaway (1993, p. 57) makes the more limited claim that popular revolts in the Soviet Union "made an important contribution to the collapse of an empire," qualifying this observation by adding that 'they did not, in my opinion, represent an authentic revolution."

10 See Chapter 8 below.

11 The referendum, discussed in Chapter 8, was held in nine of the fifteen Soviet republics. The nine participating republics represented 93 per cent of the total Soviet population.

12 A variety of other explanations for the Soviet demise are found in the scholarly literature, most of which have not penetrated the popular consciousness. Some view the Soviet demise as more-or-less inevitable, while others stress accidental developments. Dallin (1992) catalogues several developments in Soviet history, including the post-Stalin loosening of central controls and spreading corruption, which weakened the system over time, but he argues that it might nevertheless have survived. Fukuyama (1993) argues that a decay of the Soviet system's legitimacy in the eyes of the population led to its collapse, a position also taken in a later article by a previously cited analyst, Kontorovich (1993). Miller (1993) portrays the Soviet demise as a result of the rejection of the system by the rising professional and technical class. Lewin (1995) offei s a subtle and perceptive analysis which concludes that a key weakness of the Soviet system was the lack of a mechanism for self-renovation.

13 In December 1990 Vladimir Kryuchkov, head of the KGB, warned that foreign intelligence services were engaging in a "covert war" to destroy the Soviet Union (*Pravda*, 13 December 1990, p. 1).

14 Anatoly Lukyanov, the last Speaker of the Supreme Soviet and a long-time Gorbachev associate who grew increasingly critical of his policies, remarked that Gorbachev had "betrayed the party" (interview on 15 January 1994).

15 The official name of the Russian unit within the Soviet Union was the Russian Soviet Federated Socialist Republic (RSFSR). It was one of the 15 constituent republics of the Soviet Union. For simplicity, we will refer to it as the Russian Republic.

16 The Soviet party–state elite is defined in Chapter 2. It refers to the high-level officials in the Communist Party, government, and other important official organizations in the Soviet Union. Its size is estimated at about 100,000 people in the post-World War II period.

17 The expression "revolution from above" has been applied in many contexts before, including to Stalin's drastic remaking of Soviet society starting at the end of the 1920s, as well as to attempts by past Russian Tsars to transform Russian society. In this case the term refers to a revolution not by a single leader but by a ruling elite group within the society.

18 This idea is more acceptable in Russia. Kagarlitsky (1992), a Russian political analyst, argues that "In order to retain and strengthen their positions...the ruling circles had themselves to form a new model of power and a new structure of property" (p. 26). However, in contrast to the view that we present in this book, Kagarlitsky appears to believe that the Soviet system was collapsing, leaving the party–state elite no choice but to try capitalism.

19 This explains the nearly universal practice in the Western media of referring to Russian political figures who are believed to be anti-capitalist as "former Communists," whereas those who favor rapid transition to capitalism (as, for example, Boris Yeltsin himself) never earn this appellation, regardless of how many years they may have spent as top Communist officials.

20 Yegor T. Gaidar, a member of the Soviet elite who became the main architect of Russia's economic policies after 1991, spoke openly of Russia's "capitalist revolution" (*OMRI Daily Digest*, No. 98, Part I, 22 May 1995).

21 Capitalism also entails ownership of private businesses predominantly by a minority class of wealthy individuals. Advocates of privatization in the Soviet Union often presented it as a process that would lead to broad ownership of capital by the entire population, which, it could be argued, would be different from capitalism. However, in every industrialized country where

private business predominates, business ownership is highly concentrated, and there were never any grounds for expecting that a system of private business and relatively free markets in the Soviet Union could turn out any different.

22 The coverage of independent Russia goes roughly through to the end of 1995, although some data series were not available for all or part of 1995 at the time of writing.

2 SOCIALISM AND THE SOVIET SYSTEM

1 Nove (1989, p. 36).

2 Tucker (1978, p. 473).

3 Tucker (1978, pp. 476–7).

4 In a famous passage, the *Communist Manifesto* denounced the narrow self-interest and focus on material advantage of the capitalist market economy: "The bourgeoisie...has left remaining no other nexus between man and man than naked self-interest, than callous 'cash payment'...It has resolved personal worth into exchange value" (Tucker, 1978, p. 475).

5 In "Critique of the Gotha Program" Marx actually used the term "communism" for both early and late stages of the new society (Tucker, 1978, pp. 527–32). After Marx the usage shifted, with the term "communism" being reserved for the final, classless stage.

6 Despite their critique of market relations, Marx and Engels did view market forces as imposing, amidst the chaos of unplanned exchanges, a kind of order on the capitalist economy. However, compared to consciously planned economic activity, the order induced by market forces was viewed as spontaneous and potentially irrational from a social point of view.

7 The workers might exercise some influence in the legislative branch, but, in a frequently misquoted passage from the *Communist Manifesto*, they stated that "The executive of the modern state is nothing but a committee for managing the common affairs of the whole bourgeoisie" (Tucker, 1978, p. 475). That is, the capitalists are able to make the executive branch of government protect their vital interests. The common misquote is the following: "The state is the executive committee of the ruling class." This misquote has appeared in countless books, articles, and speeches by critics of Marxism, and even occasionally by supporters. The misquote attributes to Marx and Engels a cruder theory of the capitalist state, as simply a tool of the capitalist class, than they in fact believed.

8 Tucker (1978, p. 491).

9 In "Socialism: Utopian and Scientific," Engels wrote that "for the first time man, in a certain sense, is finally marked off from the rest of the animal kingdom, and emerges from mere animal conditions of existence into really human ones. The whole sphere of the conditions of life which environ man, and which have hitherto ruled man, now comes under the dominion and control of man...because he has now become master of his own social organization. Man's own social organization, hitherto confronting him as a necessity imposed by Nature and history, now becomes the result of his own free action. Only from that time will man himself, more and more consciously, make his own history...It is the ascent of man from the kingdom of necessity to the kingdom of freedom" (Tucker, 1978, pp. 715–16).

10 Stalin may well have been an exception among the Bolshevik leaders. Medvedev (1989, pp. 585–601) makes a persuasive case that Stalin, while

dedicated to socialist ideas, was, unlike the other leading Bolsheviks, primarily driven by a boundless lust for power.

11 Davies *et al.* (1994, pp. xvii, 1–2).

12 The revolution which took place in March of that year is often referred to as the "February Revolution," based on the calendar in effect in Russia at that time. Similarly, the "October Revolution," in which the Bolsheviks seized power, occurred in November according to the modern calendar.

13 The first soviets had appeared earlier, during the Revolution of 1905. The term "soviet" is a Russian word meaning "council."

14 See Chamberlin (1965, p. 278). The extent of radicalization was revealed by ward council elections in Moscow held in July and again in October 1917. All classes could vote in the ward council elections, not just workers and peasants. The Bolsheviks gained 51 per cent of the vote in October, compared to 11 per cent the previous July. Other socialist parties received another 18 per cent of the vote in October (Chamberlin, 1965, p. 279).

15 The other main socialist parties denounced the seizure of power and walked out of the Congress, although a faction of the Socialist Revolutionary Party remained.

16 The USSR was legally a federation of republics, which at the start included Russia, the Ukraine, Byelorussia, and Transcaucasia (the latter made up of Armenia, Azerbaijan, and Georgia). Later in that decade three Central Asian republics received the "Union republic" designation. The new state did not include all of the previous Russian Empire, as Finland, Estonia, Latvia, and Lithuania gained independence, and other parts of the former empire were lost to Poland, Rumania, and Turkey (Riasanovsky, 1977, p. 540.) The three Baltic republics of Latvia, Lithuania, and Estonia were later incorporated into the Soviet Union, in 1940.

17 The Bolsheviks changed the name of their party several times, but we will simply refer to it as the Communist Party, or CPSU for Communist Party of the Soviet Union. The latter name for the party was not formally adopted until 1952 (Schapiro, 1960, p. 605).

18 Lewin (1985, p. 192). The ban on factions in the Communist Party was supposed to be only temporary, but it was never rescinded. Despite the formal ban, relatively free internal debate continued on major issues within the top leadership until Stalin gained full control in the late 1920s.

19 Some critics of socialism have argued that the authoritarian Soviet system was an inevitable outcome of socialist ideas, in that state ownership of the means of production and economic planning necessarily lead to tyranny of the state over the individual. The classic statement of this view is Hayek (1944).

20 See Medvedev (1989, chs 1, 2).

21 Lewin (1985, pp. 258–66) discusses this problem.

22 Medvedev (1989, ch. 2).

23 The extreme nature of Stalin's new policies had little in common with the development strategy that had earlier been advocated by Trotsky, Zinoviev, and Kamenev. In particular, none of the latter had ever advocated forced collectivization of the peasantry (Cohen, 1985, p. 61). Cohen argues that when Stalin initiated his radical program of forced collectivization and crash industrialization, he "abandoned mainstream Bolshevik thinking about social and economic change" (1985, p. 61).

24 Collective farmers were permitted to sell produce raised on their own small private plots. Also, at various times, small private businesses of certain types were permitted, but they played an insignificant role in the economy.

25 Gosplan calculated material balances for about 2,000 broad product categories in the annual plans of the post-World War II period.
26 This description is highly simplified. In addition to the ministries responsible for particular industrial sectors, there were also a number of ministries and state committees which cut across sectoral lines. Examples include the Ministries of Finance and of Internal and Foreign Trade and the State Committees on Prices, on Labor and Wages, and on Science and Technology. The planning process also had regional dimensions, with planning organizations at the republican and local levels. In addition, the details of organization changed over time. Detailed accounts of the Soviet planning process are found in Nove (1986) and Gregory and Stuart (1990).
27 However, some non-market forces operated in the allocation of labor, such as party campaigns to persuade workers to move to newly developing regions and social pressure on urban residents to engage in "volunteer" agricultural labor at harvest time.
28 While such arrangements are not unknown in capitalist countries, they were far more prevalent in the Soviet system.
29 Hough and Fainsod (1979, chs 10–12) provide a detailed discussion of the central institutions of the Soviet political system.
30 The practice of the central committee selecting the general secretary was not actually written into the party rules until 1966 (Miller, 1993, p. 23).
31 Party congresses were held annually until 1925 and in that period were the site of important debates within the leadership. Thereafter, they were held only about every five years and allowed no debates, until the Gorbachev era.
32 The origins of the nomenklatura system are discussed in Rigby (1988, pp. 523–37).
33 For example, see Hough and Fainsod (1979, ch. 14), Rigby (1992), and Lane and Ross (1994b).
34 Hough and Fainsod (1979, p. 362).
35 That power was concentrated at the top does not entirely exclude some influences in the other direction. After the Stalin era, public opinion had some influence on the views of the millions of party members, and from there it seeped upward through the structure. As in any authoritarian form of government, the top leaders must pay some attention to public concerns if they wish to hold on to power in the long run.
36 Cohen (1985, p. 55).
37 Cohen (1985, p. 95). Major books on the Stalin terror include Medvedev (1989) and Conquest (1968).
38 Cohen (1985, p. 52).
39 The change was symbolized by Khrushchev's retirement to his dacha to write his memoirs after he was ousted by opponents in 1964 amidst harsh official criticism of his "errors."
40 In later years the formulation shifted to the claim that, as the distinctions between the three classes recognized by Soviet officialdom – workers, peasants, and white–collar employees – had become unimportant, the Soviet state had become a state of the whole people rather than a workers' state.
41 Some Western Soviet specialists viewed the system as socialist for a different reason. They interpreted socialism to simply mean a system based on state ownership and central economic planning. This attributes a narrower meaning to the term "socialism" than is found in the writings of those who have advocated it. Socialists have always considered popular sovereignty over

society's economic and political development to be an important component of socialism.

42 Despite the differences between the two systems, some analysts have argued that the Soviet system was a form of capitalism, called state capitalism. One of the first to make this case was Cliff (1988 [1948]). Another major work in this tradition is Bettelheim (1976).

43 Lane (1988) offers a somewhat similar interpretation of the Soviet system.

44 This leaves aside retirement pensions, disability payments, student stipends, and other similar non-labor incomes. But none of these derived from property ownership. The only legitimate property income in the Soviet system was rent for letting out unused space in an individually owned home.

45 However, there were bureaucratic rivalries over resources in the Soviet planning system, which did cause significant problems.

46 In some areas of the central Asian republics of the Soviet Union, unemployment did arise at some points in the postwar period, due to economic development failing to keep pace with very high birth rates. In the rest of the Soviet Union, there was almost no unemployment, except for a small number of workers who were in between jobs at any one time. Hewett (1988, pp. 39, 42) remarks that the Soviet Union achieved "as close to full employment as any industrialized economy can hope to achieve," a rate he estimated for the mid-1980s to be under 2 per cent of the labor force.

47 Urban residents typically paid 5 to 10 per cent of their income for rent.

48 Workers made up 18.1 per cent of the Supreme Soviet deputies, and peasants 17.6 per cent, in 1974 (Hough and Fainsod, 1979, p. 364).

49 The evidence indicates that the distribution of salary income in the Soviet Union was quite inegalitarian in the 1930s, but that after a wage reform launched in 1956, it became much more egalitarian (McAuley, 1977, pp. 222ff.). One study found that the ratio of the 90th percentile wage rate to the 10th percentile wage rate fell from 7.2 to 2.8 from 1946 to 1967 (Vinokur and Ofer, 1986, p. 26, citing a study by Rabkina and Rimashevskaia, 1978).

50 McAuley (1979, p. 57).

51 These data are from Vinokur and Ofer (1986, Table 10). The original data used by Vinokur and Ofer are from the widely cited study by Sawyer (1976, p. 17). The decile ratios for both the Soviet Union and Western countries are for pre-tax per capita income of households. The decile ratio of 6.7 reported for Norway, which was the smallest decile ratio for pre-tax income of the capitalist countries listed by Vinokur and Ofer, was still 49 per cent higher than the comparable Soviet ratio.

52 If one compares the distribution of wage and salary income alone in the Soviet Union to that of Western countries, the Soviet Union still appears relatively egalitarian, although less dramatically so than for total household income. The ratio of the 90th percentile wage rate to the 10th percentile wage rate was about 3.2 for the Soviet Union in the early 1970s, compared to 4.5 in the United States, 3.8 in France, and 3.7 in Japan. Furthermore, more than 20 per cent of the highest-paid decile in the Soviet Union were skilled blue-collar workers. However, the decile ratios for wages for the UK (2.8) and the Netherlands (2.8) were lower than for the Soviet Union (Vinokur and Ofer, 1986, p. 8 and Table 5; the Soviet data include public-sector wages only).

53 Some observers have reported that social relations actually closely resembling feudalism arose in some agricultural regions of Uzbekistan during the Brezhnev era, complete with castles, private police, and private prisons. See Miller (1993, p. 33).

54 Contrary to the widespread connotation of luxury which is attached to that term in the West, the Russian word "dacha" refers to a country house which can be as modest as a tiny shack erected by a family of average means in their spare time. Many urban families have some sort of dacha to which they retreat on hot summer weekends. However, the state dachas assigned to the top members of the party–state elite were large and comfortable.

55 There were some exceptions. High incomes and privileges were also accorded to some non-elite individuals, such as outstanding athletes, scientists, writers, and artists.

56 We are here leaving out of consideration a possible system of ownership and control of individual enterprises by their employees, with relations among enterprises left to the market. This possibility will be considered in Chapter 12.

57 Ticktin (1992) takes that position. In a thoughtful account of the Soviet experience, Daniels (1993, p. 175) denies any real connection between the Soviet system and the original ideas of Marx, accusing the Soviet leadership of "flying the purloined banner of Marxism." Miller (1993, p. 8) views the Soviet system as primarily driven by an autocratic tradition of modernization going back to the Tsarist era.

58 Many Western socialists who were critical of the Soviet system came to regard it as a new form of class society, neither capitalist nor socialist. An effective presentation of this view is found in Paul M. Sweezy (1980). An early statement of this view is found in Djilas (1957). Some versions of this view do not differ greatly in certain respects from the view presented in this book. However, we do not consider the ruling party–state elite of the Soviet system to be a ruling class in the traditional sense. This issue is discussed in Nove (1975, pp. 615–38)

59 The CPSU membership reached a maximum of 19.5 million in 1989 (*Izvestiia TsK KPSS*, 1989, no. 3, p. 138).

60 That list of institutions had an overlapping membership. The central committee included the members of the other bodies.

61 A few individuals in the foregoing categories would be members of the central committee.

62 Farmer (1992, p. 84) cites a wide range of estimates for the size of the Soviet ruling elite, including one by Stalin in 1937 that numbered the "first-rank leaders" of the Soviet Union at 3,000 to 4,000, the "middle-rank leaders" at 30,000 to 40,000, and the "lower Party command staff" at 100,000 to 150,000. After surveying various estimates, Farmer concludes that the ruling elite in the postwar period numbered about 100,000 (p. 85). Zimbalist *et al.* (1989, p. 258) conclude that the Soviet ruling elite numbers "less than 100,000."

63 By contrast, in capitalist systems the class of capitalists – those who own enough assets to live on the income it generates – typically represents about 1–2 per cent of the households. The Soviet party–state elite was indeed an elite group in the population.

64 *Istoriia Kommunisticheskoi Partii Sovetskogo Soiuza* (1977, p. 77), Lewin (1985, p. 200).

65 One study found that, during the Brezhnev years, 92.6 per cent of high-level Communist Party officials and 100 per cent of high-level government officials had a higher education (Kryshtanovskaya, 1994b).

66 See Farmer (1992, ch. 2), for a detailed account of the educational background of the Soviet elite. Kryshtanovskaya (1994b) found that, in the Brezhnev

years, 72.3 per cent of high-level party officials and 80.7 per cent of high-level government officials had a technical, engineering, agricultural, or military–technical education.

67 In some pre-capitalist systems, ruling group status was passed on by inheritance of both title and property, as when a feudal lord's son inherited both the lordship and the manor. Under capitalism, membership in the capitalist class is passed on through the inheritance of property alone. Of course, this does not preclude upward mobility under capitalism, as some individuals from humble backgrounds rise, through successful business or professional endeavors, into the capitalist class.

68 Some did, but the risk of being exposed and punished was real.

69 See Nove (1975), Matthews (1978), and Farmer (1992).

70 Matthews (1978, p. 159).

71 One study found that, in the late 1970s, 70 per cent of ministers and heads of state committees, and over 50 per cent of the directors of the largest state enterprises, began their working life as workers or peasants (Matthews, 1978, p. 158).

72 It is for this reason that we refer to the Soviet party–state elite as an "elite" or "group," rather than a "class." Lacking the social glue of having a common form of individual property ownership or the assured power to pass on their ruling group status to their offspring, they appear to be a looser type of social group than a traditional property-owning ruling class.

3 GROWTH, STAGNATION, AND THE ORIGINS OF PERESTROIKA

1 For example, in the early 1930s the huge Magnitogorsk steel plant was built at a then almost uninhabited location at the southern tip of the Ural Mountains, next to a previously untapped mountain of iron ore.

2 Nove (1989, p. 220).

3 Gregory and Stuart (1990, p. 12).

4 Kuznets (1963, p. 345).

5 Kuznets (1963, p. 247). Countries that industrialized late had certain advantages, such as the opportunity to borrow technologies already developed elsewhere. On the other hand, late industrializers faced the problem of stiff competition from the powerful nations which had industrialized first, a problem which made it difficult to get industrialization started in many nations.

6 Nove (1989, pp. 280–6).

7 The official Soviet data for NMP growth rates are considered to be exaggerated for two main reasons. One is the possible understatement of price increases in the official statistics, which would overstate "real" economic growth. The second factor has to do with the choice of a base year for the price index used for constructing real growth series. The computed real growth rate is affected by whether the base year chosen is early or late – it is usually the case that the earlier the base year selected, the faster the resulting computed rate of growth. This effect can be quite pronounced in an economy that is growing rapidly and undergoing major structural change. There are no objective grounds for saying what base year is the "correct" one.

All long-term growth series face this problem. The official Soviet data use a very early base year, which produces a high-end estimate of long-term growth.

 8 It can be argued that using the Western GNP concept to compare economic growth between Soviet state socialism and Western capitalism creates a bias in favor of capitalism. The Soviet use of NMP reflects the low priority placed by Soviet planners on services as compared to physical goods. Comparisons of the two systems based on GNP reflects Western capitalist priorities, which draw no distinction between goods and services. Similarly, a comparison of the two systems using NMP for both would be biased toward the Soviet system. There is no objective, unbiased way to compare economic growth rates of two systems which have different values and priorities regarding economic results.

 9 The CIA estimates of Soviet GNP appeared in annual editions of the *Handbook of Economic Statistics* published by the Directorate of Intelligence. They are most conveniently available in Joint Economic Committee (1982, 1990). The question of the reliability of these CIA estimates is discussed below.

10 In constructing Figure 3.1, to minimize the distortion that results from using a single base year for prices to measure real GNP growth over a long period, the base-year price index for GNP varied. Soviet GNP growth for 1928–50 was based on 1937 factor cost, for 1950–60 on 1970 factor cost, and for 1960–75 on 1982 factor cost. US GNP growth during 1928–50 was based on 1929 prices, for 1950–60 on 1972 prices, and for 1960–75 on 1982 prices. The (unavoidable) use of an earlier base year for US growth during 1928–40 than for Soviet growth over that period probably raises the US rate relative to the Soviet one.

11 The rapid Soviet growth was achieved with very little price inflation. According to official Soviet statistics, retail prices grew at 0.9 per cent per year during 1940–86 (Gregory and Stuart, 1990, p. 388). A more realistic estimate would be in the 1–2 per cent range, still a very low rate of price inflation compared to Western experience.

12 Becker (1994, p. 309). Becker surveys estimates of the Soviet/US GNP ratio from a variety of CIA sources. Most of the CIA estimates for 1975 fell between 58 and 62 per cent.

13 In 1970 gross investment was 28.2 per cent of Soviet GNP based on CIA estimates, while in the US it was 14.5 per cent of GNP (Joint Economic Committee, 1982, p. 67; *Economic Report of the President*, 1985, p. 232).

14 In 1980, 86.6 per cent of the population aged 15–64 worked, compared to 66.5 per cent for the US and 70.9 per cent for the European members of the OECD (Ofer, 1987, p. 1783). The direct effect of this high employment-to-population ratio is an elevated level of output per capita rather than faster growth. However, this facilitates rapid output growth over time by making the high investment rate less costly in terms of foregone consumption.

15 Education spending in the Soviet Union increased more than 6-fold in constant 1950 prices from 1928 to 1950 (Bergson, 1961, p. 85). In 1926 only 6 per cent of the population over age 15 had had schooling beyond 7th grade. By 1959 that figure had risen to 39 per cent (Gregory and Stuart, 1990, p. 360).

16 The Soviet consumption growth figure is based on 1982 established prices, reported in Joint Economic Committee (1990, pp. 89–91). The US figure is based on 1982 prices, from *Economic Report of the President* (1988, pp. 250, 283).

17 Ofer (1987, p. 1790). However, he cautions that "it should be borne in mind that this started from very low initial levels."

18 *Narodnoe khoziaistvo SSSR* (1972 [1922–72], p. 373; 1986, p. 446).
19 Directorate of Intelligence (1988a, pp. 67–72).
20 The urban share of the Soviet population rose from only 16 per cent in 1922 to 63 per cent in 1980 (*Narodnoe khoziaistvo SSSR*, 1981, p. 7; 1982 [1922–82], p. 9).
21 The agricultural share of employment fell from 71 per cent in 1926 to 26 per cent in 1980 (Ofer, 1987, p. 1792).
22 In 1981, 96 million Soviet citizens had high-school diplomas and 20 million had college degrees (*Narodnoe khoziaistvo SSSR*, 1981, p. 27).
23 Per ten-thousand of population in 1980, the Soviet Union had 37.4 physicians and 125 hospital beds while the United States had 18.2 physicians and 58.5 hospital beds (*Narodnoe khoziaistvo SSSR*, 1981, p. 88; *Statistical Abstract of the United States*, 1985, p. 844).
24 A 1987 survey article on Soviet economic growth stated there was "general agreement among researchers" that Western estimates of Soviet economic growth provided "a basically sound body of economic data" (Ofer, 1987, p. 1775).
25 This is, of course, a non sequitur. While some set of weaknesses underlay the demise of the Soviet system, one cannot deduce from that demise that any particular past dimension of Soviet performance was below its previously estimated level. This reaction to the Soviet collapse, however illogical, created a psychological predisposition to believe almost any claim that might be made which revises downward estimates of past Soviet accomplishments.
26 Khanin's original widely cited criticism of Soviet official statistics was published in Khanin and Seliunin (1987). The work of Khanin is accessible to the English reader in Harrison (1993).
27 Khanin estimated Soviet NMP growth during 1928–40 at only 3.2 per cent per year, compared to the official rate of 14.9 per cent. However, for the postwar years the differences are much smaller. Khanin estimated Soviet NMP growth as quite robust (7.2 per cent) in the 1950s and in the moderate 3 to 4.5 per cent range during 1960–75 (Joint Economic Committee, 1990, p. 46).
28 Millar *et al.* (1993, p. 38). A sort of contest developed over who could make the lowest estimate of Soviet economic accomplishments. The likely winner of this contest was Soviet scholar Victor Belkin, who, at a 1990 conference sponsored by the American Enterprise Institute, placed the Soviet GNP at 14 per cent of the US level – about equal to that of Mexico on a per capita basis (Becker, 1994, p. 312). The flavor of this effort to revise past estimates of Soviet economic performance is captured by the title of an article by a leading Western critic of the Soviet economy, Anders Åslund (1990): "How Small Is Soviet National Income?."
29 This study was mandated by the House Permanent Select Committee on Intelligence.
30 Millar *et al.* (1993, p. 34).
31 While the panel supported the CIA's estimates of the ruble value of Soviet GNP and the Soviet GNP growth rate, they did criticize some of the agency's comparative data. They concluded that estimates of the ratio of the level of Soviet GNP to that of the US may have overstated the relative size of the Soviet GNP. They noted that the CIA had been aware of the main sources of bias inherent in such a comparison, and that such biases are impossible to quantify. However, they suggested that publication of the results, despite the qualifications included in CIA reports, might have been inadvisable. See Millar *et al.* (1993, pp. 39–41).

32 Millar *et al.* (1993, p. 39).

33 Becker (1994, p. 293).

34 Alter (1994) cited in Becker (1994, p. 294).

35 *New York Times*, 1 February 1995, p. 18.

36 Boretsky (1987, p. 521). See also the CIA's comment on Boretsky's criticism (Pitzer, 1990) and Boretsky's response (Boretsky, 1990). The CIA used various fragmentary data on the Soviet economy to construct its estimates for GNP growth. Boretsky used fragmentary data on the same industries and sectors of the West German and US economies and followed the CIA methodology to construct GNP estimates. Boretsky asserted that the understatement of GNP growth was due to failure of the CIA's physical output series to take account of product improvements over time and the fact that the product lines for which the CIA obtained data grew more slowly than the remaining product lines.

37 For example, the trains in the modern, efficient Washington metro system run on rails that were made using Soviet seamless rail laying machines. Also, US military contractors purchased a technology for producing continuous-cast aluminum from the Soviet Union (Hewett, 1988, p. 33).

38 In the 1960s, the average completion time for Soviet investment projects was 7 to 8 years, more than twice the time required in Western industrialized countries (Hewett, 1988, p. 89).

39 Berliner (1976) explores the problem of slow and uneven innovation in Soviet industry in great depth. Rapid innovation occurred mainly in sectors, such as defense and space, which received a great deal of attention and resources from the top authorities, who demanded that they produce at the technological frontier. But to most Soviet enterprise managers, the disruptions and problems that attended the introduction of new products or methods of production carried the risk of preventing the enterprise from meeting its plan targets, while the rewards to the enterprise for successful innovation tended to be limited.

40 The caloric intake per capita was similar to that of Western industrialized nations by 1980, but a larger share of the Soviet diet came from potatoes and a smaller share from meat, poultry, and fresh fruit (*Narodnoe khoziaistvo SSSR za 70 let*, 1987, p. 470; *Statistical Abstract of the United States*, 1985, p. 848).

41 Japan's long-term trend rate of GNP growth fell in half during 1954–84 (Ellman, 1986, p. 532–3).

42 Pitzer and Baukol (1991) constructed the data on non-farm business-sector output for the Soviet Union. This concept is widely used for capitalist economies to measure the output growth of the commercial sector, excluding government services. They applied this concept to the Soviet economy. Their measure includes the output of all non-farm entities which receive payment for the goods and services they produce, excluding those which operate largely on a state subsidy (called "budgetary institutions"). See Pitzer and Baukol (1991, p. 49).

43 Joint Economic Committee (1990, pp. 55–6).

44 This series does show a modest slowdown in growth in 1971–75, but it remained relatively robust and well above the US rate in those years.

45 Eventually industrialization and urbanization lead to a sharp slowdown, or even a stoppage, in the growth of the labor force. Further rapid output growth depends on applying more capital goods, introducing more

advanced technologies, and raising the quality of the labor force, all of which show up as rising output per labor hour.

46 Western specialists on the Soviet economy do not all agree about the timing of the Soviet growth slowdown. Some emphasize the gradual and consistent slowdown from 1928 to 1985 (excepting the war years). However, a number of specialists have located a sharp downward break in 1975, including Hewett (1988), Schroeder (1985), and Pitzer and Baukol (1991).

47 Technological progress is not simply a matter of introducing new methods of production which boost the output of existing products. Technological progress also has an important qualitative dimension, which involves the introduction of new and better products over time. For this reason, the slowdown in Soviet technological progress in the 1970s deserves to be treated as an additional dimension of the worsening economic performance, rather than simply as a cause of the growth slowdown.

48 Some Western economists seek to measure technological progress by using an aggregate measure known as "total factor productivity" (TFP), which refers to the output of goods and services per unit of combined inputs of labor, capital goods, and natural resources. The idea is that increases in TFP show the effect of technological advance. However, there are significant conceptual and practical problems with this approach, particularly when applied to the Soviet economy. This has resulted in enormous variation in the estimates of the pattern of growth of TFP for the Soviet economy, depending on the assumptions made. The conclusion this suggests is that TFP estimates do not provide a very reliable basis for judging the pattern of Soviet technological progress over time. See Directorate of Intelligence (1988a, p. 63), Gregory and Stuart (1990, p. 365), Ofer (1987, p. 1778), and Whitesell (1985).

49 The measures Kontorovich used included the number and economic effect of innovations, inventions, and rationalizations; the share of new products in the output of the machine-building ministries; and the number of prototypes of new machines and instruments developed (Kontorovich, 1992b, pp. 220–33). For some indicators, the innovation slowdown began in the late 1960s.

50 Hauslohner (1991, p. 37).

51 The causes of the Soviet stagnation are discussed in Hewett (1988, pp. 51–78), Levine (1983, pp. 155–68), Ofer (1987, pp. 1814–19), Pitzer and Baukol (1991, pp. 74–80), and Schroeder (1985, pp. 47–67). The causal factors listed are all directed to explaining the slowdown in economic growth. The causes of the slowdown in technological innovation have proved more elusive; see Kontorovich (1992b).

52 Ofer (1987, pp. 1788–9). According to the data cited by Ofer (1987), the Soviet military burden declined in 1950–60 and then rose gradually in 1960–80. However, the slight increase after 1960 in the defense share of GNP did not cause any reduction in the share of GNP devoted to either investment or research and development, both of which increased slightly during 1960–80 (Ofer, 1987, p. 1788).

53 In the Gorbachev years, the Soviet leadership was determined to reduce the arms burden on the Soviet economy. A reduced arms burden would have aided the Soviet economy at any phase of its development. However, it is difficult to find evidence that the military burden played a role in the stagnation that began in 1975.

54 See Bowles et al. (1990, ch. 4).

55 However, in the mid-1980s oil prices fell, and this did contribute to later Soviet problems.

56 See Levine (1983, pp. 156–7).

57 The Soviet convention was to date a five-year plan period from the start of the first year through to the end of the fifth year – for example, 1981–85. For all growth data, we are following the Western convention of dating a period starting with the year that precedes the first year of the period. Following the above example, we would label a five-year period as 1980–85 rather than 1981–85. This labelling method takes account of the fact that growth in the first year of the period, 1981, is measured relative to 1980.

58 Planned investment was also sharply reduced at the same time (Hewett, 1988, p. 52).

59 The Tenth Five Year Plan for 1976–80 was launched with these words from Gosplan Chairman Baibakov: "The targets for 1976 are permeated with the idea of improving the efficiency and quality of all work" (*Pravda*, 3 December 1975, cited in Schroeder, 1985, p. 50).

60 Some lowering of growth targets might have been a good policy if it had been accompanied by other effective measures for achieving the desired improvements in efficiency and product quality. In the absence of such measures, the reduction in planned growth just made things worse.

61 In 1975 the average traffic density was 23.4 million ton-kilometers per kilometer of rail line. By contrast, US railroads carry 4.7 million ton-kilometers per kilometer (Kontorovich, 1992a, pp. 174–5).

62 See Kontorovich (1992a) for a detailed account of these developments.

63 Gustafson (1985). Gustafson attributes this investment mistake to an unduly short time-horizon on the part of the planners.

64 For evidence of such a pattern in long-term economic growth, see Gordon *et al.* (1982, pp. 41–7).

65 This interpretation of the pattern of long-run economic growth, known as the "social structure of accumulation" analysis, is explained in Kotz *et al.* (1994). Essays in that volume explain how, in various periods in the history of capitalist countries, a long stretch of rapid economic growth has ended in stagnation when the specific institutional configuration which had previously promoted rapid economic growth ceased to do so.

66 Another goal of Soviet planning was building the economic base for a strong military. The planning system was very well suited to accomplishing this goal.

67 Hewett (1988, pp. 85–6) makes a similar point. It is widely believed that a post-industrialization economy inevitably grows increasingly complex, not only in the consumer goods demanded, but in the variety of producer goods which are required.

68 Tatyana Zaslavskaya, a leading Soviet sociologist and former advisor to Gorbachev, claimed that, as of the early 1980s, "in the opinion of most managers, people are becoming more difficult to manage" (Zaslavskaya, 1990, p. 49). The sharp dropoff in labor productivity growth after 1975 may partly reflect a reduction in labor discipline, although many other factors also influenced labor productivity – particularly, the rates of investment and technological progress.

69 For somewhat similar analysis, see Zaslavskaya (1990, pp. 49–57).

70 Hewett (1988, pp. 258–73).

71 Miller (1993, pp. 60–1).

72 See the first-hand account in Ligachev (1993, ch. 1).

73 Yegor Ligachev, who was named to the post of second in command of the party by Gorbachev, made a statement to that effect at a later party conference (*Pravda*, 2 July 1988, cited in Hough, 1991, p. 248.) Ligachev claimed he was able to persuade the senior member of the politburo, Andrei Gromyko, to deliver the nominating speech for Gorbachev by stressing the overwhelming support for him among regional party leaders (Ligachev, 1993, pp. 72–5).

74 Contrary to the impression of some observers, Ligachev was not an opponent of reform of the old system. However, he favored moving slowly and cautiously, and he always held to the view that the aim of reform should be to renew and strengthen socialism, not replace it with capitalism. See Stephen Cohen's introduction to Ligachev's memoirs in Ligachev (1993, pp. vii–xxxvi) and Surovell (1991).

75 Hewett (1988, p. 261).

76 "Yakovlev is said by knowledgeable insiders to have been the architect of Gorbachev's domestic and foreign policy since the summer of 1985" (Hough, 1987, p. 34).

77 Ligachev (1993, pp. 95–6).

78 See Miller (1993, p. 42).

79 The late Ed Hewett, a careful student of Soviet economic policy, wrote in 1985 that "it is now quite clear that Gorbachev has no intention whatsoever of introducing radical reforms in the Soviet economy, at least in this decade" (Hewett, 1991a, p. 16).

80 Cited in Hewett (1988, p. 288).

81 See especially Gorbachev's report to the party central committee on 25 June 1987 (Gorbachev, 1987) and his book *Perestroika* (Gorbachev, 1988, originally published in November 1987).

82 Gorbachev (1987, pp. 4, 36, 37; 1988, pp. 4–5).

83 Gorbachev (1988, pp. 27, 32, 37).

84 Gorbachev (1987, p. 39).

85 Gorbachev (1988, pp. 20, 76).

86 Gorbachev (1987, p. 41).

87 Gorbachev (1987, p. 7; 1988, p. 18).

88 Gorbachev (1987, pp. 42, 43; 1988, pp. 71–2, 76).

89 Gorbachev (1987, pp. 9, 41).

90 Gorbachev (1988, pp. 23, 69, 72).

PART II PERESTROIKA AND THE DEMISE OF THE SOVIET SYSTEM

1 Independent Russia does have a popularly elected president, unlike the former USSR. However, in many respects democracy became more constricted after 1991. This is discussed in Chapter 11.

4 GLASNOST AND THE INTELLIGENTSIA

1 This definition of the term "intelligentsia" differs from the traditional Soviet usage, which is much broader and includes all white-collar workers having a high level of formal education.

2 Gwertzman and Kaufman (1992, pp. 11–12, 27).

3 Hewett and Winston (1991a, p. 502).

4 Brudny (1991, p. 162).
5 "Informal associations" sprang up across the Soviet Union under glasnost. By the end of 1987 an estimated 30,000 such groups had formed and by 1989 more than 60,000. Some were quasi-political groups concerned with issues such as the environment, while others promoted sports or music (Miller, 1993, p. 102).
6 See Lewin (1991, chs 5, 6).
7 Extreme Russian nationalist ideas had attracted a significant underground following prior to perestroika, not just among the intelligentsia but also within the party and state bureaucracies (Bilenkin, 1995, p. 25).
8 Ligachev (1993, pp. 95–7).
9 During 1990–91 Yakovlev shifted his views dramatically from his initial support for the reform of socialism. At a Party Congress in 1990, Yakovlev remarked to a group of delegates, "I have made my choice. I am in favor of joint-stock capital" (Daniels, 1993, p. 168). In the summer of 1991 he resigned as a senior advisor to Gorbachev and publicly renounced Marxism and socialism. See the interview with Yakovlev entitled "Why I'm Giving up on Marxism," *Sovetskaya Rossiya*, 3 August 1991, p. 1, reported in *The Current Digest of the Soviet Press*, vol. 43, no. 31, 1991, p. 11.
10 Ligachev (1993, pp. 96–7). Korotich confirmed the accuracy of Ligachev's account in a conversation with the authors on 3 December 1994.
11 Every social system has ways of eliciting support from its intelligentsia. Western democratic capitalism is no exception. However, the means used by the latter to encourage intellectuals to support the social system are more subtle. They involve mainly the effects of a system in which those with reasonably orthodox views and methods have easier access to grants, publishers, academic positions, and a favorable reputation, rather than the outright censorship and coercion employed by the Soviet system.
12 Nina Andreyeva, "I Cannot Forgo Principles," *Sovetskaya Rossiya*, 13 March 1988, p. 3.
13 Glasnost passed from policy into law during 1989–90. In July 1989 the prohibition against "anti-Soviet agitation and propaganda" was removed from the Criminal Code, and in 1990 a law "On the Press and Other Media of Mass Information" declared censorship abolished (Miller, 1993, p. 99).
14 Vasily Seliunin, "Sources," *Novy Mir*, No. 5, 1988. This article is reprinted in English in Tarasulo (1989).
15 See Steele (1994, pp. 41–42).
16 Interview with Tatyana Zaslavskaya, 19 October 1992.
17 White (1992, p. 232).
18 After a new law on the media went into effect on 1 August 1990, many leading newspapers and magazines broke their affiliation with the state or party institution to which they had previously been formally subordinate and converted to independent cooperatives (Miller, 1993, pp. 99–100).
19 Not all of the Soviet mass media followed the "liberal" direction that was attracted to Western democratic capitalism as the new model for the Soviet Union. Some veered off in a different direction, toward Russian nationalism.
20 From 1960 to 1985 the average pay in science and research fell in relative terms, from 23 per cent more than that of the average industrial worker to 4 per cent less (*Narodnoe khosziaistvo SSSR za 70 let*, 1987, p. 431). During 1960–85 the broader group of highly educated employees also saw their pay decline relative to that of manual workers (Miller, 1993, p. 31). A professor

at Moscow State University claimed that this downward trend in relative pay
had also affected university professors over that period (interview with
Alexander Buzgalin, June 1994).

21 A comment made to Fred Weir by a Soviet friend.

22 Some conservative think-tanks in the United States and Britain actively
sought to influence the thinking of Soviet economists and other intellectuals.
Examples are the Heritage Foundation and Britain's Institute of Economic
Affairs. These institutions held conferences to bring together Western free-
market thinkers and Soviet intellectuals, and they invited Soviet economists
to spend time visiting them. In any event, most Soviet economists were ready
to adopt the free-market view and did not need much prodding.

23 Barnett (1991, pp. 1087–98).

24 Abalkin's views, and his important role in economic policy-making in the
later perestroika years, are discussed in Chapter 5.

25 Interview with Nikolai Ryzhkov, 27 October 1992.

26 Interview with Alexander Savitsky, Magnitogorsk, 7 June 1994.

5 ECONOMIC REFORM

1 That consumption began to grow faster than total output (GNP or NMP)
indicates a sharp reduction in the growth of aggregate investment, discussed
below.

2 Noren (1990).

3 International Monetary Fund (1992a, p. 52). Gross fixed investment (in constant prices), based on official Soviet statistics, rose by 7.0 per cent per year
during 1985–87, compared to an annual rate of 3.4 per cent during 1975–85.

4 The important Law on State Enterprise had the somewhat awkward official
name, when translated into English, of "The Law on the State Enterprise
(Association)." The shortened name will be used here.

5 Schroeder (1987). Certain sectors were to be excluded from wholesale trade,
remaining under central allocation. These included electricity, crude oil, gas,
metal ores, and certain specialized equipment.

6 Schroeder (1987). Enterprise employees' right to elect managers was rescinded in 1990.

7 In an interview with the authors on 17 January 1994, Soviet economist and
former deputy prime minister Leonid Abalkin asserted that, while the Law
on State Enterprise "was a progressive law," its working was disrupted by
the failure to pass accompanying tax legislation. What had been required, he
asserted, were new taxes on both enterprises and the population, including
an excess profits tax. After Abalkin became deputy prime minister in 1989, he
pushed through new tax legislation in November of that year. However,
Abalkin stated that, by that date, it was too late to be effective.

8 One study of rationing in various Soviet localities found that, by the end of
1989, sugar was rationed in 97 per cent of the localities, butter in 62 per cent,
and beef in almost 40 per cent. See Noren (1990).

9 The figures cited are official Soviet data from International Monetary Fund
(1992a, p. 49). They differ slightly from the official Soviet consumption data
in Table 5.1 and Figure 5.1 in that the data cited here are for household
consumption only, excluding communal consumption. The 1989 consumption level was given a boost by the leadership's decision in mid-1988 to
increase the availability of consumer goods by cutting back and reorienting
military production and simultaneously increasing consumer goods imports.

Consumer goods imports rose by about 8–9 billion rubles in 1989, which amounted to about 2 per cent of the preceding year's total consumption level (Schroeder, 1990; International Monetary Fund, 1992a, p. 57).

10 It is a good approximation if the stocks of unsold consumer goods do not change much from year to year.

11 The data in Figure 5.2 probably understate the increase in the gap between household income and consumer goods available. It can be shown that, when stocks of consumer goods in the stores begin to decrease, as occurred during 1988–89, then the growth in real private consumer spending somewhat *overstates* the increase in the volume of consumer goods available.

12 The average real wage, which had grown at the modest rate of 1.4 per cent per year during 1980–87, suddenly grew at 7.5 per cent per year during 1987–89. Non-wage remuneration from state enterprises grew even faster. See International Monetary Fund (1992a, pp. 56, 62).

13 Gross domestic product (GDP) is a measure of total output that is very similar to GNP, particularly for the Soviet Union. The differences between the two measures involve earnings abroad by citizens of the country and in-country earnings by foreign nationals.

14 State expenditures during 1985–88 grew more slowly than they had during 1981–85; the rising deficit was due to problems on the revenue side (Noren, 1990).

15 The Soviet budget deficit was financed not by selling bonds but by means that increased the money in circulation. During 1987–89 the money supply (M1) grew at an annual rate of 14.8 per cent (International Monetary Fund, 1992a, p. 70).

16 International Monetary Fund (1992a, p. 58).

17 During 1988–89 retail inventories reached their lowest levels relative to sales since before 1950 (Schroeder, 1992, p. 99).

18 A survey found that, in early 1989, 90 per cent of Soviet families were stockpiling goods at home, compared to 25 per cent a year earlier (Schroeder, 1992, p. 99).

19 International Monetary Fund (1992a, p. 49).

20 The article was written under the name Larisa Popkova (Popkova, 1987).

21 The arguments made by advocates of privatization in the Soviet Union were frequently very simplistic, seeming to have nineteenth-century small-business capitalism as their point of reference. If it were in fact true that only the private owner of a business can efficiently manage it and produce high-quality products that consumers want, then the marketplace success of the giant corporations that dominate the economies of the United States, Western Europe, and Japan is very puzzling, since such corporations are typically run by hired managers, not the main shareholders.

22 Åslund (1991, pp. 343–344).

23 Interview with Vladimir Faminsky, 26 October 1992. Faminsky was the head of a department at the Institute of Economics in Moscow and an editor of the journal *Voprosy Ekonomiki* (Problems of Economics). He was acquainted with Shatalin during the 1980s and observed the evolution of his views.

24 According to a Western Soviet specialist, by the fall of 1989 Shatalin was "unambiguously in favour of the gradual conversion of the Soviet economy into a mixed market economy in which the capitalist sector is predominant" (Davies, 1991, p. 126). In an interview Shatalin praised the "progress in England...associated with the conservative Thatcher" (*Literaturnaya gazeta*, 11 October 1989, cited in Davies, 1991, p. 126).

25 Abalkin (1991, pp. 61, 62). The article by Abalkin was originally published in Russian in 1989.
26 By 1989 the Soviet economy had been outperformed by Western capitalism for a period of nearly fifteen years. This cumulative experience may have played a role in persuading some participants in the Soviet policy debate that capitalism was a superior alternative to any version of socialism.
27 *New York Times*, 17 November 1989, p. A16.
28 *New York Times*, 14 February 1990, p. A2.
29 *New York Times*, 16 March 1990, A6. Gorbachev was vague about exactly how perestroika should be radicalized in the sphere of economic reform, beyond stating "We must get down to creating a full-blooded domestic market".
30 *New York Times*, 14 May 1990, pp. A1, A8.
31 These comments were made in a speech in an industrial region of the Urals, reported in the *New York Times*, 14 May 1990, p. 1.
32 *New York Times*, 23 May 1990, p. A1.
33 *New York Times*, 14 May 1990, p. A8.
34 From the text of Gorbachev's speech, distributed by TASS and reprinted in the *New York Times*, 3 July 1990, p. A10.
35 In a conversation with the authors, Russian economist Stanislav Menshikov asserted that the 500 Day Plan actually originated earlier. By Menshikov's account, Yavlinsky had drawn up what was substantially the same proposal some months earlier, when he was working under Soviet Deputy Prime Minister Abalkin. Abalkin did not support the plan, leading Yavlinsky to turn to Boris Yeltsin, who gave his approval. When Gorbachev and Yeltsin named the team to come up with a new economic strategy in August 1990, the plan they produced was substantially the same as Yavlinsky's earlier plan, except a 400 day timetable had been expanded to 500 days, according to Menshikov. (Conversation with Stanislav Menshikov, Washington, DC, 9 January 1995).
36 Yavlinksy *et al.* (1991, pp. 7, 14, 15, 44, 62).
37 *New York Times*, 18 September 1990, p. A6.
38 *New York Times*, 17 October 1990, p. A1. The official title of this piece of legislation was "Basic Guidelines for Stabilization of the National Economy and Transition to a Market Economy".
39 *New York Times*, 17 October 1990, p. A8.
40 Noren (1990).
41 One Western observer remarked, "In the course of 1990, the centralized supply system (*Gossnab*), has slowly disintegrated, and enterprises have been left to fend for themselves through 'direct contacts'" (Rutland, 1991, p. 302).
42 Many cases of unofficial privatization apparently took place in the Soviet Union much earlier in the perestroika period, as directors of enterprises took advantage of the declining power of the state authorities to informally privatize their enterprise. Similarly, some private financial institutions began to function in the late 1980s before they had achieved official sanction. For example, see the case of Menatep Bank discussed in Chapter 7.
43 The chaos was deepened by the withdrawal of the Communist Party apparatus from its former role in the management of the economy over the period 1988–90. This is discussed in Chapter 6.
44 International Monetary Fund (1992a, p. 49).
45 The full dismantling of socialist economic institutions only took place in Russia after it became an independent state in 1992.

46 International Monetary Fund (1992a, p. 78). These percentages are calculated in rubles at the official exchange rate.

47 Imports from the developed capitalist countries also fell in 1991, accounting for 21 per cent of the USSR's total import reduction (International Monetary Fund 1992a, p. 78).

48 Yavlinsky *et al.* (1991, p. 66).

49 We have considered a number of specific internal causes of the accelerating economic contraction of 1990–91. However, lying behind most of these specific causes was a general problem that loomed larger and larger – a rapid decline in the power and authority of the leadership of the Soviet state, and of the state itself. The dismantling of economic institutions, the uncertainty about the future ownership of state enterprises, and the growing autarky of the Soviet republics – and even of regions within republics – were all manifestations of the declining authority of Gorbachev and the central Soviet government. In Chapter 8 we examine the political processes that were at work undermining the Soviet state, and, as a result, the Soviet economy and Gorbachev's economic reform effort.

50 Jones and Moskoff (1989, p. 29).

51 By September 1989 about 400 independent cooperative and commercial banks were in operation. By September 1991 the number had risen to 1,535 (Kozlov, forthcoming).

6 DEMOCRATIZATION

1 Gorbachev (1988, p. 18).
2 Gorbachev (1988, p. 18).
3 Gorbachev (1988, p. 22).
4 White (1990, p. 3).
5 White (1990, p. 3).
6 Robinson (1992, p. 426).
7 Tolz and Newton (1990, p. 48) citing a Radio Moscow report of 26 January 1989.
8 Moses (1992, pp. 485–6).
9 White (1990, pp. 18, 24, note 177).
10 For example, the process of delegate selection for the important Nineteenth Party Conference of June 1988 followed the traditional practice of selection from above, by territory- and province-level party committees, and in smaller republics, by republican central committees (Unger, 1991). Two years later the Twenty-eighth Party Congress in July 1990 was packed with full-time party officials, who made up more than 40 per cent of the delegates. More than 49 per cent of the delegates to that party congress had joined the party before 1970 (Chiesa, 1990, p. 26).
11 White (1990, p. 5).
12 White (1990, p. 6).
13 The Communist Party and the trade unions which it controlled each had the right to choose 100 of the public organization delegates (Miller, 1993, p. 113).
14 *Pravda*, 29 November 1988, p. 1.
15 Tolz and Newton (1990, p. 123).
16 Other prominent advocates of radical change elected from the Academy of Sciences included Academician Roald Sagdeev and economists Nikolai Shmelev, Nikolai Petrakov, and Pavel Bunich (Tolz and Newton, 1990, p. 213).

17 Gwertzman and Kaufman (1992, pp. 169–70).
18 Hough (1991, pp. 257, 260).
19 Hough (1991, p. 263). The study covered the Moscow and Leningrad areas, the 6 largest provinces of Russia, and its 16 autonomous republics. The category "intellectuals" included people in education, science, medicine, law, and the media.
20 Embree (1991, p. 1069, table 1). The figures cited include as intellectuals only the following occupations from Embree's list: professors and teachers, journalists, lawyers and judges, scientists and scholars, engineers, writers and artists, and medical doctors. In addition to those occupations, Embree also included industrial and agricultural managers as part of the intelligentsia.
21 This claim was made by Anatoly Lukyanov, then vice-president of the Supreme Soviet. See Tolz and Newton (1990, p. 329, citing TASS, 26 June 1989).
22 Tolz and Newton (1990, p. 348) and Hough (1991, pp. 269–71).
23 *Izvestiia TsK KPSS*, 1989, no. 3, p. 138.
24 *Kommunist* (1988) no. 1, p. 6.
25 Di Leo (1991, p. 436). Di Leo notes that "The paradox lies precisely in the fact that it was the secretary [Gorbachev] of the vanquished party who was bringing this about" (pp. 436–7).
26 Ligachev (1993, pp. 109, 110).
27 Ligachev (1993, p. 110).
28 *Pravda*, 6 July 1990.
29 Article 6 of the 1977 Soviet Constitution contained the following wording: "The Communist Party of the Soviet Union is the leading and guiding force of Soviet society, nucleus of its political system, of social and state organizations. The Communist Party of the Soviet Union exists for the people and serves the people."
30 Gwertzman and Kaufman (1992, pp. 232–4, 249–50).
31 Gwertzman and Kaufman, (1992, pp. 249–50). The decision to select the first president in the parliament, rather than by popular election, was justified by a perceived need to avoid a divisive national election at that time of instability and turmoil.
32 Lane and Ross (1994a, p. 37, note 22).
33 Lane and Ross (1994b, p. 54, table F).
34 Cited in Chiesa (1990, p. 29).
35 See the public-opinion polling data discussed in Chapter 8.
36 See Miller (1993, pp. 87–8) for a discussion of this point.

7   THE PARTY–STATE ELITE AND THE PRO-CAPITALIST COALITION

1 Interview with Tatyana Zaslavskaya, 19 October 1992.
2 The Soviet official, Nikolai L., made this statement to one of the authors. Nikolai had served in many world trouble spots over the years, including Cuba and Ethiopia. In July 1991 he was working as an official of Znaniye, an educational organization affiliated with the Communist Party. A few years later he was working as a high-level administrator in Yeltsin's presidential administration, while his wife worked at a private bank.
3 Interview with Nikolai Ryzhkov, 27 October 1992.
4 A review of Ligachev's memoirs (Ligachev, 1993) in the *New York Times Book Review* described Ligachev as "rigidly honest." Ligachev was widely pictured

as an opponent of perestroika and an advocate of retaining the old state socialist system with no significant changes. Some even characterized him as an unreconstructed Stalinist. It is difficult to maintain that view after reading his memoirs, including Stephen Cohen's insightful introduction (Ligachev, 1993). See also Surovell (1991). Ligachev appears to have been a supporter of the original ideas of perestroika, but he came to oppose the speed at which reforms were taking place, fearing that the whole system was being destabilized and that there was a danger that socialism would be defeated by capitalism. He turned out to be correct on that point. Despite his unhappiness with the direction of events during 1991, Ligachev did not show any support for the attempted coup of August 1991.

5 Folbre (1995, table 1.6). In 1993 the average CEO's pay in the United States was $3,772,000, while the average factory worker made $25,317, a ratio of 149 to 1.

6 Korotich's estimate was reported in Tolz and Newton (1990, p. 58, citing a report in the *Washington Post*, 31 January 1989).

7 These pay comparisons leave out the special job perquisites of the Soviet elite. However, these were not large enough to come close to erasing the gap in relative economic standing between the Soviet elite and their Western counterparts.

8 Hough (1991, pp. 276–7).

9 Hough (1991, pp. 277, 276). However, Hough concluded, wrongly as it turned out, that revolution was unlikely to occur.

10 The shift to support for capitalism by some members of the party–state elite may have been for reasons other than just perceived material self-interest. Western capitalism's generally superior economic performance after 1975, together with the failure to successfully reform the Soviet state socialist economy in the following fifteen years, may have led some members of the party–state elite to conclude that a capitalist economy was simply superior to a socialist economy. However, given the materialistic nature of most members of the Soviet party–state elite, it is not likely that a very large proportion of those shifting to support for capitalism did so based on a disinterested comparison of the two systems.

11 Marshal Sergei F. Akhromeyev, Gorbachev's chief military advisor, committed suicide on 25 August 1991 when it became apparent that the Soviet Union and its socialist features were rapidly disappearing. Upon learning of the suicide, Admiral William J. Crowe, retired chairman of the US Joint Chiefs of Staff, who knew Akhromeyev, remarked that "He wanted to moderate the harsher features of Communism but didn't want to see the Socialist state disappear" (*New York Times*, 26 August 1991, p. A13). Alexander Savitsky was the first secretary of the party committee in the steel city of Magnitogorsk, which was a symbol of Soviet achievements in industry and urban construction. A believer in socialism, Savitsky was hospitalized for depression for several months when the Soviet system was disbanded in 1991 (interview with Alexander Savitsky, 7 June 1994). Savitsky reported that the party leader of the Chelyabinsk region "died of stress" at that time.

12 Kullberg (1994). The ideology labelled "capitalist" in Figure 7.1 combines two categories that Kullberg refers to as "Westernizer" and "Moderate Reformer." She describes the Westernizers as believing that "the practices and institutions of Western societies had almost universal applicability." Members of this group expressed "faith in the powers of the market and private property to solve their country's economic crisis". They were

distinguished by "fierce criticism of socialism" and "a propensity to dismiss its accomplishments and viability" (p. 941). The Moderate Reformers "also stressed the importance of Western institutions, particularly economic institutions, as models for the future development." The Moderate Reformers "shared the impatience of the Westernizers to break out of reform socialism" (p. 942). The Moderate Reformers differed from the Westernizers in their favoring a more gradual shift to capitalism, with greater attention to the peculiarities of the Soviet context in making this transition. In a conversation with Kullberg, she agreed that her categories of Westernizer and Moderate Reformer both corresponded to our category of those who favored replacement of socialism by a system based on private owner-ship of business and markets – which we refer to as "capitalism." Wester-nizers were 19.2 per cent of the sample and Moderate Reformers 57.5 per cent (p. 941).

13 The sample consisted of 73 people drawn from mid-to-upper levels of offi-cialdom. It included military officers, enterprise directors, Communist Party officials of the Moscow regional party organization, diplomats, economists, members of the intelligentsia, journalists, and leaders of independent parties. Thus, it did not fully correspond to our definition of the party–state elite, since it apparently included some individuals whom we would consider members of the intelligentsia. However, the intellectuals "were scientific department heads or project managers," which suggests they were on the borderline of intelligentsia and party–state elite (Kullberg, 1994, p. 950, note 11). Of the sample, 63 per cent were current or past members of the Com-munist Party (p. 930). Because the sample membership was not selected by a random process, Kullberg admits that the results "are not statistically repre-sentative of the actual distribution of opinion within the Moscow elite" (p. 950, note 6).

14 Those holding the Democratic Socialist position "adhered to the ideals of the *perestroika* period and the political and social philosophy of Gorbachev" (Kullberg, 1994, p. 944).

15 Kullberg (1994) wrote that "the positions of the nationalists and communists were remarkably similar," with both believing that "the *perestroika* years had brought nothing to the country but a concomitant economic and military vitiation" (p. 945).

16 Johnson and Kroll (1991, pp. 289–91) provide an interesting account of the evolution of state enterprises and ministries into private businesses during 1989–91.

17 Androshin (1992, pp. 28–30).

18 Batsanova (1992, pp. 82–3).

19 Radaev (1993, p. 8, table 5). The remaining 6 per cent of the firms were headed by former white-collar employees, workers, farmers, or those with no previous regular employment.

20 Kryshtanovskaya (1994b) uses the Russian word "samorodki." The literal translation is "nuggets" but it is used figuratively to refer to a person pos-sessing exceptional natural talents.

21 Interview with Vadim Biryukov, 17 January 1994.

22 Interview with Viktor Mironenko, 23 October 1992.

23 Kryshtanovskaya (1994b).

24 The information presented on the evolution of Menatep Bank is from an interview with Mikhail Khodorkovsky on 14 June 1994.

25 Zhilsotsbank not only helped launch Menatep Bank. Its Moscow branch later

directly evolved into one of the largest private banks in Russia, Mosbiznes-bank (Kozlov, forthcoming).

26 Interview with Olga Kryshtanovskaya, 15 June 1994.

27 The source of information about Vladislav Sedlenek, Sergei Potapenko, and Finist Bank is the *Wall Street Journal*, 9 January 1992, p. A6. The information about Alexander Shcherbakov is from Russica database, Moscow. Shcherbakov is also a board member of the Union of Young Entrepreneurs, as is former Komsomol central committee official Alexander Ivanov. Former Komsomol apparatchiks are found scattered across the upper echelons of Russia's new private banks and other businesses.

28 The information about Yuri Edelman is from an interview on 19 January 1994.

29 Interview with Olga Kryshtanovskaya, 15 June 1994, and *Business World Weekly*, 8 August 1994. Gazprom was formerly the Soviet state natural gas monopoly. Victor Chernomyrdin, Russia's prime minister since December 1992, was previously its director.

30 Interview with Gennady Ashin, 20 January 1994. Ashin is a Russian political scientist who studies the Russian elite. Another of the Soviet Union's largest automotive enterprises, KAMAZ, also was privatized under the control of its general director at that time (Kryshtanovskaya, 1994a).

31 Interview with Pavel M., 7 August 1991. Pavel M. was a top assistant to Vladimir S.

32 *Wall Street Journal*, 1 March 1993, p. A9.

33 Interview with Olga Kryshtanovskaya, 15 June 1994.

34 Russica database, Moscow.

35 Batsanova (1994, pp. 28–30).

36 *Business World Weekly*, 27 June 1994, p. 5.

37 Interview with Olga Kryshtanovskaya, 15 June 1994; and *Business World Weekly*, 8 August 1994.

38 The first edition of the Russian *Reader's Digest* featured an article, "Ten Myths about Homelessness in America," which sought to dispel the impression that the United States had a serious problem of homelessness.

39 Interview with Anatoly Lukyanov, 15 January 1994.

40 One of the authors, Fred Weir, knows both individuals.

41 *Kto est' kto v Rossii*, (1993, p. 752).

42 *Delovie lyudi*, May 1994, p. 88.

43 There was one significant exception to this trend. No one has reported capitalists emerging from the Soviet military ranks, although instances of large-scale corruption have been reported in the Soviet and Russian armed forces. The military was perhaps the most heavily indoctrinated in socialist beliefs of any part of the old elite, and the nature of military life tended to select against individuals who would be drawn by the financial attractions of capitalism.

44 McAuley (1992).

45 Kryshtanovskaya (1994a, table 9). What we term the "party–state elite" Kryshtanovskaya refers to as the "nomenklatura." Her concept of the Soviet nomenklatura appears to be identical to our concept of party–state elite.

46 *Kto est' kto v Rossii* (1993, p. 56) and Hewett (1991b, p. 248).

47 The information about Ivan Silayev comes from *Kto est' kto v Rossii* (1993, p. 593), *New York Times*, 25 August 1994, p. 14, and McFaul and Markov (1993, p. 303, note 6).

48 The information about Arkady Volsky is from *Kto est' kto v Rossii* (1993,

p. 147) and Tolz and Newton (1990, p. 51, citing a TASS report of 28 January 1989).

49 Interview by the authors with John Lloyd, Moscow correspondent for the *Financial Times* of London, 18 January 1994.

50 Lohr (1993, p. 828, note 13).

51 Gwertzman and Kaufman (1992, p. 426). In independent Russia Volsky became an important political figure, one of the founders of the Civic Union grouping of centrist political forces.

52 Interview with Vladimir Faminsky, 26 October 1992. Faminsky was the head of a department at the Institute of Economics in Moscow and an editor of the journal *Voprosy ekonomiki* (Problems of Economics). He was a student with Gaidar and had observed the evolution of Gaidar's views during the 1980s.

53 This account of Gaidar's evolution is from an interview by the authors with John Lloyd, Moscow correspondent for the *Financial Times* of London, 18 January 1994.

54 For example, in the industrial city of Magnitogorsk during 1991, most of the top party officials shifted to top jobs either in the steel works that dominated the city or in the city administration. The former top party official in the steel works, A. I. Starikov, became director of the enterprise (interview with Alexander Savitsky, former party secretary for Magnitogorsk, 7 June 1994). It was widely reported that this pattern was repeated all over Russia.

55 *Delovie lyudi*, May 1994, p. 88. However, he later resigned and re-entered politics.

56 While the power of organized crime grew during the perestroika years, it remained limited. The so-called mafias do not appear to have played a significant role in the demise of the Soviet system. However, once the system met its end, the economic role of the mafias greatly expanded and they became a significant force in the post-Soviet states. The reasons for this will be discussed in Chapter 10.

57 There was overlap among the four groups supporting the pro-capitalist coalition. The highest-ranked intellectuals and economists were part of the party–state elite. The most important private businessmen were from the elite. However, it is still useful to think of the coalition as having these four separate supporting groups.

58 Boris Yeltsin, leader of the pro-capitalist coalition, also won significant support from ordinary workers. However, because few of his supporters from that quarter favored building a capitalist system, they should not be considered supporters of the pro-capitalist coalition in the same sense as the four groups enumerated above.

8 THE STRUGGLE FOR POWER

1 There is some dispute about the events surrounding Yeltsin's departure from the top leadership. Yeltsin delivered an unscheduled speech at the close of the central committee meeting of October 1987 which caused an uproar. It is agreed that in the speech Yeltsin criticized the manner in which perestroika was being carried out and also singled out deputy party leader Yegor Ligachev for sharp criticism. The following month Yeltsin was removed from the leadership. Two issues are in dispute about these events. One is what his complaint was concerning the implementation of perestroika. It was reported at the time that Yeltsin had objected that the pace of change was too slow

(Gwertzman and Kaufman, 1992, pp. 75–6, 79). In the following years this became a major theme for Yeltsin. However, in a recent book Jonathan Steele stated that at that central committee meeting Yeltsin had "called for a slowing down" of reform (Steele, 1994, p. 237). The official text of Yeltsin's speech, published in Yeltsin (1990, pp. 144–7), allows either interpretation. Second, there is some dispute about whether Yeltsin voluntarily resigned or was expelled against his will. It is agreed that Yeltsin had offered his resignation as Moscow party chief one month before the central committee meeting, and at the meeting he offered his resignation from the politburo. But he was sharply denounced both in the central committee and in the Moscow party committee following his speech, and the public perception was that he had been expelled from the leadership.

2 The term "Russian" is used here, rather than "Soviet," because Yeltsin became a specifically Russian political figure whose image and popularity outside the Russian part of the Soviet Union was quite different from what it was in Russia.

3 Gwertzman and Kaufman (1992, pp. 31–2). Later, when Yeltsin became president of independent Russia, his critics contrasted such early speeches to Yeltsin's well-known love of luxury and his reported toleration of corruption.

4 As we shall see in Chapter 11, Yeltsin's credentials as a democrat grew severely tarnished after two years as president of independent Russia.

5 When campaigning for the parliament of the Russian Republic in March 1990, Yelstin said "We must make Russia and all the republics more independent" (Gwertzman and Kaufman, 1992, p. 245).

6 A deal was arranged whereby one of the newly chosen Supreme Soviet deputies resigned to make a space for Yeltsin. Alexei I. Kazannik, a university law lecturer from Omsk, offered his seat to Yeltsin. Gorbachev, presiding over the Congress, hastily arranged a vote to approve this substitution, and Yeltsin was added to the Supreme Soviet (Gwertzman and Kaufman, 1992, pp. 182–3).

7 Like the new Soviet parliament, the reformed Russian parliament had two bodies, a Congress of People's Deputies and a standing legislature called the Supreme Soviet. For simplicity the term "parliament" will generally be used here, except in cases where it is necessary to distinguish between the two parliamentary bodies.

8 Gwertzman and Kaufman (1992, pp. 244–6).

9 Brudny (1993, pp. 143–4).

10 In early 1991 Democratic Russia would openly call for the dissolution of the Soviet Union. It tried (unsuccessfully) to persuade Yeltsin to campaign for a "no" vote in the referendum that year on preserving the Soviet Union (Brudny, 1993, pp. 151–2).

11 Brudny estimated that "democrats" numbered "at best only thirty percent" of the Russian Republic deputies elected in March 1990 (Brudny, 1993, p. 145). Another source estimated that candidates associated with Democratic Russia won "more than 20 per cent of the seats" (White et al., 1994, p. 285). Since Democratic Russia was not a formal political party with a membership list, it was difficult to determine precisely how many parliamentary deputies were associated with it.

12 Brudny (1993, p. 146).

13 Gwertzman and Kaufman (1992, pp. 232–3). Some later accounts claimed a turnout of over 300,000 for that demonstration (Hewett and Winston, 1991b, p. 518).

14 Miller (1993, p. 152).
15 Sakwa (1993, p. 6).
16 Brudny (1993, p. 146).
17 Gwertzman and Kaufman (1992, pp. 343–4). In the preceding several months, Gorbachev had seemed to move away from his alliance with the rapid marketizers in his entourage and closer to those favoring slower reform and strong steps to preserve the Union.
18 It was the higher body of the Russian parliament, the Russian Congress of People's Deputies, which was to meet. It had the authority to replace the current chairman of the Supreme Soviet.
19 Gwertzman and Kaufman (1992, pp. 351–2). Democratic Russia was able to organize pro-Yeltsin demonstrations in cities across Russia, but its limited strength outside Moscow and Leningrad was illustrated by the turnouts. In Yaroslavl and Volgograd an estimated 10,000 demonstrated, in Tula 6,000, and in Smolensk 1,500 (Brudny, 1993, p. 151).
20 Gwertzman and Kaufman (1992, p. 354).
21 The plan to create a directly elected Russian Republic presidency had at first not been controversial, having originated in June 1990 with support from all of the factions of the Russian Republic parliament. The plan was approved by nearly 70 per cent of Russian Republic voters in a referendum earlier in March 1991 (White et al., 1994, pp. 285, 287).
22 Urban (1992, p. 192).
23 White et al. (1994, p. 288). In the critical March 1991 meeting of the Russian parliament, Rutskoi had led a group that broke from the anti-Yeltsin Communists of Russia faction and joined the pro-Yeltsin camp in the parliament (Urban, 1992, p. 189).
24 By April 1991 Democratic Russia claimed to have 1.3 million members across Russia (Urban 1992, p. 191).
25 Brudny (1993, p. 152), White et al. (1994, pp. 288–90).
26 Interview with Nikolai Ryzhkov, 27 October 1992. Gennady Burbulis, Yeltsin's campaign chairman and perhaps his closest advisor and most important strategist, was interviewed on television by the well-known Soviet commentator Vladimir Pozner. According to Ryzhkov, when Pozner asked Burbulis whether Yeltsin in fact favored capitalism, Burbulis avoided a direct answer.
27 Yeltsin was not the first revolutionary in history to be circumspect about his full agenda. Fidel Castro initially promised Cubans a nationalist, reformist revolution. Successful revolutionaries have often only won support from the public for their full program through the process of carrying out that program. We will consider whether Yeltsin succeeded in doing this in Russia in Part III.
28 The name of the Soviet Union's second city, Leningrad, was changed to St Petersburg in June 1991.
29 The poll overrepresented residents of Moscow and St Petersburg (formerly Leningrad). Voting returns have consistently shown the population of those two cities to be much more favorable toward free markets and privatization than the population elsewhere in Russia. The poll also excluded the Asian portion of Russia, where the population was generally more traditionalist in its views.
30 White (1992, pp. 249–50) cites a poll in April 1991 which found that only 3 per cent favored "undisguised capitalism" for the Russian Republic. Poll responses vary depending on how a question is worded, but no one has

reported a survey of the general Russian population which found majority support for capitalism at that time.

31 "The Pulse of Europe" (1991, pp. 88–90, 120, 139).

32 Had the public realized the direction that Yeltsin would ultimately take Russia, they might have voted differently in the election of June 1991. A study of a sample of Russian voters 18 months after that election, in December 1992, found that only half of those who had vcted for Yeltsin for president originally would vote for him again. By December 1992 Russians had lived through 12 months of an attempted transition to capitalism. One of the characteristics of those who had abandoned support for Yeltsin, the study found, was opposition to a system which allowed the accumulation of private wealth (White *et al.*, 1994, pp. 294–5).

33 White *et al.* (1994, p. 290).

34 Rutland (1991, p. 291).

35 Gwertzman and Kaufman (1992, p. 190).

36 A strike leader from Prokopyevsk stated that "our major problem is that we don't have a proper wholesale price for our coal. Hence, we are giving the lion's share of our profit to the state" which results in the miners being "kept at a subsistence level of existence." He added that "When we will get a decent wholesale price for our coal, bypassing state bodies, then we can begin to talk about real independence" (*Canadian Tribune*, 4 September 1989, p. 12).

37 The Soviet government agreed to this transfer a few days later (Gwertzman and Kaufman, 1992, pp. 360–1).

38 Rutland (1991, p. 311), Filtzer (1994, pp. 101–8), Clarke *et al.* (1993, ch. 7). Despite the alliance that formed between many of the miners' leaders and Yeltsin, not all of the miners were Yeltsin supporters. In May 1991 the miners in Keremovo held a rally under the slogan "Yeltsin and Gorbachev – two boots from the same pair" (Urban, 1992, pp. 203–4). In the June 1991 Russian presidential election, Yeltsin was outpolled in the Kuzbass by another candidate, A. Tuleev, the head of the regional soviet and a miner himself (Clarke *et al.*, 1993, p. 167; White *et al.*, 1994, p. 290).

39 Clarke *et al.* (1993, p. 163), Gwertzman and Kaufman (1992, p. 361).

40 The analysis in this section was greatly influenced by the seminal work of Ronald Suny on nationality issues in the Soviet Union (Suny, 1993).

41 In 1989 Russians were 38 per cent of the Kazakh SSR population, compared to 40 per cent for those of Kazakh nationality. In Latvia Russians were 34 per cent compared to 52 per cent for Latvians.

42 Lewin (1995, p. 271).

43 Hobsbawm (1990, ch. 1), Suny (1993), Gellner (1983).

44 Suny (1993, ch. 3).

45 In addition, the Russian Republic itself had a federative form, having sixteen ethnically defined "autonomous republics" within it. Suny (1993) argues that the federative form of the Soviet state was actually a violation of earlier Bolshevik thinking on nationalities, which held that, while minority nationalities should have the right to secede from a state, a socialist state itself should have a unitary rather than a federative character for those nationalities that chose to remain part of it.

46 Even Estonia and Latvia had not been independent states prior to 1917.

47 In 1897 Byelorussian speakers made up only 9 per cent of the population of Minsk, which would become the capital of the Byelorussian Soviet Republic. The majority spoke Yiddish. In neighboring Lithuania at that time, 40 per

cent of the population of Vilnius was Jewish and 31 per cent Polish. (Suny, 1993, p. 31, 36.)
48 Suny (1993, pp. 40, 43).
49 Many Armenians resented the failure of the Soviet authorities to side with their claim to Nagorno-Karabakh.
50 The demand for sovereignty meant the devolution of significant state power to the republic level while still remaining part of the Soviet federation.
51 In addition to the Baltics, the March 1990 republican elections also produced parliaments with pro-independence majorities in Armenia, Georgia, and Moldavia (Miller, 1993, p. 157).
52 The USSR Supreme Soviet passed a law in April 1990 that required a two-thirds vote of the electorate for a republic to secede (Miller, 1993, pp. 157, 235 note 36). Gorbachev insisted that a vote of the republic's legislature was insufficient.
53 The other three republics that were leaning toward independence at that point – Armenia, Georgia, and Moldavia – had a total of 4.6 per cent of the Soviet population.
54 Interview with former prime minister Nikolai Ryzhkov, 27 October 1992.
55 Brudny (1993, p. 145).
56 Gwertzman and Kaufman (1992, p. 274–6).
57 The eastern Ukraine was very Russified, while the western portion was much less so. Parts of the western Ukraine had once been part of Poland.
58 *New York Times*, 30 August 1991, pp. A1, A11.
59 Gwertzman and Kaufman (1992, p. 299).
60 Gwertzman and Kaufman (1992, p. 332).
61 The wording of the question was as follows: "Do you support the preservation of the union as a renewed federation of sovereign republics in which the rights of a person of any nationality are fully guaranteed?" (Gwertzman and Kaufman, 1992, p. 348; Suny, 1993, p. 150). The active campaign against the referendum by Democratic Russia in Moscow and Leningrad produced votes of only 50.0 per cent and 50.5 per cent in favor respectively in those cities (Brudny, 1993, p. 152).
62 Karasik (1992, p. 400). The "yes" vote was 70.2 per cent in Ukraine, 71.3 per cent in Russia, 82.7 per cent in Byelorussia, and over 90 per cent in Azerbaijan and in each of the Central Asian republics.
63 Miller (1993, p. 186).
64 The same was true of the leaderships in some of the other republics, particularly the Baltics and Georgia where the nationalist movements sought not just independence but a capitalist economy.
65 Surovell (1994) provides an interesting analysis of Gorbachev's "shift to the right" in this period.
66 Miller (1993, p. 173).
67 *Pravda*, 1 March 1991, p. 2.
68 The "9 plus 1" referred to the heads of the nine republics willing to negotiate a new union treaty plus Soviet president Gorbachev. The remaining six republics – the three Baltic states and Armenia, Georgia, and Moldavia – did not participate.
69 Hewett and Winston (1991b, p. 531). The agreement also implicitly accepted the right of the six non-participating republics to leave the Union.
70 In his presentation of the draft program to the Party Congress, Gorbachev sought to pacify the traditionalists by asserting that "The Party should express and protect the interests of the working people" and assuring the

delegates that "We have been and remain adherents of a socialist structure for the life of society." However, he went on to jettison many traditional Communist positions that had hitherto survived the process of perestroika. For example, admitting that communism was barely mentioned in the draft program, he denied that the goal of communism 'is realistically attainable in the foreseeable future' (Gorbachev, 1991).

71 However, some analysts believe they began discussing a coup several months earlier (Miller, 1993, pp. 176–7).

72 *New York Times*, 20 August 1991, p. A13. Despite their clear opposition to capitalism, the statement was very cautious and did not actually mention the word "socialism."

73 *New York Times*, 20 August 1991, pp. A12, A13.

74 Initial news reports identified the vehicle, atop which Yeltsin delivered his defiant anti-coup speech, as an armored truck. However, in later accounts it was transformed into a tank, to greater dramatic effect. Compare *New York Times*, 20 August 1991, p. A1, with later news accounts.

75 However, Yeltsin was no more able to rouse the working class at this moment than were the supporters of socialist reform. No general strike materialized. Russia's workers remained largely passive observers at this juncture.

76 *New York Times*, 20 August 1991, p. A10. As with other Moscow demonstrations of 1989–91, the numbers rose in later accounts.

77 *New York Times*, 22 August 1991, p. A14.

78 Miller (1993, p. 181).

79 Interview with Konstantin Borovoi, head of the Russian Commodities Exchange, 12 January 1994. According to American Soviet specialist Marshall Goldman, "a surprising number of new entrepreneurs" were present in the crowd outside the White House (Goldman, 1994, p. 27).

80 *New York Times*, 23 August 1991, p. A1, A12.

81 There was some irony to this, in that the coup was carried out by Soviet state officials, not party officials. Yeltsin replaced the temporary suspension of the Communist Party with a permanent ban on 6 November 1991 (Sakwa, 1993, p. 419).

82 Gwertzman and Kaufman (1992, p. 446).

83 On 1 December 1991 almost 90 per cent of Ukrainian voters approved independence in a referendum (*New York Times*, 3 December 1991, p. A1). Without Ukraine, the second most populous republic and source of much of the Soviet Union's grain production, the Union was not viable.

84 *New York Times*, 18 September 1991, p. A1.

85 However, the intelligentsia did not fare well under the new system that so many of them had struggled to bring about, as we shall see in Chapter 10.

86 Garraty and Gay (1985, pp. 1028–31).

87 While the pro-capitalist coalition's political agenda was, in our view, the primary factor that led to the Soviet breakup, other centrifugal forces have also operated in Eastern Europe and the former Soviet Union during the period under consideration. For a modern large nation-state to be stable, it appears to require the presence of a type of economic system that can bind the nation-state together. Both capitalism and state socialism have proved able to serve this function. As state socialism was dismantled in Eastern Europe and the Soviet Union, and a capitalist market system failed to develop right away, the resulting absence of any cohesive economic system promoted tendencies toward regional fragmentation of nation-states.

PART III AFTERMATH OF THE SOVIET DEMISE

1 Russia's official name is the Russian Federation, but for simplicity it will be referred to as Russia.
2 Specifically, any presidential decree in matters of economic reform would automatically become law unless the parliament voted to reject it within seven days, in which case negotiation would be required with the parliament. This special power to rule by decree, which later became a focus of contention between president and parliament, was accorded to President Yeltsin for thirteen months, until 1 December 1992. (Sakwa, 1993, p. 216).
3 See Chapter 7 above, especially Figure 7.1, which showed a large majority of a sample of the Moscow elite supporting capitalism in June 1991.
4 While the terms "shock therapy" and "neoliberalism" are sometimes interpreted as having somewhat different meanings, in this work the two terms will be used interchangeably.

9 SHOCK THERAPY

1 The term "fiscal policy," derived from the archaic word "fisc," meaning the public treasury, is used in modern economics to refer to a national government designing its spending and tax policies so as to regulate the rates of economic growth and price inflation. This is distinguished from monetary policy, which involves the manipulation of money, credit, and interest rates by the central bank, with the same aims of influencing growth and inflation in the economy.
2 It is acknowledged that some parts of the transition take longer than others to complete. For example, privatization is bound to take longer than price liberalization. But all are to be begun simultaneously.
3 The problem with adages is that, for each adage, there is usually another with the opposite lesson to offer. Opponents of shock therapy pointed out that, if the chasm is wide, first building a bridge across it might be wiser, if slower, than trying to jump across.
4 In addition to the five specific policies listed on p. 162, one could add the elimination of the system of universal social protection (guaranteed employment, universal pensions, subsidized child care, free health care, cheap vacations, and so forth) and its replacement by a more limited social safety net narrowly targeted at the most needy individuals. This provision of the shock therapy strategy had an important impact on the population, but it was less central to the economic logic of shock therapy than the five policies listed on p. 162.
5 Had a large stabilization fund been available to the Russian government, it would have been consistent with shock therapy for such a fund to be used to reduce the fluctuations in the market value of the ruble. However, no such fund was provided by the international community.
6 During the perestroika years 1985–91, the Soviet population had accumulated an estimated 551 billion rubles in savings, which it held largely in cash and savings banks. This represented 62 per cent of the 1991 level of total expenditure by the population (International Monetary Fund 1992a, p. 55).
7 The most prominent developer of Monetarist theory is Milton Friedman, Emeritus Professor from the University of Chicago. This theory became influential among Western economists in the 1970s and has remained so. The main competing theory of inflation and its control is the Keynesian approach, which

views excessive monetary expansion as only one possible cause of inflation, and monetary stringency as only one possible method of anti-inflation policy. In the Keynesian view, monetary tightening may or may not be an advisable means of combating inflation, depending on the circumstances.

8 Free trade was also expected, over the longer run, to lead Russia to produce according to its "comparative advantage." This means that Russia would specialize in producing those goods which it was relatively best at producing, while importing goods in which other countries had a comparative advantage. According to traditional Western international trade theory, this process benefits all participants in international trade.

9 On 7 November Yeltsin appointed Gaidar to the position of deputy prime minister for economic reform. Gaidar was the chief economic policy figure in the Yeltsin administration for the first year of shock therapy. He became first deputy prime minister on 2 March 1992 and acting prime minister on 15 June 1992 (prior to that President Yeltsin had served as his own prime minister). Gaidar was dismissed and replaced by Victor Chernomyrdin on 14 December 1992. However, Gaidar remained an important figure in the administration, with increasing influence as Yeltsin's conflict with the parliament heated up in the summer of 1993. Gaidar, along with the like-minded economist Boris Fyodorov, finally departed from the administration in January 1994.

10 This assertion was made by two sources: John Lloyd, the Moscow correspondent of the *Financial Times* of London, in an interview on 18 January 1994; and John Foglizzo, the former representative of the International Monetary Fund in Moscow, in an interview on 13 June 1995.

11 *New York Times*, 29 October 1991, pp. A1, A12; Bush (1991, pp. 1–6).

12 Bush (1991, p. 2).

13 Bush (1991, p. 1).

14 The account of meetings between IMF personnel and Russian government leaders presented here is from an interview with John Foglizzo, 13 June 1995. Foglizzo, the first IMF representative in Moscow, served from October 1991 until the spring of 1995 and was a participant in the meetings referred to.

15 Interview with Ruslan Khasbulatov, 17 June 1994.

16 Interview with John Foglizzo, 13 June 1995.

17 Interview with John Foglizzo, 13 June 1995. While the IMF and the Western economists it brought to Moscow did not have to force shock therapy on Russia, the ideas upon which shock therapy is based derive from Western economic thought.

18 Interview with John Foglizzo, 13 June 1995.

19 The goods excluded from the price liberalization included some basic consumer necessities (such as bread, milk, baby food, apartment rents, and electricity) and a few key producer goods (such as fuels and precious metals). However, the prices for those goods were raised by about three to five times. (International Monetary Fund, 1992b, p. 9.)

20 International Monetary Fund (1993, p. 88).

21 In July 1992 the IMF agreed to the modified goal of bringing the budget deficit down to 5 per cent of GDP by year-end (*New York Times*, 6 July 1992, p. A7).

22 *New York Times*, 3 April 1992, p. A7. Not all of that aid package actually reached Russia.

23 The most important departures from the original targets have been the refusal to allow fuel prices to rise to world market levels and monetary and

budget policies that have varied over time in the degree of their conformity to the IMF's targets.

24 The surplus of 0.9 per cent of GDP cited was for a measure of the deficit known as the general balance on a cash basis. If measured on a domestic bank financing basis, the surplus was 2.3 per cent of GDP (International Monetary Fund, 1993, p. 93).

25 *Economic Report of the President* (1995, pp. 274, 372).

26 International Monetary Fund (1995a, p. 18).

27 International Monetary Fund (1993, pp. 88, 100).

28 Foreign currencies are widely used as a medium of exchange in Russia. If foreign exchange deposits are included in the money supply, it does not have any significant effect on the results of this analysis. Price inflation still exceeds money growth by margins very close to those shown in Figure 9.2.

29 Determining the degree of restrictiveness of monetary policy in an economy undergoing very rapid inflation is not a straightforward matter. A good indicator under such conditions is the relative rates of increase of money and prices. If the central bank allows the money supply to increase as fast as or faster than the rate of price increase – which translates into a rising real money supply – that indicates an easy monetary policy, since the central bank is fully accommodating the rising price level, or more than accommodating it. If the money supply grows more slowly than prices, that indicates restrictive monetary policy, since the central bank is failing to accommodate the inflation. In the latter situation, the economy's spending units on aggregate have decreasing monetary means to purchase a given real level of output, which exerts a restraining impact on the price level.

In a more stable economy, one would look at interest rates to help determine how tight monetary policy had been. But in an economy undergoing very rapid inflation, it is difficult to draw any conclusion from interest rates about the degree of tightness of monetary policy. For example, during 1992 the interest rate charged by banks on loans to state enterprises gradually rose from 32 per cent to 95 per cent per year. These sound like very high rates, which in a stable economy would imply very tight monetary policy. But the inflation rate during 1992 was 2,509 per cent, which means that the real (inflation-corrected) interest rate was actually negative. A negative interest rate would normally imply a very easy monetary policy. In 1993 the bank lending rate rose to 204 per cent, but with inflation at 840 per cent, real interest rates were again negative. To Russians considering borrowing to finance normal productive activities, these rates appeared impossibly high. To speculators, these interest rates were quite enticing. Interest rates tell us little during rapid inflation because, to calculate the real interest rate at any moment in time, one must know the future rate of inflation, which is very uncertain under conditions of rapid inflation.

30 International Monetary Fund (1995a, p. 56). The date for this estimate is apparently the middle of 1994.

31 International Monetary Fund (1994, p. 128).

32 International Monetary Fund (1995a, pp. 56, 128).

33 *Statisticheskoe obozrenie* (1995, No. 4, p. 41). However, the owners of the shares of these newly privatized enterprises were primarily enterprise employees and managers rather than the outside investors that some privatization enthusiasts had foreseen.

34 International Monetary Fund (1995a, p. 130). No data were available for later

years. The subsidy figures cited include both central bank credits and direct government subsidies and credits.

35 International Monetary Fund (1993, p. 40).
36 Potential foreign investors faced significant obstacles from ambiguous and conflicting laws and regulations, as well as unsatisfactory enforcement of laws and contracts.
37 International Monetary Fund (1993, p. 35).

10 THE RESULTS OF SHOCK THERAPY

1 International Monetary Fund (1992b, p. 10).
2 Inflation by itself does not reduce the purchasing power of the population as a whole. This matter is discussed below.
3 Advocates of shock therapy frequently argue that the official statistics overstate the decline in Russia's economy. Two main problems exist with the data. First, enterprises may have an incentive to underreport output to the authorities, to avoid taxation (or prosecution for illegal production). This may understate the level of output in any given year, but it should not bias the growth rate of output over time. Second, critics charge that Goskomstat undercounts the growing private sector. If true, this could lead to understating both levels and growth rates of output, since private activity has grown as a percentage of total economic activity. However, defenders of Goskomstat assert that the agency has made a serious effort to accurately estimate private economic activity since 1993, when it became a significant portion of total economic output.
4 The rapid inflation in Russia makes it difficult to construct meaningful estimates of the rate of change in the "real" (that is, inflation-corrected) values of economic variables. This is so because the prices of different products have grown at dramatically different rates, making real growth-rate series very sensitive to the type of price index used and the base year selected. The sudden burst of inflation in the single month of January 1992 poses a particularly difficult problem for measuring "real" values of economic variables.
5 Gross national product (GNP) is the measure of total economic output that economists in the US used until recently, when it was supplanted by the slightly different measure, gross domestic product (GDP).
6 Figure 10.2 shows the decline from base year 1991 to final year 1995, which covers the shock therapy years of 1992 through 1995.
7 In addition to the problems common to the rest of industry, which are discussed below, the textile industry has faced a continuing shortage of cotton, which formerly came from what is now independent Uzbekistan.
8 Some observers of the Russian economy have suggested that the large reported declines in production mainly, or even entirely, represent a decline in output by the military–industrial complex. The pervasiveness of the production decline, which the data reveal, shows this belief to be mistaken.
9 International Monetary Fund (1992a, p. 58). Some specialists argue that price controls produced effects which made the official inflation statistics understate the actual rate of Soviet price inflation.
10 The consumer price series used for Figure 10.4 is based on a retail price index for 1991, a hybrid consumer price index for 1992, and an expanded consumer price index thereafter. No single consumer price index is available for the whole period, and most specialists use the series presented in Figure 12.4. For a discussion of these price indices, see Koen (1994). The monthly inflation

rates cited in this book refer to the increase from the beginning to the end of a month, and annual inflation rates refer to inflation over the course of the year, unless otherwise noted.

11 Producer prices appear to have risen even faster than consumer prices, although the Russian producer price index has serious problems (Koen, 1994).

12 Canadian Press Service, Moscow Bureau files.

13 Inflation itself redistributes real income, rather than reducing it. However, wage earners and pensioners as a whole have lost, as inflation has transferred their real buying power to other groups.

14 International Monetary Fund (1993, p. 91); *Statisticheskoe obozrenie* (1995, No. 12, p. 60).

15 Calculated from *Statisticheskoe obozrenie* (1995, No. 4, pp. 57–8), International Monetary Fund (1995b, p. 15).

16 The average real pension was calculated from *Statisticheskoe obozrenie* (1995, No. 4, p. 61, and No. 12, p. 62) and the sources cited above for Figure 10.5. Data for calculating the average real pension for 1992–93 were not available.

17 International Monetary Fund (1995b, p. 11).

18 *Statisticheskoe obozrenie* (1995, No. 4, p. 11).

19 Hough (1994, p. 27).

20 Reported by the Associated Press, New York, 10 May 1995. The remaining 18 per cent said their situation was unchanged.

21 The study was by Vox Populi and the Economic News Agency for the newspaper *Nezavisimaya Gazeta*, reported in *Business World Weekly*, 9 August 1994. Of the top five names on the list, four were bankers.

22 An account of money-making activities of the two mayors is found in the *Wall Street Journal*, 13 February 1994, pp. A1, A7.

23 There are exceptions. Mosbiznesbank now claims to devote a majority of its assets to productive loans. Some Russian banks were created by manufacturing enterprises for the main purpose of providing credit to the founding enterprise; even banks of this type typically make most of their profits from asset speculation. It is difficult to make profits from lending to productive enterprises in conditions of depression and rapid inflation.

24 Yuri Melnikov, head of the Russian bureau of Interpol, estimated the capital flight from Russia at $80 billion as of year-end 1994 (OMRI Daily Digest, Part I, No. 122, 23 June 1995).

25 During the three-year period 1992–94, gross foreign direct investment in Russia was $3.9 billion and official grants and credits (excluding debt deferral) totalled $15.5 billion (Economic Commission for Europe, 1995, p. 148).

26 The income distribution in the United States became significantly more unequal between the mid-1970s and the early 1990s. Today income is more unequally distributed in the United States than in the other leading industrialized capitalist countries.

27 For the former Soviet Union, McAuley (1979, p. 57); for Russia, *Statisticheskoe obozrenie* (1995, No. 12, p. 58).

28 *New York Times*, 2 October 1994, p. 9.

29 *New York Times*, 25 July 1995, p. A4. High school students from New Jersey and Long Island, gearing up for the Westinghouse science competition, were able to pay to spend a summer under the tutelage of some of Russia's top molecular biologists, protein physiologists, and biochemists in Pushchino, Russia. Under normal conditions, their own graduate students would be lucky to get such access.

30 In May 1992, Bell Labs paid for two Russian physicists, leading experts in waves and nonlinear optics at the huge General Physics Institute, to do research for Bell Labs. They were paid 5,000 rubles per month, or $11 at the current exchange rate. In that same month Corning, Inc., hired 115 scientists and technicians from two Russian research institutes. Sun Microsystems has hired large numbers of Russian computer scientists. (*New York Times*, 11 January 1993, pp. D1, D2.)

31 See Hersh (1994).

32 It will be argued below that the rise of organized crime after 1991 was related to the shock therapy strategy of economic transformation.

33 *New York Times*, 30 January 1994, p. 1.

34 *Boston Globe*, 9 May 1994, p. 6. Russians use the term "mafia" for organized crime groups.

35 *Boston Globe*, 9 May 1994, pp. 1, 6.

36 *New York Times*, 16 August 1993, p. A6.

37 Russian legislator Andrei Aizderdzis was shot to death at his home after the newspaper he owned printed the names of 266 organized crime figures (*New York Times*, 28 April 1994, p. A7). Sergei Skorochkin, a businessman and parliamentary deputy, was kidnapped and slain on 1 February 1995. In a previous incident, Mr. Skorochkin had shot dead a man whom he had identified as a mafia agent (*New York Times*, 3 February 1995, p. A11).

38 When Moscow apartments were privatized, they were generally given to their current occupants. Those living in apartments in choice locations have been offered generous cash deals to trade their apartment for one in a less desirable location, along with an offer of transportation to the new apartment. However, they would not arrive at the new home. Moscow police reported the confirmed murder of 32 Muscovites, with an additional 1,750 unaccounted for, in such apartment scams in the first three months of 1994. One police official suggested that city officials in charge of apartment registrations were bribed to look the other way in such murderous scams (*Moscow Times*, 4 June 1994, p. 1).

39 *Moscow Times*, 4 June 1994, p. 2, displayed a photograph of masked Interior Ministry police with automatic weapons arresting suspected organized crime leaders in the lobby of the American-owned Radisson Slavyanskaya Hotel in Moscow.

40 *Moscow News Weekly*, 1992, no. 50, p. 9.

41 Interview with Vadim Radaev, 13 June 1995. Radaev, head of the Department of Economic Sociology and Labor Economics at the Institute of Economics in Moscow, conducted the study of a sample of 277 Moscow enterprises.

42 *New York Times*, 2 August 1995, p. A1. Women were affected less; their life expectancy was 71.1 years in 1994 (OMRI Daily Reports, Part I, 23 August 1995).

43 A number of less doctrinaire Western economists, who realized the mismatch between the theory underlying shock therapy and the institutional reality facing the former Soviet Union and the nations of Eastern and Central Europe, advised against shock therapy from the beginning. One example is Galbraith (1990). However, such warnings were ignored.

44 For example, see Amsden *et al.* (1994), Goldman (1994), Millar (1994), Kregel and Matzner (1992), Weisskopf (1992a), Murrell (1993). Despite the economic depression in Russia following the introduction of shock therapy, this strategy still has many defenders. Perhaps the best example is Åslund (1995).

Åslund argues that the problems associated with shock therapy are relatively minor compared to its achievements.

45 The cost squeeze was worsened by an effect of the economic contraction. When enterprises reduce production during an economic contraction, the presence of fixed costs, such as plant depreciation and management salaries, raises the average cost per unit of output. This problem afflicts firms during business downturns anywhere, but in Russia the reluctance to lay off workers despite declining production turned their salaries into fixed costs of production.

46 Net exports are the fourth component of aggregate demand, but for a large country such as Russia, net exports normally are quite small compared to the other three components.

47 During 1989–91, household consumption represented between 44.4 per cent and 46.7 per cent of gross domestic product (International Monetary Fund, 1993, p. 91).

48 From Figure 10.5.

49 The new rich, who gained from the price liberalization, had a great deal of spending money, but they did not spend much of it on domestically produced consumer goods, preferring foreign imports.

50 The non-economist might wonder why professional economists would recommend policies that assure an economic depression. The answer is found in a key belief held by the Monetarists who designed shock therapy, a belief which derives from classical Western economic thought from the period before the Keynesian revolution. This is the view that aggregate demand is never a problem – that "supply creates its own demand," as Say's law states. According to this doctrine, the production of goods and services by the private sector necessarily generates sufficient income and demand to sell the resulting output. Government spending does not affect demand in the long run, so the belief goes, because the taxes and borrowing required to finance it will reduce private spending by an equal amount. And monetary policy is believed to affect only prices, not real output, in the long run.

These are the underlying beliefs that enabled Monetarist economists to recommend very tight monetary and fiscal policies to stop inflation while insisting that, at the same time, price liberalization would stimulate production. However, as Keynes so persuasively argued sixty years ago, this is not how modern economies actually behave. When demand falls, so does production; and public spending affects total demand just like private consumption or investment. These lessons, learned at great cost in the 1930s, had been forgotten by many in the economics profession by the 1980s.

51 Tight monetary and fiscal policies can be effective instruments for stopping inflation in a booming economy. Under such conditions, those policies can restrain excessive total demand, to bring it in line with the economy's productive capacity. However, even in that case there is a risk that the boom will be turned into a recession.

52 The monthly inflation rate in Russia fell more or less steadily during the first half of 1992, reaching 11 per cent per month in July and 9 per cent in August. However, the August rate still translates into an annual rate of 181 per cent. To stop the inflation, the severe policy would have had to continue for a good deal longer.

53 Gerashchenko had been the head of the state bank in the Soviet days. His father had been a central banker under Stalin.

54 For example, the automobile enterprise VAZ (Volga Automobile Associated

Works) has had some success in international markets with its Lada model. But tight monetary policy has blocked the access to credit it needs to raise its product to world standards. A company official remarked bitterly, "The IMF is not interested in Russian car production. Why keep car production going here, when car companies in the United States and Japan can't sell all the cars they make?" (*New York Times*, 23 July 1992, p. A10).

55 For an elaboration of this view, see Amsden *et al.* (1994, chs 1, 5) and Berliner (1992).

56 Weisskopf (1994).

57 The official privatizations of large enterprises, which most frequently took the form of employee buyouts, typically handed effective ownership and control to the top managers rather than the work force as a whole. In addition, many former officials from the old Soviet central economic ministries have ended up as top officials of the more valuable newly privatized enterprises.

58 To some extent this resulted from Russian consumers' fascination with long-denied Western goods. But it is also partly due to the weak marketing and financial resources of domestic farmers and manufacturers.

59 In the nineteenth century, the United States imposed high tariffs on superior British and German goods, particularly those which would compete directly with important developing American industrial products. America's first major capitalist industry – textiles – developed for decades behind a high tariff wall.

60 Total direct foreign investment in Russia during 1992–94 amounted to $3.9 billion (*Economic Commission for Europe*, 1995, p. 148). That averaged about $9 per capita per year for the Russian population.

61 Cynthia Taft Morris has shown that the state played an important role in the development of capitalist economies in many countries that developed after Britain in the nineteenth century. She singles out the role of national and local governments in early capitalist development in providing "market places, transportation, education, protection against fraud, public health, and in rural areas, investment in rural physical overhead capital and help transmitting improved techniques" (Morris, 1992, p. 11). Her study included the Netherlands, Germany, Australia, Canada, and New Zealand.

62 For an account of the highly interventionist role of the government in South Korea's industrialization, see Amsden (1989).

63 The highly abstract type of theorizing which dominates modern Western economics does not lend itself to understanding the complex process of institutional change and development which characterizes a transition from one economic system to another.

64 Some of the Western advisors knew little about the former Soviet economy, believing that the characteristics of the economic system inherited from the Soviet period were irrelevant to designing a transition strategy. A Russian official, Peter Aven, the Minister of Foreign Economic Relations, once echoed this view, stating that "There are no special countries from the point of view of economists. If economics is a science, with its own laws – all countries and all economic stabilization plans are the same" (*Nezavisimaya Gazeta*, 27 February 1992, p. 5, cited in Goldman, 1994, p. 106).

65 In this respect the Soviet system differed from the state socialist systems in other countries of the Warsaw Pact, several of which already had industrialized economies when Soviet-backed Communist parties took power after World War II.

66 One study estimated that 80 per cent of the output of the Soviet machinery industry was produced by monopolists (Yavlinsky et al., 1991, p. 66). Gossnab, the state supply agency, estimated that in 1991 "out of 7,664 products manufactured in the machine-building, metallurgical, chemical, timber, and construction sectors, 77 percent, or 5,884, were monopolies" (Goldman, 1994, p. 13).
67 This problem is explored in Leijonhufvud (1993).
68 As we noted above, the new private banks are mainly involved in speculative activities, not the financing of production. The few that are trying to finance productive activity, which includes both some descendants of the former state banking system and some new banks created and controlled by industrial enterprises, lack the financial resources to make much of an impact.
69 Such a two-sector strategy is based on a key assumption: that the giant state enterprises built under the state socialist system can only be operated effectively, for the foreseeable future, with state support and under state control. Whatever the inefficiencies that result from continuing state subsidization and control, they are believed to be less harmful than the collapse which results from turning them loose from state support and direction.
70 Berliner (1992).
71 It is unclear whether China is evolving into a capitalist system, as many outside observers believe, or is developing a form of market socialism. Most of the non-state enterprises in China are not conventional capitalist firms but rather are owned by villages or townships or are worker collectives.
72 During 1980–93, the real GDP of China grew at the rate of 9.6 per cent per year, the highest rate that any country recorded over that period (World Bank, 1995, pp. 164–5; this same rate was also achieved by Botswana). While the non-state sector of China's economy has grown much faster than the state sector, and many problems afflict the large state enterprises, there have been some improvements in the state sector. During 1980–89 output per worker in state-owned industry grew by 52 per cent (Berliner, 1992).
73 In the 1970s and 1980s Western experts tried to convince the Chinese of the virtues of privatization and price liberalization, but they failed to do so.

11 RUSSIA'S POLITICAL EVOLUTION

1 *Financial Times*, 19 December 1991, p. 1.
2 *New York Times*, 14 January 1992, p. A3.
3 In February 1992 Rutskoi escalated his criticism of the government's economic program, delivering a condemnatory speech at a convention of extreme nationalists on 8–9 February (Hahn, 1994, pp. 314–15). However, these attacks found little support at that time outside the isolated nationalist and Communist political groups.
4 The career of Arkady Volsky, a former high-level CPSU apparatchik who became a Yeltsin supporter in 1991, was discussed in Chapter 7 above. Civic Union was originally made up of three political parties: the All-Russian Union "Renewal," led by Volsky; the Democratic Party of Russia, led by Nikolai Travkin; and the National Party of Free Russia, led by Vice-President Rutskoi and V. Lapitsky (Hahn, 1994, p. 314).
5 Some Civic Union leaders, including Volsky, talked openly about the advantages of the "Chinese model." They argued that the Chinese economic strategy could be carried out in Russia within the framework of democratic political institutions.

6 For a discussion of Civic Union's economic program, see Ellman (1993). None of the several versions of this economic program was ever formally adopted by Civic Union, yet they played a major role in the debates over economic policy in 1992.

7 Weir (1993–94, p. 14).

8 The Moderate Reformers "were significantly less optimistic about the feasibility of rapid change, and urged that attention be given to the peculiarities of the Soviet context in the formulation of reform" (Kullberg, 1994, p. 943).

9 Kullberg (1994) argues that this was a major reason for the division that arose between the parliament and the president.

10 *New York Times*, 15 December 1992, p. A16.

11 Fyodorov demanded that Yeltsin show his commitment to shock therapy by firing central bank president Viktor Gerashchenko, threatening to resign if his demand were not fulfilled. Yeltsin instead accepted Fyodorov's resignation.

12 *Moscow Times*, 21 January 1994, p. 1, and *New York Times*, 22 January 1994, p. 4. Western economic advisor Anders Åslund remarked that "Russia has now really abandoned the course of fundamental reforms" (*New York Times*, ibid.).

13 After July 1992 Gerashchenko eased monetary policy somewhat from the extremely tight policy of the first half of 1992, but, as was shown in Chapter 9, monetary policy still remained relatively tight. Fiscal policy also eased somewhat over time, yet it remained close to the IMF targets.

14 The one exception was privatization, which could not be completed without the cooperation of the parliament. It was only after the parliament was dissolved that privatization was largely completed.

15 Russia differs from China in a number of ways that are relevant here. Critics of the centrists' call for a China-like model note that Russia no longer had a strong political party to guide the state and economy, its population is largely urban rather than rural, and it does not have a large supply of very cheap rural labor to draw on for new industries. Supporters of such a direction for Russia argue that, despite these differences, a version of gradual transformation tailored to Russia's conditions could work effectively.

16 Gaidar has received financial and political support from a number of leading bankers. One is Oleg Boyko, the chief executive of Konsern Olbi, a financial holding company, and president of Bank Natsionalni Kredit. Boyko was a key backer of Gaidar who served as deputy chairman and chief financial officer of Gaidar's Russia's Choice political party. Boyko later broke with Gaidar after Gaidar condemned Yeltsin's Chechnya action in December 1994 (interview with Boyko in *Kommersant Daily*, 14 September 1995, and interview with Gennady Ashin, a Russian political scientist, on 7 June 1995).

17 In 1995 Grigory Yavlinsky, a liberal economist and aspiring presidential contender, criticized the Yeltsin government for "its capitulation to a small business elite that is getting rich on its economic policies" (*New York Times* Op Ed page, 14 September 1995, p. A27).

18 Teague (1992).

19 Shortly after Yeltsin had named former enterprise director Vladimir Shumeiko to the post of first deputy prime minister in June 1992, Shumeiko remarked, "There is a need for a class of owners, and ... all who are now concerned with production are entitled to high rank in this class" (Hahn, 1994, p. 315, citing *Moscow News*, 24, 15–22 June 1992, p. 6.) Some of the opposition to Gaidar's program from industrialists may have resulted from a fear, probably well-grounded, that Gaidar intended that the new class of capitalists in Russia would largely exclude the enterprise directors. While

Civic Union called for an entirely different strategy for building capitalism, some of its enterprise director support may have been based mainly on concern that they be included in the new capitalist class, rather than any deeply held opposition to shock therapy.

20 One well-placed Russian economist, Anatoly I. Miliukov, estimated that 10 per cent of Russian industry had done "relatively well" in the shock therapy years, primarily by finding export markets in which they could compete effectively. Miliukov was the head of the Expert Analytical Service of the Supreme Soviet in 1992–93 and later became a vice-chairman of Mosbiznesbank (interview, 15 June 1994).

21 See Figure 10.3.

22 Prime Minister Chernomyrdin "is reported to hold a large financial stake" in Gazprom (*New York Times*, 9 September 1995, p. 3). Chernomyrdin founded Gazprom, and its chairman, Rem Vyakhirev, "is a Chernomyrdin protege" (*Washington Post*, 3 December 1995, p. A1). Gazprom holds between 20 and 35 per cent of the world's natural gas reserves and produces about 94 per cent of all Russian gas (*Russian Petroleum Investor Market Intelligence Report*, 1995). The value of Gazprom's reserves has been estimated at between $400 and $900 billion (*Washington Post*, op. cit.). If Chernomyrdin's share in Gazprom were only a few per cent, it would make him one of the world's richest men.

23 The flagship enterprise of the Russian steel industry, the Magnitogorsk Metallurgical Works, has been able to obtain hundreds of millions of dollars in foreign funds (from Germany) to build cold-rolled mills and electric furnaces. As of June 1994 the workers in the Magnitogorsk works still had a living standard similar to that of Russian industrial workers in the 1980s, well above that of industrial workers in other Russian industries in 1994 (interviews with enterprise managers and workers in Magnitogorsk, June 1994).

24 Some argue that the former industrialists in the government have, in practice, been more effective at implementing shock therapy than the liberal economists. Russian economist and former Soviet deputy prime minister Leonid Abalkin remarked that, in practice, Chernomyrdin had been a stricter Monetarist than Fyodorov (interview, 14 June 1995). It is said that both Gaidar and Fyodorov talked sternly but often gave in to pressure for more credits from industry and agriculture, whereas Chernomyrdin spoke of the need to support industry while staunchly resisting demands for subsidies.

25 Initially the two largest were the Russian Communist Workers' Party, a Leninist organization, and the Socialist Party of Working People, which had a reformist program and appeal similar to that of the CPSU at the end of the perestroika period.

26 The two most influential at first were Sergei Baburin's Russian All People's Union and the more extreme Russian National Assembly (or Sobor, as it was called).

27 The two sides to this alliance disagreed about socialism, which the Communists of course favored but many of the nationalists did not, and internationalism, which many Communists still believed in. Perhaps the most important unifying theme was the call for a strong Russian state.

28 According to Ludmilla Vartazarova, a leader of the Socialist Party of Working People, the CPRF has three main factions within it: a statist–patriotic faction, an orthodox communist faction, and a democratic socialist faction. (Interview with Ludmilla Vartazarova, 13 June 1995.)

29 Yavlinsky criticized various policies of the Yeltsin government, but his group maintained a strongly pro-Western orientation and appeared to have only

minor differences over economic policy with the government. After the war in Chechnya began in December 1994, Yavlinsky became much sharper in his criticisms of the government.

30 To win any seats from the vote for political parties, a party had to receive at least 5 per cent of the total votes cast for parties.

31 Each party that surpassed the 5 per cent threshold in the party vote received a proportionate number of duma seats from its party list, and parties could also win duma seats by entering candidates in the 225 geographical constituency contests. Part (b) of Figure 11.1 shows the total percentage of duma seats won through both means.

32 Zhirinovsky received a great deal of coverage on the state-controlled television, prompting some analysts to speculate that Yeltsin hoped Zhirinovsky would draw from the Communist vote, dividing and weakening the opposition.

33 Central Election Commission final results reported in the *New York Times*, 26 December 1993, p. 18.

34 While Gaidar, the leader of Democratic Choice, was a sharp critic of the Chechnya war, on other issues he was a strong supporter of the government.

35 Duma Press Service report, February 1996.

36 It was often said that Yeltsin was the only figure elected by the entire Russian electorate, the parliamentary deputies having been elected in individual election districts. However, strictly speaking that was not true. Yeltsin was elected president as part of a two-candidate team: Yeltsin for president and the popular military officer Rutskoi for vice-president. When Rutskoi sided with the leadership of the parliament against Yeltsin's policies, it weakened Yeltsin's claim to superior democratic legitimacy.

37 Remark made to Fred Weir.

38 Weir (1993, p. 56).

39 A presidential anti-corruption commission accused Rutskoi of putting millions of dollars of state funds in a Swiss bank account (*New York Times*, 19 August 1993, p. A15). The Moscow Procurator's Office later dismissed the charges as groundless, concluding that they had been trumped-up based on faked documents (OMRI Daily Digest, Part I, No. 242, 14 December 1995).

40 For example, see Weir (1993–94).

41 The Western media regularly referred to the parliament as the "Soviet-era parliament," yet it was no more a Soviet-era institution than was the Yeltsin presidency. The parliament was the first ever in Russia selected entirely by multi-candidate contests in equal-size electoral districts.

42 Weir (1993–94, p. 62).

43 The features of the new Russian constitution described here are from Levy (1994a) and (1994b). Levy is an attorney based in Moscow.

44 *Rossiiskie vesti*, 25 December 1993, p. 1.

45 The *New York Times* reported that the eligible electorate, as reported by the Central Election Commission, went from 107 million to 106.3 million to 105.284 million in the few days after the election (*New York Times*, 15 December 1993, p. A18).

46 The *New York Times* reported that opinion polls in *Izvestia* showed little support for military action in Chechnya (24 December 1994, p. 4).

47 Gaidar complained that, after his criticism of the military action, he could not even reach Yeltsin by telephone (*New York Times*, 16 December 1994, p. A16).

48 Dawisha and Parrott (1994, p. 68).

49 *New York Times*, 10 December 1994, p. 4, reported that President Yeltsin's

decree authorizing the use of "all measures available to the state" to end the Chechen insurgency was the formalization of a decision by the National Security Council.

50 In a nationwide survey of 1,035 people in Russia conducted in April 1995 for the magazine *U.S. News and World Report*, only 9 per cent of respondents thought Yeltsin deserved to be re-elected as president (Associated Press, 28 April 1995, Washington).

51 When the Chechnya war began, Yeltsin checked into a hospital, reportedly for elective surgery on his nose. He remained secluded there for several weeks.

52 *New York Times*, 24 December 1994, p. 4. Former federal prosecutor Alexei Kazannik (the same person who had given up his seat in the USSR Supreme Soviet to make room for Yeltsin in 1989) remarked that "Everyone knows you have to go to Gen. Korzhakov if you want a doubtful decision made or an illegal decree signed." Opposition from Korzhakov was reported to have sunk a World Bank-backed plan to liberalize Russia's oil export quotas (Associated Press, 23 December 1994, Moscow).

53 *New York Times*, 20 December, 1994, p. A14.

54 However, there are also conflicts between a capitalist economy and a democratic state in the West. The economic inequality of capitalism runs counter to the political equality of citizens which must be the basis of any genuine democracy. And a capitalist economy allows unelected heads of large business firms to make important decisions affecting the population without much input from democratic political institutions. Some argue that, in contemporary capitalism, the conflicts between capitalism and democracy may be growing (Bowles and Gintis, 1987).

55 This refers to the military coup in Chile in 1973 led by General Augusto Pinochet. Pinochet overthrew the elected socialist government of Salvador Allende and proceeded to implement an economic program designed by Monetarist followers of the conservative University of Chicago Economics Department. Pinochet carried out his coup with enormous violence and repression; tens of thousands of supporters of the Allende government were killed by the military. It is unclear whether Russian advocates of the 'Pinochet' option are advocating ruthless suppression and violence akin to what happened in Chile, or rather a milder form of authoritarianism directed at rapidly creating capitalist institutions in Russia.

56 According to a newspaper report, Zhirinovsky won 72 per cent of the vote in the strategic missile forces, 46 per cent in the Moscow military district, 40 per cent in the air force, and 74 per cent in the Kantemirovskaya division. The latter was used by Yeltsin for the October assault on the White House (*Moscow Times*, 18 December 1993, p. 2).

57 Mikhail Khodorkovsky, the president of Menatep Bank, one of the leading new private banks, reportedly called for the Russian state to play a bigger role in directing the economy, particularly in encouraging more investment, in a public speech in June 1995 (interview with John Lloyd, former correspondent of the *Financial Times* of London, 12 June 1995). That same month a top officer of Mosbiznesbank said that the major banks have been pressing the government "to implement a more active economic policy" (interview with Anatoly Miliukov, vice-chairman of Mosbiznesbank, 16 June 1995).

58 The published program of the CPRF, dated 22 January 1995, is a relatively radical call for building democratic socialism in Russia. Following an initial

period in which they would focus on reversing the collapsing economy, they call for returning property to public ownership which was "taken against public interests," making "social forms of property in the means of production dominant," and operating the economy "on the basis of scientific planning and management." They call for working people to "participate in a more active and wider way in management of the state's affairs through soviets, trade unions, worker self-management, and other institutions of direct people's power." They claim as their goal a "classless society liberated from exploitation of man by man," in which "the free development of each is the precondition of the free development of all." They also proclaim a commitment to peacefully reconstituting a union with as many of the former Soviet republics as are willing to participate. However, it is impossible to foretell what relation this program might have to the policies that a CPRF-led government would actually follow.

59 The Polish and Hungarian reformed Communist parties did not make any great changes in economic policy, contrary to election promises. The Polish successor to the Communist Party even continued shock therapy when in office.

60 Yuri Voronin, the head of the Committee on Social and Economic Development of the central committee of the CPRF, rejected the moderate, even neoliberal, policies which the reformed Communists followed in Poland and Hungary, stating "We will not follow that path. We will use new mechanisms to develop a socialist direction of reforms, to provide a healthy entrance into the world market" (interview, 14 June 1995).

61 Another obstacle is the history of authoritarian, top-down methods of operation that the CPRF may have inherited from the CPSU, from which it is descended. Success in building democratic socialism would require a decisive break with that tradition of party operation, a break which the CPSU was never able to make under Gorbachev's leadership.

62 Some Russians believe that if former Soviet leader Leonid Brezhnev somehow arose from the grave and appeared on a ballot for president, he would score a convincing victory at the polls.

12 LESSONS FOR THE FUTURE OF SOCIALISM

1 By comparison, the New Deal social reformers in the United States, who began their efforts in 1933, required about fifteen years to complete a successful restructuring of American capitalism.

2 It may seem obvious that single-party rule is inconsistent with democracy, but in the past many Marxists argued that a single party could reflect the needs and wishes of the working-class majority.

3 Weisskopf (1992b, p. 1).

4 Lange (1938 [1936–37]) was an early pioneer of market socialist theory. A large literature on market socialism arose in the post-World War II period, partly in response to Yugoslavia's adoption of some features of that model. Examples are Ward (1967) and Horvat (1982). Nove (1983, 1991) provided a particularly influential statement of the market socialist position, drawing on the problems of Soviet economic planning. In response to the Soviet demise, a new wave of market socialist theory has arisen, including Bardhan and Roemer (1992), Weisskopf (1992b), Schweickart (1992), and Roemer (1994).

5 In Roemer's (1994) widely discussed version, enterprises are owned by mutual funds, with the shares of the latter owned by the citizenry. Shares

can neither be traded for money nor passed on to heirs. Each citizen receives an equal quantity of special chits that can be used only to purchase shares in mutual funds.

6 However, significant inequality of reward must be allowed to remain in order to provide the incentives that are the basis of the market system's claim to economic efficiency and technological progressivity.

7 Not all advocates of market socialism favor worker control of enterprises. Some, such as Roemer (1994), favor more traditional control by top managers.

8 Devine (1988, 1992), Albert and Hahnel (1991a, 1991b, 1992). See also Laibman (1992) for a somewhat different conception of democratic planned socialism.

9 Devine (1988, ch. 9).

10 See Dobb (1963, pp. 157–61) and Postan and Rich (1952, pp. 289–354). According to Dobb, in 1338 Florence had 200 workshops employing 30,000 wage earners making cloth (p. 157), yet this relatively developed capitalism ultimately did not survive.

Bibliography

Abalkin, Leonid (1991) "The Market in a Socialist Economy," in Anthony Jones and William Moskoff (eds) *The Great Market Debate in Soviet Economics*, Armonk, NY: M. E. Sharpe.

Albert, Michael and Hahnel, Robin (1991a) *Looking Forward: Participatory Economics for the Twenty-First Century*, Boston: South End Press.

—— (1991b) *The Political Economy of Participatory Economics*, Princeton, NJ: Princeton University Press.

—— (1992) "Socialism As It Was Always Meant To Be," *Review of Radical Political Economics* 24, 3–4: 46–66.

Alter, J. (1994) "Not-So-Smart Intelligence," *Newsweek* 7 March.

Amsden, Alice (1989) *Asia's Next Giant: South Korea and Late Industrialization*, Oxford: Oxford University Press.

Amsden, Alice, Kochanowicz, Jacek, and Taylor, Lance (1994) *The Market Meets Its Match: Restructuring the Economies of Eastern Europe*, Cambridge, Mass.: Harvard University Press.

Androshin, Alexandr (1992) "Hermes Takes on the World," *Delovie lyudi* (Business People), February.

Åslund, Anders (1990) "How Small Is Soviet National Income?' in Henry S. Rowen and Charles Wolf, Jr. (eds) *The Impoverished Superpower: Perestroika and the Soviet Military Burden*, San Francisco: Institute for Contemporary Studies Press.

—— (1991) "The Making of Economic Policy in 1989 and 1990," in Hewett and Winston (1991a).

—— (1995) *How Russia Became a Market Economy*, Washington, DC: Brookings.

Bardhan, Pranab and Roemer, John E. (1992) "Market Socialism: A Case for Rejuvenation," *Journal of Economic Perspectives* 6, 3: 101–16.

Barnett, Vincent (1991) "Conceptions of the Market among Russian Economists: A Survey," *Soviet Studies* 44, 6: 1087–98.

Batsanova, Galina (1992) "Mikhail Gura's American Dream," *Delovie lyudi* (Business People), June.

—— (1994) "Yakov Dubenetsky: Not the Average Banker," *Delovie lyudi* (Business People), April.

Becker, Abraham C. (1994) "Intelligence Fiasco or Reasoned Accounting?: CIA Estimates of Soviet GNP," *Post-Soviet Affairs* 10, 4: 291–329.

Bergson, Abram (1961) *The Real National Income of Soviet Russia since 1928*, Cambridge, Mass.: Harvard University Press.

Berliner, Joseph S. (1976) *The Innovation Decision in Soviet Industry*, Cambridge, Mass.: The MIT Press.

—— (1992) "The Pace of Privatization," in U.S. Congress Joint Economic Committee *The Economies of the Former Soviet Union*, Washington DC: US Government Printing Office.

Bettelheim, Charles (1976) *Class Struggles in the USSR*, volumes 1 and 2, New York: Monthly Review Press.

Bilenkin, Vladimir (1995) "The Ideology of Russia's Rulers in 1995: Westernizers and Eurasians," *Monthly Review* 47, 5: 24–36.

Boretsky, Michael (1987) "The Tenability of the CIA Estimates of Soviet Economic Growth," *Journal of Comparative Economics* 11: 517–42.

—— (1990) "Reply: CIA's Queries about Boretsky's Criticism of Its Estimates of Soviet Economic Growth," *Journal of Comparative Economics* 14: 315–26.

Bowles, Samuel and Gintis, Herbert (1987) *Democracy and Capitalism: Property, Community, and the Contradictions of Modern Social Thought*, New York: Basic Books.

Bowles, Samuel, Gordon, David M., and Weisskopf, Thomas E. (1990) *After the Wasteland: A Democratic Economics for the Year 2000*, Armonk, NY: M. E. Sharpe.

Brudny, Yitzhak M. (1991) "The Heralds of Opposition to Perestroyka," in Hewett and Winston (1991b).

—— (1993) "The Dynamics of 'Democratic Russia', 1990–1993," *Post Soviet Affairs* 9, 2: 141–70.

Bush, Keith (1991) "El'tsin's Economic Reform Program," *Report on the USSR* 3, 46: 1–6.

Chamberlin, William Henry (1965) *The Russian Revolution 1917–1921*, volume 1, New York: Grosset and Dunlap.

Chiesa, Giulietto (1990) "The 28th Congress of the CPSU," *Problems of Communism* 39, 4: 24–38.

Clarke, Simon, Fairbrother, Peter, Burawoy, Michael, and Krotov, Pavel (1993) *What about the Workers? Workers and the Transition to Capitalism in Russia*, London: Verso.

Cliff, Tony (1988 [1948]) *State Capitalism in Russia*, London: Bookmarks.

Cohen, Stephen F. (1985) *Rethinking the Soviet Experience: Politics and History since 1917*, New York: Oxford University Press.

Compendium of Social Statistics and Indicators (1988), New York: United Nations, Department of International Economic and Social Affairs, Statistical Office.

Conquest, Robert (1968) *The Great Terror: Stalin's Purge of the Thirties*, London: The Macmillan Company.

Dallin, Alexander (1992) "Causes of the Collapse of the USSR," *Post Soviet Affairs* 8, 4: 279–302.

Daniels, Robert V. (1993) *The End of the Communist Revolution*, London: Routledge.

Davies, R. W. (1991) "Soviet Economic Reform in Historical Perspective," in Catherine Merridale and Chris Ward (eds) *Perestroika: The Historical Perspective*, London: Edward Arnold.

Davies, R. W., Harrison, Mark, and Wheatcroft, S. G. (eds) (1994) *The Economic Transformation of the Soviet Union 1913–1945*, Cambridge: Cambridge University Press.

Dawisha, Karen and Parrott, Bruce (1994) *Russia and the New States of Eurasia: The Politics of Upheaval*, Cambridge: Cambridge University Press.

Devine, Pat (1988) *Democracy and Economic Planning*, Cambridge: Polity Press.

—— (1992) "Market Socialism or Participatory Planning," *Review of Radical Political Economics* 24, 3–4: 67–89.

Di Leo, Rita (1991) "The Soviet Union 1985–1990: After Communist Rule the Deluge?," *Soviet Studies* 43, 3: 429–49.

Directorate of Intelligence (1988a) *Handbook of Economic Statistics: 1988*, Washington, DC: Central Intelligence Agency.

—— (1988b) *Revisiting Soviet Economic Performance under Glasnost: Implications for CIA Estimates*, SOV 88–10068, Washington, DC: Central Intelligence Agency, September.

Djilas, Milovan (1957) *The New Class: An Analysis of the Communist System*, London: Thames and Hudson.

Dobb, Maurice (1963) *Studies in the Development of Capitalism*, New York: International Publishers.

Economic Commission for Europe (1995) *Economic Survey of Europe in 1994–1995*, New York and Geneva: United Nations.

Economic Report of the President Washington, DC: United States Government Printing Office, various years.

Ellman, Michael (1986) "The Macro-economic Situation in the USSR – Retrospect and Prospect," *Soviet Studies* 38, 4: 530–42.

—— (1993) "Russia: The Economic Program of the Civic Union," *RFE/RL Research Report* 2, 11–12: 34–45.

Ellman, Michael and Kontorovich, Vladimir (eds) (1992a) *The Disintegration of the Soviet Economic System*, London and New York: Routledge.

—— (1992b) "Overview," in Ellman and Kontorovich (1992a).

Embree, Gregory J. (1991) "RSFSR Election Results and Roll Call Votes," *Soviet Studies* 43, 6: 1065–84.

Farmer, Kenneth C. (1992) *The Soviet Administrative Elite*, New York: Praeger.

Filtzer, Donald (1994) *Soviet Workers and the Collapse of Perestroika: The Soviet Labour Process and Gorbachev's Reforms, 1985–1991*, Cambridge: Cambridge University Press.

Folbre, Nancy (1995) *The New Field Guide to the U.S. Economy: A Compact and Irreverent Guide to Economic Life in America*, New York: The New Press.

Fukuyama, Francis (1993) "The Modernizing Imperative: The USSR as an Ordinary Country," *The National Interest* special issue, 31: 10–18.

Galbraith, John Kenneth (1990) "Revolt in Our Time: The Triumph of Simplistic Ideology," in Gwyn Prins (ed.) *Spring in Winter: The 1989 Revolutions*, Manchester: Manchester University Press.

Garraty, John A. and Gay, Peter (eds) (1985) *The Columbia History of the World*, New York: Harper and Row.

Gellner, Ernst (1983) *Nations and Nationalism*, Ithaca, NY: Cornell University Press.

Goldman, Marshall, I. (1994) *Lost Opportunity: Why Economic Reforms in Russia Have Not Worked*, New York: W. W. Norton.

Gorbachev, Mikhail (1987) "On the Party's Tasks in Fundamentally Restructuring Management of the Economy," *Reprints from the Soviet Press* 45, 2–3: 3–65.

—— (1988) *Perestroika: New Thinking for Our Country and the World*, New York: Harper and Row.

—— (1991) "On the Draft of the New CPSU Program," report to the Plenary Session of the CPSU Central Committee on 25 July 1991 *The Current Digest of the Soviet Press* 43, 30: 2–6.

Gordon, David M., Edwards, Richard, and Reich, Michael (1982) *Segmented Work, Divided Workers: The Historical Transformation of Labor in the United States*, Cambridge: Cambridge University Press.

Gregory, Paul R. and Stuart, Robert C. (1990) *Soviet Economic Structure and Performance*, fourth edition, New York: Harper and Row.

Gustafson, Thane (1985) "The Origins of the Soviet Oil Crisis, 1970–1985," *Soviet Economy* 1, 2: 103–35.

Gwertzman, Bernard and Kaufman, Michael T. (eds) (1992) *The Decline and Fall of the Soviet Empire* [selected articles from *The New York Times*], New York: Times Books.

Hahn, Gordon M. (1994) "Opposition Politics in Russia," *Europe–Asia Studies* 46, 2: 305–35.

Hanson, Philip (1990) "Property Rights in the New Phase of Reforms," *Soviet Economy* 6, 2: 95–124.

Harrison, Mark (1993) "Soviet Economic Growth since 1928: The Alternative Statistics of G. I. Khanin", *Europe–Asia Studies* 45, 1: 141–67.

Hauslohner, Peter A. (1991) "Gorbachev's Social Contract," in Hewett and Winston (1991b).

Hayek, F. A. (1944) *The Road to Serfdom*, Chicago: University of Chicago Press.

Hersh, Seymour M. (1994) "The Wild East," *The Atlantic Monthly* June: 61–80.

Hewett, Ed A. (1988) *Reforming the Soviet Economy: Equality versus Efficiency*, Washington DC: The Brookings Institution.

——(1991a) "Gorbachev's Economic Strategy: A Preliminary Assessment," in Hewett and Winston (1991a).

——(1991b) "Radical Perceptions of Perestroyka," in Hewett and Winston (1991a).

Hewett, Ed A. and Winston, Victor H. (eds) (1991a) *Milestones in Glasnost and Perestroyka: The Economy*, Washington, DC: The Brookings Institution.

——(1991b) *Milestones in Glasnost and Perestroyka: Politics and People*, Washington, DC: The Brookings Institution.

Hobsbawm, E. J. (1990) *Nations and Nationalism since 1780: Programme, Myth, Reality*, Cambridge: Cambridge University Press.

Horvat, Branko (1982) *The Political Economy of Socialism: A Marxist Social Theory*, Oxford: Martin Robertson.

Hough, Jerry F. (1987) "Gorbachev Consolidating Power," *Problems of Communism* 36, 4: 21–43.

——(1991) "The Politics of Successful Economic Reform", in Hewett and Winston (1991b).

——(1994) "Russia – On the Road to Thermidor," *Problems of Post-Communism* 41, Fall: 26–32.

Hough, Jerry F. and Fainsod, Merle (1979) *How the Soviet Union Is Governed*, Cambridge, Mass.: Harvard University Press.

International Monetary Fund (1992a), *Economic Review: The Economy of the Former USSR in 1991*, Washington, DC: The International Monetary Fund.

——(1992b) *Economic Review: Russian Federation*, Washington DC: The International Monetary Fund.

——(1993) *Economic Reviews 1993: Russian Federation*, Washington DC: The International Monetary Fund.

——(1995a) *Economic Reviews 1994: Russian Federation*, Washington DC: The International Monetary Fund.

——(1995b) *Russian Federation – Statistical Appendix*, IMF Staff Country Report 95/107, Washington DC: International Monetary Fund.

Istoriia Kommunisticheskoi Partii Sovetskogo Soiuza (1977), second edition, Institut Marksizma–Leninizma pri TsK KPSS, Glavnoe upravlenie geodezii i kartografii pri Sovete Ministrov SSSR, Moscow: GUGK.

Johnson, Simon and Kroll, Heidi (1991) "Managerial Strategies for Spontaneous Privatization," *Soviet Economy* 7, 4: 281–316.

Joint Economic Committee, US Congress (1982) *USSR: Measures of Economic Growth and Development, 1950–1980*, Washington DC: US Government Printing Office, December.

—— (1990) *Measures of Soviet Gross National Product in 1982 Prices*, Washington DC: US Government Printing Office, November.

—— (1993) *The Former Soviet Union in Transition*, volume 1, Washington DC: US Government Printing Office.

Jones, Anthony and Moskoff, William (1989) "New Cooperatives in the USSR," *Problems of Communism* 38, 6: 27–39.

Kagarlitsky, Boris (1992) *The Disintegration of the Monolith*, trans. Renfrey Clarke, London: Verso.

Karasik, Theodore W. (1992) *USSR Facts and Figures Annual*, volume 17, Gulf Breeze, Fla: Academic International Press.

Karklins, Rasma (1994) "Explaining Regime Change in the Soviet Union," *Europe–Asia Studies* 4, 1: 29–45.

Khanin, G. I. and Seliunin, V. (1987) "Lukavayay tsifra," *Novyi mir* 2.

Koen, Vincent (1994) "Measuring the Transition: A User's View on National Accounts in Russia," IMF Working Paper, January.

Kontorovich, Vladimir (1992a) "The Railroads," in Ellman and Kontorovich (1992a).

—— (1992b) "Technological Progress and Research and Development," in Ellman and Kontorovich (1992a).

—— (1993) "The Economic Fallacy," *The National Interest* special edition, 31: 35–45.

Kotz, David M., McDonough, Terrence, and Reich, Michael (eds) (1994) *Social Structures of Accumulation: The Political Economy of Growth and Crisis*, Cambridge: Cambridge University Press.

Kozlov, Nicholas N. (forthcoming) "Financial Reform in the Former USSR," in A. Ugrinsky and J. Hickey *Government Structures in the USA and the Sovereign States of the Former USSR*, Westport, Conn.: Greenwood Press.

Kregel, Jan A. and Matzner, Egon (1992) "Agenda for Reconstruction of Central and Eastern Europe," *Challenge* September–October: 33–40.

Kryshtanovskaya, Olga (1994a) "Transformatsiia staroi nomenklatury v novuiu rossiiskuiu elitu: Doklad," (Transformation of the Old Nomenklatura into a New Russian Elite: Report) unpublished conference paper: Moscow, November.

—— (1994b) "Transformatsiia staroi nomenklatury v novuiu rossiiskuiu elitu: Tezisy doklada," (Transformation of the Old Nomenklatura into the New Russian Elite: Thesis of the Report) unpublished paper: Moscow, May.

Kto est' kto v Rossii (1993) Moscow, Izdatel'skii Dom "Novoe Vremia."

Kullberg, Judith S. (1994) "The Ideological Roots of Elite Political Conflict in Post-Soviet Russia," *Europe–Asia Studies* 46, 6: 929–53.

Kuznets, Simon (1963) "A Comparative Appraisal," in Abram Bergson and Simon Kuznets (eds) *Economic Trends in the Soviet Union*, Cambridge, Mass.: Harvard University Press.

Laibman, David (1992) "Market and Plan: Socialist Structures in History and Theory," *Science and Society* 56, 1: 60–91.

Lane, David (1970) *Politics and Society in the USSR*, London: Weidenfeld and Nicolson.

—— (1988) "Ruling Class and Political Elites: Paradigms of Socialist Societies," in David Lane (ed.) *Elites and Political Power in the USSR*, Aldershot, Hants: Edward Elgar.

Lane, David and Ross, Cameron (1994a) "The Composition of the Politburo of the CPSU: 1966 to 1991," *Coexistence* 31: 29–61.

—— (1994b) "Limitations of Party Control: The Government Bureaucracy in the USSR," *Communist and Post-Communist Studies* 27, 1: 19–38.

Lange, Oskar (1938 [1936–37]) "On the Economic Theory of Socialism," in Oskar Lange and Fred M. Taylor *On the Economic Theory of Socialism*, New York: McGraw-Hill.

Leijonhufvud, A. (1993) "Depression in Russia," *New Left Review* 199: 120–6.

Levine, Herbert S. (1983) "Possible Causes of the Deterioration of Soviet Productivity Growth in the Period 1976–1980," in Joint Economic Committee, United States Congress *Soviet Economy in the 1980's: Problems and Prospects*, part 1, Washington DC: US Government Printing Office.

Levy, M. (1994a) "The Legislative Bodies: Who Takes Precedence?," *Moscow Times* 12 January: 9.

—— (1994b) "Lawmaking Loopholes: Who Takes Precedence?," *Moscow Times* 19 January: 9.

Lewin, Moshe (1985) *The Making of the Soviet System: Essays in the Social History of Interwar Russia*, New York: Pantheon Books.

—— (1991) *The Gorbachev Phenomenon*, Berkeley: University of California Press.

—— (1995) *Russia/USSR/Russia: The Drive and Drift of a Superstate*, New York: The New Press.

Ligachev, Yegor (1993) *Inside Gorbachev's Kremlin: The Memoirs of Yegor Ligachev*, New York: Pantheon Books.

Lohr, Eric (1993) "Arkadii Volsky's Political Base," *Europe–Asia Studies* 45, 5: 811–29.

McAuley, Alastair (1977) "The Distribution of Earnings and Incomes in the Soviet Union," *Soviet Studies* 29, 2, April: 214–37.

—— (1979) *Economic Welfare in the Soviet Union*, Madison: University of Wisconsin Press.

McAuley, Mary (1992) "Politics, Economics, and Elite Realignment in Russia: A Regional Perspective," *Soviet Economy* 8, 1: 46–88.

McFaul, Michael and Markov, Sergei (eds) (1993) *The Troubled Birth of Russian Democracy*, Stanford, Calif.: The Hoover Institution Press.

Malia, Martin (1994) *The Soviet Tragedy: A History of Socialism in Russia, 1917–1991*, New York: The Free Press.

Matthews, Mervyn (1978) *Privilege in the Soviet Union: A Study of Elite Life-Styles under Communism*, London: George Allen and Unwin.

Medvedev, Roy (1989) *Let History Judge: The Origins and Consequences of Stalinism*, New York: Columbia University Press.

Menshikov, Stanislav (1990) *Catastrophe or Catharsis: The Soviet Economy Today*, Moscow and London: Inter-Verso.

Millar, James R. (1994) "The Failure of Shock Therapy," *Problems of Post-Communism* 41, Fall: 21–5.

Millar, James R., Berkowitz, Daniel M., Berliner, Joseph S., Gregory, Paul R., and Linz, Susan J. (1993) "An Evaluation of the CIA's Analysis of Soviet Economic Performance, 1970–90," *Comparative Economic Studies* 35, 2, Summer: 33–57.

Miller, John (1993) *Mikhail Gorbachev and the End of Soviet Power*, London: St Martin's Press.

Mises, Ludwig von (1935 [1920]) "Economic Calculation in the Socialist

Commonwealth," in F.A. Hayek (ed.) *Collectivist Economic Planning*, London: Routledge.

Morris, Cynthia Taft (1992) "Insights from Early Capitalism for Eastern Europe Today," unpublished paper.

Moses, Joel C. (1992) "Soviet Provincial Politics in an Era of Transition and Revolution, 1989–91," *Soviet Studies* 44, 3: 479–509.

Murrell, Peter (1993) "What Is Shock Therapy? What Did It Do in Poland and Russia?," *Post-Soviet Affairs* 9, 2: 111–40.

Narodnoe khoziaistvo SSSR, statisticheskii ezhegodnik, Tsentralnoe Statisticheskoe Upravlenie SSSR, Moscow: Finansy i statistika, various years.

Narodnoe khoziaistvo SSSR za 70 let (1987), statisticheskii ezhegodnik, Tsentralnoe Statisticheskoe Upravlenie SSSR, Moscow: Finansy i statistika.

Noren, James H. (1990) "The Economic Crisis: Another Perspective," *Soviet Economy* 6, 1: 3–55.

Nove, Alec (1975) "Is there a Ruling Class in the USSR?," *Soviet Studies* 17, 4: 615–38.

—— (1983) *The Economics of Feasible Socialism*, London: Allen and Unwin.

—— (1986) *The Soviet Economic System*, third edition, Boston: Allen and Unwin.

—— (1989) *An Economic History of the USSR*, London: Penguin Books.

—— (1991) *The Economics of Feasible Socialism Revisited*, London: Harper-Collins Academic.

OECD (1995) *Short-Term Economic Indicators: Transition Economies*, Paris: Centre for Co-Operation with the Economies in Transition, various issues.

Ofer, Gur (1987) "Soviet Economic Growth: 1928–1985," *Journal of Economic Literature* 15, 4: 1767–1833.

Pitzer, John S. (1990) "The Tenability of CIA Estimates of Soviet Economic Growth: A Comment," *Journal of Comparative Economics* 14: 301–14.

Pitzer, John S. and Baukol, Andrew P. (1991) "Recent GNP and Productivity Trends," *Soviet Economy* 7, 1: 46–82.

Popkova, Larisa (1987) "Gde pyshneye pirogi," (Where the Pies are More Scrumptious) *Novyi mir* 63, 5: 239–41.

Postan, M. and Rich, E. E. (1952) *The Cambridge Economic History of Europe: Trade and Industry in the Middle Ages*, volume 2, Cambridge: Cambridge University Press.

"The Pulse of Europe: A Survey of Political and Social Values and Attitudes" (1991) Washington, DC: Times Mirror Center for the People and the Press.

Rabkina, N. E. and Rimashevskaia, N. M. (1978) "Raspredelitel'nye otnosheniia i sotsial'noe razvitie," *Economika i organizatisiia promyshlennogo proizvodstva* 5.

Radaev, V. (1993) "Novoe predprinimatel'stvo v rossii" (New Entrepreneurs in Russia), Moscow: Institute of Economics of the Russian Academy of Sciences.

Reddaway, Peter (1993) 'The Role of Popular Discontent' *The National Interest* 31, special issue: 57–63.

Riasanovsky, Nicholas V. (1977) *A History of Russia*, third edition, New York: Oxford University Press.

Rigby, T. H. (1988) "Staffing USSR Incorporated: The Origins of the Nomenklatura System," *Soviet Studies* 40, 4: 523–37.

—— (1992) "The Government in the Soviet Political System," in Eugene Huskey (ed.) *Executive Power and Soviet Politics: The Rise and Decline of the Soviet State*, Armonk, NY: M. E. Sharpe.

Robinson, Neil (1992) "Gorbachev and the Place of the Party in Soviet Reform, 1985–91," *Soviet Studies* 44, 3: 423–43.

Roemer, John E. (1994) *A Future for Socialism*, Cambridge, Mass.: Harvard University Press.

Rossiiskii statisticheskii ezhegodnik (1994) Moscow: Goskomstat rossii.

Rutland, Peter (1991) "Labor Unrest and Movements in 1989 and 1990," in Hewett and Winston (1991b).

Sakwa, Richard (1993) *Russian Politics and Society*, London: Routledge.

Sawyer, M. (1976) "Income Distribution in OECD Countries," *OECD Economic Outlook: Occasional Studies* July.

Schapiro, Leonard (1960) *The Communist Party of the Soviet Union*, New York: Random House.

Schroeder, Gertrude E. (1985) "The Slowdown in Soviet Industry, 1976–1982," *Soviet Economy* 1: 42–74.

—— (1987) "Anatomy of Gorbachev's Economic Reform," *Soviet Economy* 3, 3: 219–41.

—— (1990) "Crisis in the Consumer Sector: A Comment," *Soviet Economy* 6, 1: 56–64.

—— (1991) "Perestroyka in the Aftermath of 1990," *Soviet Economy* 7, 1: 3–13.

—— (1992) "Soviet Consumption in the 1990s: A Tale of Woe," in Ellman and Kontorovich (1992a).

Schweickart, David (1992) "Economic Democracy: A Worthy Socialism that Would Really Work," *Science and Society* 56, 1: 9–38.

Statistical Abstract of the United States Washington DC: US Government Printing Office, various years.

Statisticheskoe obozrenie, Goskomstat rossii, various issues.

Steele, Jonathan (1994) *Eternal Russia: Yeltsin, Gorbachev, and the Mirage of Democracy*, Cambridge, Mass.: Harvard University Press.

Suny, Ronald Grigor (1993) *The Revenge of the Past: Nationalism, Revolution, and the Collapse of the Soviet Union*, Stanford, Calif.: Stanford University Press.

Surovell, Jeffery (1991) "Ligachev and Soviet Politics," *Soviet Studies* 43, 2: 355–74.

—— (1994) "Gorbachev's Last Year: Leftist or Rightist?," *Europe–Asia Studies* 46, 3: 465–87.

Sweezy, Paul M. (1980) *Post-Revolutionary Society: Essays*, New York: Monthly Review Press.

Tarasulo, Issac J. (ed.) (1989) *Gorbachev and Glasnost: Viewpoints from the Soviet Press*, Wilmington, Del.: Scholarly Resources Books.

Teague, Elizabeth (1992) "Splits in the Ranks of Russia's 'Red Directors'," *RFE/RL Research Report* 1, 35: 6–10.

Ticktin, Hillel (1992) *Origins of the Crisis in the USSR: Essays on the Political Economy of a Disintegrating System*, Armonk, NY: M. E. Sharpe.

Tolz, Vera and Newton, Melanie (eds) (1990) *The USSR in 1989: A Record of Events*, Boulder, Colo.: Westview Press.

Tucker, Robert C. (ed.) (1978) *The Marx–Engels Reader*, second edition, New York: W. W. Norton.

Unger, A. L. (1991) "The Travails of Intra-Party Democracy in the Soviet Union: The Elections to the 19th Conference of the CPSU," *Soviet Studies* 43, 2: 329–54.

Urban, Michael E. (1992) "Boris El'tsin, Democratic Russia and the Campaign for the Russian Presidency," *Soviet Studies* 44, 2: 187–207.

US Bureau of the Census (1961) *Historical Statistics of the United States: Colonial Times to 1957*, statistical abstract supplement, Washington DC: US Government Printing Office.

Vinokur, Aaron and Ofer, Gur (1986) "Inequality of Earnings, Household

Income and Wealth in the Soviet Union in the 70's," Soviet Interview Project, Working Paper 25, University of Illinois at Urbana-Champaign.

Ward, Benjamin N. (1967) *The Socialist Economy: A Study of Organizational Alternatives*, New York: Random House.

Weir, Fred (1993) "Interview: Fred Weir in Russia," *Covert Action* 45: 54–60.

—— (1993–94) "Russia in the Winter of Democracy," *Covert Action* 47: 10–64.

Weisskopf, Thomas E. (1992a) "Russia in Transition: Perils of the Fast Track to Capitalism," *Challenge* 35, 6: 28–37.

—— (1992b) "Toward a Socialism for the Future, in the Wake of the Demise of the Socialism of the Past," *Review of Radical Political Economics* 24, 3–4: 1–28.

—— (1994) "Myths and Realities of Privatization in Russia," *Review of Radical Political Economics* 26, 3: 32–40.

White, Stephen (1990) " 'Democratization' in the USSR," *Soviet Studies* 42, 1: 3–25.

—— (1992) *Gorbachev and After*, Cambridge: Cambridge University Press.

White, Stephen, McAllister, Ian, and Kryshtanovskaya, Olga (1994) "El'tsin and his Voters: Popular Support in the 1991 Russian Presidential Elections and After," *Europe–Asia Studies* 46, 2: 285–303.

Whitesell, Robert S. (1985) "The Influence of Central Planning on the Economic Slowdown in the Soviet Union and Eastern Europe: A Comparative Production Function Analysis," *Econometrica* 52: 235–44.

The World Bank (1995) *World Development Report 1995: Workers in an Integrating World*, Oxford: Oxford University Press.

Yavlinsky, G., Fedorov, B., Shatalin, S., Petrakov, N., Aleksashenko, S., Vavilov, A., Grigoriev, L., Zadornov, M., Machits, V., Mikhailov, A., and Yasin, E. (1991) *500 Days: Transition to the Market*, New York: St Martin's Press.

Yeltsin, Boris (1990) *Against the Grain: An Autobiography*, trans. Michael Glenny, London: Jonathan Cape.

Zaslavskaya, Tatyana (1990) *The Second Socialist Revolution: An Alternative Soviet Strategy*, trans. S. M. Davies, Bloomington and Indianapolis: Indian University Press.

Zimbalist, Andrew, Sherman, Howard J., and Brown, Stuart (1989) *Comparing Economic Systems: A Political-Economic Approach*, second edition, New York: Harcourt Brace Jovanovich.

Index

consumer goods 35, 38, 41, 51–2, 77–8,
133–4, 140, 164, 188; crisis in market 80–3; rationing 23, 73, 80
consumer prices 177, 179
consumption 37, 38; growth rate 75–7
cooperatives 21, 92–3, 116
Corning Inc. 273(30)
corruption 47, 53, 191, 213
cost–price spiral 188, 189
Council of Ministers 24–5, 31, 54, 93,
103, 124, 127, 136
coup attempt (August 1991) 4, 5, 13,
132, 148–52, 158
CPSU Central Committee News 98
credit policy 162, 164–5, 169, 190
crime 184–5, 191
Crowe, Admiral William 259(11)

dachas 29, 66
Daily Worker 67
Dallin, Alexander 240(12)
Daniels, Robert V. 245(57), 253(9)
Davies, R.W. 242(11), 255(24)
Dawisha, Karen 279(48)
death rate (shock therapy) 185–6
decile ratio 28, 182–3
Delovie Lyudi (Business People) 119,
123, 261(42), 262(55)
democracy 3, 4, 15–16, 19, 216–18
democratic centralism 17, 19, 230
Democratic Choice of Russia 209, 210
Democratic Party of Russia 208,
276(4)
democratic planning 231–3
Democratic Russia 60, 126, 135–6, 137,
140–1, 145
democratic socialism 58, 60, 111–12,
138, 221–2; lessons for future 9,
224–35
democratization 5, 56–7, 60, 133, 143;
Communist Party 97–107;
effects 107–8; of state 99–103
demographic data (shock therapy)
185–6
Devine, Pat 282(8–9)
Di Leo, Rita 104
Directorate of Intelligence 44, 46, 50,
250(48)
Djilas, Milovan 245(58)
Dobb, Maurice 282(10)
Dubenetsky, Yakov 123
duma elections 208, 209–10

Economic Commission for Europe 272(25), 275(60)
economic contraction (contributory
factors) 90–2
economic growth 3; perestroika and
34–42; planned and actual 49–50
Economic News Agency 272(21)
economic performance, Soviet
(1928–75) 34–42
economic policies (in 1920s) 20–1
economic proposals (1990–91) 86–90
economic reform 73–95
Economic Report of the President 37, 43,
44, 46, 247(13), 247(16), 270(25)
economic restructuring (policy evolution 1985–9) 75–80
economic stagnation 42–53, 55, 56
economic structure of Soviet system
21–3
economic transformation: shock
therapy 161–72; shock therapy
(results) 173–99; shock therapy
effects 200–23
Economics Institute 85
economists (influence) 69–71
Edelman, Yuri 121, 122
education 32, 33, 37–8
elections: democratization process
99–103, 108; duma seats 208, 209–10;
new constitution 215; Yeltsin's rise
to power 133–7
elite: families 118, 119–20; ideology
of 114–15, 118–19; privilege system 29–30, 33, 66, 112–13, 133–4;
support for capitalism 5–7, 110–15;
see also party–state elite
Ellman, Michael 239(5), 249(41), 277(6)
Embree, Gregory J. 258(20)
employment 37–8; full employment
27, 35; unemployment 14, 15, 16, 37,
180–1, 231; peasants/workers 17–18,
19–21, 25; *see also* labor
Engels, Friedrich 13–16
enterprise: autonomy 79–80; directors 201, 205–6, 220, 228; managers 195–7; ownership 230–1
environment 41–2, 229
Estonian Front 144
exports 48, 93, 163, 172, 218

Faces of Hatred (Korotich) 65
Fainsod, Merle 243(29), 244(48)